THE POETICAL WORKS
OF
ROBERT BROWNING

General Editor: IAN JACK

TO ROBERT BROWNING.

There is delight in singing, though none hear
Beside the singer ; and there is delight
In praising, though the praiser sit alone
And see the praised far off him, far above.
Shakespeare is not *our* poet, but the world's,
Therefore on him no speech ; and short for thee,
Browning ! Since Chaucer was alive and hale,
No man hath·walk'd along our roads with step
So active, so inquiring eye, or tongue
So varied in discourse. But warmer climes
Give brighter plumage, stronger wing ; the breeze
Of Alpine heights thou playest with, borne on
Beyond Sorrento and Amalfi, where
The siren waits thee, singing song for song.

Sent out to New Zealand time in 1845
by R. Browning.
a Donnett

WALTER SAVAGE LANDOR.

Morning Chronicle, Nov. 22, 1845.

Robert Browning Sr. had a few copies of these lines printed for distribution to
friends. See pp. 9–10, below.

THE POETICAL WORKS
OF
ROBERT BROWNING

Volume IV

BELLS AND POMEGRANATES
VII–VIII
(*Dramatic Romances and Lyrics*,
Luria, *A Soul's Tragedy*)
and
CHRISTMAS-EVE AND EASTER-DAY

EDITED BY

IAN JACK
ROWENA FOWLER
AND
MARGARET SMITH

CLARENDON PRESS · OXFORD
1991

Burgess
PR
4203
. J3
1983
c. 1
v. 4

Oxford University Press, Walton Street, Oxford OX2 6DP

Oxford New York Toronto
Delhi Bombay Calcutta Madras Karachi
Petaling Jaya Singapore Hong Kong Tokyo
Nairobi Dar es Salaam Cape Town
Melbourne Auckland

and associated companies in
Berlin Ibadan

Oxford is a trade mark of Oxford University Press

Published in the United States
by Oxford University Press, New York

© Ian Jack, Rowena Fowler, and Margaret Smith 1991

British Library Cataloguing in Publication Data
Browning, Robert, 1812–1889
The poetical works of Robert Browning.—(Oxford English
texts).
Vol. 4, Bells and pomegranates VII–VIII: (Dramatic
romances and lyrics, Luria, A Soul's tragedy) and
Christmas-Eve and Easter-Day
I. Title   II. Jack, Ian   III. Fowler, Rowena   IV. Smith,
Margaret, 1931–
821.8
ISBN 0–19–812789–8

Library of Congress Cataloging in Publication Data
(Revised for vol. 4)
Browning, Robert, 1812–1889.
The poetical works of Robert Browning.
Includes bibliographical references and index.
Vol. 3 edited by Ian Jack and Rowena Fowler;
vol. 4—   edited by Ian Jack, Rowena Fowler, and
Margaret Smith.
Contents: vo. 1. Pauline; paracelsus—v. 2. Straf-
ford; Sordello—[etc.]—v. 4. Bells and pomegranates,
VII–VIII (dramatic romances and lyrics, Luria, a
soul's tragedy) and Christmas-Eve and Easter-Day.
I. Jack, Ian Robert James.   II. Smith, Margaret,
1931–   .   III. Fowler, Rowena.   IV. Title.
PR4203.J3   1983 821'.8   82–12603
ISBN 0–19–812789–8

Set by Joshua Associates Limited, Oxford
Printed and bound in
Great Britain by Biddles Ltd.
Guildford and King's Lynn

PREFACE AND
ACKNOWLEDGEMENTS

I N the present volume, as before, Ian Jack is responsible for the principal part of the introductions, the explanatory notes, and the appendices. Margaret Smith is responsible for the textual work on *Dramatic Romances and Lyrics*, Rowena Fowler for that on *Luria*, *A Soul's Tragedy*, and *Christmas-Eve and Easter-Day*; while together they have produced a revised form of the Textual Introduction first published in Volume I, taking account of the discoveries of Michael Meredith and others. In practice, of course, the division of labour has not been clear-cut: Ian Jack would particularly like to thank his co-editors for their vigilant scrutiny of his part of the work.

We are grateful to the authorities of the English Poetry Collection of Wellesley College Library, who have permitted us to reproduce in full, for the first time, Elizabeth Barrett's comments on the poems in *Dramatic Romances and Lyrics*. In deciphering the handwriting, which is often difficult, we have been indebted to the advice of Dr Philip Kelley, who will be reproducing the notes in another form in his indispensable edition of the *Correspondence*, and who has been generous enough to make no objection to our different use of the material.

Miss Myrtle Moulton-Barrett and Col. R. A. Moulton-Barrett have kindly permitted us to make brief quotations from unpublished letters in their collection.

For permission to reproduce other material, and for help of many kinds, we are further indebted to the authorities of the Armstrong Browning Library of Baylor University, the Beinecke Library at Yale, the Robert H. Taylor Collection at Princeton, the Thomas Fisher Rare Book Collection of the University of Toronto, the Pierpont Morgan Library, the Harold B. Lee Library of Brigham Young University, the Berg Collection at the New York Public Library, the Humanities Research Center at Texas, and the William Andrews Clark Memorial Library, University of California, Los Angeles.

In this country we are greatly indebted to the staffs of Cambridge University Library, the Forster Collection in the Victoria and Albert Museum, the John Rylands Library, the British Library, and Balliol College Library. Mr R. M. Andrewes of the Pendlebury Music Library in Cambridge has been particularly helpful.

Our greatest personal debt has again been to Dr Philip Kelley. Mr Ronald Hudson also has most kindly come to our assistance. We have been helped on particular points by Professor Mary Lefkowitz and Mr Michael Meredith (both of whom have joined the small team of editors), Professor Timothy Webb, the Rev. Dr Allan Doig, Dr Kevin Van Anglen, and a number of present and past Fellows of Pembroke College, Cambridge: among them Professor Malcolm Lyons, Professor Michael Reeve, Dr A. V. Grimstone, Dr Richard Hunter, Dr Jane Stevenson, and Dr Rivkah Zim. The assistance of several other scholars is acknowledged in the appropriate part of the volume.

Once again we wish to thank Dr Leofranc Holford-Strevens, a man of learning who is untiring in the assistance which he gives to others.

It should perhaps be mentioned that two poems ('She was fifteen, had great eyes' and 'Æschylus' Soliloquy') and a set of 'Anacreonta' attributed to Browning by Pettigrew and Collins and others are omitted here, since they have been shown to be by Elizabeth Barrett.[1]

This volume contains a list of the titles and first lines of the poems published in *Dramatic Lyrics* (included in our Vol. III) as well as of those published in *Dramatic Romances and Lyrics*. A list including the poems in *Men and Women* will be included in Vol. V.

I.J., R.F., M.S.

20 January 1989

[1] *Index of English Literary Manuscripts*, Vol. IV, compiled by Barbara Rosenbaum and Pamela White (Mansell, London and New York, 1982). See too *Collections*.

CONTENTS

TEXTUAL INTRODUCTION IX

REFERENCES AND ABBREVIATIONS XIX

INTRODUCTION TO *DRAMATIC ROMANCES AND LYRICS* 1

DRAMATIC ROMANCES AND LYRICS 15

INTRODUCTION TO *LURIA* 179

LURIA 193

INTRODUCTION TO *A SOUL'S TRAGEDY* 271

A SOUL'S TRAGEDY 281

INTRODUCTION TO *CHRISTMAS-EVE AND EASTER-DAY* 317

CHRISTMAS-EVE AND EASTER-DAY 331

APPENDICES

A. Browning's Essay on Shelley 421

B. Fugitives 443

C. Index of the titles and first lines of the poems in *Dramatic Lyrics* and *Dramatic Romances and Lyrics* 447

ADDITIONS AND CORRECTIONS TO VOLS. I–III 450

TEXTUAL INTRODUCTION

D URING Browning's lifetime his poems and plays were published, some of them in many different editions, over a span of fifty-six years. The textual editor has the challenging task of presenting the evolution of the poet's art in a way that will enable the reader to perceive clearly its direction and pattern. The editor must also attempt to evaluate each edition in order to assess the likelihood of accuracy in those deriving from it, and especially in the author's last revised text; necessary emendations will be made in the light of such informed evaluation. While acknowledging Browning's concern for accuracy, the editor will be aware of the possibility of errors in works with a long and sometimes complex textual history, including final corrections made by the poet in the last year of his life.

We give here a brief account of the publication and transmission through later editions of the major poems and plays first published up to and including the year 1850, so that our more detailed textual introductions to individual works may be seen in perspective. For a fuller account of Browning's early works to 1844, the reader should turn to the first three volumes of the present edition.

Pauline was published (anonymously) in 1833, *Paracelsus* in 1835, *Strafford* in 1837, and *Sordello* in 1840. Browning's fair copy manuscript of *Paracelsus* survives, as does a transcript by two unknown copyists of *Strafford*, made for the licensing of the play by the Lord Chamberlain's office before the first performance (see p. 452 below). Other annotated copies of all four works provide evidence of Browning's revisions, actual or intended, and have been used in the preparation of the text and in our notes.

Bells and Pomegranates, Browning's next venture in publishing, took the form of a series of eight pamphlets, published by Edward Moxon between April 1841 and April 1846. The first six have been presented in Volume III of this edition; *Dramatic Romances and Lyrics*, *Luria*, and *A Soul's Tragedy* (the contents of the last two pamphlets) are the concern of the present volume. Several of the poems in *Dramatic Romances and Lyrics* had first appeared in *Hood's Magazine* in 1844 and 1845; Browning's revision of these in the light of Elizabeth Barrett's highly intelligent criticisms, which we record in our notes, forms a particularly interesting aspect of their history.

By December 1846 Browning had decided to produce a carefully revised new edition of his poems—an edition which should do justice to the varied range of his talents since he had become renowned as the 'Author of *Paracelsus*'. The two volumes, published by Chapman and Hall, were prepared by July 1848, and a proof-copy survives with '1848' on the title-page;[1] but 'The POETICAL WORKS... With numerous Alterations and Additions', advertised in the *Athenæum* on 2 December of that year, did not appear until the end of the month, and were dated 1849. The edition was not intended to be complete: *Pauline*, *Strafford*, *Sordello*, and two short pieces from *Dramatic Romances and Lyrics* ('Claret and Tokay' and the lines 'Here's to Nelson's Memory') were omitted; but the major poems in the collection—notably *Paracelsus* and *Pippa Passes*—had, as Browning had promised, been very thoroughly revised.

Christmas-Eve and Easter-Day, published by Chapman and Hall on 1 April 1850, had been printed from the fair-copy manuscript in the hands of Robert and Elizabeth Barrett Browning now in the Forster collection in the Victoria and Albert Museum. It was included, along with *Sordello* and *Paracelsus*, in the third of the three volumes of Robert Browning's *Poetical Works* in 1863. This was a more comprehensive edition, restoring to the corpus most of the poems (but not *Pauline*) omitted in 1849, rearranging them, and adding the poems first published as *Men and Women* in 1855. These included the revised and extended version of *Saul*, the first part of which had appeared in *Dramatic Romances and Lyrics*. Although Browning told Moncure Conway on 17 September 1863 that there were 'no changes of importance in any of the poems', he had in fact made a thorough revision of *Paracelsus*, *Sordello*, and *Strafford*, and of the *Men and Women* poems,[2] and he had carefully supervised the

---

[1] On this copy, first discovered and reported on by Ian Jack, see John Pettigrew, 'Baylor's 1848 *Poems*', BN, Spring 1972, pp. 46–7.

[2] See A. C. Dooley, 'The Textual Significance of Robert Browning's 1865 *Poetical Works*', *Papers of the Bibliographical Society of America*, 71, pp. 212–18.

production of the edition. When a line was omitted from 'A Lovers' Quarrel' 'through a blunder of the printer's', the sheet was cancelled 'before many copies had been issued', and the correct text was printed.[1] Browning noticed other errors, but *1863* is on the whole a reliable text, and is of special significance in the development of *Christmas-Eve and Easter-Day* and of several poems in *Dramatic Romances and Lyrics* as well as of the works mentioned above: notably, a number of readings first introduced in *1849* were either re-phrased or removed in favour of the original text.

The volume of selections published in 1863 by Chapman and Hall and edited by John Forster and Bryan W. Procter was, they explained,[2] published 'with Mr. Browning's sanction', although 'for the choice of the particular pieces he [was] in no respect responsible'. While it is possible that Forster and Procter consulted Browning on some details of the text, it is evident that he did not have editorial control; there are in any case several obvious errors in, for example, 'The Flight of the Duchess'; most of the punctuation variants are out of line with the direction of Browning's revision, and were not used by him in later editions. We have, therefore, not recorded variants from this edition for the poems in Volume IV.

Early in 1865, however, Browning prepared for Chapman and Hall his own selection of the 'lightest' of his poems, to be 'tied together after the pretty device of [his] old publishers, Messrs. MOXON. Not a single piece here [he added] belongs to the Selection already issued.'[3] Revised proofs of Browning's preface, dated 21 March 1865, and corrected copy for some of the poems, survive to show that he took some care with the presentation of this selection. *1865S* consequently has its place in the sequence of authorially controlled editions, and in the recording of variants in our Volume IV.

Browning also revised the three-volume edition of 1863. In a letter of 26 November in that year he told Mrs William Wetmore Story that he 'did *not* send her' a copy of the 1863 collection 'because

---

[1] See N. I. Hart, 'A Browning Letter on "The Poetical Works" of 1863', NQ, June 1974, pp. 213–15.

[2] See their preface on p. v of the *Selections*.

[3] See Browning's preface, and the proofs with his revisions in the Humanities Research Center, Austin, Texas.

a prettier one is in prospect'. This was the fourth edition, dated 1865 and adorned with a photograph of the poet, but not issued until January 1866. Browning corrected the errors he had noticed in *1863*, and introduced some hundreds of revisions, those in *Strafford* and the poems originally in *Men and Women* being of particular interest.[1] He paid less attention to the original *Dramatic Romances and Lyrics*, though he made minor corrections in 'The Flight of the Duchess' and 'The Bishop Orders his Tomb', and revised some half-dozen lines in 'Pictor Ignotus'. Unfortunately the fourth edition as a whole is less reliable than the third; it has a number of careless misprints, including 'blooming' for 'booming' in *Sordello*, i. 317, and it is likely that Browning gave it less than his usual attention. He had edited a selection of Elizabeth's poems for Chapman, and had been preoccupied with his 'Roman murder story'—'16,000 lines, or over,—done in less than two years, Isa!', as he wrote to Miss Blagden on 19 May 1866.[2] We have therefore regarded with suspicion doubtful readings which first entered the text in *1865*, and in the few instances where corruption seems certain, we have restored the readings of *1863*.

Dissatisfied on other grounds with Chapman as a publisher, Browning turned to George Smith of Smith, Elder & Co., who produced a new collected edition in six volumes, issued monthly from March to August 1868. The copy-text for all the poems except *Pauline* and *Dramatis Personæ* was *1865*, prepared by Browning, who introduced some hundreds of revisions of punctuation and slight changes of wording designed to improve rhythm, clarity, and style in general. *Pauline* was thoroughly revised, in spite of Browning's disclaimer '(no syllable is changed)' in the preface. Among the *Dramatic Romances and Lyrics*, 'The Englishman in Italy', 'The Italian in England', and 'Time's Revenges', for example, show small but significant verbal revisions. Nevertheless Browning was dissatisfied with the edition: complaining of two 'vile misprints' in *Colombe's Birthday*,[3] he asserted that the volumes were 'full of such', adding:

[1] From *1863* onwards the poems originally in *Men and Women*, *Dramatic Lyrics*, and *Dramatic Romances and Lyrics* were comprehensively 'redistributed'. See our Vol. III, pp. 8–9.
[2] *Dearest Isa*, p. 239.
[3] W. J. Rolfe, 'An Unpublished Browning Letter', *Nation*, 17 February 1910; cited by John Maynard in his review of the Ohio *Works of Robert Browning*, SBC, Fall 1974, p. 87. Neither error is corrected in later editions within Browning's lifetime.

'They come of the printer's laziness, who, if the type gets misplaced, prefers to replace it as he best can, without troubling the "Reader" who may not be at hand.' Browning himself had failed to notice several of the errors of 1865, and had left them uncorrected.

Thanks to the work of Warner Barnes[1] and Michael Meredith,[2] we are now aware of the subsequent publishing history of the six-volume *Poetical Works*. In 'Learning's Crabbed Text' Meredith notes that the 1868 volumes sold briskly, so that 'in eighteen months the edition was almost exhausted and a reprint was needed'. Because the type had been redistributed, resetting was needed, and Browning took the opportunity to revise the text for the edition of 1870. Most of his revisions, which occur mainly in the lyrics and dramatic monologues, are minor matters of punctuation and elision (typically, 'Of the' becoming 'O' the'), serving to produce smoother sound and movement. Because of the number of the revisions (some 200), and because two distinct lines of textual descent derive from it, 1870 is a significant edition, and its variants have been recorded.

One of the lines of descent is that of the first and second series of *Selections*, published respectively in 1872 and 1880. While most of the poems followed closely the text of 1870, a few were inter-estingly revised. 'The Englishman in Italy', for example, was newly set out in long lines, with effective additional revisions of punctuation and phrasing. The first series, Browning explained in a preface dated 14 May 1872, was formed by '*simply stringing together certain pieces on the thread of an imaginary personality*' to provide a companion-volume to the selections he had made from Elizabeth's poems; and he added that he did not '*apprehend any more charges of being wilfully obscure, unconscientiously careless, or perversely harsh*'—an emphasis which may help to explain the direction of some of his revisions. The second series (1880) was a complementary volume of (on the whole) rather longer pieces. The two series, which had been frequently reprinted, were published as a new two-volume edition in 1884. The 1872 preface was reprinted, and most of the poems

---

[1] See Warner Barnes, 'Two Robert Brownings: The Edition of 1868' in *The Warden's Meeting: A Tribute to John Sparrow* (Oxford University Society of Bibliophiles, 1977), pp. 58–60.

[2] Michael Meredith, 'Learning's Crabbed Text: A Reconsideration of the 1868 Edition of Browning's *Poetical Works*', SBC 13 (1985), 97–107.

were unchanged; but others, such as 'The Flight of the Duchess' and 'Time's Revenges', received still further revision. The 1884 volumes and their corrected reprints in 1886 and 1888 proved very popular, sold well, and could be obtained enhanced 'with photographic illustrations by Payne Jennings' in a version produced by Suttaby & Co. in 1886.[1] They were reproduced for many years after Browning's death.

The six-volume edition had nevertheless continued to sell, and the text of *1870* was reprinted in *1872* without alteration. When another reprint was called for in 1875, Browning realized for the first time that the text was distressingly inaccurate, with ludicrous misprints such as 'human hair' for 'human air' in l. 432 of *Christmas-Eve*, and the unmetrical 'speckled' for 'specked' in l. 18 of 'The Englishman in Italy'. He therefore corrected the stereotypes for the edition of 1875, adding also a small number of new revisions. A few errors escaped his notice, and were therefore perpetuated in the nine reprints[2] of the edition, which also acquired an increasing number of flaws deriving from the worn plates and their inadequate repairs. Michael Meredith explains that 'This deterioration of the plates was one reason which led George Smith in May 1884 to propose publishing an entirely new expanded edition which would include all Browning's recent poetry.'[3] He remarks that 'It took Smith and Browning over three years to complete the task, three years in which the [six-volume] edition continued to be reprinted, until in May 1888 the first volume was ready, followed by the fifteen remaining volumes at monthly intervals.'[4]

For this expanded edition Browning scrutinized his poems yet again, using *1875* or one of its reprints as his copy for much of the work, and therefore incorporating the revisions he had made in that text. For *King Victor and King Charles*, *The Return of the Druses*, *Luria*, *A Soul's Tragedy*, *Dramatis Personæ*, *Christmas-Eve and Easter-Day*, and *Men and Women* he corrected the copies of *1870* and *1872* now in the Gordon Ray collection in the Pierpont Morgan Library. By

---

[1] British Library C. 60. e. 2.
[2] Eight reprints only for vol. i: see Meredith, op. cit., p. 102.
[3] Loc. cit.
[4] Ibid., pp. 102–3.

December 1887 he found that he had 'gone over' his poems so often that he saw 'little or nothing to amend . . . except in the punctuation'.[1] This was generally true: his revisions tended to make the end-of-line punctuation slightly heavier, but there were few more substantial changes save in the *Bells and Pomegranates* plays mentioned above and in *Pauline*, where Browning claimed permission to diminish the faults of 'juvenile haste'. Readings from the *Selections* were rarely used—an exception being the adoption of '—Chew, abbot's own cheek!' in place of the *1875* text in l. 244 of 'The Englishman in Italy'. Unfortunately some of the errors as well as the revisions of the ill-printed *1870* found their way into *1888*, despite Browning's scrutiny, either directly through its use as copy, or via *1875*. The erroneous 'used' in l. 408 and 'his friend' in l. 729 of 'The Flight of the Duchess' entered the *1888* text in this way via *1875*; it is therefore possible, and indeed likely, that 'loathy' at *Sordello*, iv. 23 is a misprint, not a revision, deriving from the unreliable text of *1870*, where it first appeared, and uncorrected in *1875*.

While it is true then that Browning checked the proofs carefully for 'every volume of the first impression of the 1888–1889 edition'[2] and that when he returned the proofs for vol. iii on 6 May 1888 he praised the 'scrupulous accuracy of the Printers',[3] he noticed a number of errors in the published volumes. In the spring of 1889 he told his friend James Dykes Campbell that he had been sending George Smith 'corrections for the stereotype plates' of the early volumes, already out of print, 'preparatory to reprinting'.[4] In the latter part of August he told Campbell that he 'had revised the first ten volumes, and repeated his kind offer to transcribe' his corrections into Campbell's copy. This was accordingly done by 28 August, the day before Browning left England on what was to be his last journey to Italy. The copy, with about 300 very neatly inserted corrections, is the large paper copy now in the British

---

[1] Letter to George Smith, 31 Dec. 1887, quoted by Michael Hancher in 'Browning and the *Poetical Works* of 1888–1889', BN, Spring 1971, p. 25.

[2] See A. C. Dooley, 'Browning's *Poetical Works* of 1888–1889', SBC, Spring 1979, pp. 45–6.

[3] Letter to George Smith, 6 May 1888, quoted by Michael Hancher, op. cit., p. 26.

[4] See Browning's letter and Campbell's manuscript notes in the latter's copy of the *Poetical Works* of 1888–9, British Library C. 116. d. 1.

Library. A second list of corrections for vols iv–x can be found in Brown University Library. Most, but not all, of these corrections were incorporated in the corrected reprint published after Browning's death, of which all the volumes were dated 1889 (issued early in 1890).[1]

Though this reprint derives from corrected stereotype plates, it is not a satisfactory basis for an authoritative edition, since Browning did not read the proofs to ensure that his corrections had been accurately carried out. Even in the early states of the second impression the end-of-line punctuation is unreliable.[2] We agree with Messrs Kelley and Peterson[3] that the first impression should be used, and have based our edition on the text of 1888–9 as given in the earliest copies, collated with extant MSS, with the authoritative editions of each poem previous to 1888, and with the 1889 reprint. Our emendations are based wherever possible on Browning's own corrections, or, when the 1888–9 text is unquestionably faulty, on the readings of previous editions.

General note on the recording of variants in this edition

Printed editions

We aim to record substantive variants, and variants in accidentals which significantly affect the meaning. Variants not recorded are, for example, apostrophes denoting omission of letters (shouldst/should'st, adored/ador'd); capitalization and spelling variants of no special importance (East/east—unless personification is involved; Thy/thy when unambiguously referring to God; ancles/ankles; recognise/recognize etc.); alternation between colons and semi-

---

[1] The corrections in the Dykes Campbell copy, transcribed by Browning from his own copy, do not tally precisely with those in the Brown University list, nor with the alterations made in the 1889 reprint. Either the lists sent by Browning to the printers differed from the others, or the printers misinterpreted or misprinted them: cf. for example our textual notes to *Pauline*, l. 332 and *King Charles*, l. 31—where the *1889* reading, 'give the pretext' looks like a printer's error. We have assessed individual discrepancies on their merits in the light of the poem's textual history, giving weight to the authenticated lists.

[2] On the subsequent deterioration of the impressions, see A. C. Dooley, op. cit., SBC, Spring 1979, pp. 54–5.

[3] See P. Kelley and W. S. Peterson, 'Browning's Final Revisions', in BIS 1 (1973), 87–118.

colons, with a few exceptions; hyphenation unless it indicates a different meaning; and commas with a minimal influence on meaning. A one-word lemma will normally be a punctuation variant. The words before and after substantive variants are given to aid identification, except where the variant begins or ends a line, when only one accompanying word or phrase is given. The date of the edition(s) in which variants occur is stated; the readings of editions not specified are normally the same as those in the basic text (in most cases, that of 1888).

Manuscripts

Our recording varies according to the nature of the manuscript and its relation to the printed editions; selection criteria are explained in the textual introductions to individual poems. Angle brackets indicate deletions: ⟨ ⟩; square brackets additions or substitutions: [ ]; ogee brackets enclose comments by the editors: { }.

Primary texts and editions of Browning's works consulted for Vol. IV

Manuscript: *Christmas Eve and Easter Day*. Forster Collection, Victoria and Albert Museum.

First Editions: *Hood's Magazine*, June 1844: 'Claret and Tokay' and 'The Laboratory'; July 1844: 'Garden-Fancies'; August 1844: 'The Boy and the Angel'; March 1845: 'The Tomb at St. Praxed's'; April 1845: 'The Flight of the Duchess'.

Bells and Pomegranates, No. VII. November 1845. *Dramatic Romances and Lyrics*. Moxon.

Bells and Pomegranates, No. VIII. April 1846. *Luria*; and *A Soul's Tragedy*. Moxon.

Christmas-Eve and Easter-Day, 1850. Chapman and Hall.

Collected Poetical Works and later editions

1849. *Poems*, 2 vols. Chapman and Hall. 'A New Edition'.
1863. *The Poetical Works*, 3 vols. Chapman & Hall. 'Third Edition'.
1865. *A Selection from the Works of Robert Browning*. Moxon. '*1865S*'.
1865. *The Poetical Works*, 3 vols. Chapman & Hall. 'Fourth Edition'. (Issued January 1866).

1868. *The Poetical Works*, 6 vols. Smith, Elder & Co. Vols. iii, iv, v.

1870. *The Poetical Works*, 6 vols. Smith, Elder & Co. Revised edition of *1868*.

1872. *Selections from The Poetical Works of Robert Browning*, First Series. Smith, Elder & Co. '*1872S*'.

1875. *The Poetical Works*, 6 vols. Smith, Elder & Co. Revised edition of *1870*.

1880. *Selections from The Poetical Works of Robert Browning*, Second Series. Smith, Elder & Co. '*1880S*'.

1884. *Selections from The Poetical Works of Robert Browning*, First and Second Series, 'New Edition'. Smith, Elder & Co. [and corrected reprints, 1886, 1888]. '*1884S, 1886S, 1888S*'.

1888–9. *The Poetical Works*, 16 vols. Smith, Elder & Co. Issued monthly from April 1888 to July 1889. Vols. iii, iv, v, vi (1888).

1889. *The Poetical Works*, 16 vols. Smith, Elder & Co. A corrected reprint of the 1888–9 edition. All volumes dated 1889; issued early 1890.

For secondary texts (copy manuscripts, manuscript fragments, annotated and proof copies), see the textual introductions to the individual poems.

REFERENCES AND ABBREVIATIONS

Note: the place of publication is given if it is not London or Oxford

Berdoe   *The Browning Cyclopædia*, by Edward Berdoe, 2nd ed., 1892.

Biographie universelle   Biographie universelle, ancienne et moderne, 52 vols., Paris, 1811–28.

BIS   *Browning Institute Studies*, New York.

Browning and Domett   Robert Browning and Alfred Domett, ed. Frederic G. Kenyon, 1906.

BN   *The Browning Newsletter*, Armstrong Browning Library, Waco, Texas.

BSN   *Browning Society Notes* (published by the Browning Society of London).

Checklist   The Browning's Correspondence: A Checklist, compiled by Philip Kelley and Ronald Hudson, The Browning Institute and Wedgestone Press, 1978. (Supplements in later vols. of BIS).

Collections   see Kelley and Coley.

Collier   *The Great Historical . . . Dictionary*, Vol. I, 2nd ed., revised by Jeremy Collier, 1701.

Collins and Shroyer   *The Plays of Robert Browning*, ed. Thomas J. Collins and Richard J. Shroyer, Garland Publishing, New York and London, 1988.

Cook, Eleanor   *Browning's Lyrics: An Exploration*, Toronto, 1974.

Cooke, George Willis   *A Guide-Book to the Poetic and Dramatic Works of Robert Browning*, Boston and New York, 1891.

Correspondence   The Brownings' Correspondence, ed. Philip Kelley and Ronald Hudson, Wedgestone Press, Winfield, Kansas, 1984 (in progress).

Courtship   The Courtship of Robert Browning and Elizabeth Barrett, by Daniel Karlin, 1985.

Dearest Isa: Robert Browning's Letters to Isabella Blagden, ed. Edward C. McAleer, Austin, Texas, and Edinburgh, 1951.

DeVane   *A Browning Handbook*, by William Clyde DeVane, 2nd ed., New York, 1955 (1st ed., 1935).

Domett   *The Diary of Alfred Domett 1872–1885*, ed. E. A. Horsman, 1953.

Drew   *Robert Browning: A Collection of Critical Essays*, ed. Philip Drew, 1966.

EBB   Elizabeth Barrett Browning.

Encyclopædia Britannica   *The Encyclopædia Britannica*, 11th ed., 29 vols., 1910–11.

Furnivall, Frederick J., *A Bibliography of Robert Browning, from 1833 to 1881*, 2nd ed., Browning Society, 1881.

Gosse   *Robert Browning: Personalia*, by Edmund Gosse, Boston and New York, 1890. (Part of the impression was sold in London in 1891, under the imprint of T. Fisher Unwin.)

Griffin and Minchin   *The Life of Robert Browning*, by W. Hall Griffin, completed and edited by H. C. Minchin, 3rd ed., revised and enlarged, 1938 (1st ed., 1910).

Handbook   *A Handbook to the Works of Robert Browning*, by Mrs Sutherland Orr, 7th ed., 1896 (1st ed., 1885).

Harrison   'Birds in the Poetry of Browning', by Thomas P. Harrison: *Review of English Studies*, NS, vol. vii, no. 28 (October 1956), 393–405.

Hood   'Browning's Ancient Classical Sources', by T. L. Hood: *Harvard Studies in Classical Philology*, Cambridge, Mass., 33 (1922), 79–180.

Hudson   *Browning to his American Friends*, ed. Gertrude Rees Hudson, 1965.

Johnson   *A Dictionary of the English Language*, by Samuel Johnson, 9th ed., 2 vols., 1806.

Kelley and Coley   *The Browning Collections: A Reconstruction with Other Memorabilia*, compiled by Philip Kelley and Betty A. Coley, Armstrong Browning Library, Baylor University, Texas, 1984.

Kelley and Hudson   *see Checklist*.

Kintner   *The Letters of Robert Browning and Elizabeth Barrett Barrett 1845–1846*, ed. Elvan Kintner, 2 vols., Cambridge, Mass., 1969.

Landis   *Letters of the Brownings to George Barrett*, ed. Paul Landis, Urbana, Illinois, 1958.

Learned Lady: Letters from Robert Browning to Mrs. Thomas FitzGerald, ed. Edward C. McAleer, Cambridge, Mass., 1966.

Lemprière   *A Classical Dictionary*, by J. Lemprière, 5th ed., 1804.

Letters   *Letters of Robert Browning Collected by Thomas J. Wise*, ed. Thurman L. Hood, 1933.

Letters of EBB   *The Letters of Elizabeth Barrett Browning*, ed. Frederic G. Kenyon, 2 vols., 1898.

Life   *Life and Letters of Robert Browning*, by Mrs Sutherland Orr, new ed., rev. . . . by Frederic G. Kenyon, 1908 (1st ed., 1891).

Litzinger and Smalley   *Browning: The Critical Heritage*, ed. Boyd Litzinger and Donald Smalley, 1970.

Maynard   *Browning's Youth*, by John Maynard, Cambridge, Mass., 1977.

Meredith   *More Than Friend: The Letters of Robert Browning to Katharine de Kay Bronson*, ed. Michael Meredith, Armstrong Browning Library and Wedgestone Press, 1985.

MLQ   *Modern Language Quarterly*.

More than Friend   see Meredith.

New Letters   *New Letters of Robert Browning*, ed. William Clyde De Vane and Kenneth Leslie Knickerbocker, New Haven, 1950.

New Poems   *New Poems by Robert Browning and Elizabeth Barrett Browning*, ed. Sir Frederic G. Kenyon, 1914.

NQ   *Notes and Queries*.

ODEP   *Oxford Dictionary of English Proverbs*, 3rd ed., ed. F. P. Wilson, 1970.

OED   *Oxford English Dictionary*.

OED²   *Oxford English Dictionary*, 2nd ed., ed. J. A. Simpson and E. S. C. Weiner, 20 vols., 1989.

OED *Supplement*   *Supplement to the Oxford English Dictionary*, ed. R. W. Burchfield, 4 vols., 1972–86.

Ohio Edition   *The Complete works of Robert Browning*, ed. Roma A. King, Jr., and others, vols. iv and v, Athens, Ohio, 1973, 1981.

Parleyings   *Browning's Parleyings: The Autobiography of a Mind*, by William Clyde DeVane, New Haven, 1927.

Personalia   see Gosse.

Pettigrew *or* Pettigrew and Collins   *Robert Browning: The Poems*, vol. i, ed. John Pettigrew, supplemented and completed by Thomas J. Collins, 1981 (Penguin English Poets: Yale University Press).

PK   References in the style 'PK 48:24' are to letters listed in *Checklist*.

PMLA   *Publications of the Modern Language Association of America*.

Porter and Clarke   *The Complete Works of Robert Browning*, ed. Charlotte Porter and Helen A. Clarke, 12 vols., New York, 1898 (published in different formats, at different times, and under various titles, e.g. as the Florentine Edition, the Camberwell Edition, etc.).

PQ   *Philological Quarterly*.

Raymond and Sullivan   *The Letters of Elizabeth Barrett Browning to Mary Russell Mitford 1836–1854*, ed. Meredith B. Raymond and Mary Rose Sullivan, Armstrong Browning Library, etc., 3 vols., 1983.

RES   *The Review of English Studies*.

SBC   *Studies in Browning and his Circle*, Armstrong Browning Library, Waco, Texas.

SP   *Studies in Philology*.

Tilley   *A Dictionary of the Proverbs in England in the Sixteenth and Seventeenth Centuries*, by Morris Palmer Tilley, Ann Arbor, Michigan, 1950.

TLS   *Times Literary Supplement*.

Trumpeter   *Browning's Trumpeter: The Correspondence of Robert Browning and Frederick J. Furnivall 1872–1889*, ed. William S. Peterson, Washington, DC, 1979.

UTQ   *University of Toronto Quarterly*.

VP   *Victorian Poetry*.

Wedgwood   *Robert Browning and Julia Wedgwood*, ed. Richard Curle, 1937.

Note: references to Shakespeare are to *William Shakespeare: The Complete Works* (Tudor Edition), ed. Peter Alexander, 1951.

Abbreviations and signs used in the textual notes

*	Emendation.
†	So in text (e.g. four dots appear in the text and do not indicate an omission by the editors).

. . . .	Omission by the editors.[1]
{ }	Comment by the editors.
[ ]	Addition or substitution in MS.
⟨ ⟩	Deletion in MS.
|	Division between lines.
BrU	Brown University list of corrections in RB's hand to vols. iv–x of *1888–9*.
DC	British Library copy of Browning's *Poetical Works* (1888–9), formerly belonging to James Dykes Campbell and corrected by Browning.
Domett 1845	Copy of *Bells and Pomegranates*, No. VII presented to Alfred Domett and annotated by Browning, now in Humanities Research Center, Texas.
Hood (or *Hood's*)	Hood's Magazine and Comic Miscellany, 1844, 1845.
Howard MS	Copy of 'The Lost Leader' in Browning's hand at Castle Howard, Yorkshire.
LC Transcript	British Library Add. MS. 42941.
Morgan MS	Copy of 'Home Thoughts, from Abroad' in Browning's hand in Pierpont Morgan Library, New York.
1845	*Dramatic Romances and Lyrics (Bells and Pomegranates VII).*
1846	*Luria* and *A Soul's Tragedy (Bells and Pomegranates VIII).*
1849	*Poems by Robert Browning. In Two Volumes . . . A New Edition.*
1850	*Christmas-Eve and Easter-Day.*
1863	*The Poetical Works of Robert Browning . . . Third Edition*, 3 vols.
1865S	*A Selection from the Works of Robert Browning.*
1865	*The Poetical Works of Robert Browning . . . Fourth Edition*, 3 vols.
1868,1870,1875	*The Poetical Works of Robert Browning*, 6 vols., 1st, 2nd., and 3rd eds.
1872S	*Selections from the Poetical Works of Robert Browning, First Series.*
1880S	*Selections from the Poetical Works of Robert Browning, Second Series.*

---

[1] It should be noted that RB and EBB often used '. .' as a form of punctuation in their letters. The normal '. . .' is used in this edition to indicate an omission, except in the textual notes, where '. . . .' is used.

1884S	*Selections from the Poetical Works of Robert Browning, First and Second Series, New Edition*, 2 vols.
1886S,1888S	Corrected reprints of *1884S*.
1888–9	*The Poetical Works of Robert Browning*, 16 vols.
1889	*The Poetical Works of Robert Browning*, 16 vols. Revised reprint of *1888–9*.

INTRODUCTION TO
DRAMATIC ROMANCES AND LYRICS

BROWNING and his friends had been pleased with *Dramatic Lyrics*, published in 1842 as the third of the *Bells and Pomegranates*. When he sent a copy of these 'verses' to Alfred Domett in New Zealand, Browning wrote: 'I shall have more ready ere long, I hope,—and better.'[1] It is clear that what he had in mind was another collection of short and middle-length poems.

We know more about the history of the poems in *Dramatic Romances and Lyrics* than we do about that of the pieces in the earlier collection. In 1844–5 Browning wrote a number of letters to Frederick Oldfield Ward, who was exerting himself to help Thomas Hood, now nearing the end of his life in sickness and poverty. Ward solicited contributions to *Hood's Magazine* not only from Hood's friends but also from others who knew him only 'at second hand',[2] through his writings; and Browning was sufficiently moved by Hood's situation to 'break a rule . . . kept these ten years' and contribute. 'The Laboratory' and 'Claret and Tokay' appeared in the number for June 1844, 'Garden-Fancies' in that for July, and 'The Boy and the Angel' in that for August. After his return from a journey to Italy which lasted from August to December, Browning contributed 'The Tomb at St. Praxed's' to the number for March 1845, and the first part of 'The Flight of the Duchess' to that for the following month.

On 22 May 1844 Browning wrote to Ward: 'I will this minute set about transcribing the best of whatever I can find in my desk likely to suit you—and will send it in the course of the day .. morning, I hope. I love Mr Hood heartily and grieve I can do him no other good

---

[1] *Correspondence*, vi. 221.
[2] PK 45:65; 45:32. 'Do you remember F. [O.] Ward?', Joseph Arnould asked Domett in July 1844. 'He is now sub-editor of *Hood's Magazine*, and in this capacity has acted well in wrenching from our Robert several little morceaux, sketches by a master, which have appeared in said Magazine, and being more exoteric than even his *sketches* generally are, may do him some further service with the public': *Browning and Domett*, p. 103.

turn.'[1] From the poems which he had by him he seems to have sent
'The Laboratory' at once and 'Claret and Tokay' a few days later.
'How do you like these?', he asked of the latter. '*Lilt* them a little,
for the music. But, of all things, print them together. Do as you like
about putting in, or out, the one you have already. Take counsel
with yourself, too, about the line I have noted: nor forget to send
proofs & copy.' We have no clue to 'the line ... noted'. A letter
dating from June or July 1844 is even more tantalizing:

so far from 'boring me' with corrections, you helped me essentially—but
here was the blunder, your last note, with the good 'gossamer' emenda-
tion, came *after* the proof had been received and corrected according to
the *last-but-that* (in which you said—'Hood thinks that '*not too much*' is
better than '*never a*',.. and he would omit '*whole*', as making a long line of
it &c &c—) When the proof had been duly returned, your note reached
me, after some inexplicable delay—and I thought it no use to counter-
mand what I had written. Another time we will manage better.

The word 'gossamer' occurs nowhere in Browning's poems, so we
know that the proposed emendation was not adopted, and can only
guess which poem was in question: possibly the second of the
'Garden-Fancies', as T. L. Hood suggested.[2] The words 'never a'
occur in neither poem, so revision must have taken place; but not
revision to 'not too much'. Shortly before he left for Italy, it seems,
Browning sent Ward 'Theocrite' (i.e. 'The Boy and the Angel'),
asking to see a proof of it.[3]

During the voyage he wrote 'How they Brought the Good News'.
While he was abroad it seems likely that he wrote, or conceived,
'The Tomb at St. Praxed's', and perhaps other poems. Further pieces
must have been written after his return.

[1] PK 44:145; 44:152; 44:173.
[2] *Letters*, p. 342 (note to 44:2–2).
[3] PK 44:200.1. The sincerity of Browning's desire to help Hood is shown by a letter he
wrote Ward the day before he sailed: 'I will try—try, really, to write you some letters from
the sea-way to Naples—and then you may advertise after what fashion you will, so that it
be your fashion and not mine. Not one, that is, which takes the matter out of the inconse-
quential shape of a few letters to a friend, and bookmaker on it ... I can put down more
interesting things that have already happened to me in the midland sea—but you shall
judge. I looked again and again over my romances but they would not bear cutting and
were too long without it.' We know nothing of any such publication. Cf. *Correspondence*, iv.
67–8, for one of the 'interesting things' which Browning had already described in a letter,
an occurrence from his first voyage to Italy.

In February 1845 Browning wrote two more letters to Ward which have survived.[1] About 7 February he refers to the danger of Hood's being arrested for debt, and includes an important sentence: 'if you can let me have four or five pages, I will despatch two of my new Lyrics—(two for the *same* number, because *one* will be a some- what startling affair, and the other must contrast—and show by its opposite tone that I speak *dramatically* in both cases.)' In the event he did not send 'two . . . new Lyrics', and we are unable to identify the 'startling' piece. On 18 February he wrote again to Ward: 'I send you *one* poem as long as the two I promised', no doubt 'The Tomb at St. Praxed's', with its stage-direction '(*Rome*, 15—)', which occupies three pages of the March number.

Browning first wrote to Elizabeth Barrett on 10 January 1845, and we hear a great deal throughout the year of the poems which were to appear together early in November. On 27 January he refers to 'three or four half-done-with "Bells"' on his desk,[2] while a month later he tells her that when he has finished his present work he will follow her advice and write in his own person: 'but first I have some Romances and Lyrics, all dramatic, to dispatch, and *then*, I shall stoop of a sudden under and out of this dancing ring of men & women hand in hand' and set about 'this First Poem of mine to be'.[3] It is clear that he has already realized that certain of his shorter poems cannot suitably be described as 'Lyrics'. He tells her that 'The Flight of the Duchess', which she had seen in *Hood's* in April, 'is one of my Dramatic Romances.'[4] 'So', he adds, 'is a certain "Saul" I should like to show you one day—an ominous liking,—for nobody ever sees what I do till it is printed. But as you *do* know the printed little part of me, I should not be sorry if, in justice, you knew all I have *really* done,—written in the portfolio there,—tho' that would be far enough from *this* me, that writes to you now.' She admitted to being 'overjoyed' at the prospect of 'revelations' from the portfolio. He had succeeded in his bid to interest her more deeply in his work, and his poetic career entered a new phase.

---

[1] PK 45:32; *New Letters*, pp. 35–6.
[2] Kintner, i. 11. [3] Kintner, i. 26.
[4] Kintner, i. 55–6, 58. In fact the completed 'Saul' was to be classified as a Dramatic Lyric.

On 13 May he told her that she 'must help [him] with all [his] new Romances and Lyrics, and Lays & Plays, and read them and heed them and end them and mend them!' Immediately after her rebuff of his premature proposal of marriage we find him telling her that he means, 'on the whole, to be a Poet, if not *the* Poet .. for I am vain and ambitious some nights'. He explains his evident surge of spirits on 14 June:

You do not understand what a new feeling it is for me to have someone who is to like my verses or I shall not ever like them after! So far differently was I circumstanced of old, that I used rather to go about for a subject of offence to people; writing ugly things in order to warn the ungenial & timorous off my grounds at once. I shall never do so again at least! As it is, I will bring all I dare, in as great quantities as I can—if not next time, after then—certainly. I must make an end, print this Autumn my last four 'Bells,' Lyrics, Romances, The Tragedy, & Luria, and then go on with a whole heart to my own Poem—indeed, I have just resolved not to begin any new song, even, till this grand clearance is made.[1]

We notice that *Luria* and *A Soul's Tragedy* were to appear separately, and that Browning planned one *Bell* for his new Dramatic Lyrics and another for Dramatic Romances.

Of course Elizabeth felt anxious at the responsibility he was thrusting on her. On 19 June she wrote: 'if when your poems come, you persist in giving too much importance to what I may have courage to say of this or of that in them, you will make me a dumb critic & I shall have no help for my dumbness . . . I shall do what I can—as far as *impressions* go, you understand—& *you* must promise not to attach too much importance to anything said.' 'I will finish & transcribe the "Flight of the Duchess",' he replied, 'since you spoke of that first.' This worried her, since she was deeply concerned about his health at this point. '*Don't bring the Duchess with you on Wednesday*,' she wrote emphatically, '. . . try to get well *first*, we will do the "Bells" afterwards.' If only he will agree to this, 'I will promise to be ready afterwards to help you in any thing I can do .. transcribing or anything .. to get the books through the press in the shortest of times.' By 7 July she had received the greater part of the poem; but two days later, delighted as he was that she deeply

---

[1] Kintner, i. 63, 75, 95.

admired it, he told her that he would 'not be able to bring . . . the rest' the following day. But he was going to 'transcribe the other things', which she was 'to judge'.[1]

A few days later he sent her 'all the Hood poems', on which she commented with admiration on 21 July, making one observation of particular interest:

I object a little to your tendency . . which is almost a habit . . & is very observable in this poem ['The Laboratory'] I think, . . of making lines difficult for the reader to read . . see the opening lines of this poem. Not that music is required everywhere, nor in *them* certainly, but that the uncertainty of rhythm throws the reader's mind off the *rail* . . & interrupts his progress with you and your influence with him. Where we have not direct pleasure from rhythm, & where no peculiar impression is to be produced by the changes in it, we sh.[d] be encouraged by the poet to *forget it altogether*; should we not?[2]

She sought his assurance that all these poems would be in his next pamphlet. Three days later she went on to give him what she termed her 'querulous queries' on 'The Flight of the Duchess', insisting that they were no more than 'passing thoughts, . . some right, it may be . . some wrong, it must be'. He immediately replied that all her criticisms were 'true, except the overrating', adding: 'all the suggestions are to be adopted, the improvements accepted'. We quote further from this letter in the introduction to the poem, below. He now wished her to criticize other short poems, 'to work very hard', as she observed. As soon as she looked at these further pieces she commented that they were 'full of various power & beauty & character'. A week later he thanked her for 'correcting [his] verses', which elicited a predictably embarrassed response: 'My correcting your verses!!!—Now is *that* a thing for you to say?'[3]

Elizabeth was worried that he was too impatient, and attempting too much. She was afraid that he would struggle to prepare his two tragedies for the printers, and feared that 'even to complete the preparation of the lyrics & take them through the press, [might] be

<hr />

[1] Kintner, i. 99–102, 118. [2] Kintner, i. 127, 131–5.
[3] Kintner, i. 145–6, 159. See pp. 144–5 for an anecdote which illustrates the depth of her concern for these poems. She had a habit of omitting question-marks where they might be expected, in her tentative suggestions: we have not supplied them.

too much' for him: '—& if so, why you will not do it—will you? ..
you will wait for another year, .. or at least be satisfied for this, with
bringing out a number of the old size, consisting of such poems as
are fairly finished & require no retouching. "Saul" for instance, you
might leave— —!' In fact the seventh of the *Bells*, with its short
poems, was to amount to twenty-four pages, while the completion
of 'Saul' was postponed, only part of it being published on this occa-
sion. Meanwhile he acknowledged her 'new notes on my verses'.[1]

Browning was beginning to consider the arrangement of the
poems. On 2 October he sent Elizabeth some 'easy' verses taken
from 'a paper-full' and 'meant to go between poem & poem in my
next number and break the shock of collision'. After her unsuccess-
ful attempt to persuade him to supply titles for the three 'Home-
Thoughts, from abroad' (see pp. 61–2 below), we find Browning
reporting a visit to the publisher Edward Moxon on 12 October: 'he
spoke rather encouragingly of my ... prospects', he wrote. 'I send
him a sheetful tomorrow, I believe, and we are "out" on the 1st. of
next month.' Three days later he told Elizabeth that his poems had
duly gone to press, commenting:

there is not much *correctable* in them,—you make, or you spoil, one of
these things,—that is, *I* do. I have adopted all your emendations, and
thrown in lines and words, just a morning's business; but one does not
write plays so. You may like some of my smaller things, which stop inter-
stices, better than what you have seen .. I shall wonder to know: I am to
receive a *proof* at the end of the week—will you help me & over-look it.[2]

The 'smaller things' included 'Earth's Immortalities', 'Song', and
'Night and Morning', on none of which have we queries or sugges-
tions by Elizabeth.

In her he had a friend as deeply interested in the outcome as he
was himself. 'So now let us talk of the first of November', she wrote
in her next letter, '& of the poems which are to come out then, & of
the poems which are to come after them ... Oh yes—do let me see
the proof'.[3] Her next letter included her celebrated question about
the meaning of the title of the series,[4] and expressed impatience to

[1] Kintner, i. 185. 209.   [2] Kintner, i. 221, 229, 236.
[3] Kintner, i. 238.   [4] See Vol. III, pp. 3 ff.

see the proof, which reached Browning the following evening. 'This arrived on Saturday night', he wrote on 20 October, '—I just correct it in time for this our first post—will it do, the new matter? I can take it to-morrow—when I am to see you—if you are able to glance thro' it by then.'[1] He asked if she liked the dedication to John Kenyon, and wished that he had been at liberty to have a motto from one of her poems, apparently 'The Lost Bower'.

On 22 October she wrote to supplement what she had already said and written about the poems:

their various power & beauty will be striking and surprising to your most accustomed readers. St. Praxed—Pictor Ignotus—the ride—the Duchess! —Of the new poems I like supremely the first & last .. that 'Lost Leader' which strikes so broadly & deep .. which nobody can ever forget—& which is worth all the journalizing & pamphleteering in the world!—& then, the last 'Thought' which is quite to be grudged to that place of fragments .. those grand sea-sights in the long lines—Should not these fragments be severed otherwise than by numbers?—The last stanza but one of the 'Lost Mistress' seemed obscure to me. Is it so really? The end you have put to 'England in Italy' gives unity to the whole . . . The Duchess appears to me more than ever a new-minted golden coin—the rhythm of it answering to your own description,

"Speech half asleep, or song half awake?"

You have right of trove to these novel effects of rhythm. Now if people do not cry out about these poems, what are we to think of the world?[2]

'The proof does not come?', she asked the following day, clearly with reference to a 'revise'.[3] Four days later Browning complained that he had heard nothing of it, and would have to go to enquire. 'In the other', he wrote, 'I have corrected all the points you noted,—to their evident improvement.' Later that day the proof did arrive: 'I . . . have just run thro' it', he told her the following morning, sending it on for her scrutiny 'that time may not be lost': he had found in it 'Faults, faults' and reported that he had 'got

[1] Kintner, i. 241–2.
[2] Kintner, i. 244. For her further comments on 'England in Italy' cf. pp. 39 ff. below, and for his later attempts to improve 'The Lost Mistress' see pp. 59–60.
[3] Kintner, i. 247, 251.

tired of this'. On the 29th she wrote to him 'in haste, not to lose time about the proof':

You will see on the papers here my doubtfulnesses such as they are—but silence swallows up the admirations . . & there is no time. 'Theocrite' over-takes that wish of mine which ran on so fast—and the 'Duchess' grows and grows the more I look—and 'Saul' is noble and must have his full royalty some day . . . For the new poems—they are full of beauty. You throw largesses out on all sides without counting the coins—how beautiful that 'Night & Morning' . . and the 'Earth's Immortalities' . . & the 'Song' too.[1]

Her praise of 'The Glove' and her remarks on 'The Flight of the Duchess' are quoted elsewhere. 'Am I not to thank you for all my pleasure & pride in these poems?', she asks: '—while you stand by and try to talk them down, perhaps.' The same day Browning thanked her for 'all this trouble and correcting', adding: 'When you see the pamphlet's self, you will find your own doing,—but where will you find the proofs of the best of all helping and counselling and inciting, unless in new works which shall justify the *unsatisfaction*, if I may not say shame, at these, these written before your time, my best love.' On the 31st she asked when the pamphlet would appear, the 1st being no longer the aim. On the 4th he told her that 'Moxon promises the books for to-morrow, Wednesday—so towards evening yours will reach you.' The next day she waited for this 'true living breathing book, let the writer say of it what he will', but it was the 6th before he was able to send her a copy, lamenting (at the same time) that 'friend A. & B. & C. must get their copy, and word of regard, all by next post!' In at least one case he found that a friend had received 'proof-sheets' direct from Moxon, without his own direction: he told Eliot War-burton that he hoped to go on 'to do more & better', and assured him that he would send him 'a clean copy in a day or two'.

As soon as she received her copy, Elizabeth sat down to reread everything 'with new delight', hoping that no harm had been done by her 'meddling'. She wrote to Browning the same day:

I do hold that nobody with an ordinary understanding has the slightest pretence for attaching a charge of obscurity to this new number—there are lights enough for the critics to scan one another's dull blank of visage

---

[1] Kintner, i. 252–3, 253, 256, 257, 258; PK 45:273.

by . . . people who shall complain of darkness are blind . . I mean, that the construction is clear & unembarrassed everywhere. Subtleties of thought which are not directly apprehensible by minds of a common range, are here as elsewhere in your writings—but if to utter things 'hard to understand' from *that* cause, be an offence, why we may begin with 'our beloved brother Paul,' you know, & go down through all the geniuses of the world, & bid them put away their inspirations.

She was afraid that he would overtask himself in the attempt to complete *Luria*, soon urging him to 'let the people have time to learn the last number by heart'. She continued:

I . . . hold that as far as construction goes, you never put together so much unquestionable, smooth glory before, . . not a single entanglement for the understanding . . unless 'the snowdrops' [in 'The Lost Mistress'] make an exception—while for the undeniableness of genius it never stood out before your readers more plainly than in that same number!—Also you have extended your sweep of power . . . The rhythm (to touch one of the various things) the rhythm of that 'Duchess' does more & more strike me as a new thing . . . Then the Ride—with that touch of natural feeling at the end, to prove that it was not in brutal carelessness that the poor horse was driven through all that suffering . . yes, & how that one touch of softness acts back upon the energy & resolution & exalts both, instead of weakening anything, as might have been expected by the vulgar of writers or critics. And then 'Saul'—& in a first place 'St. Praxed'—& for pure description, 'Fortù' and the deep 'Pictor Ignotus'—& the noble, serene 'Italy in England', which grows on you the more you know of it—& that delightful 'Glove'—and the short lyrics . . for one comes to *'select' everything* at last, & certainly I do like these poems better & better.[1]

None of the other friends to whom Browning sent presentation copies of *Dramatic Romances and Lyrics* replied as memorably as Landor. 'What a profusion of imagery, covering what a depth of thought!', he wrote. 'You may stand quite alone if you will—and I think you will.'[2] On 22 November Landor printed in the *Morning Chronicle* his famous compliment to Browning:

[1] Kintner, i. 259–60, 267, 267–8.

[2] See R. H. Super, *Walter Savage Landor* (London ed., 1957), p. 357. In Domett's copy of Landor's complimentary poem the words 'to me in 1845' seem to have been added. In fact Browning sent the lines with a letter dated 19 March 1846: *Browning and Domett*, p. 124. The MS of the poem is at Yale. (In his *Works*, 1846, Landor substituted 'brief' for 'short' in l. 6).

Browning was able to take EBB a packet of 'good-natured letters' from other admiring readers: see Kintner, i. 277.

TO ROBERT BROWNING.

There is delight in singing, though none hear
Beside the singer; and there is delight
In praising, though the praiser sit alone
And see the prais'd far off him, far above.
Shakespeare is not *our* poet, but the world's,
Therefore on him no speech; and short for thee,
Browning! Since Chaucer was alive and hale,
No man hath walk'd along our roads with step
So active, so inquiring eye, or tongue
So varied in discourse. But warmer climes
Give brighter plumage, stronger wing; the breeze
Of Alpine heights thou playest with, borne on
Beyond Sorrento and Amalfi, where
The Siren waits thee, singing song for song.

Nov. 19, 1845.   W. S. LANDOR.

It is not surprising that Browning's father was so proud of these lines that he had them printed for circulation among his friends. The only copy of this printing known to survive is reproduced as the frontispiece to the present volume, by permission of the Harry Ransom Humanities Research Center of the University of Texas at Austin.

Beside such poet's praise the reviews must have seemed something of an anticlimax, yet several spoke well of the pamphlet. The writer in the *Examiner* was 'disposed to admire this little book . . . very much', rejoicing that Browning had 'found the path again' after the 'metaphysics' of some of his earlier work: 'His writing has always the stamp and freshness of originality,' the reviewer commented. 'It is in no respect imitative or commonplace. Whatever the verse may be, the man is in it: the music of it echoing to his mood.' The December number of the *New Monthly Magazine* announced the publication as one which would give pleasure to the 'admirers of Robert Browning's poetry . . . now very numerous'. Elizabeth sent him a cutting of this observation, which may have helped to console him for Moxon's remark that the pamphlet had been 'going off "rather heavily"'. The *English Review* praised the *Bells and Pomegranates* so far published, in spite of their 'fantastic name', and stated that the 'two lyrical numbers . . . would and will alone vindicate his fame'. On 17 January the *Athenæum* hailed 'yet another proof of Mr. Browning's fertility', quoted extensively from several of the pieces, and concluded that 'these Romances will add to the poet's reputation'.[1]

The Text

As has already become evident, the most interesting period in the textual history of these poems is that preceding their publication as the seventh of the *Bells and Pomegranates* pamphlets. For the great majority of them we have earlier readings and comments by Elizabeth Barrett which almost always led to revisions.

In her criticisms of the poems which had been published in *Hood's Magazine* we notice in particular her concern about the rhythm of the verse. 'Will you read this line with the context', she asks of l. 31 of 'The Laboratory', '& see if the rhythm is not perplexed in it?'; while she also comments on the rhythm of two other lines. She objects to the words 'lest horror then springs' in the penultimate line because they 'are clogged, I think . . & the expression seems forced'. The word 'clogged' also appears in relation to 'Mind the pink shut mouth opens never' in 'The Flower's Name', and in her comments on other of the poems. She criticizes the rhythm, the occasional use of short lines, and the obscurity of 'The Boy and the Angel', and suggests that 'a little dilation' of the later stanzas would help the reader. In response to her criticisms, Browning revised all six poems, paying particular attention to 'The Boy and the Angel', in which nineteen lines were rewritten and five new couplets added for the 1845 version. Elizabeth had questioned a Shakespearian locution in 'The Tomb at St. Praxed's'; Browning duly revised it and also wrote three new lines elaborating on the tomb ornaments. He improved the rhythm of a number of lines in 'The Flower's Name' and 'The Laboratory', and made slighter revisions in 'Sibrandus' and 'Claret and Tokay'.

Elizabeth's comments on the poems first published in *1845*

---

[1] *Examiner*, 15 November 1845, p. 723; *New Monthly Magazine*, December 1845 (last page); Kintner, i. 345; *English Review*, December 1845, iv. 274, 277; *Athenæum*, 17 January 1846, pp. 58–9.

provide our only evidence of readings in Browning's manuscripts. Impressed as she was by 'Pictor Ignotus', she made several objections, being particularly worried by an 'obscurity in the expression' in one place. Many of her numerous comments on 'England in Italy' relate to the rhythm. She queried the original version of l. 122, to the advantage of the poem as published. The last stanza of 'The Confessional' might, she considered, be cleared 'by a moment's attention'. She found l. 225 of 'The Flight of the Duchess' unsatisfactory—'there is something forced in the expression, or appears to *me* to be so'—and the following line 'too short to the ear'. Her comments on these and other poems may be found in the footnotes to them below.

The most important revisions after *1845* were those in the two-volume edition of 1849, a collection to which Browning attached great importance. His treatment of the poems originally published in *Hood's* (and already once revised for *1845*) varied considerably. He left 'The Bishop Orders his Tomb' and 'Sibrandus Schafnaburgensis' comparatively unchanged, and omitted 'Claret and Tokay' altogether; but he made a number of important revisions in 'The Flower's Name' and 'The Laboratory', and (among other improvements) added two new lines to 'The Boy and the Angel'. Of the poems first published in *1845*, he revised 'Pictor Ignotus' with exceptional thoroughness, concentrating mainly on the first fifty lines. He focused on particular lines in several of the other poems—leaving the first three sections of 'Saul' intact, for example, but revising the rest, with notable improvements in rhythm; similarly he concentrated on the second stanza of 'The Lost Leader' and the fourth stanza of 'The Lost Mistress'. 'The Flight of the Duchess' was revised with especial care for *1849*: many of the forty substantive changes benefited the rhythm as well as the sense.

While Browning seems to have reread the poems carefully for *1863*, in which he classified his shorter poems for the first time, the revisions are minor—except perhaps in the last section of 'The Flight of the Duchess', where the tone and tempo were modified by a fairly thorough revisal of the punctuation. These aspects seem to have influenced his alterations especially in the more dramatic poems: judicious verbal and punctuation changes were made at key points in 'The Italian in England', 'The Englishman in Italy', and 'Time's Revenges', for example, though the revision of 'The Lost Leader' was less happy. The last line of 'Nationality in Drinks' (the new title under which 'Claret and Tokay' had been revived) was amusingly emended to remove Browning's mistaken notion that 'Ausbruch' was a place. The *1849* text of 'Saul' had already been greatly changed, extended, and metrically reworked in 1855 for *Men and Women*; Browning left this version more or less intact, save for a little lightening of the punctuation, in 1863. The full textual history of this poem will be presented in Volume V.

The 'Fourth Edition' of 1865 was a revised version of *1863* with some notable improvements in, for example, 'Pictor Ignotus' and 'The Englishman in Italy'; but, as often in this edition, several of the poems were marred by printing errors. We have emended the text of 'The Flight of the Duchess' and 'Time's Revenges' where such misprints escaped Browning's own attention in his later editions. The 1865 text evidently formed the basis of Browning's manuscript copy of 'The Lost Leader' made for the autograph album of Rosa-lind Howard, ninth Countess of Carlisle; we have recorded its minor variants from this text in our notes as 'Howard MS'. The *Selection* of 1865 included seven poems from *Dramatic Romances and Lyrics*: 'The Lost Mistress', 'Song', 'Claret and Tokay' (printed as two separate pieces), 'Time's Revenges', 'The Englishman in Italy', and the two 'Home-Thoughts'. There are in the *Selection* one or two interesting readings which, though clearly authorial, were not perpetuated in later texts. Corrected pages of copy for the *Selection* survive in the Humanities Research Center at Texas, and (for 'Time's Revenges') at Princeton; they have been noted where appro-priate as 'proof' readings.

1868 is a slightly revised version of *1865*. Here again attention was paid to the phrasing and punctuation of particular groups of lines rather than to reworking complete poems: thus in 'The Flight of the Duchess' Browning concentrated on the Gipsy's speech, and there were improvements in the rhythm and clarity of certain lines in 'The Englishman in Italy', 'The Boy and the Angel', and 'Time's Revenges'.

As Michael Meredith has shown,[1] Browning revised the text of

---

[1] In 'Learning's Crabbed Text': SBC 13 (1985), 97–107.

1868 for a second six-volume edition in 1870. He made some twenty slight changes in the poems of *Dramatic Romances and Lyrics*, chiefly in punctuation. Unfortunately *1870* proved to be full of errors, not all of which were noticed by Browning when he revised it in 1875, and we have emended various faulty readings deriving from it, notably in 'The Flight of the Duchess'. One curiosity of this textual sequence is Browning's acceptance of a misprint in the *1870* text of 'The Englishman in Italy' ('speckled with' for 'specked with'), and his transformation of the error into a new version of the line in *1875*.

Using *1870* as his copy, Browning also made two series of *Selections* in 1872 and 1880, covering between them all the *Dramatic Romances and Lyrics* except 'The Confessional', 'Home Thoughts from the Sea', and 'Nationality in Drinks'. Many of the poems were interestingly revised, and both 'The Lost Mistress' and 'The Glove' gained considerably in clarity. Most of these improvements were retained in the two-volume *Selections* of 1884 and in the reprints of 1886 and 1888, but not in the *Poetical Works* of 1888–9. 'The Flight of the Duchess' had been revised yet again for the *Selections* of 1884, and it is perhaps surprising that Browning incorporated so few of the new readings in his final text. *1888* was based on the six-volume *1875* edition, and evidently satisfied Browning, for he made only a handful of slight corrections in the Dykes Campbell copy and the Brown University list. These were carried out in 1889, and have been used in our text, along with necessary emendations (mainly of punctuation), which we have based wherever possible on the most reliable of the earlier texts.

DRAMATIC ROMANCES
AND LYRICS

title *1845* BELLS AND POMEGRANATES. No. VII. DRAMATIC ROMANCES &
LYRICS. BY ROBERT BROWNING, Author of "Paracelsus." LONDON: EDWARD
MOXON, DOVER STREET. MDCCCXLV.

[The reverse of the title-page of *1845* bears the following dedication: 'ℑnscribed to JOHN KENYON, Esq., in the hope that a recollection of his own successful "RHYMED PLEA FOR TOLERANCE" may induce him to admit good-naturedly this humbler prose one of his very sincere friend, R. B. *Nov.* 1845.' This is repeated at the beginning of the *Dramatic Romances and Lyrics* in *1849* (being the collections of *1842* and *1845* together), with the variant 'his very grateful and affectionate friend,' and the deletion of the date. In Vol. i of *1863*, which is dedicated to John Forster and which consists of the poems published in *1842*, *1845*, and *1855* (in *Men and Women*), redistributed and classified, the note opposite the first page of the text reads: 'Part of these {*1868* Part of the Poems} were inscribed to my dear friend John Kenyon: I hope the whole may obtain the honour of an association with his memory'. Unlike the *Dramatic Lyrics* of 1842, the *Dramatic Romances and Lyrics* of 1845 has a list of Contents, below the dedication.]

JOHN KENYON: Born in 1784, Kenyon was a wealthy philanthropist who had been at school with Browning's father. He was on cordial terms with Wordsworth, Coleridge, Lamb, Landor, and numerous other men of letters, many of whom experienced his discreet and thoughtful generosity. He was a distant relation of Elizabeth Barrett. He met Browning in 1839, and later attempted, without success, to introduce him to EBB. On their marriage he made them an allowance, and in his will he left them a large legacy. In the dedication of *Aurora Leigh*, which appeared in the year of his death, 1856, EBB wrote: 'you have believed in me, borne with me, and been generous to me, far beyond the common uses of mere relationship or sympathy of mind'. *A Rhymed Plea for Tolerance* (1833), advocating charity as a moderator of religious zeal, was the first of his three volumes of verse.

'HOW THEY BROUGHT THE
GOOD NEWS FROM GHENT TO AIX'

BROWNING was often asked about this poem. On 20 October 1871 he told one enquirer who wished to know 'the antecedents of the journey' that there were 'none but the sitting down under the bulwark of a ship off the coast of Tangiers, and writing it on the fly-leaf of Bartoli's *Simboli*; the whole "Ride" being purely imaginary'.[1] On 23 January 1881 he told another correspondent that there was 'no sort of historical foundation' for the poem, adding that he 'had been at sea long enough to appreciate even the fancy of a gallop on the back of a certain good horse "York", then in [his] stable at home'.[2] At the end of the same year he wrote to the Revd. V. D. Davis:

All the circumstances were imaginary—the places inserted by conjecture—and the date given as an indication of the time and manner of the 'galloping' on which attention was meant to be concentrated. Would the object of the ride be clearer if you suppose that Ghent was invested and reduced to extremity, that help was about to arrive in some unexpected way, and that the intelligence of this—which would 'save the city from its fate' of surrendering—must reach Ghent at once by some road still open—by an accident perhaps?[3]

He added a comment which is of interest in relation to more than this particular poem: 'A film or two, even so slight as the above, may sufficiently support a tolerably big spider-web of a story—where there is ability and good will enough to look most at the main fabric in the middle.'

In another letter Browning mentioned that he had no map by him as he

[1] *New Letters*, p. 203. On another occasion Browning told 'A Friend' that he had been 'in a sailing vessel slowly making [his] way from Sicily to Naples in calm weather' when he longed for 'a breezy gallop' and wrote the poem: *Pall Mall Gazette*, 31 December 1889, p. 3.

[2] Frederick J. Furnivall, *A Bibliography of Robert Browning*, 2nd ed., 1881 (Browning Society Papers), p. 49 n.

[3] TLS, 8 February 1952, p. 109. In this letter, dated 30 December 1881, Browning writes 'Ghent' for 'Aix'. Ghent is in the NW of Belgium, Aix-la-Chapelle (Aachen) in Germany near the borders of Belgium and Holland. As Pettigrew observes, the other places mentioned in the poem are 'more or less between the two points'. Griffin and Minchin point out that there were no railways in Belgium when Browning accompanied the Chevalier George de Benkhausen to Russia in 1834: 'For fifteen hundred miles, therefore, the travellers journeyed day and night as fast as horses could take them.' It is no doubt true that it was from the outward and homeward journeys on that occasion that he 'acquired the knowledge of localities' in the poem: pp. 61–2.

wrote, so that 'the places mentioned' are 'remembered or guessed at loosely enough'.[1] In one of several further replies to questions he stressed that he had written 'with a merely general impression of the characteristic warfare and besieging which abound in the Annals of Flanders', and that this accounted for 'some difficulties in the time and space occupied by the ride in one night'.[2] James Russell Lowell acknowledged that it was disheartening 'That anybody should suppose that the quadrupedans sonitus of your Courier's famous horse ever resounded on more solid fields than those of [the] imagination, or that a poem was less authentic because unsupported by any evidence in Haydon's Dictionary of Dates', yet begged him to 'make an honest admirer happy' by sending an unknown reader a line of explanation.[3]

DeVane states that the copy of *Simboli* in which Browning originally wrote the poem is that at Balliol. So it seems; but unfortunately the writing is erased, and is now illegible.[4]

The statement by Mrs Orr and Griffin and Minchin that Browning wrote the poem on his first voyage to Italy in 1838 has rightly been opposed by Kenyon and others.[5] Browning told Fanny Haworth that, but for 'a scene in a play', he had not written 'six lines' while abroad,[6] and if 'How they Brought the Good News' had existed before 1842 he would surely have included it in *Dramatic Lyrics*. The poem was no doubt written during his second voyage to Italy in 1844, from which he returned about the middle of December.

Like 'Lochinvar' in *Marmion*, 'Lochiel's Warning' by Thomas Campbell, and indeed 'Through the Metidja to Abd-el-Kadr' in *Dramatic Lyrics*, 'How they Brought the Good News' is a poem in which the metre mimes the rhythm of riding. In her first comment on it Elizabeth Barrett mentioned a less obvious literary parallel: 'You have fairly distanced the rider in Rookwood here', she wrote, '—not that I sh^d think of saying so, if we had not talked of him before. You hear the very "trampling & breathing" of the horses all through—& the sentiment is left in its right place through all the physical force-display. Then the difficult management of the *three* horses, of the *three* individualities, . . & Roland carrying the

---

[1] *New Letters*, p. 300.   [2] *Letters*, pp. 215–16.   [3] Hudson, p. 360.

[4] Kelley and Coley, A 168. It is tantalizing that Browning's other copy of the book (A 167), now at Wellesley, lacks its flyleaves.

[5] *Life*, p. 94; Griffin and Minchin, p. 20, p. 95 n.; *The Works of Robert Browning*, ed. F. G. Kenyon (10 vols., 1912, repr. Ernest Benn, n.d.), iii, p. xiii; DeVane, p. 154. On p. 128, contradicting their earlier statement, Griffin and Minchin assign the poem to Browning's second Italian voyage.

[6] *Correspondence*, iv. 67.

interest with him triumphantly!—I know you must be fond of this poem; & nobody can forget it who has looked at it once.' In *Rookwood: A Romance*, by Harrison Ainsworth (1834), we find a celebrated (but unhistorical) account of a ride to York by the highwayman Dick Turpin on his mare Black Bess. Elizabeth is probably referring to the anapaestic poem 'Black Bess', of which one stanza may be quoted:

> Brake, brook, meadow, and plough'd field, Bess fleetly bestrode,
> As the crow wings her flight, we selected our road,
> We arrived at Hough Green in five minutes or less,
> My neck, it was saved, by the speed of Black Bess.[1]

1849 Dramatic Romances and Lyrics; 1863 Lyrics; 1868– Dramatic Lyrics.

'HOW THEY BROUGHT THE GOOD NEWS FROM GHENT TO AIX.'

[16—.]

I.

I SPRANG to the stirrup, and Joris, and he;
I galloped, Dirck galloped, we galloped all three;
'Good speed!' cried the watch, as the gate-bolts undrew;
'Speed!' echoed the wall to us galloping through;

---

1 *1845* and He;   2 *1845* Three;

Title: *from Ghent to Aix*: see Introduction.
1 *Joris*: like 'Dirck' (Eng. Derek), a name found in the Low Countries.
2 *I galloped*: 'By the way, how the word "galloping" is a good galloping word!', EBB commented: '& how you felt it, & took the effect up & dilated it by repeating it over & over in your first stanza, .. doubling, folding one upon another, the hoof-treads'. She writes out 2–5 with variants which must be earlier readings: 'as the east gate undrew— / Good speed from the wall ... / The gate, shut the porter'.
3 *undrew*: cf. Mrs Radcliffe, *The Mysteries of Udolpho*, ch. xxxiv: 'Emily ... heard ... the bolts undraw of a small postern door.'

---

[1] *Rookwood*, iii. 242.
For an account of Browning's unwilling attempt to record his poem during the last months of his life, and what came of it, see Michael Hancher and Jerrold Moore, '"The Sound of a Voice that is Still": Browning's Edison Cylinder': BN, Spring 1970, pp. 21–33 and Fall, 1970, pp. 10–18.

Behind shut the postern, the lights sank to rest,   5
And into the midnight we galloped abreast.

II.

Not a word to each other; we kept the great pace
Neck by neck, stride by stride, never changing our place;
I turned in my saddle and made its girths tight,
Then shortened each stirrup, and set the pique right,   10
Rebuckled the cheek-strap, chained slacker the bit,
Nor galloped less steadily Roland a whit.

III.

'T was moonset at starting; but while we drew near
Lokeren, the cocks crew and twilight dawned clear;
At Boom, a great yellow star came out to see;   15
At Düffeld, 't was morning as plain as could be;
And from Mecheln church-steeple we heard the half-chime,
So, Joris broke silence with, 'Yet there is time!'

IV.

At Aerschot, up leaped of a sudden the sun,
And against him the cattle stood black every one,   20
To stare thro' the mist at us galloping past,
And I saw my stout galloper Roland at last,

---

8 *1845* stride for stride,   17 *1884S–8S* half chime,   18 *1845–65* So Joris
*19 {reading of *1845–65*} *1868–89* At Aershot,

10 *pique*: OED considers this an erroneous form of 'peak'. Porter and Clarke similarly
gloss it as 'the pommel of the saddle', with the pleasing comment: 'We state this on
authority of an army officer, although the meaning is in none of the dictionaries.'

13 *moonset*: perhaps coined by Browning: subsequently used by William Morris.

14 *Lokeren*: since, on Browning's admission, the places were 'inserted by conjecture',
'remembered or guessed at loosely enough', we content ourselves with referring the reader
who wishes to follow this imaginary journey to an atlas.

and twilight: EBB has '& twilight seemed clear', and comments: 'I doubt about 'twilight
seeming clear'. Is it a happy expression? But I only *doubt*, you know. The leaping up of the
sun afterward, & the cattle standing black against him, & staring through the mist at the
riders,... all that,... I do not call it *picture*, because it is so much better.. it is the very sun &
mist & cattle themselves.'

With resolute shoulders, each butting away
The haze, as some bluff river headland its spray:

V.

And his low head and crest, just one sharp ear bent back   25
For my voice, and the other pricked out on his track;
And one eye's black intelligence,—ever that glance
O'er its white edge at me, his own master, askance!
And the thick heavy spume-flakes which aye and anon
His fierce lips shook upwards in galloping on.   30

VI.

By Hasselt, Dirck groaned; and cried Joris, "Stay spur!
"Your Roos galloped bravely, the fault's not in her,
"We'll remember at Aix"—for one heard the quick wheeze
Of her chest, saw the stretched neck and staggering knees,
And sunk tail, and horrible heave of the flank,   35
As down on her haunches she shuddered and sank.

VII.

So, we were left galloping, Joris and I,
Past Looz and past Tongres, no cloud in the sky;
The broad sun above laughed a pitiless laugh,
'Neath our feet broke the brittle bright stubble like chaff;   40
Till over by Dalhem a dome-spire sprang white,
And "Gallop," gasped Joris, "for Aix is in sight!"

---

24 *1845* The haze as . . . . spray. *1849–65* The haze, as . . . . spray.   37 *1845* So left were we galloping, *1849–65* So we were left galloping,   42 *1872S–88S* sight!

25 *one sharp ear*: 'And I like the description of Roland, . . I like *him* . . seeing him, . . with one sharp ear bent back & the other pricked out!', EBB commented: 'it is so lovingly the horse . . even to me who know nothing of horses in the ordinary way of sitting down & trying to remember what I know, but who recognize this for a real horse galloping.'

29 *spume-flakes*: no other example in OED.

40 *'Neath our feet*: cf. Virgil, *Æneid*, viii. 596: 'quadrupedante putrem sonitu quatit ungula campum', translated by Dryden: 'And shake with horny Hoofs the solid ground'.

41 *dome-spire*: apparently Browning's coinage.

VIII.

"How they'll greet us!"—and all in a moment his roan
Rolled neck and croup over, lay dead as a stone;
And there was my Roland to bear the whole weight   45
Of the news which alone could save Aix from her fate,
With his nostrils like pits full of blood to the brim,
And with circles of red for his eye-sockets' rim.

IX.

Then I cast loose my buffcoat, each holster let fall,
Shook off both my jack-boots, let go belt and all,   50
Stood up in the stirrup, leaned, patted his ear,
Called my Roland his pet-name, my horse without peer;
Clapped my hands, laughed and sang, any noise, bad or good,
Till at length into Aix Roland galloped and stood.

X.

And all I remember is—friends flocking round   55
As I sat with his head 'twixt my knees on the ground;
And no voice but was praising this Roland of mine,
As I poured down his throat our last measure of wine,
Which (the burgesses voted by common consent)
Was no more than his due who brought good news from
          Ghent.   60

---

43 *1845* us"—   53 *1888* {some copies} noise. bad {faulty type} {DC as text}
55 *1845–88S* is, friends   56 *1845,1849* sate . . . . ground,

44 *croup*: 'The buttocks of a horse': Johnson.

58 *As I poured*: 'Raising her head upon his shoulder, Dick poured the contents of the bottle down the throat of his mare': *Rookwood*, iii. 333.

59 *Which* (*the burgesses voted*: EBB preserves an earlier reading: 'One query at the last stanza: "That they saved to have drunk our Duke's health in, but grieved—" You mean to say . . "would have grieved" . . do you not? The construction seems a little imperfect.'

60 *Was no more*: for EBB's praise of 'that touch of natural feeling at the end', see above, p. 9.

PICTOR IGNOTUS

UNDERSTANDING of this poem has been advanced by Dr J. B. Bullen's discovery of Browning's debt to accounts of the life of Fra Bartolommeo (Baccio della Porta 1472/1475–1517).[1] We do not know exactly when it was written, but it is natural to associate it with Browning's visit to Italy in the later part of 1844. The sources are literary rather than pictorial, however, and it may have been the publication of the first of the two volumes of Mrs Anna Jameson's *Memoirs of the Early Italian Painters* on 12 July 1845[2] which prompted him to write. In any event, Browning will have turned to Vasari's *Lives of the Painters*, and perhaps to other early authorities. There are no important verbal parallels to any of the possible sources: 'Pictor Ignotus' is a work of the imagination the nature of whose speaker was simply suggested by Bartolommeo. It has two themes: it is a study of a neurotic psychological type, and an imaginative commentary on a turning-point in the history of art.

Bartolommeo occupies a prominent position in Mrs Jameson's work, coming last in the first volume. She introduces him in these words:

Before we enter on the golden age of painting—that splendid æra which crowded into a brief quarter of a century (between 1505 and 1530) the greatest names and most consummate productions of the art—we must speak of one more painter justly celebrated.[3]

She groups Bartolommeo with Perugino and Francia as one of the men who 'were still living at this period; but [who] belonged to a previous age, and were informed ... by a wholly different spirit'. These three 'contributed in some degree to the perfection of their great contemporaries and

[1] 'Browning's "Pictor Ignotus" and Vasari's "Life of Fra Bartolommeo di San Marco"': RES, August 1972, pp. 313–19. See too the exchange between Bullen and M. H. Bright, *English Language Notes* (Boulder, Colorado), March 1976, pp. 192–4, 206–15.
  It is of interest that Heinrich Wölfflin devotes a chapter of his *Classic Art* (1st ed., in German, 1899) to Fra Bartolommeo, describing him as 'The type of the monastic painter in the High Renaissance'.

[2] It was advertised as published 'This day' in the *Athenæum* for that date: p. 702c. Vol. ii was published on 26 July. The *Memoirs* had been published anonymously, as 'Essays', in the *Penny Magazine* in 1844, that on Fra Bartolommeo having appeared on 9 and 16 March. If one believes that 'Pictor Ignotus' was the poem mentioned by Browning to EBB in mid-July 1845 as having been 'written some time ago' (Kintner, i. 128 and 129 n.; Bullen, 315 n.) this earlier publication might be of interest; but the identification is very doubtful.

[3] *Memoirs*, i. 218–25.

successors, but . . . owed the sentiment which inspired their own works to influences quite distinct from those which prevailed during the next half-century'.

Following Vasari, Mrs Jameson writes: 'From his earliest years he appears to have been a religious enthusiast, and this turn of mind not only characterised all the productions of his pencil, but involved him in a singular manner with some of the most remarkable events and characters of his time.' He had lived on to a period when a new spirit 'was rapidly corrupting the simple and pious taste which had hitherto prevailed in art': with the encouragement of the Medici family, there now prevailed a 'pagan taste in literature and art and a general laxity of morals, a licence of conduct, and a disregard of all sacred things'.

It was at this time, when Florence had become 'one of the most magnificent, but also one of the most dissolute of cities', that Savonarola was preaching. The conclusive evidence for Bullen's hypothesis is that it explains the 'voice' which changed the life of the speaker. Here is Mrs Jameson's account of the matter:

The natural taste and character of Bartolomeo placed him far from this luxurious and licentious court; but he had acquired great reputation by the exquisite beauty and tenderness of his Madonnas, and he was employed by the Dominicans of the convent of St. Mark to paint a fresco in their church, representing the Last Judgment. At this time Savonarola, an eloquent friar in the convent, was preaching against the disorders of the times, the luxury of the nobles, the usurpation of the Medici, and the vices of the popes, with a fearless fervour and eloquence which his hearers and himself mistook for direct inspiration from heaven. The influence of this extraordinary man increased daily; and among his most devoted admirers and disciples was Bartolomeo. In a fit of perplexity and remorse, caused by an eloquent sermon of Savonarola, he joined with many others in making a sacrifice of all the books and pictures which related to heathen poetry and art on which they could lay their hands; into this funeral pyre, which was kindled in sight of the people in one of the principal streets of Florence, Bartolomeo flung all those of his designs, drawings, and studies which represented either profane subjects or the human figure undraped, and he almost wholly abandoned the practice of his art for the society of his friend and spiritual pastor.

The celebrated 'burning of the vanities' in the Piazza della Signoria in Florence took place in 1497. The next year Savonarola himself was tortured and burnt on the orders of the Pope.

As a result of the preaching of Savonarola and the 'tumult and horrors' at the time of his execution, Bartolommeo 'took the vows and became a

Dominican friar, leaving to his friend Albertinelli the task of completing those of his frescoes and pictures which were left unfinished'. He spent the next four years 'without touching a pencil, in the austere seclusion of his convent'; but then his Superior persuaded him 'to resume the practice of his art'. Mrs Jameson's next sentences leave no doubt about the identity of the youth in the first line of the poem:

Timid by nature, and tormented by religious scruples, he at first returned to his easel with languor and reluctance; but an incident occurred which re-awakened all his genius and enthusiasm. Young Raphael, then in his twenty-first year, and already celebrated, arrived in Florence. He visited the Frate in his cell, and between these kindred spirits a friendship ensued which ended only with death, and to which we partly owe the finest works of both.

Mrs Jameson here quotes *An Account of Some of the Statues, Bas-Reliefs, Drawings and Pictures in Italy*, by Jonathan Richardson and his son (1722): 'at this time Fra Bartolomeo seems to have been the greater man, and might have been *the* Raphael, had not Fortune been determined in favour of the other'. She goes on to quote the Scots painter Sir David Wilkie: 'Here a monk in the retirement of his cloister, shut out from the taunts and criticism of the world, seems to have anticipated in his early time all that his art could arrive at in its most advanced maturity.'[1]

The metrical form of the poem is unusual, the cross-rhymed iambic pentameters being heavily enjambed. Alliteration is prominent. From *1863* Browning printed it immediately before 'Fra Lippo Lippi' and 'Andrea del Sarto'.

Fifteen of the first fifty lines were revised in *1849*, almost all to diminish the obscurity of the original text: ll. 47–8 are a good example. Elsewhere, as in ll. 9–10, revision of the punctuation helped matters. One of the changes in *1868*, that in l. 69, permits a slight difference of interpretation.

1849 Dramatic Romances and Lyrics; 1863– Men and Women.

---

[1] *Memoirs*, i. 231.

PICTOR IGNOTUS.

FLORENCE, 15—.

I COULD have painted pictures like that youth's
    Ye praise so. How my soul springs up! No bar
Stayed me—ah, thought which saddens while it soothes!
    —Never did fate forbid me, star by star,
To outburst on your night with all my gift   5
    Of fires from God: nor would my flesh have shrunk
From seconding my soul, with eyes uplift
    And wide to heaven, or, straight like thunder, sunk
To the centre, of an instant; or around
    Turned calmly and inquisitive, to scan   10
The licence and the limit, space and bound,
    Allowed to truth made visible in man.
And, like that youth ye praise so, all I saw,
    Over the canvas could my hand have flung,

3–3 *1845* soothes! | Never *1849* soothes!— | Never   5 *1872S–88S* night,
6–7 *1845* would this flesh .... seconding that soul,   8 *1845,1849* Heaven,
9–10 *1845* centre of an instant, or around | Sent calmly and inquisitive   12 *1845–65*
Truth .... Man.

Title: 'Painter unknown' or 'An unknown painter', as in an art gallery.

1 *that youth's*: Raphael's (see Introduction).

2–3 *No bar* / *Stayed me*: cf. the Richardsons' remark quoted above, p. 25.

4 *star by star*: a recent critic has commented tellingly on the ambiguity of this phrase: 'The stars were presumably to be his fiery gift to the grateful world . . ., but there is also an astrological connection that would link his "star by star" back to the idea of "fate"': Herbert F. Tucker, Jr., *Browning's Beginnings: The Art of Disclosure* (Minneapolis, 1980), p. 166.

5 *To outburst*: a 'rare' verb (OED), which is common in Browning: e.g. *Paracelsus*, ii. 286, *Sordello*, iii. 353.

6 *fires from God*: cf. Matt. 3:11.

my flesh: cf. Matt. 26:41: 'the spirit indeed is willing, but the flesh is weak'.

7 *uplift*: as in *Paradise Lost*, i. 193.

8 *straight like thunder*: EBB quotes with 'a thunder', and asks: 'Is there not something obscure in the expression? And it is all so fine here, that you should let the reader stand up as straight as he can, to look round.'

9 *To the centre,*: Browning made 9–10 much clearer in *1849*, which was very carefully revised, as shown in our textual notes.

Each face obedient to its passion's law,   15
    Each passion clear proclaimed without a tongue;
Whether Hope rose at once in all the blood,
    A-tiptoe for the blessing of embrace,
Or Rapture drooped the eyes, as when her brood
    Pull down the nesting dove's heart to its place;   20
Or Confidence lit swift the forehead up,
    And locked the mouth fast, like a castle braved,—
O human faces, hath it spilt, my cup?
    What did ye give me that I have not saved?
Nor will I say I have not dreamed (how well!)   25
    Of going—I, in each new picture,—forth,
As, making new hearts beat and bosoms swell,
    To Pope or Kaiser, East, West, South, or North,
Bound for the calmly-satisfied great State,
    Or glad aspiring little burgh, it went,   30
Flowers cast upon the car which bore the freight,
    Through old streets named afresh from the event,

16 *1872S* tongue· {faulty semicolon?} *1884S–8S* tongue.   19 *1845* eyes
20 *1845,1849* place,   23 *1845* Men, women, children, hath *1849* O Human faces,
hath   27 *1845* And making   28 *1845* As still to Pope and Kaiser, South and
North, *1849–68* {as *1888* except 'South'}   29 *1845–88S* calmly satisfied
31 *1845* freight   32 *1845–63* from its event,

15 *Each face*: Raphael's 'Cartoons' (the seven great paintings in the Victoria and Albert
Museum, which are designs for tapestries) have long been recognized as a repertoire of the
expression of emotions.

18 *A-tiptoe*: cf. Dryden, *The Sixth Satyr of Juvenal*, 650: 'That she must rise on Tip-toes
for a kiss'.

19 *Or Rapture*: 'A most exquisite image, & perfect in the expression of it I think': EBB
(whose quotation has 'her eyes').

23 *my cup*: biblical in suggestion: cf. Ps. 23:5.

27 *As, making new hearts beat*: EBB quotes as 'Ever new hearts made beat' and comments:
'The construction seems to me to be entangled a little by this line, . . & the reader pauses
before he clears the meaning to himself—Why not clear it for him by writing the line thus
. . for instance. . ? "New hearts being made to beat, & breasts to swell" or something better
which will strike you—Will you consider?'

31 *car*: chariot.

32 *streets named afresh*: Vasari tells us that the Virgin painted by Cimabue for the church
of Santa Maria Novella in Florence 'was carried in solemn procession, with the sound of
trumpets and other festal demonstrations', from his own house to the church; and that the
place in which he had worked on it was 'ever afterwards called . . Borgo Allegri': *Lives*,
trans. Mrs Jonathan Foster, i (1850), p. 41.

Till it reached home, where learned age should greet
    My face, and youth, the star not yet distinct
Above his hair, lie learning at my feet!—   35
    Oh, thus to live, I and my picture, linked
With love about, and praise, till life should end,
    And then not go to heaven, but linger here,
Here on my earth, earth's every man my friend,—
    The thought grew frightful, 't was so wildly dear!   40
But a voice changed it. Glimpses of such sights
    Have scared me, like the revels through a door
Of some strange house of idols at its rites!
    This world seemed not the world it was before:
Mixed with my loving trusting ones, there trooped   45
    . . . Who summoned those cold faces that begun
To press on me and judge me? Though I stooped
    Shrinking, as from the soldiery a nun,
They drew me forth, and spite of me . . . enough!
    These buy and sell our pictures, take and give,   50

---

33 *1845* —Of reaching thus my home, where Age should greet *1849–65S* {as *1888* except
'Age'}   34 *1845* Youth, the star as yet *1849–65S* Youth, the star not yet
35 *1845* feet,—   36 *1845* pictures, linked   38 *1845* Heaven *1849* Heaven,
39 *1845* earth, its every man my friend,— *1872S–88S* {as *1888* except 'friend,'}
40 *1845* Oh, that grows frightful, 'tis so   41 *1845–63* changed it!   42 *1845,*
1849 thro'   43 *1845–63* House of Idols at its rites; *1865,1865S* House of Idols at its
rites!   44 *1845,1849* was before! *1872S* was, before: *1884S–8S* was, before.
45 *1845* my loving ones there trooped—for what? *1849–68* {as *1888* except 'ones'}
46 *1845* Who . . . . faces which begun   47,48 *1845* me? As asquat | And shrinking
from the soldiery a nun, *1849* {as *1888* except 'Tho''}

---

33 *Till it reached home*: EBB quotes as 'And thus to reach my home, where Age sh.ᵈ greet',
and asks: 'Should you not write it . . "Of reaching thus my home" &c the construction
taking you back to what he dreamed of—First he dreamed "of going"—& then of "reach-
ing" his home &c—.'
    38 *And then not go to heaven*: 'Fine, all this!': EBB.
    41 *But a voice changed it*: that of Savonarola: cf. Introduction.
    47 *asquat* (*1845*): as in *Sordello*, i. 599.
    50 *These buy and sell*: quoting an earlier wording, 'These men may buy us, sell us', EBB
comments: 'Meaning pictures, by "*us*"—But the reader cannot see it until afterwards, &
gets confused. Is it not so? And moreover I do think that by a touch or two you might give a
clearer effect to the previous verses about the "gibing" &c. This poem is so fine, . . so full of
power, . . as to claim every possible attention to the working of it—It begins greatly,
grandly, & ends so—the winding up winds up the soul in it. The versification too is noble . .

Count them for garniture and household-stuff,
    And where they live needs must our pictures live
And see their faces, listen to their prate,
    Partakers of their daily pettiness,
Discussed of,—"This I love, or this I hate,   55
    "This likes me more, and this affects me less!"
Wherefore I chose my portion. If at whiles
    My heart sinks, as monotonous I paint
These endless cloisters and eternal aisles
    With the same series, Virgin, Babe and Saint,   60
With the same cold calm beautiful regard,—
    At least no merchant traffics in my heart;
The sanctuary's gloom at least shall ward
    Vain tongues from where my pictures stand apart:
Only prayer breaks the silence of the shrine   65
    While, blackening in the daily candle-smoke,
They moulder on the damp wall's travertine,
    'Mid echoes the light footstep never woke.

52 *1845* {as *1888* except 'pictures live,'} *1849* And where they live our pictures needs must live, *1863* {as *1849* except 'must live'}   55 *1845* love   56 *1845* more 57 *1865S* I choose my   58 *1845* sinks   60 *1845,1849,1872S–88S* Babe, 61 *1845–65S* cold, calm, beautiful regard,   64 *1845* apart;   66 *1845* While, blackening . . . . candle smoke, *1868* While blackening . . . . candle-smoke,

& altogether it classes with your finest poems of the length—does it not, in your own mind? I cannot tell you how much it impresses mine.'
    Bullen aptly quotes Sir Francis Turner Palgrave's *Handbook for Travellers in Northern Italy* (1842): 'Before the sixteenth century, it may be doubted whether any *cabinet pictures*, that is to say, moveable pictures, intended merely to hang upon the wall . . . as ornaments, . . . ever existed': p. 428. Fresco paintings could not be 'bought and sold'.

  56 *likes*: pleases.
  61 *regard*: 'Look; aspect directed to another': Johnson.
  63–4 *ward* / . . . *from*: cf. *Titus Andronicus*, III. i. 195–6.
  67 *travertine*: limestone. Cf. 'The Bishop Orders his Tomb', 66.
  68 *light*: frivolous. Cf. Vasari on the Saint Sebastian which Fra Bartolommeo painted to show that he could paint nude figures: 'It is said that when this painting was put up in the church, . . . the grace and beauty of the vivid imitation of life, . . . had given occasion to the sin of light and evil thoughts; they consequently removed it to the Chapter House, but it did not remain there long, having been purchased by Giovanni Batista della Palla, who sent it to the King of France': *Lives*, trans. Mrs Foster, ii (1851), 455.

So, die my pictures! surely, gently die!
    O youth, men praise so,—holds their praise its worth?   70
Blown harshly, keeps the trump its golden cry?
    Tastes sweet the water with such specks of earth?

69 *1845–65S* So die, my pictures;   70 *1845* Oh youth men praise so, *1849,1863* Oh,
youth, men praise so,—

    71–2 *Blown harshly*: cf. the ending of 'Popularity' in *Men and Women*.

THE ITALIAN IN ENGLAND

BROWNING'S interest in Italy began early. About 1829 he followed his sister Sarianna in having Italian lessons with an exile, Angelo Cerutti,[1] and soon he sympathized with the struggle of the Italians for independence from the Austrians. Part III of *Pippa Passes* is a dialogue between a young revolutionary and his mother: at the end of it he leaves her to attempt to assassinate the Austrian Emperor Franz, proclaiming: ''Tis God's voice calls'.

When he made his second journey to Italy in 1844 Browning will have heard of the recent execution of two brothers, Attilio and Emilio Bandiera, who had raided the Neapolitan coast in a rising to liberate political prisoners. Betrayed by one of their own company, they had been executed on 25 July. Browning was in Naples soon afterwards. In November of the next year we find him lending Elizabeth Barrett a memorial volume to the two brothers, *Ricordi dei fratelli Bandiera e dei loro compagni di Martirio in Cosenza* (Paris, 1844), a book edited by Giuseppe Mazzini which includes some of their correspondence.[2] The poem was probably written in 1845.

The speaker may be thought of as a member of 'La Giovane Italia', an association which was working to free Italy from foreign and domestic tyranny and to bring about its unification under a republican form of government. 'God and the People' was its motto. Mazzini had arrived in England in 1837; subsequently he met the Carlyles, and on 19 June 1844 Carlyle wrote a powerful letter to *The Times* protesting against the opening of his correspondence by the English government. Although he dissociated himself from the Young Italy movement, Carlyle wrote: 'I have had the honour to know Mr. Mazzini for a series of years, and whatever I may think of his practical skill in worldly affairs, I can with great freedom testify to all men that he, if I have ever seen one such, is a man of genius and virtue ... one of those rare men ... who are worthy to be called martyr souls.'

When she read the poem in manuscript EBB wrote: 'A serene noble

---

[1] For a useful account of Cerutti, see Maynard, pp. 304 ff.

[2] Kintner, i. 278. Mazzini presented Browning with a copy of the book (Kelley and Coley, A 1577), but that was no doubt later. He would surely have mentioned that the copy he lent to Elizabeth was a presentation, if it had been.

poem this is—an heroic repose in it—but nothing to imagine queries out of, with whatever goodwill—I like the simplicity of the greatheartedness of it, (though perhaps half Saxon in character) with the Italian scenery all round—It is very impressive.' She did query the first form of ll. 121–2, however (see below).

Mrs Orr tells us that Browning was 'proud to remember that Mazzini informed him he had read this poem to certain of his fellow-exiles in England to show how an Englishman could sympathize with them' (*Handbook*, p. 306 n.).

In *1849* Browning changed the title from 'Italy in England', and made seven verbal revisions, as well as changes in punctuation. Lines 54–5 had been misleading: l. 115 now lost its rather pointless inversion: while four other lines were also improved. Changes of punctuation in *1863* included a full stop instead of an exclamation mark at the end of the poem. In *1868* ll. 116–17 were revised.

1849 Dramatic Romances and Lyrics; 1863 Romances; 1868– Dramatic Romances.

THE ITALIAN IN ENGLAND

THAT second time they hunted me
From hill to plain, from shore to sea,
And Austria, hounding far and wide
Her blood-hounds thro' the country-side,
Breathed hot and instant on my trace,—   5
I made six days a hiding-place
Of that dry green old aqueduct
Where I and Charles, when boys, have plucked
The fire-flies from the roof above,
Bright creeping thro' the moss they love: 10

Title *1845* ITALY IN ENGLAND.   4 *1863* through the country-side *1865–72S* thro' the country-side   5 *1845* trace, *1884S–8S* trace.—   6 *1872S–88S* made, six days,   8 *1863* boys   10 *1845,1849* thro' .... love. *1863* through .... love.

3–4 *hounding . . . / Her blood-hounds*: 'He who only lets loose a Greyhound out of the slip, is said to hound him at the Hare': Bp John Bramhall *a.p.* Hobbes (1656), cited in OED, 'Hound', *v.* 3.
5 *instant*: urgent. Cf. the title of the poem, 'Instans Tyrannus'.

—How long it seems since Charles was lost!
Six days the soldiers crossed and crossed
The country in my very sight;
And when that peril ceased at night,
The sky broke out in red dismay   15
With signal fires; well, there I lay
Close covered o'er in my recess,
Up to the neck in ferns and cress,
Thinking on Metternich our friend,
And Charles's miserable end,   20
And much beside, two days; the third,
Hunger o'ercame me when I heard
The peasants from the village go
To work among the maize; you know,
With us in Lombardy, they bring   25
Provisions packed on mules, a string
With little bells that cheer their task,
And casks, and boughs on every cask
To keep the sun's heat from the wine;
These I let pass in jingling line,   30
And, close on them, dear noisy crew,
The peasants from the village, too;
For at the very rear would troop
Their wives and sisters in a group
To help, I knew. When these had passed,   35
I threw my glove to strike the last,
Taking the chance: she did not start,
Much less cry out, but stooped apart,
One instant rapidly glanced round,

16 *1845–63* signal-fires; well, *1884S–8S* signal-fires. Well,   24 *1884S–8S* maize:
25 *1845,1849* With us,   26 *1872S–88S* string,   35 *1845–88S* I knew; when
38–9 *1845–65* apart | One instant,

   19 *Metternich*: born in Koblenz in 1773, Metternich was appointed minister for foreign
affairs by the Emperor Franz I in 1809. He was strongly anti-democratic, suppressing
liberal aspirations by persecution and press censorship. He was driven from office in March
1848 and died in 1859, believing to the end that an absolute monarchical system of govern-
ment best served the interests of the people. He was detested by those who were struggling
to free Italy from the Austrian yoke. Cf. 121–3.

And saw me beckon from the ground.   40
A wild bush grows and hides my crypt;
She picked my glove up while she stripped
A branch off, then rejoined the rest
With that; my glove lay in her breast.
Then I drew breath; they disappeared: 45
It was for Italy I feared.

    An hour, and she returned alone
Exactly where my glove was thrown.
Meanwhile came many thoughts: on me
Rested the hopes of Italy.   50
I had devised a certain tale
Which, when 't was told her, could not fail
Persuade a peasant of its truth;
I meant to call a freak of youth
This hiding, and give hopes of pay,   55
And no temptation to betray.
But when I saw that woman's face,
Its calm simplicity of grace,
Our Italy's own attitude
In which she walked thus far, and stood,   60
Planting each naked foot so firm,
To crush the snake and spare the worm—
At first sight of her eyes, I said,
"I am that man upon whose head
"They fix the price, because I hate   65
"The Austrians over us: the State
"Will give you gold—oh, gold so much!—
"If you betray me to their clutch,

---

*40 (reading of *1884S–8S, DC, 1889*) *1845–88,   1872S* ground: 44 *1845–88S*
breast: 45 *1845–63* breath: 49 *1845–88S* thoughts;   50 *1845–88S*
Italy;   54–5 *1845* This hiding was a freak of youth; | I meant to give her hopes of
pay,   64–5 *1845* that person on whose head . . . . price   66 *1884S–8S* over
us;   67 *1845–65* so much,   68 *1845, 1849* clutch! *1863* clutch

    41 *crypt*: hiding-place.

"And be your death, for aught I know,
"If once they find you saved their foe. 70
"Now, you must bring me food and drink,
"And also paper, pen and ink,
"And carry safe what I shall write
"To Padua, which you'll reach at night
"Before the duomo shuts; go in, 75
"And wait till Tenebræ begin;
"Walk to the third confessional,
"Between the pillar and the wall,
"And kneeling whisper, *Whence comes peace?*
"Say it a second time, then cease; 80
"And if the voice inside returns,
"*From Christ and Freedom; what concerns*
"*The cause of Peace?*—for answer, slip
"My letter where you placed your lip;
"Then come back happy we have done 85
"Our mother service—I, the son,
"As you the daughter of our land!"

Three mornings more, she took her stand
In the same place, with the same eyes:
I was no surer of sun-rise 90
Than of her coming. We conferred
Of her own prospects, and I heard
She had a lover—stout and tall,
She said—then let her eyelids fall,
"He could do much"—as if some doubt 95
Entered her heart,—then, passing out,
"She could not speak for others, who
"Had other thoughts; herself she knew:"

71 *1865* "Now you must   75 *1845–65* Duomo   77 *1845–65* Third Confes-
sional,   79 *1845,1849* whisper *whence*   80 *1845,1849* time;   81 *1849*
returns.   91 *1845–88S* coming: we   97 *1845,1849* others—who

75 *duomo*: cathedral.
76 *Tenebrae*: 'The name given to the office of matins and lauds of the following day,
usually sung in the afternoon or evening of Wednesday, Thursday and Friday in Holy
Week': OED. Here probably used generally for the evening service.

And so she brought me drink and food.
After four days, the scouts pursued   100
Another path; at last arrived
The help my Paduan friends contrived
To furnish me: she brought the news.
For the first time I could not choose
But kiss her hand, and lay my own   105
Upon her head—"This faith was shown
"To Italy, our mother; she
"Uses my hand and blesses thee."
She followed down to the sea-shore;
I left and never saw her more.   110

　　How very long since I have thought
Concerning—much less wished for—aught
Beside the good of Italy,
For which I live and mean to die!
I never was in love; and since   115
Charles proved false, what shall now convince
My inmost heart I have a friend?
However, if I pleased to spend
Real wishes on myself—say, three—
I know at least what one should be.   120
I would grasp Metternich until
I felt his red wet throat distil
In blood thro' these two hands. And next,
—Nor much for that am I perplexed—
Charles, perjured traitor, for his part,   125
Should die slow of a broken heart

101 *1845,1849* path: 103 *1845,1849* news: 107 *1845,1849* mother;—
108 *1845–65* thee!"   115 *1845* In love I never was; and   116–17 *1845,1849*
false, nothing could convince|....I had a friend; *1863,1865* false, nothing could convince|
....I had a friend.   119 *1845,1849* Three—   120 *1845–65* should be;
123 *1845–65* hands: and

　122 *I felt*: EBB quotes 121—2, with an earlier wording of this line: 'I felt his throat, &
had my will'. She comments: 'After all the abjuring of queries [cf. above, p. 32], .. is not
"had my will" a little wrong—*I would what I would*—? There is a weakness in the expression
.. is there not?'

Under his new employers. Last
—Ah, there, what should I wish? For fast
Do I grow old and out of strength.
If I resolved to seek at length   130
My father's house again, how scared
They all would look, and unprepared!
My brothers live in Austria's pay
—Disowned me long ago, men say;
And all my early mates who used   135
To praise me so—perhaps induced
More than one early step of mine—
Are turning wise: while some opine
"Freedom grows license," some suspect
"Haste breeds delay," and recollect   140
They always said, such premature
Beginnings never could endure!
So, with a sullen "All's for best,"
The land seems settling to its rest.
I think then, I should wish to stand   145
This evening in that dear, lost land,
Over the sea the thousand miles,
And know if yet that woman smiles
With the calm smile; some little farm
She lives in there, no doubt: what harm   150
If I sat on the door-side bench,
And, while her spindle made a trench
Fantastically in the dust,
Inquired of all her fortunes—just
Her children's ages and their names,   155
And what may be the husband's aims

127 *1845* employers—last *1849–65* employers: last   138 *1845* should one wish?
129 *1845* strength; *1849* strength.—   138 *1845* wise; while part opine *1849–63*
wise; while some opine   139 *1845* License," part suspect *1849–65* License," some
suspect   140 *1845–65* Delay,"   141–2 *1845* said .... endure:
149 *1845* smile—   150 *1845* doubt— *1849,1863* doubt;   151 *1845,1849* sate

140 *"Haste breeds delay"*: proverbial. 'More haste, less speed.'

For each of them. I'd talk this out,
And sit there, for an hour about,
Then kiss her hand once more, and lay
Mine on her head, and go my way.   160

So much for idle wishing—how
It steals the time! To business now.

157 *1845,1849* them—   162 *1845,1849* now! *1870* now

THE ENGLISHMAN IN ITALY

On his second visit to Italy, in 1844, Browning landed at Naples at some time in September and was soon exploring the neighbouring countryside.[1] In April of the following year we find him attempting a tiny sketch— 'Three scratches with a pen'—to give Elizabeth an impression of the view of 'the green little Syrenusæ where I have sate and heard the quails sing',[2] these being the 'three small rocky islands near the coast of Campania, where the Sirens were supposed to reside'.[3] It seems clear, as Mrs Sutherland Orr remarks, that 'every detail of the poem' is 'given from personal observation'.[4] This is exemplified by the passage in another letter in which he describes how his mule 'walked into a sorb-tree, not to tumble sheer over Monte Calvano', and he 'felt the fruit against [his] face', his 'little ragged bare-legged guide' laughing at his identifying the type of tree so surely. He tells Elizabeth how 'all Naples-bay and half Sicily, shore and inland, come flocking once a year to the Piedigrotta fête', and continues, in a satirical description of that occasion, that he would 'engage to bring the whole of the Piano (of Sorrento) in likeness to a red . . . dressing gown properly spangled over, before the priest that held it out on a pole had even begun his story . . .'.[5] Whatever the syntax of the sentence, it is evident that the Piano di Sorrento had made a deep impression on him.

We do not know when Browning began the poem—perhaps in April or early May 1845—but it is clear that he wrote much of it in July. On 7 August Elizabeth gave him her detailed comments on it, adding (a few days later) that she 'understood perfectly, through it all, that it is *unfinished*, & in a rough state round the edges'.[6] In the last of her comments on the manuscript, she wrote: 'I think it will strike you when you come to finish this unfinished poem, that all the rushing & hurrying life of the descriptions of it, tossed in one upon another like the grape-bunches in the early part, & not 'kept under' by ever so much breathless

---

[1] We know from EBB's comments on the manuscript that the original title was 'England in Italy. Autumn at Sorrento'. For Browning's project of writing some travel letters which might be published to help Hood, see above, p. 2 n.

[2] Kintner, i. 46 (text corrected from facing facsimile).

[3] Lemprière. Cf. *Æneid*, v. 864.

[4] *Handbook*, p. 287 n.

[5] Kintner, i. 54–5. The Piedigrotta fête is celebrated on 8 September.

[6] Kintner, i. 155.

effort on the poets part, .. can be very little adapted to send anybody to
sleep .. even if there were no regular dinner in the middle of it all. Do
consider. For giving the *sense of Italy*, it is worth a whole library of travel-
books.'[1]

She often referred to the poem in her letters. On 22 October she wrote:
'The end you have put to "England in Italy" gives unity to the whole .. just
what the poem wanted. Also you have given some nobler lines to the
middle than met me there before.'[2] The 'end' is no doubt the seven-line
conclusion we know: the new passage in the middle can only be guessed
at. The personal significance which the poem came to have for them is
evident when she tells him that they would 'be nearer the sun .. & further
from the world' in Italy, '. . . out of hearing of the great storm of gossiping,
when "scirocco is loose"'.[3]

In his essay, 'The Sources of "The Englishman in Italy"',[4] Daniel Karlin
develops the personal theme in detail, suggesting (for example) that
Elizabeth's fear of the wind may correspond to little Fortù's panic at the
Scirocco, allayed by the speaker. He stresses the importance of the storm,
and the relationship of this poem to 'Saul', which was well under way by
this time: the first part of it was published in this same *Bell*.

Browning revised carefully for *1849*, changing the title from the
original 'England in Italy'. The opening lines become more affectionate
and immediate, and more regular in metre, while a clearer (and more
conventional) line replaces 'All the Plain saw me gather, I garland' at the
end of the opening section. Other changes show Browning intensifying
the impression of drought, and then of hasty effort as the rain begins (29,
41, 43). The 'kings' of l. 100 become 'popes', presumably after the events
of 1848, while the 'strings' of maccaroni give way to 'ropes' of lasagne. In
1863, surprisingly, line 11 at the end of the opening section reverts to its
original wording. In l. 243 'windfalls' becomes 'windfall': revision or
misprint, it so remained. In the *Selection* of *1865* we find unique readings
in ll. 32 and 161. The most interesting revision in *1868* (139–40) is due to
Browning's realization that he had confused the colour and texture of
sorb-apples with those of the fruit of the strawberry-tree.

Like 'Cristina', this poem is given in long lines in the *Selections* of 1872
to 1888, with a few resultant minor changes in punctuation, and some
interesting verbal revisions. In l. 191 'the flat sea-pine' becomes 'black', a
reading not found in the collected editions.

---

[1] All her other comments are printed in our notes.
[2] Kintner, i. 244.   [3] Kintner, i. 426.
[4] BSN, Winter 1984–5, pp. 23–43.

In *1888* 'So' is revised to 'Till' in l. 170, a comma is omitted in error in 187, while a full stop disappears from the end of 249 (to be restored in *1889*).

1849 Dramatic Romances and Lyrics; 1863 Romances; 1868– Dramatic Romances.

THE ENGLISHMAN IN ITALY

PIANO DI SORRENTO

FORTÙ, Fortù, my beloved one,
    Sit here by my side,
On my knees put up both little feet!
    I was sure, if I tried,
I could make you laugh spite of Scirocco.   5
    Now, open your eyes,
Let me keep you amused till he vanish
    In black from the skies,
With telling my memories over
    As you tell your beads;   10
All the Plain saw me gather, I garland
    —The flowers or the weeds.

Title: *1845* ENGLAND IN ITALY. | (*Piano di Sorrento.*)   1–2 *1845* my loved one, | Sit by   4 *1884S–8S* I am sure,   5 *1845,1849* Scirocco: 6 *1845,1849* eyes—   7 *1872S–8S* amused,   9 *1872S–8S* over,   11 *1849* All the memories plucked at Sorrento   12 *1845* —Flowers prove they, or weeds. *1849* —The flowers, or the weeds.

    Sub-title: see Introduction, n. 1. *Piano*: plain.
    1 *Fortù*: the intimate form of 'Fortuna', a girl's name.
    5 *Scirocco*: a hot wind, properly from the SE, which many find agitating and depressing.
    7 *Let me keep you*: EBB quotes as 'While I talk you asleep till he's oer, / With his black in the skies', and comments: 'I dont like "he's oer" much, or at all perhaps. There is something to me weak & un-scirocco-like in the two contractions—Would "till he carries / His black from the skies" be more *active*.'
    11 *All the Plain*: 'a fiend of a line for ambiguity!', Domett complains '. . . every body sticks at that line . . . Who would think of "garland" being a *verb*? . . . You should alter this. It is a capital specimen of the cause of obscurity—*carelessness* or cramming too much into a given space': PK 46:378. Browning revised in *1849*, but in *1863* reverted to his original reading. For 'garland' as a verb, cf. the dedication to *Queen Mab*, st. iii.
    12 This line ends the first verse-paragraph.

Time for rain! for your long hot dry Autumn
    Had net-worked with brown
The white skin of each grape on the bunches,   15
    Marked like a quail's crown,
Those creatures you make such account of,
    Whose heads,—speckled white
Over brown like a great spider's back,
    As I told you last night,—   20
Your mother bites off for her supper.
    Red-ripe as could be,
Pomegranates were chapping and splitting
    In halves on the tree:
And betwixt the loose walls of great flintstone,   25
    Or in the thick dust
On the path, or straight out of the rock-side,
    Wherever could thrust
Some burnt sprig of bold hardy rock-flower
    Its yellow face up,   30
For the prize were great butterflies fighting,
    Some five for one cup.
So, I guessed, ere I got up this morning,
    What change was in store,
By the quick rustle-down of the quail-nets   35
    Which woke me before

13 *1845* 'Twas time, for .... Autumn *1865S* Time for rain! for .... autumn
18 *1845–68,1865S–88S* heads,—specked with white *1870* heads,—speckled with white
21 *1845,1849* supper;   22 *1849* be.   24 *1872S–88S* tree.   25 *1845*
And 'twixt   29 *1845* Some starved sprig   32 *1845* Some five for one cup:
1865S Five foes for one cup.   33 *1845* So I guessed,

    13 *Time for rain!*: EBB quotes as ''Twas time, for your long dry autumn', and comments:
'I just doubt if "and dry" might not improve the rhythm—doubt. Only if the emphasis is
properly administered to "long", nothing of course is wanted—only, again, it is trusting to
the reader!'

    14 *net-worked*: the first example of the verb in OED² dates from 1887 (USA).

    16 *a quail's crown*: which has three streaks of ochreous white.

    34 *What change*: EBB quotes as 'What was in store', and comments: 'Surely "what
change" or "what fate" or some additional word sh^d assist the rhythm in this place. The line
is brokenly short.'

    35 *the quail-nets*: 'Nets spread to catch quails as they fly to or from the other side of the
Mediterranean. They are slung by rings on to poles, and stand sufficiently high for the
quails to fly into them': *Handbook*, p. 287 n.

I could open my shutter, made fast
    With a bough and a stone,
And look thro' the twisted dead vine-twigs,
    Sole lattice that's known.   40
Quick and sharp rang the rings down the net-poles,
·   While, busy beneath,
Your priest and his brother tugged at them,
    The rain in their teeth.
And out upon all the flat house-roofs   45
    Where split figs lay drying,
The girls took the frails under cover:
    Nor use seemed in trying
To get out the boats and go fishing,
    For, under the cliff,   50
Fierce the black water frothed o'er the blind-rock.
    No seeing our skiff
Arrive about noon from Amalfi,
    —Our fisher arrive,
And pitch down his basket before us,   55
    All trembling alive
With pink and grey jellies, your sea-fruit;
    You touch the strange lumps,
And mouths gape there, eyes open, all manner
    Of horns and of humps,   60
Which only the fisher looks grave at,
    While round him like imps

---

39 *1872S–88S* through   40 *1845* known; *1849* known!   41 *1845* Sharp rang
. . . . down the bird-poles   43 *1845* brother were working,   44 *1849* teeth:
47 *1865S* cover   50–1 *1845* For under the cliff . . . . blind-rock—   53–
4 *1872S–88S* Amalfi!—our   56 *1872S–88S* alive,   57 *1845, 1849* sea-fruit,
58 *1845* —Touch the *1849* —You touch the

    47 *frails*: baskets made of rushes.
    51 *blind-rock*: concealed rock. Cf. OED, 'Blind', *a.*, 9.
    57 *jellies*: jellyfish.
    58 *You touch the strange lumps*: EBB comments: 'I do like all this living description—living
description which never lived before in poetry, . . & now will live always. These fishes have
suffered no earthchange though they lie here so grotesquely plain between rhyme &
rhyme—And the grave fisher too!—& the children "brown as his shrimps"!'

Cling screaming the children as naked
    And brown as his shrimps;
Himself too as bare to the middle   65
    —You see round his neck
The string and its brass coin suspended,
    That saves him from wreck.
But to-day not a boat reached Salerno,
    So back, to a man,   70
Came our friends, with whose help in the vineyards
    Grape-harvest began.
In the vat, halfway up in our house-side,
    Like blood the juice spins,
While your brother all bare-legged is dancing   75
    Till breathless he grins
Dead-beaten in effort on effort
    To keep the grapes under,
Since still when he seems all but master,
    In pours the fresh plunder   80
From girls who keep coming and going
    With basket on shoulder,
And eyes shut against the rain's driving;
    Your girls that are older,—
For under the hedges of aloe,   85
    And where, on its bed
Of the orchard's black mould, the love-apple
    Lies pulpy and red,

64 *1845* shrimps,   65 *1849* middle—   69 *1872S–88S* Salerno:
70 *1845,1849* So back to a man   72 *1845,1849* began: 73–4 *1845* vat half-
way .... house-side .... spins *1849* vat, half-way .... house-side, ... spins,
77 *1845,1849* Dead-beaten,   79 *1845* For still .... master   83 *1845,1849*
driving,

    66 *You see round his neck*: 'Why not "And you see round his neck" .. for rhythm—The
line stops you: & you need not stop, when you are looking at him, to "see round his neck".'
    69 *But to-day*: the 'exceeding truth' of this part of the poem was pointed out by Ruskin to
Mary Russell Mitford: see her *Recollections of a Literary Life* (3 vols., 1852), i. 290.
    Salerno: some 30 miles SE of Naples.
    72 *Grape-harvest*: 'The treading of the grapes is admirable painting—that "breathless he
grins", so true to life—& the effort to "keep the grapes under"—all, admirable': EBB.
    77 *Dead-beaten*: the first of the two examples in OED[2] is from 1875.
    87 *love-apple*: tomato.

All the young ones are kneeling and filling
    Their laps with the snails   90
Tempted out by this first rainy weather,—
    Your best of regales,
As to-night will be proved to my sorrow,
    When, supping in state,
We shall feast our grape-gleaners (two dozen,   95
    Three over one plate)
With lasagne so tempting to swallow
    In slippery ropes,
And gourds fried in great purple slices,
    That colour of popes.   100
Meantime, see the grape bunch they've brought you:
    The rain-water slips
O'er the heavy blue bloom on each globe
    Which the wasp to your lips
Still follows with fretful persistence: 105
    Nay, taste, while awake,
This half of a curd-white smooth cheese-ball
    That peels, flake by flake,
Like an onion, each smoother and whiter;
    Next, sip this weak wine   110
From the thin green glass flask, with its stopper,
    A leaf of the vine;
And end with the prickly-pear's red flesh
    That leaves thro' its juice

---

91 *1845* by the first   95–8 *1845* grape-gleaners—two dozen, | Three over one plate,— | Maccaroni so tempting to swallow | In slippery strings,   100 *1845* That colour of kings,—   101 *1845,1849* grape-bunch....you,—   105 *1845,1849* persistence— *1872S–88S* persistence.   106 *1845* taste   107 *1845,1849* cheese-ball,   108 *1865S* flake by flake   109 *1845* onion's, each .... whiter— *1849* onion's, each .... whiter; *1872S–88S* onion, each .... whiter: 110 *1845* Next sip   112 *1845,1849* vine,—

92 *regales*: feasts.

97 *With lasagne*: Daniel Karlin compares these lines, appositely, with 'Saul' (*1845*), 145–8: BSN, Winter 1984–5, p. 29.

105 *Still*: always.

The stony black seeds on your pearl-teeth.   115
          Scirocco is loose!
Hark, the quick, whistling pelt of the olives
          Which, thick in one's track,
Tempt the stranger to pick up and bite them,
          Tho' not yet half black!   120
How the old twisted olive trunks shudder,
          The medlars let fall
Their hard fruit, and the brittle great fig-trees
          Snap off, figs and all,
For here comes the whole of the tempest!   125
          No refuge, but creep
Back again to my side and my shoulder,
          And listen or sleep.

O how will your country show next week,
          When all the vine-boughs   130
Have been stripped of their foliage to pasture
          The mules and the cows?
Last eve, I rode over the mountains;
          Your brother, my guide,
Soon left me, to feast on the myrtles   135
          That offered, each side,
Their fruit-balls, black, glossy and luscious,—
          Or strip from the sorbs

115 *1845,1849* pearl-teeth   116 *1845* ... Scirocco *1849* .. Scirocco   {*1884S–8S* have a line-space between 115 and 116}   117 *1845* Hark! the quick pelt *1849–65S* Hark! the quick, whistling pelt   121 *1845* And how their old twisted trunks shudder! *1849,1863* How the old twisted olive trunks shudder!   123 *1845* fruit—the brittle   124 *1849* all,—   126 *1845* refuge   133 *1845* Last eve I .... mountains—   135 *1845* left me   137 *1845* luscious,

117 *pelt*: pelting.

127 *Back again to my side*: EBB quotes without 'again'; and asks: 'Is not some word, some dissyllable, (as if you were to write "Back again" &c,) wanted for rhythm, reading it with the preceding line?'

138 *sorbs*: sorb-apples, which are greenish-brown in colour and smooth in texture. Browning originally described them as rosy, hairy, and gold. In *1868* he changed the construction of l. 139 so that a third fruit, which was of this kind (that of *Arbutus unedo*, the strawberry-tree) was added to the myrtle fruits and the sorbs.

A treasure, or, rosy and wondrous,
    Those hairy gold orbs!   140
But my mule picked his sure sober path out,
    Just stopping to neigh
When he recognized down in the valley
    His mates on their way
With the faggots and barrels of water;   145
    And soon we emerged
From the plain, where the woods could scarce follow;
    And still as we urged
Our way, the woods wondered, and left us,
    As up still we trudged   150
Though the wild path grew wilder each instant,
    And place was e'en grudged
'Mid the rock-chasms and piles of loose stones
    Like the loose broken teeth
Of some monster which climbed there to die   155
    From the ocean beneath—
Place was grudged to the silver-grey fume-weed
    That clung to the path,
And dark rosemary ever a-dying
    That, 'spite the wind's wrath,   160
So loves the salt rock's face to seaward,
    And lentisks as staunch

139–41 1845–65S A treasure, so rosy . . . . | Of hairy . . . . | sure, sober   145 1845–63
faggots, ... water; 1872S–88S faggots . . . . water.   147 1845 plain where . . . . fol-
low, 1872S–88S plain where . . . . follow;   148–50 1872S–88S and still, ... left us.
Up, up . . . . trudged,   153 1845,1849 rock-chasms,   154 1849 (Like
155 1845,1849 monster, ... die 1872S–88S monster . . . . die,   156 1849 beneath)
159 1845,1849 rosemary, ever a-dying, 1872S–88S rosemary ever a-dying, 160 1845
Which, 'spite   161 1845,1849 rock's face to seaward,— 1865S rock-face to sea-
ward, 1872S–88S rock's face to seaward:

    140 gold orbs: the fruit of the strawberry-tree. Cf. Kintner, i. 54, where Browning quotes
from Shelley's 'Marenghi', st. xiii: 'those globes of deep-red gold / Which in the woods the
strawberry-tree doth bear'. The fruit is studded with little points all over, and may perhaps
be described as 'hairy'.
    149 The woods wondered: cf. 'By the Fire-side', 236: 'The forests had done it.'
    157 fume-weed: not in OED. Pettigrew suggests fumitory.
    159 rosemary: rosemary is used as an emblem at funerals. Cf. Hamlet, iv. v. 172.
    162 lentisks: the lentisk is the mastic tree: cf. Sordello, iv. 823 ff.

To the stone where they root and bear berries,
        And . . . what shows a branch
Coral-coloured, transparent, with circlets   165
        Of pale seagreen leaves;
Over all trod my mule with the caution
        Of gleaners o'er sheaves,
Still, foot after foot like a lady,
        Till, round after round,   170
He climbed to the top of Calvano,
        And God's own profound
Was above me, and round me the mountains,
        And under, the sea,
And within me my heart to bear witness   175
        What was and shall be.
Oh, heaven and the terrible crystal!
        No rampart excludes
Your eye from the life to be lived
        In the blue solitudes.   180
Oh, those mountains, their infinite movement!
        Still moving with you;
For, ever some new head and breast of them
        Thrusts into view

163 *1849* berries,— *1872S–88S* berries: 164 *1845* And—what   166 *1845,*
1849 leaves— *1863* leaves: 168 *1845* gleaners o'er sheaves: *1865S* gleaner o'er
sheaves, *1872S–88S* gleaners o'er sheaves.   169 *1845* Foot after .... lady— *1849*
Still, foot after .... lady— *1863–8,1865S* Still, foot after .... lady: *1872S–88S* Still, foot
after .... lady,   170 *1845–68,1865S* So, round *1872S–88S* still, round
171 *1872S–88S* Calvano: 175 *1845* And with me, *1849–65S* And within me,
176 *1845–63* shall be!   177 *1845,1849* Oh heaven, *1865S* Oh heaven
179 *1845* The eye   180 *1845–63* solitudes!   181 *1865S* Oh those
182 *1845* with you—   183 *1845* For ever

164 *a branch*: perhaps the Judas-tree, *Cercis siliquastrum*.
171 *Calvano*: Browning referred to 'Monte Calvano' in the letter in which he described
his visit to the area to EBB: Kintner, i. 54. Furnivall wrote that Browning 'is far from sure
that this is the right name', adding: 'it was the one he heard applied in Sorrento to the great
mountain opposite; but the names are greatly changed in the dialect there': *A Bibliography of
Robert Browning*, 2nd ed. (1881), p. 170.
172 *profound*: furthest space. Cf. Virgil, *Georgics*, iv. 222: 'caelumque profundum'.
177 *the terrible crystal*: Ezek. 1:22.
183 *ever some new head and breast of them*: 'Should it not be written . . "With ever some"
&c—?', EBB asked, adding: 'These mountains & their "infinite movement" are finely true'.

To observe the intruder; you see it   185
    If quickly you turn
And, before they escape you, surprise them.
    They grudge you should learn
How the soft plains they look on, lean over
    And love (they pretend)   190
—Cower beneath them, the flat sea-pine crouches,
    The wild fruit-trees bend,
E'en the myrtle-leaves curl, shrink and shut:
    All is silent and grave:
'T is a sensual and timorous beauty,   195
    How fair! but a slave.
So, I turned to the sea; and there slumbered
    As greenly as ever
Those isles of the siren, your Galli;
    No ages can sever   200
The Three, nor enable their sister
    To join them,—halfway

---

185 *1845,1849* intruder—   *187 {reading of *1872S–88S*} *1845,1849* you, surprise
them— *1863–75,1865S* you, surprise them: *1888,1889* you surprise them.   189–
90 *1845* lean over, | And love, they pretend,   191 *1845* them—the flat sea-pine
1849 them; the flat sea-pine *1872S–88S* them, the black sea-pine   193–4 *1845,1849*
shut— | All is silent and grave— *1863–65S* shut, | All is silent and grave,   195 *1845,*
1849 'Tis . . . . beauty— *1872S–88S* 'T is . . . . beauty,—   196 *1845–63* fair, but a
slave!   197 *1845* So I turned to the sea,—and there slumbered *1849* {as *1888* except
'sea,—'} *1872S–88S* {as *1888* except 'slumbered,'}   199 *1845* syren, your Galli;
1872S–88S siren, your Galli.   201 *1845* Three—

189–90 *lean over / And love (they pretend)*: EBB transcribes as '& love so / As they would
pretend / Lower beneath them', and comments: 'I do not see the construction. Is "lower"
put here as a verb? & if correctly, is it clearly, so, put?' On 12 August Browning replied: 'So
you can decypher my *utterest* hieroglyphic? Now droop the eyes while I triumph: the plains
Cower, *Cower* beneath the mountains their masters': Kintner, i. 153. She replied: '"Cower"
puts it all right of course': p. 154.

194 *All is silent and grave*: EBB quotes as 'All's silent & grave', and asks: 'Why not "All *is*
silent & grave", without abbreviation. The rhythm gains by it, I think'.

198 *As greenly*: EBB quotes as 'Greenly as ever', suggesting that '*As* greenly as ever'
would 'take the rhythm on better'.

199 *Galli*: or 'Syrenusæ', as Browning calls them in a letter: see our Introduction.

200 *No ages can sever*: EBB quotes as 'Years cannot sever' and comments: 'Quære . . "And
years"—or "For years".'

201 *The Three*: Il Gallo Lungo, La Castelluccia, and La Rotunda: 'their sister' is Vetara,
and the 'small one' just offshore Isca.

On the voyage, she looked at Ulysses—
  No farther to-day,
Tho' the small one, just launched in the wave,   205
  Watches breast-high and steady
From under the rock, her bold sister
  Swum halfway already.
Fortù, shall we sail there together
  And see from the sides   210
Quite new rocks show their faces, new haunts
  Where the siren abides?
Shall we sail round and round them, close over
  The rocks, tho' unseen,
That ruffle the grey glassy water   215
  To glorious green?
Then scramble from splinter to splinter,
  Reach land and explore,
On the largest, the strange square black turret

---

204 *1849* farther to-day; *1863,1865* further to-day; *1872S–88S* farther to-day!
207 *1872S–88S* rock her bold sister,   209 *1845* O when shall .... together *1872S–*
88S Fortù, shall .... together,   210 *1872S–88S* see, from the sides,
211 *1845,1849* faces—   213 *1845* Oh, to sail   216 *1845* green,—
218 *1845* land and explore *1872S–88S* land, and explore,

 205 *Tho' the small one*: EBB quotes as 'Though the one breast-high in the water', and
comments: 'quære .. "bosom-high" for rhythm'. In her notes on the proof she copies out
the words 'in the water / Watches—' without comment. Browning revised 205–6, but did
not adopt 'bosom-high'.
 209 *Fortù, shall we sail there together*: EBB quotes as 'When shall we sail there together',
commenting: 'You have effaced .. "oh .. when shall we"—but the exclamation seems
wanted for rhythm & expression—does it not?'
 213 *Shall we sail round*: EBB has 'Oh to sail round them, close over', with the comment:
'The line is broken I think. Should it not either be "And oh, to sail round them", or "Oh, to
sail round & round them".'
 215 *That ruffle*: EBB has 'That ruffle the grey sea-water', asking: 'Why not "the grey
ocean-water" for rhythm'. She adds: 'All beautiful description.'
 219 *On the largest*: EBB quotes as 'The square black tower on the largest', asking: 'Did you
write "*built* on the largest"—because the eternal rhythm!', adding: 'How tired you are!—*as
you said once to me*'. In a note on the proofs she copied out, without comment: 'The strange
square-black turret on the largest / Built with never a door'. On 6 November, sending EBB
her copy of *Dramatic Romances and Lyrics*, Browning wrote: 'See your corrections .. and
understand that in one or two instances in which they would seem not to be adopted, they *are*
so, by some modification of the previous, or following line .. as in one of the Sorrento lines ..
about a "turret"—see!' She replied: 'I see how the "turret" stands in the new reading, triumph-
ing over the "tower", & unexceptionable in every respect': Kintner, i. 258, 259–60.

With never a door,   220
Just a loop to admit the quick lizards;
     Then, stand there and hear
The birds' quiet singing, that tells us
     What life is, so clear?
—The secret they sang to Ulysses   225
     When, ages ago,
He heard and he knew this life's secret
     I hear and I know.

Ah, see! The sun breaks o'er Calvano;
     He strikes the great gloom   230
And flutters it o'er the mount's summit
     In airy gold fume.
All is over. Look out, see the gipsy,
     Our tinker and smith,
Has arrived, set up bellows and forge,   235
     And down-squatted forthwith
To his hammering, under the wall there;
     One eye keeps aloof
The urchins that itch to be putting
     His jews'-harps to proof,   240
While the other, thro' locks of curled wire,
     Is watching how sleek

220–1 *1845* door— | Just a loop that admits .... lizards; *1872S–88S* (as *1888* except
'lizards?')   222 *1845* —To stand   224 *1845* clear; *1849* clear!
225 *1845,1849* The secret .... Ulysses,   226 *1845* When ages ago
227 *1849,1872S–88S* secret,   228 *1845–63* know!   229 *1845* Ah see! O'er
Calvano the sun breaks: *1849* (as *1888* except 'Calvano—') *1872S–88S* (as *1888* except 'Cal-
vano.')   231 *1845* And flutters it over his summit   232 *1845–63* fume!
233 *1845* over. Look out, see the gypsy, *1849* over! Look out, see the gypsy, *1872S–88S*
over. Look out, see, the gipsy,   237 *1845* hammering .... there; *1872S–88S* ham-
mering .... there!   240 *1872S–88S* jews'-harp   241 *1845* other thro' ....
wire

225 *The secret*: a reference to *Hydriotaphia, Urne Buriall*, by Sir Thomas Browne, ch. v:
'What Song the *Syrens* sang, or what name *Achilles* assumed when he hid himself among
women, though puzling Questions, are not beyond all conjecture.' Both problems are said
to have been put to scholars by the Emperor Tiberius.
     230 *He strikes*: EBB quotes without 'He', commenting: 'For clearness, the personal
pronoun is wanted, I fancy. What "strikes?"'

Shines the hog, come to share in the windfall
　—Chew, abbot's own cheek!
All is over. Wake up and come out now,   245
　And down let us go,
And see the fine things got in order
　At church for the show
Of the Sacrament, set forth this evening.
　To-morrow's the Feast   250
Of the Rosary's Virgin, by no means
　Of Virgins the least,
As you'll hear in the off-hand discourse
　Which (all nature, no art)
The Dominican brother, these three weeks,   255
　Was getting by heart.
Not a pillar nor post but is dizened
　With red and blue papers;
All the roof waves with ribbons, each altar
　A-blaze with long tapers;   260
But the great masterpiece is the scaffold
　Rigged glorious to hold
All the fiddlers and fifers and drummers
　And trumpeters bold,

243 1845,1849 windfalls 1872S–88S windfall.   244 1845,1849 —An abbot's own
cheek! 1863–75,1865S —An abbot's own cheek. 1872S–88S Chew, abbot's own cheek!
245 1845 All is over! wake .... now, 1849,1863 All is over! Wake .... now,
247 1845 And see all the fine things set in order   248 1849–65 Church
*249 {reading of 1872S–88S, DC, 1889} 1845–75,1865S evening; 1888 evening
251–2 1845 virgin, by no means | Of virgins the least— 1872S–88S Virgin, by no means |
Of Virgins the least: 253 1845 As we'll hear   255 1845 brother these three
weeks   257 1845,1849 Not a post nor a pillar but's dizened   259 1845 each
altar's   260 1872S–88S tapers.   264–5 1872S–88S bold | .... Auber:

244 —Chew: revision (taken over, unusually, from the Selections) has made the line
obscure.
245 Wake up: EBB quoted as 'And now come out, you best one', adding: 'quære, if it wᵈ
not be well to repeat the "come out—" "And now come out, come out &c—".'
250 the Feast: 'the anniversary of the battle of Lepanto [7 October 1571], where the
Turkish fleet was destroyed by the Catholic powers of Europe, and for which victory Our
Lady of the Rosary receives annual thanks': Porter and Clarke. The feast is held on the first
Sunday in October: in 1844 this was the 6th.
257 dizened: decorated, decked out. Johnson terms it 'a low word'.

Not afraid of Bellini nor Auber,   265
    Who, when the priest's hoarse,
Will strike us up something that's brisk
    For the feast's second course.
And then will the flaxen-wigged Image
    Be carried in pomp   270
Thro' the plain, while in gallant procession
    The priests mean to stomp.
All round the glad church lie old bottles
    With gunpowder stopped,
Which will be, when the Image re-enters,   275
    Religiously popped;
And at night from the crest of Calvano
    Great bonfires will hang,
On the plain will the trumpets join chorus,
    And more poppers bang.   280
At all events, come—to the garden
    As far as the wall;
See me tap with a hoe on the plaster
    Till out there shall fall
A scorpion with wide angry nippers!   285

---

271 *1872S–88S* while, in gallant procession,   273 *1845* And all .... church stand
old *1849–65S* And all .... church lie old   276 *1845–65,1865S–88S* popped.
278 *1872S–88S* hang: 280 *1845–63* bang!   281 *1845–70,1872S–88S*
garden,   282 *1845,1849* wall,

    265 *Bellini nor Auber*: Vincenzo Bellini (1801–35) and Daniel François Esprit Auber
(1782–1871), composers particularly popular at the time.
    269 *Image*: of the Blessed Virgin Mary.
    272 *stomp*: 'But is this word stamp', asked EBB, '& is it to rhyme to "pomp". I object to
that rhyme—*I*!!' Browning strengthened the word, in blacker ink, and wrote in a letter that
'the Priests stomp over the clay ridges, (a palpable plagiarism from two lines of a legend that
delighted my infancy . . . "In London town, when reigned King Lud, His lords went stomp-
ing thro' the mud" . . .)': Kintner, i. 154. EBB wrote in reply: 'But is there an English word
of a significance different from "stamp," in "stomp"? Does not the old word King Lud's
men stomped withal, claim identity with our "stamping." The *a* and *o* used to "change
about," you know, in the old English writers—see Chaucer for it. Still the "stomp" with the
peculiar significance, is better of course than the "stamp" even with a rhyme ready for it, &
I dare say you are justified in daring to put this old wine into the new bottle': Kintner,
i. 154–5. OED[2] (which cites this passage) is notably more interested in this word, originally
dialectal and then American, than the original OED.
    285 This line ends the verse-paragraph.

—"Such trifles!" you say?
Fortù, in my England at home,
    Men meet gravely to-day
And debate, if abolishing Corn-laws
    Be righteous and wise   290
—If 't were proper, Scirocco should vanish
    In black from the skies!

286 *1845* ... "Such trifles" *1849* ... "Such trifles"—   290 *1849* Is .... wise
1872S–88S be .... wise!   291 *1845* —If 'tis proper *1849* —If 'tis proper,

289 *abolishing Corn-laws*: the Corn Laws restrained the importation of cereals and so
caused severe suffering among the poor. In 1838 the Anti-Corn-Law League had been
formed. In 1845 the wet summer affected the harvest, and the potato-crop was seriously
damaged by rot. On 1 November Peel told the Cabinet that the Laws would have to be
changed: they were repealed in June 1846.

THE LOST LEADER

'I HAVE been asked the question you now address me with, and as duly answered it, I can't remember how many times,' Browning wrote to A. B. Grosart on 24 February 1875: 'there is no sort of objection to one more assurance, or rather confession, on my part that I *did* in my hasty youth presume to use the great and venerable personality of Wordsworth as a sort of painter's model; one from which this or the other particular feature may be selected and turned to account: had I intended more, above all, such a boldness as portraying the entire man, I should not have talked about "handfuls of silver and bits of ribbon." These never influenced the change of politics in the great poet; whose defection, nevertheless, accompanied as it was by a regular face-about of his special party, was to my juvenile apprehension, and even mature consideration, an event to deplore. But just as in the tapestry on my wall I can recognise figures which have *struck out* a fancy, on occasion, that though truly enough thus derived, yet would be preposterous as a copy, so, though I dare not deny the original of my little poem, I altogether refuse to have it considered as the "very effigies" of such a moral and intellectual superiority.'[1]

Later the same year he wrote to a young lady who, with two other members of her family, asked him 'in verse' the same question:

I have been asked ... I suppose a score of times: and I can only answer, with something of shame and contrition, that I undoubtedly had Wordsworth in my mind—but simply as "a model;" you know, an artist takes one or two striking traits in the features of his "model," and uses them to start his fancy on a flight which may end far enough from the good man or woman who happens to be "sitting" for nose and eye.

I thought of the great Poet's abandonment of liberalism, at an unlucky juncture, and no repaying consequence that I could ever see. But—once call my fancy-portrait *Wordsworth*—and how much more one ought to say,—how much more would not I have attempted to say![2]

The poem may well have been prompted by Wordsworth's acceptance of the Poet Laureateship in April 1843, after the death of Southey. Browning's attitude to Wordsworth at this time resembled that of Byron and Shelley thirty years before. 'Was ever such a *"great"* poet before?', he demanded rhetorically of Elizabeth Barrett shortly after publishing the

---

[1] *Letters*, pp. 166–7.   [2] *Life*, p. 123.

poem.[1] It is aptly placed after 'The Italian in England' and 'The English-man in Italy', with its final indignant reference to those who were gravely debating 'if abolishing Corn-laws / Be righteous and wise'; Elizabeth par-ticularly admired it. DeVane points out that the speaker's attitude to Wordsworth may be compared with that of Pym to Strafford (*Strafford*, v. ii. 272 ff.).

Browning made some striking verbal changes in the second stanza when he revised the poem for *1849*. There were a few later revisions: we note that in *1868*, l. 23, already twice recast, returned almost to its original form. The holograph in the Castle Howard archives[2] is based on *1865*, with some minor variants.

1849 Dramatic Romances and Lyrics; 1863 Lyrics; 1868– Dramatic Lyrics.

THE LOST LEADER.

I.

JUST for a handful of silver he left us,
    Just for a riband to stick in his coat—
Found the one gift of which fortune bereft us,
    Lost all the others she lets us devote;
They, with the gold to give, doled him out silver,   5
    So much was theirs who so little allowed:
How all our copper had gone for his service!
    Rags—were they purple, his heart had been proud!
We that had loved him so, followed him, honoured him,
    Lived in his mild and magnificent eye,   10
Learned his great language, caught his clear accents,

2 *1845* ribband   3 *1845* Got the one   4 *1870–88S* others, she
6 *1845,1849* their's   7 *Howard MS* Now all   8 *1845* they purple his *Howard*
MS they ribands, his

1 *a handful of silver*: probably a reminiscence of the thirty pieces of silver which Judas received for betraying Christ: Matt. 27:3.
2 *riband*: referring to the Laureateship.

[1] Kintner, i. 464. Cf. ii. 986.
[2] We are grateful to the Howard family, and to Mr Eeyan Hartley, the Keeper of Archives at Castle Howard, for their assistance.

Made him our pattern to live and to die!
Shakespeare was of us, Milton was for us,
    Burns, Shelley, were with us,—they watch from their graves!
He alone breaks from the van and the freemen,   15
    —He alone sinks to the rear and the slaves!

II

We shall march prospering,—not thro' his presence;
    Songs may inspirit us,—not from his lyre;
Deeds will be done,—while he boasts his quiescence,
    Still bidding crouch whom the rest bade aspire: 20
Blot out his name, then, record one lost soul more,
    One task more declined, one more footpath untrod,
One more devils'-triumph and sorrow for angels,
    One wrong more to man, one more insult to God!
Life's night begins: let him never come back to us!   25
    There would be doubt, hesitation and pain,
Forced praise on our part—the glimmer of twilight,
    Never glad confident morning again!
Best fight on well, for we taught him—strike gallantly,
    Menace our heart ere we master his own;   30

15 *Howard MS* freemen.   16 *1845–88S,Howard MS* He alone   18 *1845* may
excite us,—   20 *1872S* aspire; *1884S–8S* aspire.   21 *1845,1849* then,—
record   22 *1845* task unaccepted, one footpath   23 *1845* One more devils'-
triumph and sorrow to angels, *1849* One more triumph for devils, and sorrow for angels,
1863,1865,Howard MS (as *1849* except 'devils') *1872S–88S* (as *1888* except 'devil's-triumph')
29 *1845* him,—come gallantly, *1849–65* him,—strike gallantly, *1889* (some copies) him—
strike gallantly. (faulty type)   30 *1845* Strike our face hard ere we shatter his own;
1849 Aim at our heart ere we pierce through his own;

14 *Burns, Shelley*: 'Burns was with us', EEB wrote on reading the proof, perhaps indicat-
ing an earlier reading.
    15 *the van*: 'The chief of men is he who stands in the van of men': Carlyle, *Past and
Present* (1843), Book III, ch. viii (in which an attack on 'these mad and miserable Corn-
Laws' is part of Carlyle's argument).
    the freemen: cf. Cowper, *The Task*, v. 733: 'He is the freeman whom the truth makes
free, / And all are slaves beside.'
    24 *One wrong more*: EEB jotted this line down, on reading the proof, without comment.
    29–30 *Best fight on well*: quoting as 'Best fight on bravely', Domett commented: 'it does
not appear at first *who* had best fight on bravely—the renegade or the lamenters of his
apostasy who speak or sing. "Such trifles!" you say—but in *such trifles exactly* is it that the
difference between obscurity & perspicuity in writing consists': PK 46:378. The meaning is
no doubt that 'The Lost Leader' had 'Best fight on well'.

Then let him receive the new knowledge and wait us,
Pardoned in heaven, the first by the throne!

31 *1845* him get the   32 *1845–65* in Heaven, the

32 *Pardoned in heaven*: EBB wrote these three words in her notes on the proofs, again without comment.

THE LOST MISTRESS

W E do not know when this poem was written. As DeVane observes, if it had been composed before he left for Italy in 1844 Browning would probably have offered it to *Hood's Magazine*. It is tempting to associate it with his premature declaration of his love for Elizabeth Barrett in May 1845, but there is no hard evidence. It seems probable that she did not see the poem in manuscript, since initially she made no comment on it. When she saw it in proof she merely jotted down the words 'For though no glance &c', presumably because she found the penultimate stanza obscure, as she acknowledged on 22 October, when she asked Browning if it 'really' was. 'One verse indeed in that expressive lyric . . . does still seem questionable to me', she wrote on 6 November, 'though you have changed a word since I saw it; & still I fancy that I rather leap at the meaning than reach it—but it is my own fault probably . . I am not sure.' Browning revised the passage five times, but the best of his improvements (for *Domett 1845* and for the later *Selections*) were not used in *1888–9*.

1849 Dramatic Romances and Lyrics; 1863 Lyrics; 1868– Dramatic Lyrics.

THE LOST MISTRESS.

I.

ALL's over, then: does truth sound bitter
  As one at first believes?
Hark, 't is the sparrows' good-night twitter
  About your cottage eaves!

II.

And the leaf-buds on the vine are woolly,   5
  I noticed that, to-day;

---

1 *1845,1849* then—   4 *1845* eaves.   6 *1845* that

One day more bursts them open fully
    —You know the red turns grey.

III.

To-morrow we meet the same then, dearest?
    May I take your hand in mine?   10
Mere friends are we,—well, friends the merest
    Keep much that I resign:

IV.

For each glance of the eye so bright and black,
    Though I keep with heart's endeavour,—
Your voice, when you wish the snowdrops back,   15
    Though it stay in my soul for ever!—

V.

Yet I will but say what mere friends say,
    Or only a thought stronger;
I will hold your hand but as long as all may,
    Or so very little longer!   20

7–8 *1845* fully | —You . . . . gray. *1880S–88S* fully: | You . . . . grey.   9 *1865S* dearest
12 *1845–65,1865S* that I'll resign: *1880S–88S* that I resign.   13 *1845* For tho' no
glance of the eyes so black *1849–65,1865S* For each glance of that eye so bright and black,
1880S–88S Each glance of the eye so bright and black,   14 *1845* But I keep
15 *1845* If you only wish . . . . back *Domett 1845* {RB inserts (in ink before 'If'}
16 *1845* That shall stay . . . . ever! *Domett 1845* {RB underlines 'That' and adds)— in ink at
the end of the line} *1849* Though it stays . . . . ever!— *1880S–88S* Though it stay . . . .
ever,—   17 *1845,1849* —Yet I will   19 *1845* but so long

HOME-THOUGHTS, FROM ABROAD

HOME-THOUGHTS, FROM ABROAD
'HERE'S TO NELSON'S MEMORY!'
HOME-THOUGHTS, FROM THE SEA

THE first reference to 'Oh, to be in England', originally published in *1845* as the first of three poems yoked under the common title 'Home-Thoughts, from abroad', occurs in a letter from Browning in response to a request from Elizabeth that he should write out 'a verse or two' for the album of 'a very young friend' of hers.[1] Next day he sent her 'some easy [verses] out of a paper-full meant to go between poem & poem in my next number and break the shock of collision'. 'Your spring-song is full of beauty as you know very well', she wrote in acknowledgement, '—& "that's the wise thrush," so characteristic of you (& of the thrush too) that I was sorely tempted to ask you to write it "twice over," . . & not send the first copy to Mary Hunter notwithstanding my promise to her.' What follows strongly suggests that Elizabeth had also received 'Here's to Nelson's memory!' and the poem later entitled 'Home-Thoughts, from the Sea', which appeared in *1845* as the second and third parts of 'Home-Thoughts, from Abroad':

And now when you come to print these fragments, would it not be well if you were to stoop to the vulgarism of prefixing some word of introduction, as other people do, you know . . a title . . a name? You perplex your readers often by casting yourself on their intelligence in these things—and although it is true that readers in general are stupid & cant understand, it is still more true that they are lazy & wont understand . . & they dont catch your point of sight at first unless you think it worth while to push them by the shoulders & force them into the right place. Now these fragments . . you mean to print them with a line between . . & not one word at the top of it . . now don't you!—And then people will read

"Oh, to be in England"

and say to themselves . . 'Why who is this? . . who's out of England?' . . . you will see what I mean . . & often I have observed how some of the very most beautiful of your lyrics have suffered just from your disdain of the usual tactics of writers in this one respect.

'Thank you, thank you', he replied: '—I will devise titles—I quite see what

[1] Kintner, i. 219.

you say, now you do say it. I am . . . looking over & correcting what you read—to press they shall go.'[1]

Her letter of 22 October, written after she had seen a proof of *Dramatic Romances and Lyrics*, repeats her plea: 'Should not these fragments be severed otherwise than by numbers?';[2] but when the pamphlet appeared the three poems were merely printed with the common title and numbered 'I.', 'II.', and 'III.' In *1849* 'Home-Thoughts, from Abroad' is the title of the first poem, the second disappears, while the third becomes 'Home-Thoughts, from the Sea'. In *1863* and subsequently the second piece was printed as the last of a trio of poems grouped together as 'Nationality in Drinks'.

DeVane wrongly states that Mrs Orr assigns the first poem to Browning's first visit to Italy: in fact she is referring to the third of them.[3] Griffin and Minchin do associate it with his first journey, however, remarking that 'the contrast between an Italian June and the English April which had witnessed his departure' had suggested the piece; but if he had written it as early as that he would surely have printed it in *Dramatic Lyrics*, and perhaps before that in *Hood's Magazine*. He may well have written the lines in England in the spring of 1845, remembering both his Italian tours. On 27 January 1845 he mentions to Elizabeth that 'the whitethroat is come and sings now'.[4]

Lines 2–4 of 'Here's to Nelson's memory!' state that that poem was written at sea, no doubt during Browning's second voyage to Italy, in the autumn of 1844.[5] He will have heard a great deal about Nelson, since 'dear old [Captain James] Pritchard' and a number of his other early friends had been sailors or in some other way closely connected with the sea.[6]

According to Mrs Orr, Sarianna Browning told her that 'Home-Thoughts, from the Sea' was written 'at the same time, and in the same manner' as 'How they Brought the Good News from Ghent to Aix':[7] on Browning's first voyage to Italy, that is to say, and 'on the cover of Bartoli's De' Simboli trasportati al Morale'. Griffin and Minchin accept this, pointing out that he passed sixteen miles SE of Cape St Vincent on 27 April 1838. We have already discounted Browning's own statement that 'How

---

[1] Kintner, i. 221–2, 223.   [2] Kintner, i. 223, followed by i. 244.
[3] *Life*, p. 94 (she does not refer to 'Home-Thoughts, from Abroad'); Griffin and Minchin, p. 128.   [4] Kintner, i. 11.
[5] James F. Loucks, however, has suggested that this poem may have been written as late as August 1845, prompted by 'the recent donation, to Greenwich Hospital, of the coat in which Lord Nelson was wounded at the Battle of Trafalgar': SIB, Fall 1976, pp. 71–2.
[6] See Maynard, pp. 99 ff.
[7] *Life*, p. 94; Griffin and Minchin, pp. 95 n., 127–8.

they Brought the Good News' had been written on that voyage, however, while Kenyon rightly observes that Browning had been ill during the first two weeks of it, and had later told Fanny Haworth that he had written very little.[1] The poem was probably written during his second voyage. Elizabeth singled this out from the three pieces, praising 'those grand sea-sights in the long lines'.[2]

In BN, Fall 1969, pp. 24–5 Douglas C. Ewing described the Pierpont Morgan manuscript of 'Oh, to be in England' as 'the first draft' of this poem. It seems to antedate 1845, in any case, and may even be the copy which Browning wrote out for Mary Hunter. Browning revised the piece in 1849 and 1863, and then left it virtually intact.

In 1863 the three poems were classified as 'Lyrics', and from 1868 as 'Dramatic Lyrics'. For details, see above.

HOME-THOUGHTS, FROM ABROAD.

I.

O H , to be in England
Now that April's there,
And whoever wakes in England
Sees, some morning, unaware,
That the lowest boughs and the brushwood sheaf   5
Round the elm-tree bole are in tiny leaf,
While the chaffinch sings on the orchard bough
In England—now!

1–2 [printed as one line in *1872S–88S*, reading] 'now that'   3–4 *Morgan MS, 1845* And who wakes in England | Sees, some *1872S–88S* [as *1888*, but printed as one line, reading] 'sees, some'   5 *1845–68,1865S* brush-wood   7 *Morgan MS* fruit tree bough   8–9 *1845* [has a space between these lines, but no section-number.] *1872S–88S* printed without a break or section-number after l. 8, and reading 'May follows'

[1] Above, p. 18; *The Works of Robert Browning*, ed. F. G. Kenyon (Centenary ed., 10 vols., 1912, repr. Ernest Benn, n.d.), iii, p. xxi.
[2] Kintner, i. 244.

II.

And after April, when May follows,
And the whitethroat builds, and all the swallows!   10
Hark, where my blossomed pear-tree in the hedge
Leans to the field and scatters on the clover
Blossoms and dewdrops—at the bent spray's edge—
That's the wise thrush; he sings each song twice over,
Lest you should think he never could recapture   15
The first fine careless rapture!
And though the fields look rough with hoary dew
All will be gay when noontide wakes anew
The buttercups, the little children's dower
—Far brighter than this gaudy melon-flower!   20

II.

Here's to Nelson's memory!
'T is the second time that I, at sea,
Right off Cape Trafalgar here,
Have drunk it deep in British Beer.
Nelson for ever—any time   5
Am I his to command in prose or rhyme!
Give me of Nelson only a touch,
And I save it, be it little or much:
Here's one our Captain gives, and so
Down at the word, by George, shall it go!   10
He says that at Greenwich they point the beholder
To Nelson's coat, "still with tar on the shoulder:

10 *Morgan MS,1845,1849* whitethroat . . . . swallows— *1872S–88S* white-throat . . . . swallows!   11 *Morgan MS* Hark! where the blossomed pear tree *1845,1849* Hark! where my blossomed pear-tree   14 *Morgan MS,1845* thrush; . . . . over *1872S–88S* thrush: . . . . over   17 *Morgan MS,1845* fields are rough . . . dew, *1849–88S* fields look rough . . . . dew,   18 *1872S* And will   19 *Morgan MS,1845,1849* dower,
II. 4 *1845* British beer: 8 *1845* And I guard it, ... much;   9 *1845* one the Captain   11–12 *1845* they show the beholder | Nelson's . . . . shoulder, *1863–75* [as *1888* except 'shoulder,']

II. 6 *his to command*: a polite formula; but here emphatic.
7 *only a touch*: perhaps an echo of *Henry V*, Prologue to Act IV, 47.

"For he used to lean with one shoulder digging,
"Jigging, as it were, and zig-zag-zigging
"Up against the mizen-rigging!"   15

III.

HOME-THOUGHTS, FROM THE SEA

NOBLY, nobly Cape Saint Vincent to the North-west died
          away;
Sunset ran, one glorious blood-red, reeking into Cadiz Bay;
Bluish 'mid the burning water, full in face Trafalgar lay;
In the dimmest North-east distance dawned Gibraltar grand
          and gray;
"Here and here did England help me: how can I help
          England?"—say,   5
Whoso turns as I, this evening, turn to God to praise and pray,
While Jove's planet rises yonder, silent over Africa.

---

title *1845* (prints as 'III.', with no separate title)   1 *1845* Nobly Cape Saint Vincent
to the north-west died away; *Domett 1845* (RB adds 'Nobly,' in pencil at the beginning of
the line) *1849* (as *1888* except 'north-west') *1863–75* (as *1888* except 'North-West') *1865S*
Nobly, nobly Cape St. Vincent to the North-West died away;   3 *1845–63,1865S*
mid . . . . water, *1865* mid . . . . water;   4 *1845,1849* north-east distance, *1863–65S*
North-East distance, *1868–75* North-East distance   5 *1845,1849* help me,—
7 *1845* Yonder where Jove's planet rises silent over Africa.

II. 15 *mizen-rigging*: the mizen-mast is the 'aftermost mast' of a three-masted ship.
III. 1 *Cape Saint Vincent*: the SW point of Portugal, off which Nelson (under the com-
mand of Sir John Jervis) defeated the Spanish fleet on 14 February 1797.
2 *reeking*: smoking.
3 *Trafalgar*: Cape Trafalgar, between Cadiz and Gibraltar, off which Nelson defeated
the French on 21 October 1805, dying in the action on his ship 'Victory'.
7 *Jove's planet*: Jupiter.

THE BISHOP ORDERS HIS TOMB
AT SAINT PRAXED'S CHURCH

ON 18 February 1845 Browning wrote to F. O. Ward: 'I send you *one* poem as long as the two I promised—(about 4 pages, I think) and I pick it out as being a pet of mine, and just the thing for the time—what with the Oxford business, and Camden Society and other embroilments.'[1] The poem was published in *Hood's Magazine* for March. The title was simply 'The Tomb at St. Praxed's', followed by '(Rome, 15—.)'

The 'Oxford business' refers to the latest developments of the Tractarian Movement, which had begun in 1833, when, as a sequel to a sermon by John Keble on 'National Apostasy', Newman and others began to publish a series of *Tracts for the Times*. On 13 February 1845 W. G. Ward was publicly condemned in Convocation in Oxford for writing *The Ideal of a Christian Church Considered*, on the ground that it was inconsistent with his subscription to the Thirty-Nine Articles of the Church of England. Newman's secession to Rome was to occur in October of the same year. The Camden Society had been founded in 1838 for the publication of documents relating to the early history and literature of the British Empire: Browning may have been thinking rather of the Cambridge Camden Society, founded the following year for the study of ecclesiology.[2]

If Browning did not write the poem in Italy, he may well have begun it there, since it was ready for publication within six weeks or so of his return. It is possible that he refers to it on 13 January, when he tells Elizabeth Barrett: 'I don't think I shall let *you* hear, after all, the savage things about Popes and imaginative religions that I must say.'[3]

While he had no doubt visited the church of Santa Prassede, and been struck by its ornate interior, there is very little correspondence between it and the descriptions in the poem. It has no 'aery dome', but only a half-

---

[1] *New Letters*, p. 35. For Ward and *Hood's Magazine*, see above, pp. 1 ff.

[2] See Robert A. Greenberg, 'Ruskin, Pugin, and the Contemporary Context of "The Bishop Orders his Tomb"': PMLA 84 (1969), 1588–94. Greenberg's article provides useful background material, whether or not one accepts his view that the poem is influenced by A. W. Pugin's *Contrasts: or a Parallel between the Noble Edifices of the Fourteenth and Fifteenth Centuries, and Similar Buildings of the Present Day* (1836; 2nd ed., with modified title, 1841).

[3] Kintner, i. 7.

dome above the altar.[1] As for the Bishop's tomb, it is (as Mrs Orr observes) 'entirely fictitious',[2] and a careful reader will realize that his sons would on no account have constructed the elaborate and expensive structure which he desired.

As B. W. Fuson pointed out, deathbed monologues are common in the minor poetry of the late eighteenth century and the early nineteenth;[3] yet the passages which scholars have cited as possible influences on this poem are mostly in prose. K. I. D. Maslen suggested that Browning may have remembered an anonymous review of Ranke's *History of the Popes* in the *Edinburgh Review* for October 1840.[4] Macaulay (who wrote it) deplores men like Leo X, 'who, with the Latinity of the Augustan age, had acquired its atheistical and scoffing spirit' and who 'spoke of the Incarnation, the Eucharist, and the Trinity, in the same tone in which Cotta and Velleius talked of the oracle of Delphi, or of the voice of Faunus in the mountains. Their years glided by in a soft dream of sensual and intellectual voluptu-ousness. Choice cookery, delicious wines, lovely women, hounds, falcons, horses, newly-discovered manuscripts of the classics . . . these things were the delight and even the serious business of their lives.'

Since it was common for men of importance to leave directions about their monuments, it is difficult to assess the relevance of any particular example. J. D. Rea cited a passage describing a nobleman called Vespasiano Gonzaga lying on his bed in an upper room of his palace and ordering that his daughter should 'be bound and obligated to erect in that church a tomb of marble, . . . on the construction and adornment of which she will be bound and obligated to spend fifteen hundred scudi, besides the stones necessary to adorn the aforesaid tomb, which I have brought from Rome'.[5] Since it is no longer believed that Irenio Affó's biography of Vespasiano Gonzaga, Duke of Sabbioneta, is the source of 'My Last Duchess', as Rea was arguing, even the occurrence of the name 'Gandolfo' and the verb 'elucescebat' elsewhere in that work fail to convince us of its relevance to the present poem. Barbara Melchiori's case for the influence of *The Art of Painting in all its Branches*, by Gérard de Lairesse (translated by

[1] The interior of the church is admirably illustrated in Fascicolo 14 (Bologna, 21 May 1966) in the series *Tesori d'arte cristiana*.

[2] *Handbook*, p. 247 n. For a contrary view, see Charles Flint Thomas, 'Real Sources for the Bishop's Tomb in the Church of St. Praxed': SBC, Spring/Fall 1984, pp. 160–6.

[3] *Browning and his English Predecessors in the Dramatic Monolog* (State University of Iowa, 1948), pp. 37 ff.

[4] 'Browning and Macaulay': NQ, December 1980, pp. 525–7, referring to the *Edinburgh Review*, lxxii. 242.

[5] '"My Last Duchess"': SP xxix (1932), 120–2. Cf. our Vol. III, p. 184.

J. F. Fritsch) is rather more persuasive. Browning wrote on the fly-leaf of his copy of the edition of 1778: 'I read this book more often and with greater delight, when I was a child, than any other: and still remember the main of it most gratefully for the good I seem to have got by the prints, and wondrous text.'[1] In Book VI, ch. 16, de Lairesse describes 'an ancient Tomb or sepulcher of light red marble, intermixed with dark grey, and white eyes and veins, with a lid or cover of lapis lazuli'. Emphasis is laid on the importance of valuable stones of contrasting colours. Another passage in Book VI (ch. 14, pp. 249 ff.) gives a description of a landscape—'*Sweet Repose disturbed by Lewdness. An Emblem*'—which is close in spirit, and sometimes in diction, to ll. 56 ff. of the poem.[2] Other scholars have suggested that Trimalchio's specifications for his own tomb in the *Satyricon* of Petronius Arbiter may have been in Browning's memory as he wrote. Trimalchio wishes to have his dog at his feet, and garlands and jars of perfume. He wants to have a frieze (very different from that desired by the Bishop, however), and he suddenly becomes suspicious of his heirs.[3]

Since we know that the Brownings owned two copies of the *Anecdotes* of Joseph Spence, this inconclusive list of conceivable influences may close with a reminiscence of Pope's in that book which is likely enough to have struck Browning as bizarre—a passage not so far adduced (so far as we know) in relation to this poem:

I paid Sir Godfrey Kneller a visit but two days before he died; I think I never saw a scene of so much vanity in my life. He was lying in his bed, and contemplating the plan he had made for his own monument. He said many gross things in relation to himself, and the memory he should leave behind him. He said he should not like to lie among the rascals at Westminster; a memorial there would be sufficient; and desired me to write an epitaph for it.[4]

On 21 July 1845 Elizabeth gave high praise to 'the Hood poems which have delighted me so—& first to the St. Praxed's which is of course the finest & most powerful .. & indeed full of the power of life .. and of death'.[5] Ruskin wrote of the poem memorably in *Modern Painters*: 'I know no other piece of modern English, prose or poetry, in which there is so

---

[1] Kelley and Coley, A 1379.

[2] The passages cited by Barbara Melchiori, in *Browning's Poetry of Reticence* (1968), are from pp. 255 and 327 ff. In VP 8 (1970), 209–18 George Monteiro suggests that the types of stone mentioned in Browning's poem have a symbolical significance deriving from the Bible.

[3] *Satyricon*, 71.

[4] *Anecdotes, Observations, and Characters, of Books and Men*, collected by Joseph Spence, ed. S. W. Singer (1820), p. 165. Cf. Kelley and Coley, A 2186–7.

[5] Kintner, i. 130.

much told, as in these lines, of the Renaissance spirit,—its worldliness, inconsistency, pride, hypocrisy, ignorance of itself, love of art, of luxury, and of good Latin.'[1]

Having been brought up as a Dissenter, Browning must have been surprised and perhaps shocked by the rich interiors of the Italian churches—whether that of Santa Prassede or (even more) that of 'the Jesu Church so gay'.[2] 'I have no kind of concern as to where the old clothes of myself shall be thrown', he once wrote on the subject of his own burial.[3]

1846 Dramatic Romances and Lyrics; 1863 Men, and Women; 1868– Men and Women.

THE BISHOP ORDERS HIS TOMB AT SAINT PRAXED'S CHURCH.

ROME, 15—.

VANITY, saith the preacher, vanity!
Draw round my bed: is Anselm keeping back?
Nephews—sons mine . . . ah God, I know not! Well—
She, men would have to be your mother once,
Old Gandolf envied me, so fair she was!   5
What's done is done, and she is dead beside,
Dead long ago, and I am Bishop since,

title *Hood,1845* THE TOMB AT ST. PRAXED'S. *1849* THE BISHOP ORDERS HIS TOMB AT ST. PRAXED'S CHURCH.   1 *Hood* Preacher,   7 *Hood* And long

Title: see Introduction.

Date: we are no doubt to associate the poem with the period before the Counter-Reformation.

1 *Vanity*: 'Vanity of vanities, saith the Preacher, vanity of vanities; all is vanity': Eccles. 1:2.

3 *Nephews*: 'how was it that the popes and cardinals always had so many nephews?', young Daniel Deronda asks his tutor in George Eliot's novel (ch. xvi). The word was the usual euphemism for the illegitimate sons of a pope or other ecclesiastic. Titian's painting of Pope Paul III with his 'nipoti' is a celebrated example.

6 *What's done is done*: proverbial: cf. *Macbeth*, III. ii. 12.

[1] *The Works*, ed. E. T. Cook and A. D. O. Wedderburn (39 vols., 1902–12), vi. 449.
[2] See 49n.
[3] *Life*, p. 244.

And as she died so must we die ourselves,
And thence ye may perceive the world's a dream.
Life, how and what is it? As here I lie   10
In this state-chamber, dying by degrees,
Hours and long hours in the dead night, I ask
"Do I live, am I dead?" Peace, peace seems all.
Saint Praxed's ever was the church for peace;
And so, about this tomb of mine. I fought   15
With tooth and nail to save my niche, ye know:
—Old Gandolf cozened me, despite my care;
Shrewd was that snatch from out the corner South
He graced his carrion with, God curse the same!
Yet still my niche is not so cramped but thence   20
One sees the pulpit o' the epistle-side,
And somewhat of the choir, those silent seats,
And up into the aery dome where live
The angels, and a sunbeam's sure to lurk:
And I shall fill my slab of basalt there,   25
And 'neath my tabernacle take my rest,
With those nine columns round me, two and two,

13 *Hood,1845* seems all: 14 *Hood–1849* St. Praxed's   17–19 *Hood* —Old
Gandolf came me in, despite my care, | For a shrewd snatch out of the corner south | To
grace his carrion with, God curse the same!   21 *1872S–88S* pulpit on the
23 *1872S–88S* aëry

9 *the world's a dream*: one of the great commonplaces (e.g. *The Tempest*, iv. i. 156–8),
recently expressed in Longfellow's 'A Psalm of Life' (1839): 'Tell me not, in mournful
numbers, / Life is but an empty dream!'

11 *this state-chamber*: the dying were often moved to some particular room. By the end of
his monologue the Bishop believes that he is in his church.

16 *niche*: in *Easter-Day* (l. 835) this rhymes with 'which', as was normal in Browning's
day.

17 *Old Gandolf cozened me*: copying out 'Old Gandolf *came me in* ... / For a shrewd
snatch', from *Hood's*, EBB asked: 'Is that "came me in" a correct expression .. or rather, does
it *express* .. does it not make the meaning hard to get at?' Like 'cozened' (cheated), 'come me
in' is Shakespearian: see *1 Henry IV*, iii. i. 98.

21 *the epistle-side*: to the right of the altar, from which the Epistle is read.

23 *the aery dome*: Browning (or the Bishop) is not accurate in his description: S. Prassede
has only a half-dome, at the eastern end of the church.

26 *my tabernacle*: a tabernacle is 'An ornate canopied structure, as a tomb or shrine':
OED. Pettigrew draws attention to Exod. 26:30 ff.

The odd one at my feet where Anselm stands:
Peach-blossom marble all, the rare, the ripe
As fresh-poured red wine of a mighty pulse.   30
—Old Gandolf with his paltry onion-stone,
Put me where I may look at him! True peach,
Rosy and flawless: how I earned the prize!
Draw close: that conflagration of my church
—What then? So much was saved if aught were missed!   35
My sons, ye would not be my death? Go dig
The white-grape vineyard where the oil-press stood,
Drop water gently till the surface sink,
And if ye find . . . Ah God, I know not, I! . . .
Bedded in store of rotten fig-leaves soft,   40
And corded up in a tight olive-frail,
Some lump, ah God, of *lapis lazuli*,
Big as a Jew's head cut off at the nape,
Blue as a vein o'er the Madonna's breast . . .
Sons, all have I bequeathed you, villas, all,   45
That brave Frascati villa with its bath,
So, let the blue lump poise between my knees,
Like God the Father's globe on both his hands
Ye worship in the Jesu Church so gay,
For Gandolf shall not choose but see and burst!   50

29 *Hood* Peachblossom-marble   30 *Hood* fresh-pour'd . . . . pulse *1845–65* fresh-
poured . . . . pulse   38 *Hood–1863* sinks,   39 *Hood–1865* . . Ah, God I
46 *Hood* Frescati   47 *Hood,1845* So let   48 *1863,1865* His hands

31 *onion-stone*: from It. *cipollino*, 'a kind of greenish-white marble splitting into coats
like an onion, *cipolla*': Porter and Clarke.
41 *olive-frail*: a frail is a kind of basket made of rushes. Cf. 'The Englishman in Italy', 47.
42 *lapis lazuli*: 'The *lapis lazuli*, or azure stone, is a copper ore, very compact and hard, so
as to take a high polish, [which] is worked into a great variety of toys [ornaments]. It is
found in detached lumps, of an elegant blue colour variegated with clouds of white, and
veins of a shining gold colour': Johnson, quoting [Dr John] Hill.
43 *a Jew's head*: such as that of John the Baptist, often portrayed in paintings.
46 *Frascati*: a town outside Rome which commands a fine view of the Campagna.
Wealthy noblemen and ecclesiastics built villas there: the Villa Falconieri was planned by
Cardinal Ruffini before 1550. They usually had a bath or ornamental pond in the middle of
the atrium.
49 *the Jesu Church*: the Chiesa del Gesù, which has a representation of the Trinity in
which (as Pettigrew observes) an angel, not God, holds a large globe of *lapis lazuli*.

Swift as a weaver's shuttle fleet our years:
Man goeth to the grave, and where is he?
Did I say basalt for my slab, sons? Black—
'T was ever antique-black I meant! How else
Shall ye contrast my frieze to come beneath?   55
The bas-relief in bronze ye promised me,
Those Pans and Nymphs ye wot of, and perchance
Some tripod, thyrsus, with a vase or so,
The Saviour at his sermon on the mount,
Saint Praxed in a glory, and one Pan   60
Ready to twitch the Nymph's last garment off,
And Moses with the tables . . . but I know
Ye mark me not! What do they whisper thee,
Child of my bowels, Anselm? Ah, ye hope
To revel down my villas while I gasp   65
Bricked o'er with beggar's mouldy travertine
Which Gandolf from his tomb-top chuckles at!
Nay, boys, ye love me—all of jasper, then!

53 *1872S–88S* say, basalt   60 *Hood–1849* St. Praxed   68 *Hood,1845* jasper then!

51 *Swift as a weaver's shuttle*: 'My days are swifter than a weaver's shuttle, and are spent without hope': Job 7:6.

52 *Man goeth to the grave*: Job 7:9 and 14:10.

54 *antique-black*: It. *nero antico*.

58 *Some tripod, thyrsus*: for his frieze the Bishop has in mind, incongruously juxtaposed with Christian representations, a Bacchic scene of the sort portrayed on certain Greek vases and in some of the great paintings of the Italian Renaissance, such as Bellini's Feast of the Gods. A tripod was an ornamental vessel, on three legs, often presented as a prize or a votive offering. Cf. Dryden, *Virgil's Æneis*, v. 146. A thyrsus was a staff or spear tipped with an ornament like a pine-cone, sometimes with ivy or vine branches twined round it: an emblem of revelry, commonly carried by Bacchus.

60 *Saint Praxed*: St Praxedes or Prassede was a martyr of the second century.

62 *the tables*: see Exod. 24:12: 'And the LORD said unto Moses, Come up to me into the mount, and be there: and I will give thee tables of stone, and a law, and commandments which I have written; that thou mayest teach them.' The orders given by the Lord at 25:8 ff. form an ironic parallel to the tabernacle desired by the Bishop.

64 *Child of my bowels*: i.e. my beloved child: cf. Philem. 12.

65 *To revel down my villas*: for a comparable use of the verb cf. Scott, *Rokeby*, I. xvii. 22: 'I revell'd thrice the sum away'.

66 *travertine*: limestone. Cf. 'Pictor Ignotus', 67.

68 *jasper*: Johnson quotes Addison on Italy: 'The most valuable pillars about Rome are four columns of oriental jasper in St. Paulina's chapel, and one of transparent oriental jasper in the vatican library.' Cf. the description of the heavenly Jerusalem in Rev. 21:11, 18, 19.

'T is jasper ye stand pledged to, lest I grieve
My bath must needs be left behind, alas!   70
One block, pure green as a pistachio-nut,
There's plenty jasper somewhere in the world—
And have I not Saint Praxed's ear to pray
Horses for ye, and brown Greek manuscripts,
And mistresses with great smooth marbly limbs?   75
—That's if ye carve my epitaph aright,
Choice Latin, picked phrase, Tully's every word,
No gaudy ware like Gandolf's second line—
Tully, my masters? Ulpian serves his need!
And then how I shall lie through centuries,   80
And hear the blessed mutter of the mass,
And see God made and eaten all day long,
And feel the steady candle-flame, and taste
Good strong thick stupefying incense-smoke!
For as I lie here, hours of the dead night,   85
Dying in state and by such slow degrees,
I fold my arms as if they clasped a crook,
And stretch my feet forth straight as stone can point,
And let the bedclothes, for a mortcloth, drop

---

*69 {reading of *1863–88S,DC,1889*} Hood 'Tis . . . . pledg'd . . . . grieve *1845,1849* 'Tis . . . . pledged . . . . grieve *1888* 'T is . . . . pledged . . . . grieve.   73 *Hood* And I shall have St. Praxed's *1845,1849* And have I not St. Praxed's   75 *Hood* limbs   78 *Hood* line   79 *Hood* —Tully . . . . need! *1870,1875* Tully, ... need *1888* {some copies have a very faint exclamation-mark}   84 *Hood–1868* stupifying   89 *Hood* bed-clothes for a mortcloth *1845–65* bedclothes for a mortcloth

---

78 *gaudy ware*: meretricious stuff.

79 *Tully . . . Ulpian*: Marcus Tullius Cicero (106–43 BC) has always been the model for those who wish to write Latin prose in the manner of the classical period. Domitius Ulpianus (d. AD 223) was an important jurist; although he is a good and lively writer, he admits words and constructions foreign to the Ciceronian age. Cf. 99 n.

82 *God made and eaten*: in the Eucharist, or sacrament of the Lord's supper, in which the bread becomes (the Roman Catholic doctrine) or represents the flesh of Christ: Matt. 26:26. A. C. Dooley compares *An Earnest Appeal to Men of Reason and Religion*, by John Wesley (1743, often reprinted), part 10: 'Is it now in your power to see, or hear, or taste, or feel God?': SBC, Spring 1980, pp. 54–5. While the Bishop's words may be 'An Echo of Wesley', as Dooley suggests, such questions were of course a commonplace of anti-Catholic polemic.

87 *a crook*: the pastoral staff of a bishop, commonly represented in his funerary monument.

89 *mortcloth*: funeral pall.

Into great laps and folds of sculptor's-work: 90
And as yon tapers dwindle, and strange thoughts
Grow, with a certain humming in my ears,
About the life before I lived this life,
And this life too, popes, cardinals and priests,
Saint Praxed at his sermon on the mount,   95
Your tall pale mother with her talking eyes,
And new-found agate urns as fresh as day,
And marble's language, Latin pure, discreet,
—Aha, ELUCESCEBAT quoth our friend?
No Tully, said I, Ulpian at the best!   100
Evil and brief hath been my pilgrimage.
All *lapis*, all, sons! Else I give the Pope
My villas! Will ye ever eat my heart?
Ever your eyes were as a lizard's quick,
They glitter like your mother's for my soul,   105
Or ye would heighten my impoverished frieze,
Piece out its starved design, and fill my vase

90 *1872S–88S* sculptor's work: 93 *Hood* life before this life I liv'd, *1845* life before
this life I lived,   94 *Hood–1865* Popes, Cardinals and Priests, *1870,1875* {as *1888*
except 'priests'}   95 *Hood–1849* St. Praxed .... mount, *1884S* Saint Praxed ....
mount.   103 *Hood–1865* My villas: will   106–8 {not in *Hood*}
106 *1884S–8S* frieze.

95 *his sermon on the mount*: in l. 59 the Bishop knew who preached the sermon. Pettigrew
cites a letter, unfortunately without a reference, in which Browning explained that 'the
blunder as to the sermon is the result of the dying man's haziness', adding (with reference
to the poem as a whole), 'he would not reveal himself as he does but for that'. We are no
doubt to attribute his confusion of the gender of St Praxed to the same 'haziness'.

96 *talking*: eloquent.

99 ELUCESCEBAT: Browning answered D. G. Rossetti's question on this word: '"elucesco" is
dog-latin rather,—the true word would be "eluceo"—& Ulpian, the golden jurist, is a copper
latinist' (extract from a letter dated 29 May 1856 in *Pall Mall Gazette*, 2 April 1890, p. 7). A
friend comments that *elucesco* for the Ciceronian *eluceo*, 'shine forth', is first found in the
Vulgate, long after Ulpian. As J. W. Binns has pointed out in an important article, 'Browning,
Tully and Ulpian' (SBC, Spring 1978, pp. 66–70), G. J. Vossius, *De Vitiis Sermonis et Glossema-*
tis Latino-Barbaris (Amsterdam, 1645), sig. N1[r], had observed that although *elucesco* was fre-
quently found in later Latin writing, classical authors had used *eluceo* or a synonym.

101 *my pilgrimage*: 'The days ... of my pilgrimage are an hundred and thirty years: few
and evil have the days of the years of my life been': Gen. 47:9.

103 *eat my heart*: torment me.

104 *eyes ... as a lizard's quick*: cf. Byron, *Childe Harold's Pilgrimage*, iv. 1047: Browning
may be remembering the 'nipoti' in Titian's Pope Paul III (above, 3 n.).

With grapes, and add a vizor and a Term,
And to the tripod ye would tie a lynx
That in his struggle throws the thyrsus down,   110
To comfort me on my entablature
Whereon I am to lie till I must ask
"Do I live, am I dead?" There, leave me, there!
For ye have stabbed me with ingratitude
To death—ye wish it—God, ye wish it! Stone—   115
Gritstone, a-crumble! Clammy squares which sweat
As if the corpse they keep were oozing through—
And no more *lapis* to delight the world!
Well go! I bless ye. Fewer tapers there,
But in a row: and, going, turn your backs   120
—Ay, like departing altar-ministrants,
And leave me in my church, the church for peace,
That I may watch at leisure if he leers—
Old Gandolf, at me, from his onion-stone,
As still he envied me, so fair she was!   125

---

109 *Hood* Or to the   114 *Hood* stabb'd me with *1863* stabbed with
115 *1872S–88S* To death: ye   119 *Hood–1863,1884S–8S* Well, go!
122 *1884S–8S* peace   124 *1872S–88S* Gandolf   125 *1889* {some copies}
envied me. so {faulty type}

108 *a vizor and a Term*: a visor or mask, sometimes Bacchanalian, is often found in the
sort of painting and sculpture (hardly funerary) which the Bishop has in his thoughts. A
'Term', common in art criticism, is a representation of the god Terminus, often phallic. Cf.
our note to *Strafford*, v. ii. 42 (Vol. II, p. 139).
111 *entablature*: 'That part of an order which is above the column; including the archi-
trave, the frieze, and the cornice': OED. Here the Bishop seems to be referring to a basalt
base to support his sarcophagus.
116 *Gritstone*: coarse sandstone.
121 *altar-ministrants*: boys or men who assist the priest.
122 *in my church*: cf. 11 n.
125 *so fair she was!*: on reading the MS, EBB sent a general comment: 'This is a wonderful
poem I think—& classes with those works of yours which show most power .. most
unquestionable genius in the high sense. You force your reader to sympathize positively in
his glory in being buried!' She cited 80 ff. as 'a grand passage'.

GARDEN FANCIES

THE FLOWER'S NAME

SIBRANDUS SCHAFNABURGENSIS

THESE two poems were published as a pair in *Hood's Magazine* for July 1844, and remained a pair, with their original titles. It is likely that they were written between the publication of *Dramatic Lyrics* in November 1842 and Browning's visit to Italy in the later part of 1844, but we have no firm evidence for dating them. DeVane conjectures that 'The Flower's Name' was written in June 1844, and expresses his belief that it 'celebrates . . . Browning's mother's garden'. That may be, but the piece is no doubt dramatic, and is apparently about a Spanish lady, as Elizabeth Barrett assumed (cf. 16 n.). She admired the poem, writing that 'some of the stanzas about the name of the flower, with such exquisite music in them, & grace of every kind', gave her great pleasure, as did 'that beautiful & musical use of the word "meandering", which I never remember having seen used in relation to *sound* before', adding that 'It does to mate with your "simmering quiet" in Sordello [i. 909–10], which brings the summer air into the room as sure as you read it.'[1]

Pettigrew states that 'Sibrandus' is 'based on fact', but provides no evidence. DeVane informs us that 'The incident . . . happened in his mother's garden, probably in the month of May, 1844': again without evidence. Mrs Orr realizes that the poem is dramatic, since she refers to the speaker as 'Some wag'.[2] Eleanor Cook has suggested that the germ of the piece may have been a passage in Rabelais concerning 'a great, greasy, grand, grey, pretty, little, mouldy book, which smelt more strongly but not more sweetly than roses . . . The rats and moths, or—to be more truthful—some other venomous vermin, had nibbled off the opening.'[3]

'I like your burial of the pedant so much!', Elizabeth Barrett wrote immediately after her praise of 'The Flower's Name': '—you have quite the damp smell of funguses and the sense of creeping things through and through it.' Six months later Browning was to acknowledge to her his 'odd liking for "vermin"', mentioning efts and newts. 'What a fine fellow our

---

[1] Kintner, i. 130.
[2] *Handbook*, p. 285.
[3] Cook, p. 79 n., quoting *Gargantua and Pantagruel*, i. i.

English water-eft is,' he went on: '... I always loved all those wild creatures God *"sets up for themselves"* so independently of us.'[1] They find their apotheosis in stanzas VII and VIII of 'Sibrandus'.

In *1863* and *1865* 'Soliloquy of the Spanish Cloister' became the third of the 'Garden Fancies', but from *1868* it was printed separately, immediately after them.

1849 Dramatic Romances and Lyrics; 1863 Lyrics; 1868– Dramatic Lyrics.

GARDEN FANCIES.

I. THE FLOWER'S NAME.

I.

HERE'S the garden she walked across,
    Arm in my arm, such a short while since:
Hark, now I push its wicket, the moss
    Hinders the hinges and makes them wince!
She must have reached this shrub ere she turned,   5
    As back with that murmur the wicket swung;
For she laid the poor snail, my chance foot spurned,
    To feed and forget it the leaves among.

II.

Down this side of the gravel-walk
    She went while her robe's edge brushed the box: 10
And here she paused in her gracious talk
    To point me a moth on the milk-white phlox.

Note: the stanzas were not numbered in *Hood's Magazine*   *10 {reading of *Hood–
1888S*, DC, *1889*} *1888* box   *12 {reading of *1863–88S*, DC, *1889*} *Hood–1849* flox.
1888 phlox

    10 *box*: low box-wood hedge.

[1] Kintner, i. 356.

Roses, ranged in valiant row,
　　I will never think that she passed you by!
She loves you noble roses, I know;   15
　　But yonder, see, where the rock-plants lie!

III.

This flower she stopped at, finger on lip,
　　Stooped over, in doubt, as settling its claim;
Till she gave me, with pride to make no slip,
　　Its soft meandering Spanish name: 20
What a name! Was it love or praise?
　　Speech half-asleep or song half-awake?
I must learn Spanish, one of these days,
　　Only for that slow sweet name's sake.

IV.

Roses, if I live and do well,   25
　　I may bring her, one of these days,
To fix you fast with as fine a spell,
　　Fit you each with his Spanish phrase;
But do not detain me now; for she lingers
　　There, like sunshine over the ground,   30

14 *Hood,1845* Think will I never she   15 *Hood,1845* She loves noble
16 *Hood* But this—so surely this met her eye!   17 *Hood,1845* lip;   18 *Hood*
doubt, settling its claim, *1845* doubt, as settling its claim,   20 *1849,1880S–8S* name.
21 *Hood* Was it love, *1845–65* was it love,   22 *Hood–1865* half-asleep,
23 *Hood,1845* Spanish   25 *1880S–8S* Roses,—   28 *Hood,1845* phrase!
1880S–8S phrase.

16 *But yonder*: EBB quotes the *Hood's* text, 'But this . . so surely this met her eye', and
comments: 'Is it hypercritical to complain of this "eye". I seldom like the singular "eye"—
and then, when it is a Spanish eye! The line is not a great favorite of mine altogether—and
the poem *is*—& you see the least speck on a Venice glass: and if it is "*my fancy*", at least I
speak it off my mind & have done with it. The beauty & melody we never shall have done
with . . none of us.'

20 *meandering*: see EBB's comment, in our Introduction above.

　　Spanish name: Pettigrew suggests *azucena*, a white lily very common in Spanish love-
poetry; but it is hardly a rock-plant (cf. 16–17).

23 *I must learn Spanish*: in December 1834 Browning told Ripert-Monclar that he had
'learned Spanish enough' to be able to read it: 'I *will* not learn German for instance', he then
wrote, '—& can't help learning Spanish!': *Correspondence*, iii. 111.

And ever I see her soft white fingers
    Searching after the bud she found.

V.

Flower, you Spaniard, look that you grow not,
    Stay as you are and be loved for ever!
Bud, if I kiss you 't is that you blow not: 35
    Mind, the shut pink mouth opens never!
For while it pouts, her fingers wrestle,
    Twinkling the audacious leaves between,
Till round they turn and down they nestle—
    Is not the dear mark still to be seen?   40

VI.

Where I find her not, beauties vanish;
    Whither I follow her, beauties flee;
Is there no method to tell her in Spanish
    June's twice June since she breathed it with me?
Come, bud, show me the least of her traces,   45
    Treasure my lady's lightest footfall!
—Ah, you may flout and turn up your faces—
    Roses, you are not so fair after all!

---

33 *Hood* look you   *35 {reading of DC,1889}* *Hood* you, 'tis . . . . not, *1845–65* you 'tis . . . . not, *1868–88, 1880S–8S* you 't is . . . . not,   36 *Hood* Mind the pink shut mouth *1845* Mind that the pink mouth   37 *Hood* while it pouts thus, her *1845–65* while thus it pouts, her   39 *1880S–8S* nestle;   46 *Hood* Tread in my lady's . . . . foot-fall *1845,1849* Treasure my lady's . . . . foot-fall *1863,1865* {as *1888* except 'footfall'}   47 *Hood,1845* faces!   48 *Hood* Roses, are you so fair after all? *1845* {as *1888* except 'all.'}

  33 *look that you grow not*: EBB quotes without 'that', as in *Hood's*, and suggests that it should be inserted.

  35 *blow*: bloom and become overblown.

  36 *Mind*: EBB quotes the line with 'the pink shut', as in *Hood's*, and the comment: 'A clogged line—is it not? Difficult to read.'

  47 *flout*: mock.

  48 *Roses*: EBB quotes (from *Hood's*) as 'Roses, are you so fair after all?', commenting: 'I just ask whether to put it in the affirmative thus "Roses, ye are not so fair after all" does not satisfy the ear & mind better. It is only *asking*, you know.'

II. SIBRANDUS SCHAFNABURGENSIS.

I.

Plague take all your pedants, say I!
   He who wrote what I hold in my hand,
Centuries back was so good as to die,
   Leaving this rubbish to cumber the land;
This, that was a book in its time,   5
   Printed on paper and bound in leather,
Last month in the white of a matin-prime
   Just when the birds sang all together.

II.

Into the garden I brought it to read,
   And under the arbute and laurustine   10
Read it, so help me grace in my need,
   From title-page to closing line.
Chapter on chapter did I count,
   As a curious traveller counts Stonehenge;
Added up the mortal amount;   15
   And then proceeded to my revenge.

Note: the stanzas were not numbered in *Hood's Magazine*   1 *Hood,1845* all pedants, 4 *Hood,1845* to bother the   9 *Hood,1845* read;   10 *Hood* And under these arbutes and   15 *1880S–8S* amount,

    Title: as Griffin and Minchin point out (p. 23), *Schafnaburgensis* means 'a native of Aschaffenburg'. They state that Browning found the word in Nathaniel Wanley's *Wonders of the Little World*, but give no reference. DeVane goes further, claiming that Sibrandus of Aschaffenburg is mentioned in Wanley, but similarly without a reference. 'Lamberto Schafnaburgense' occurs in Giambatista Verci's *Storia degli Ecelini* (3 vols., Bassano, 1779), at i. 141. As we mention in Vol. II, p. 175, this was an important source for *Sordello*. The pedant is imaginary, but Browning is careful to make him come from a renowned centre of learning.

    7 *in the white*: probably referring to the pure white light of early morning. Cf. Italian *alba*, 'dawn'.

    10 *the arbute and laurustine*: EBB quotes as 'these arbutus and laurustine', asking: 'Are these pluralities quite correct? You know best .. & I doubt, at worst. If you wrote "And under the arbuti and laurustines" it w^d seem to me a more *consistent* course .. but I do not attempt even to decide'. OED describes 'arbute' as archaic or poetical for 'arbutus': 'laurustine' for 'laurustinus', 'An evergreen winter-flowering shrub', occurs in OED.

    15 *mortal*: great, deadly (slang).

III.

Yonder's a plum-tree with a crevice
   An owl would build in, were he but sage;
For a lap of moss, like a fine pont-levis
   In a castle of the Middle Age,   20
Joins to a lip of gum, pure amber;
   When he'd be private, there might he spend
Hours alone in his lady's chamber:
   Into this crevice I dropped our friend.

IV.

Splash, went he, as under he ducked,   25
   —At the bottom, I knew, rain-drippings stagnate:
Next, a handful of blossoms I plucked
   To bury him with, my bookshelf's magnate;
Then I went in-doors, brought out a loaf,
   Half a cheese, and a bottle of Chablis;   30
Lay on the grass and forgot the oaf
   Over a jolly chapter of Rabelais.

V.

Now, this morning, betwixt the moss
   And gum that locked our friend in limbo,
A spider had spun his web across,   35
   And sat in the midst with arms akimbo:

---

17 *Hood–1849* plum-tree,   *19 {reading of *Hood–1888S, DC, 1889*} *1888* pont levis
20 *Hood–1888S* middle age,   26 *Hood* —I knew at the bottom rain-drippings
stagnate: *1845–65* {as *Hood* except 'stagnate;'} *1868* —I knew, at the bottom, rain-drippings
stagnate; *1870–88S* {as *1888* except 'stagnate;'}   27 *Hood–1870* Next a
28 *Hood* book-shelf's magnate: 36 *Hood–1849* sate . . . . a-kimbo:

   19 *lap*: a fold or projecting piece.
      pont-levis: drawbridge. OED's only other example is from Caxton. Browning's father
was interested in historical and military matters.
   30 *Chablis*: a French white wine. In 'A Likeness', 21–4, the region is given as 'Chablais',
and rhymed with Rabelais as here.
   32 *Rabelais*: Browning owned the three-volume edition of his *Œuvres* published in Paris
in 1820: Kelley and Coley, A 1919. His friend Joseph Arnould wrote on Rabelais in the *New
Quarterly* for January 1845.

So, I took pity, for learning's sake,
　　And, *de profundis, accentibus lætis*,
Cantate! quoth I, as I got a rake;
　　And up I fished his delectable treatise.   40

VI.

Here you have it, dry in the sun,
　　With all the binding all of a blister,
And great blue spots where the ink has run,
　　And reddish streaks that wink and glister
O'er the page so beautifully yellow: 45
　　Oh, well have the droppings played their tricks!
Did he guess how toadstools grow, this fellow?
　　Here's one stuck in his chapter six!

VII.

How did he like it when the live creatures
　　Tickled and toused and browsed him all over,   50
And worm, slug, eft, with serious features,
　　Came in, each one, for his right of trover?
—When the water-beetle with great blind deaf face
　　Made of her eggs the stately deposit,
And the newt borrowed just so much of the preface   55
　　As tiled in the top of his black wife's closet?

---

37 *Hood,1845* So I   39 *Hood,1845 Cantate*, ... rake, *1849–65 Cantate!* .... rake,
45 *Hood–1849* yellow—   46 *Hood* Oh, the droppings have played
52–3 *Hood–1849* trover; | When   55 *Hood,1845* borrowed so much
56 *Hood–1849* closet.

　　38 *de profundis*: 'From the depths, sing in glad accents!': the speaker offers a light-hearted variant on the Vulgate version of Ps. 130:1: 'De profundis clamavi ad te Domine' (Ps. 129 in Vulgate).
　　46 *Oh, well have the droppings*: Browning must have deleted 'well have' in the MS. EBB quotes the shorter version, and then the text as printed, as what he 'had written—& better written, I think'.
　　50 *toused*: Johnson gives 'To pull; to tear', as meanings of this verb, now archaic: 'tousle' is the iterative form of it.
　　51 *eft*: 'A newt; . . . a small kind of lizard that lives generally in the water': Johnson.
　　52 *trover*: 'The act of finding and assuming possession of any personal property': OED.

VIII.

All that life and fun and romping,
    All that frisking and twisting and coupling,
While slowly our poor friend's leaves were swamping
    And clasps were cracking and covers suppling!   60
As if you had carried sour John Knox
    To the play-house at Paris, Vienna or Munich,
Fastened him into a front-row box,
    And danced off the ballet with trousers and tunic.

IX.

Come, old martyr! What, torment enough is it?   65
    Back to my room shall you take your sweet self.
Good-bye, mother-beetle; husband-eft, *sufficit!*
    See the snug niche I have made on my shelf!
A.'s book shall prop you up, B.'s shall cover you,
    Here's C. to be grave with, or D. to be gay,   70
And with E. on each side, and F. right over you,
    Dry-rot at ease till the Judgment-day!

57–9 *Hood–1849* life, and fun, ... frisking, and twisting, ... swamping,   60 *Hood* Clasps cracking, *1845,1849* And clasps were cracking,   62 *Hood* To the play at Paris, Vienna, *1845,1849* To the play-house at Paris, Vienna,   64 *Hood* Ballet in trowsers and tunic. *1845* Ballet with trousers and tunic. *1849* {as *1845* except 'tunic'} 66 *Hood–1865* self!   68 *Hood,1863,1865* shelf. *1845,1849* shelf: 72 *Hood* judgment-day!

   59 *swamping*: intransitive.

   60 *And clasps*: EBB quotes 59–60 from *Hood's* and comments: 'Or query . . "While clasps were . . ."—A good deal is to be said for the abrupt expression of the "text" . . but the other is safer . . & less trusting the reader. You will judge.' She continues: 'Do you know that this poem is a great favorite with me—it is so new, & full of a creeping crawling grotesque life. Ah but . . do you know besides, it is almost reproachable in you to hold up John Knox to derision in this way!'

   61 *John Knox*: Knox (1505–72) was a leader of the Reformation in Scotland, a stern man opposed to many forms of entertainment. Browning's mother had been baptized into the Church of Scotland.

   64 *danced off the ballet*: the verb is no doubt causative: 'set the ballet-dancers going'.

   67 *sufficit*: it is enough (L.).

THE LABORATORY

'The Laboratory' and 'Claret and Tokay' were the first poems which Browning contributed to *Hood's Magazine*, appearing in the number for June 1844 (see above, p. 1). In *Dramatic Romances and Lyrics* 'The Laboratory' became the first of two poems with the preliminary joint-title, 'France and Spain'; the second was 'The Confessional', then first published. The joint-title was dropped from *1849* onwards.

No doubt the poem was written after the publication of *Dramatic Lyrics* in November 1842, in pursuance of Browning's plan to 'have more ready ere long'.[1] In the first edition of his *Handbook* (1935) DeVane stated that 'No source has been found . . . and I should not expect to find one.' Long before, however, Arthur Symons had described the speaker as 'a Brinvilliers',[2] and in his second edition (1955) DeVane acknowledges that Browning 'may have had in mind such a person of the court of Louis XIV as [this] notorious poisoner'. It is a distinct possibility. He would only have to turn to his favourite volumes, those of the *Biographie universelle*, to find seven columns on a woman who would certainly have appealed to his marked taste for 'morbid cases of the soul'.[3] She was mentioned by Voltaire and Mme de Sévigné, and had been sketched by Lebrun on her way to execution. In 1845 *Bentley's Miscellany* published a romance on the story by Albert Smith. Elizabeth Barrett referred to the water-torture to which the woman was subjected in a letter in 1846,[4] and in *Aurora Leigh* (i. 465–70).

Marie-Marguerite de Brinvilliers was a petite woman (cf. l. 29) whose lover had for some time been imprisoned in the same room in the Bastille as the notorious Exili,[5] who made a trade of the manufacture of poisons. Mme de Brinvilliers learned the art of poisoning from her lover, and her 'cupidity and desire for vengeance disposed her only too readily to profit from it': between 1666 and 1670 she poisoned her father, two brothers,

---

[1] *Correspondence*, vi. 221.

[2] *An Introduction to the Study of Browning* (1886), p. 75.

[3] *Robert Browning and Julia Wedgwood*, ed. Richard Curle (1937), p. 158. In the motive-lessness of some of her crimes the *Biographie universelle* notes 'une singularité qui tient à l'histoire du cœur humaine': p. 610a.

[4] Kintner, i. 513.   [5] *Biographie universelle*, v. 610a.

and her sister. It is said that her lover died 'while he was composing a violent poison', when the glass mask which he was wearing to protect himself from the deadly fumes fell off. After his death a veritable 'trésor de crimes' was discovered, a casket containing packets of poisons of all kinds.[1]

We have already quoted Elizabeth's acknowledgement that while she understood that the 'hideous' quality of the poem was what Browning desired, she yet found in it too much 'uncertainty of rhythm', the opening lines being particularly 'difficult for the reader to read'.[2] Two of her initial comments relate to rhythm. She also jotted down the first line and the phrase '—call you a gum?' (13) from the proof of the pamphlet, which must have followed the *Hood's* readings, as well as 'yonder soft phial' (15) and 'she would fall' (35), in each of which Browning had apparently already improved on the *Hood's* text. Our notes reveal the numerous revisions in *1845* and *1849*.

1849 Dramatic Romances and Lyrics; 1863 Lyrics; 1868– Dramatic Lyrics.

THE LABORATORY.

ANCIEN RÉGIME.

I.

Now that I, tying thy glass mask tightly,
May gaze thro' these faint smokes curling whitely,
As thou pliest thy trade in this devil's-smithy—
Which is the poison to poison her, prithee?

II.

He is with her, and they know that I know   5
Where they are, what they do: they believe my tears flow

title (see Introduction, above. The sub-title was in parentheses in *1844* and *1845*, in square brackets from *1849* to *1868*. In *1844* ('*Hood*' in the textual notes) the stanzas were not numbered.)   1 *Hood* Now I have tied thy glass mask on tightly,   3 *Hood* devil's-smithy,   5 *Hood–1865* with her;   6 *Hood* they are—

ANCIEN RÉGIME: i.e. before the French Revolution.

[1] *Biographie universelle*, v. 610b.   [2] Kintner, i. 131. Cf. p. 5 above.

While they laugh, laugh at me, at me fled to the drear
Empty church, to pray God in, for them!—I am here.

III.

Grind away, moisten and mash up thy paste,
Pound at thy powder,—I am not in haste!   10
Better sit thus, and observe thy strange things,
Than go where men wait me and dance at the King's.

IV.

That in the mortar—you call it a gum?
Ah, the brave tree whence such gold oozings come!
And yonder soft phial, the exquisite blue,   15
Sure to taste sweetly,—is that poison too?

V.

Had I but all of them, thee and thy treasures,
What a wild crowd of invisible pleasures!
To carry pure death in an earring, a casket,
A signet, a fan-mount, a filigree basket!   20

VI.

Soon, at the King's, a mere lozenge to give,
And Pauline should have just thirty minutes to live!

---

7 *Hood* laugh—laugh at me—   8 *Hood,1845* church to pray God in   10 *Hood* powder—am I in haste? *1845* powder,—am I in haste?   11 *1872S–88S* thus and 12 *Hood* me, and . . . . king's. *1872S–88S* me, and . . . . King's.   13 *Hood* mortar—call you a gum?   *14 {reading of all editions except *1888*; exclamation mark inked in in DC} *1888* come   15 *Hood* And yon soft   16 *Hood* sweetly—17,18 *Hood* treasures—|. . . . pleasures—   19 *Hood* a earring,   20 *Hood* filagree-basket! *1845,1849* fillagree-basket! *1863–8* filigree-basket!   21 *Hood* king's, but a lozenge to give, *1845* King's, but a lozenge to give *1849–75*, *1872S* King's, a mere lozenge to give

14 *brave*: one of several Gallicisms in the poem.
20 *signet*: a small seal, often a signet-ring.
22 *Pauline*: stressed on the second syllable, as in French.

But to light a pastile, and Elise, with her head
And her breast and her arms and her hands, should drop dead!

VII.

Quick—is it finished? The colour's too grim!   25
Why not soft like the phial's, enticing and dim?
Let it brighten her drink, let her turn it and stir,
And try it and taste, ere she fix and prefer!

VIII.

What a drop! She's not little, no minion like me!
That's why she ensnared him: this never will free   30
The soul from those masculine eyes,—say, "no!"
To that pulse's magnificent come-and-go.

IX.

For only last night, as they whispered, I brought
My own eyes to bear on her so, that I thought
Could I keep them one half minute fixed, she would fall   35
Shrivelled; she fell not; yet this does it all!

---

23 *Hood,1845* To light a pastille, and Elise, with her head, *1849* But to light a pastille, and
Elise, with her head, *1863,1865* {as *1888* except 'pastille,'} *1872S–88S* {as *1888* except 'Elise'}
24 *Hood–1849* breast, and her arms,   25 *Hood* grim;   26 *Hood,1845* Why
not like the   29 *Hood* little— .... like me; *1845–65* little, ... like me—
31 *Hood* those strong, great eyes: say, "No!" *1845* {as *1888*} *1849* those strong, great eyes,—
say, "no!" *1872S–88S* {as *1888* except '"No!"'}   34 *Hood* thought,   35 *Hood*
she'd fall *1845–65* she would fall,   36 *Hood* Shrivelled:

    23 *pastile*: 'A small roll of aromatic paste prepared to be burnt as a perfume': OED.
    29 *minion*: little thing (Fr. *mignonne*), here used in ironical self-depreciation.
    31 *masculine eyes*: EBB quotes with 'strong great eyes' from the *Hood's* text, and asks:
'Will you read this line with the context, & see if the rhythm is not perplexed in it?' Brown-
ing revised for *1845*, then temporarily restored 'strong great' in *1849*.
    32 *come-and-go*: cf. *A Blot in the 'Scutcheon*, II. 266 (cited in OED², with an attributive use
from 1793).
    35 *she would fall*: 'Why not "she would fall"—' EBB asked. Cf. the *Hood's* text.

X.

Not that I bid you spare her the pain;
Let death be felt and the proof remain:
Brand, burn up, bite into its grace—
He is sure to remember her dying face!   40

XI.

Is it done? Take my mask off! Nay, be not morose;
It kills her, and this prevents seeing it close:
The delicate droplet, my whole fortune's fee!
If it hurts her, beside, can it ever hurt me?

XII.

Now, take all my jewels, gorge gold to your fill,   45
You may kiss me, old man, on my mouth if you will!
But brush this dust off me, lest horror it brings
Ere I know it—next moment I dance at the King's!

---

37 *Hood* spare her pain! *1845–65* spare her the pain!   38 *Hood–1865* remain;
41 *Hood* off! Be not morose! *1845,1849* off! Nay, be not morose, *1863,1865* off! Nay, be
not morose   42 *Hood,1845* close—   43 *Hood–1865* fee—   46 *Hood*
mouth, if   47 *Hood* horror there springs   48 *Hood* king's. *1845* King's.

  37 *spare her the pain*: EBB quotes the line as in *Hood's*, and asks: 'And the rhythm here? Is
it well done that it should change?' Browning revised.
  42 *prevents*: prevents me.
  43 *fee*: reward.
  47 *But brush*: EBB quotes the line as 'But brush the dust off me, lest *horror then springs*', a
slight revision of the *Hood's* text, and comments: 'The last words are clogged, I think . . &
the expression seems forced.'

THE CONFESSIONAL

SINCE this poem was not published in *Hood's Magazine*, we conclude that it was written during or (more probably) after Browning's second journey to Italy, as a companion-piece for 'The Laboratory'. In *1845* they have the joint title 'France and Spain', being numbered 'I' and 'II'. It is conceivable that Browning set the second poem in Spain because he had published two poems as 'Italy and France' in the *Dramatic Lyrics* of 1842. Domett ironically described 'The Confessional' as 'a sugar plum for the Puseyites' (Maynard, p. 105). Unlike 'The Laboratory' the poem has no indication of period, which led DeVane to regard it as 'a contemporary utterance'. There is no known source, but the story is of a type common in the periodicals of the early nineteenth century.

1849 Dramatic Romances and Lyrics; 1863 Lyrics; 1868– Dramatic Lyrics.

THE CONFESSIONAL.

[SPAIN.]

I.

IT is a lie—their Priests, their Pope,
Their Saints, their . . . all they fear or hope
Are lies, and lies—there! through my door
And ceiling, there! and walls and floor,
There, lies, they lie—shall still be hurled   5
Till spite of them I reach the world!

title *1845* II.—SPAIN—THE CONFESSIONAL.   3 *1845,1849* thro'   5 *1845,*
1849 lie, shall still be hurled,

II.

You think Priests just and holy men!
Before they put me in this den
I was a human creature too,
With flesh and blood like one of you,   10
A girl that laughed in beauty's pride
Like lilies in your world outside.

III.

I had a lover—shame avaunt!
This poor wrenched body, grim and gaunt,
Was kissed all over till it burned,   15
By lips the truest, love e'er turned
His heart's own tint: one night they kissed
My soul out in a burning mist.

IV.

So, next day when the accustomed train
Of things grew round my sense again,   20
"That is a sin," I said: and slow
With downcast eyes to church I go,
And pass to the confession-chair,
And tell the old mild father there.

V.

But when I falter Beltran's name,   25
"Ha?" quoth the father; "much I blame
"The sin; yet wherefore idly grieve?
"Despair not—strenuously retrieve!
"Nay, I will turn this love of thine
"To lawful love, almost divine;   30

16 *1845* truest love   19 *1845* So next   21 *1845,1849* said—   26 *1845*
Ha? quoth the father; much   30 *1845–65* divine. *1868–75* divine,

11 *in beauty's pride*: cf. Thais, in Dryden's 'Alexander's Feast', 11: 'In Flow'r of Youth and
Beauty's Pride'.
13 *avaunt!*: begone!
19 *train*: sequence, course.
28 *retrieve*: atone: unusual as an intransitive verb.

VI.

"For he is young, and led astray,
"This Beltran, and he schemes, men say,
"To change the laws of church and state;
"So, thine shall be an angel's fate,
"Who, ere the thunder breaks, should roll   35
"Its cloud away and save his soul.

VII.

"For, when he lies upon thy breast,
"Thou mayst demand and be possessed
"Of all his plans, and next day steal
"To me, and all those plans reveal,   40
"That I and every priest, to purge
"His soul, may fast and use the scourge."

VIII.

That father's beard was long and white,
With love and truth his brow seemed bright;
I went back, all on fire with joy,   45
And, that same evening, bade the boy
Tell me, as lovers should, heart-free,
Something to prove his love of me.

IX.

He told me what he would not tell
For hope of heaven or fear of hell;
And I lay listening in such pride!   50
And, soon as he had left my side,
Tripped to the church by morning-light
To save his soul in his despite.

34 *1845* So thine   37 *1845* For when .... breast   40 *1845* To me
42 *1845* scourge.   46 *1845–75* boy,   50 *1845–65* Heaven .... Hell;
51 *1845,1849* pride,   54 *1849* despite

32 *Beltran*: Beltran is a common Spanish name.

44 *seemed bright*: EBB quotes with 'was bright', and the comment: '*looked* bright.. *seemed*
so .. should it not be, for the meaning?'

X.

I told the father all his schemes,   55
Who were his comrades, what their dreams;
"And now make haste," I said, "to pray
"The one spot from his soul away;
"To-night he comes, but not the same
"Will look!" At night he never came.   60

XI.

Nor next night: on the after-morn,
I went forth with a strength new-born.
The church was empty; something drew
My steps into the street; I knew
It led me to the market-place: 65
Where, lo, on high, the father's face!

XII.

That horrible black scaffold dressed,
That stapled block ... God sink the rest!
That head strapped back, that blinding vest,
Those knotted hands and naked breast,   70
Till near one busy hangman pressed,
And, on the neck these arms caressed ...

---

62 *1845,1849* new-born: 63 *1845* empty: 64 *1845* street: 65 *1845,*
1849 market-place—   66 *1845* And, lo,—on high— *1849* Where, lo,—on high—
67 *1845,1849* drest— *1863,1865* drest,   68 *1845,1849* The stapled block . . *1863–75*
That stapled block . .   70 *1845,1849* breast—   71 *1845,1849* pressed—
72 *1845,1849* And—on

57–8 *to pray / The one spot*: cf. OED, 'Pray', *vb.*, 7.

66 *Where, lo*: EBB quotes as 'And lo!—there, smiled the father's face', and comments:
'You know the best of course—but to me, it seems strange that she sh^d have seen "the
father's face" at all in the shadow of that scaffold!'

67 *dressed*: set up, prepared.

68 *sink*: an imprecation.

69 *That head strapped back*: Pettigrew suggests garrotting as the mode of execution, in
accordance with Spanish custom. The block would be 'stapled' with the iron collar of the
garrotte. The word 'hangman' can refer to any kind of executioner.

XIII.

No part in aught they hope or fear!
No heaven with them, no hell!—and here,
No earth, not so much space as pens   75
My body in their worst of dens
But shall bear God and man my cry,
Lies—lies, again—and still, they lie!

74 *1845* No Heaven .... Hell,—and here *1849* No Heaven ...: Hell,—and here,
1863,1865 No Heaven .... Hell!—and here,   75 *1845,1849* Earth,
77 *1845,1849* Man my cry— *1863,1865* Man my cry,

73 *No part*: referring to the stanza as a whole, EBB comments: 'You think at first that she
means to abjure having any part with them: but afterwards the construction seems to swing
round to another side—Does not this stanza require clearing by a moment's attention? It is
a striking, thrilling poem too, to make it quite worth while.' Browning must have revised to
clarify the meaning.

THE FLIGHT OF THE DUCHESS

THE first 215 lines were published in *Hood's Magazine* for April 1845, the verse-paragraphs being unnumbered. Elizabeth Barrett read this unfinished piece, which was headed 'Part the First', and understandably wished to know more. On 3 May Browning told her that what had been published was 'only the beginning of a story written some time ago, and given to poor Hood in his emergency at a day's notice', adding: 'the true stuff and story is all to come, the "*Flight*" and what you allude to is the mere introduction—but the Magazine has passed into other hands and I must put the rest in some "Bell" or other—it is one of my Dramatic Romances'. The apparent meaning is that much more of the story had already been written, and such was Elizabeth's understanding: she asked whether 'The Flight of the Duchess' was in the portfolio in which he kept his poems, adding: 'That poem has a strong heart in it, to begin so strongly.' After two further enquiries on her part he told her, on 22 June, that he would 'finish & transcribe' it.[1]

She was immediately worried that he might put himself under undue strain to please her, and suggested that he should either lay it aside for a while or show her 'just that one sheet—if one sh^d be written—which is finished'. A week later, however, he told her that he would bring her 'the rest of the "Duchess"—four or five hundred lines', asking if she remembered 'the main of the *first* part', and immediately adding that properly '*parts* there are none except in the necessary process of chopping up to suit the limits of a magazine' and stating that he had given *Hood's* as much as he 'could transcribe at a sudden warning': confirmation, surely that there was more which he did not transcribe. By 11 July she had the greater part of the poem: 'be sure she will be the world's Duchess', she wrote, '& received as one of your most striking poems. Full of various power the poem is .. I cannot say how deeply it has impressed me—but though I want the conclusion, I don't *wish* for it; and in this, am reasonable for once!! You will not write & make yourself ill—will you?' Excited by her praise, he told her that he would bring 'the rest of the poem' on 16 July. On the 24th she gave him numerous detailed comments on it; but she wrote the next day to express the wish that he should not be unduly influenced by her 'querulous queries', 'passing thoughts ... some right, it may

[1] Kintner, i. 55, 60, 100.

be .. some wrong, it must be . . . just impressions, & by no means pretend-
ing to be judgments'. She told him that the poem had given her 'the very
greatest pleasure', astonishing her by 'the versification, mechanically
considered,—& by the successful evolution of pure beauty from all that
roughness & rudeness of the son of the boar-pinner .. successfully
evolved, without softening one hoarse accent of his voice'.[1]

He was delighted, feared that she had overestimated his work, and
assured her that 'all the suggestions are to be adopted, the improvements
accepted'. He would leave the piece until just before printing, 'and then go
over it, alter at the places [on which she had made suggestions], and do
something for the places where I (really) wrote anyhow, almost, to get
done'. He continued:

It is an odd fact, yet characteristic of my accomplishings one and all in this kind,
that of *the poem*, the real conception of an evening (two years ago; fully)—of *that*,
not a line is written,—tho' perhaps after all, what I am going to call the acces-
sories in the story are real though indirect reflexes of the original idea, and so
supersede properly enough the necessity of its personal appearance,—so to speak;
but, as I conceived the poem, it consisted entirely of the gipsy's description of the
life the Lady was to lead with her future gipsy lover—a *real* life, not an unreal
one like that with the Duke—and as I meant to write it, all their wild adventures
would have come out and the insignificance of the former vegetation would
have been deducible only—as the main subject has become now—of course it
comes to the same thing, for one would never show half by half like a cut orange.

'Your account of the production of the poem interests me very much', she
replied, '—& proves just what I wanted to make out from your statements
the other day . . . that you are more faithful to your first *Idea* than to your
first *plan*.' On 25 July 1845, therefore, Browning dates the 'conception' of
the poem to 'an evening (two years ago; fully)', which would point to early
1843.[2]

But we also have to consider a letter which Browning wrote to Furni-
vall in 1883:

There was an odd circumstance that either mended or marred the poem in the
writing—I fancied the latter at the time. As I finished the line—which ends what
was printed in Hood's Magazine as the First Part . . . I saw from the window
where I sat a friend opening the gate to our house.

He was unable to continue work that day, and the next day 'other inter-
ruptions occurred', with the result that he 'lost altogether the thing as it
was in [his] head at the beginning, and, subsequently, gave it to Hood as a

[1] Kintner, i. 102, 109–10, 120, 123, 132–3.   [2] Kintner, i. 135, 137.

fragment'. This would seem to mean that, as late as April 1845, he had written no more than the 'fragment' printed in *Hood's* that month as 'Part the First'. Such an interpretation cannot be reconciled with the evidence already cited, however, and is also incompatible with the next part of the letter to Furnivall: 'some time afterwards [i.e. after he had finished the first 215 lines] I was staying at Bettisfield Park in Wales, and a guest, speaking of early winter, said "the deer had already to break the ice in the pond"—and a fancy struck me, which, on returning home, I worked up into what concludes the story'.[1]

We know that Browning spent the greater part of a week at the home of Sir John Hanmer in September 1842: an agreeable visit which he mentioned in a letter to Domett[2] and recalled when he was asked if he could solicit a contribution to *Hood's* from Kinglake, whom he met at Bettisfield. We know of no subsequent visit, and Griffin and Minchin are probably right in assuming that this was the occasion on which a fellow-guest (whom they identify as Kinglake) made the chance remark. According to their account of the matter, Browning resumed work on the poem when he returned home, beginning where Part I had left off. This would indicate an earlier point in 1842 for the original conception of the poem and the writing of the first 215 lines. It seems that when Browning wrote 'two years ago; fully' in 1845, he should have written 'three years ago; fully'.

It is less surprising that Browning should have confused the chronology when he wrote to Furnivall in his old age. Our tentative conclusion is that a good deal more than 215 lines were written in 1842, and that the printing of 'Part the First' three years later, and the keen interest which Elizabeth took in the poem, led him to take it up again that year and conclude it. We do not know how much revision took place before he showed it to her; but it is clear that he adopted most of her suggestions on points of detail before he published 'The Flight of the Duchess' in *Dramatic Romances and Lyrics* on 5 November 1845.

It has sometimes been asserted, notably in the second edition of DeVane's *Handbook*, that 'In depicting the imprisonment of the modern

---

[1] *Trumpeter*, pp. 70–1.

[2] *Correspondence*, vi. 88; *Checklist*, 45:32; Griffin and Minchin, p. 129. A probable reference to this visit occurs in a letter from EBB to Browning written on 2 March 1846. Kenyon had called on her and told her that 'Somebody . . . (who had spent several days with you in a house with a large library)' had come away '"quite astounded by the versatility of your learning"—& that, to complete the circle, you discoursed as scientifically on the training of greyhounds & breeding of ducks as if you had never done anything else all your life'; Kintner, i. 508.

duchess in a medieval situation and in showing her flight, Browning, forbidden at this time to speak of his love to Miss Barrett, had in mind [her] plight in Wimpole Street, and was urging her by means of the poem to flight to Italy.'[1] This seems to us to be interpreting the piece in too personal a way. The poem would surely be a tactless essay in wooing, since the Duke could only be identified with Mr Barrett. 'My Last Duchess' had already demonstrated Browning's interest in the theme of the tyrannical male more than two years before he first wrote to Elizabeth. We prefer the temperate statement in DeVane's first edition, in 1935: 'The situation and the character of the duchess as we have her finally in 1845 ... may owe something to the situation and character of Elizabeth Barrett herself.' Nothing forbids one speculating, as Pettigrew does in his note on ll. 608–41, 'Robert Browning to Elizabeth Barrett?'[2] The fact that she makes no reference to any personal application, in her voluminous comments, proves nothing: she would not have wished to do so, and her observations on this and the other poems confine themselves almost exclusively to technicalities.

Her keen interest in the poem is further shown by numerous comments in her letters. She told Browning that his 'perfect rhymes, perfectly new, & all clashing together as by natural attraction', made her feel 'shame & admiration'.[3] She considered the piece 'a new-minted golden coin—the rhythm of it answering to your own description, "Speech half asleep, or song half awake?".' She added: 'You have right of trove to these novel effects of rhythm.'

There is a minor mystery about the source of the story. In the letter from which we have already quoted Browning told Furnivall that the poem 'originally all grew out of this one intelligible line of a song that I heard a woman singing at a bonfire on Guy Faux night when I was a boy—"Following the Queen of the Gypsies, O!"'[4] He added a comment applicable to other of his poems, too: 'From so slender a twig of fact can these little singing birds start themselves for a flight to more or less distances.' Furnivall, who was an expert on ballads, must have suggested some form of the ballad of 'Johnnie Faer' as Browning's source; but he replied that the suggestion had already been made to him by Fanny Haworth, yet in fact

---

[1] DeVane had been influenced by an article by Edward Snyder and Frederic Palmer, Jr.: 'New Light on the Brownings': *Quarterly Review*, July 1937, pp. 48–63, and by two articles by Fred Manning Smith which he cites at p. 175 n. 42.

[2] Cf. Daniel Karlin in *Courtship*, p. 91.

[3] Kintner, i. 235, 244. (The line quoted is l. 22 of 'The Flower's Name').

[4] *Trumpeter*, p. 71.

he had been 'in total ignorance' of it when he wrote the poem.[1] None of the versions of the ballad in Child's great collection[2] (in which it appears as No. 200, 'The Gypsy Laddie') includes the line which Browning remembered, yet the plot—how a high-born lady runs away to the gypsies—is so close to that of his poem that we must conclude that the line he had heard came from some version of the ballad. We note that on 6 February 1846 he sent Elizabeth an 'old ballad' he had mentioned to her, 'for the strange coincidence'.[3] 'Certainly there is a likeness to your Duchess', she replied, '—it is a curious crossing.' DeVane quotes a version from *One Hundred English Folk-songs*, ed. Cecil J. Sharp (Boston ed., 1916). The line 'To follow along with my gypsies O!', which is as close to what Browning remembered as anything so far found, occurs in *The Everlasting Circle*, ed. James Reeves (1960), in his 61A, 'The Gypsy Countess', the source being a transcription made by Sabine Baring-Gould from the singing of an illiterate countryman in the late 1880s.[4]

Although the poem is set in Moldavia, there is little or no attempt at consistency. The young Duke, 'our middle-age-manners-adapter', with his foolish passion for 'all usages thoroughly worn-out', constitutes a satirical comment on the medieval enthusiasm which gave rise to the Eglinton Tournament in 1839 and led to the formation of the group of young men who gathered round Disraeli and were known as 'Young England'.[5] It is of interest that Elizabeth mentions that Browning was reading *Sybil* in July 1845, in one of the letters in which she praises this poem.[6]

'The rhythm ... of that "Duchess" does more & more strike me as a new thing',[7] Elizabeth wrote in one of her letters; 'something like (if like anything) what the Greeks called *pedestrian-metre*, .. between metre & prose .. the difficult rhymes combining too quite curiously with the easy

[1] *Trumpeter*, p. 70.

[2] *The English and Scottish Popular Ballads* ed. F. J. Child (8 vols., Boston 1857–8 and 1864, repr. (5 vols. in 3), Folklore Press, NY, [1957]).

[3] Kintner, i. 440, 478.

[4] On Baring-Gould, see Reeves, pp. 1 ff. Under 'raggle-taggle' OED[2] cites a similar ballad from Sharp and Marson, *Folk Songs from Somerset*, 1st ser. (1904), 19: 'What care I for my house and my land, / What care I for my money, O! / What care I for my new wedded lord? / I'm off with the wraggle-taggle gypsies, O!'

[5] On 6 July 1844 a critic commented on the current number of *Hood's Magazine*: 'The only fault of a capital number is, that there is somewhat too much of Young England in it': *The Letters of Thomas Hood*, ed. Peter F. Morgan (Edinburgh ed., 1973), p. 636 n. For this aspect of the background, see e.g. ch. 5 of *A Dream of Order*, by Alice Chandler (Nebraska, 1970; London, 1971).

[6] Kintner, i. 120.   [7] Kintner, i. 267.

looseness of the general measure.' We notice an affinity with 'The Pied Piper', 'Waring', and other of Browning's own poems, and with *The Ingoldsby Legends* and certain pieces by Thomas Hood.[1]

The text. When the promise of completion—'you shall hear'—at the end of the *Hood's* text was fulfilled in *1845*, Browning numbered the sections and added 700 lines, ending with a long unbroken Section XVI from l. 788 to the end. DeVane's comment that the poem 'lost eleven lines during the course of its history' is misleading: the total number of lines remained the same from *1845* onwards, and no line was revised beyond easy recognition. As our notes make clear, EBB's numerous and perceptive comments had exerted a marked influence on *1845*, leading Browning to make improvements which set the pattern for further later refining. In *1849* we find forty changes in substantives, many leading to a smoother, more regular rhythm and to greater precision or clarity, as when 'all the grace' of the Duke became 'the austere grace' (328), and 'Let her superintend' gave way to 'Let her preside at' (267). The enormously long sentences towards the end of Section XV were more distinctly divided, and Section XVI became two Sections.

In *1863* the poem was left substantially intact but for Section XVII, which Browning revised rather more thoroughly. Few changes were made in *1865* and *1868*. We notice that the *1888* text must have been based on that of 1875, or a reprint of *1875*, since in ll. 313, 358, and 446 it incorporates three of the five readings first introduced then. Further, like other long poems, 'The Flight of the Duchess' was given a new typographical layout in *1888*: certain lines were indented, usually as a guide to the irregular pattern of rhymes.

1849 Dramatic Romances and Lyrics; 1863 Romances; 1868– Dramatic Romances.

---

[1] For EBB's reference to *Christabel* see below, 727 n.

THE FLIGHT OF THE DUCHESS

I.

You're my friend:
    I was the man the Duke spoke to;
    I helped the Duchess to cast off his yoke, too;
So here's the tale from beginning to end,
My friend!   5

II.

Ours is a great wild country:
    If you climb to our castle's top,
    I don't see where your eye can stop;
For when you've passed the cornfield country,
Where vineyards leave off, flocks are packed,   10
And sheep-range leads to cattle-tract,
And cattle-tract to open-chase,
And open-chase to the very base
Of the mountain where, at a funeral pace,
Round about, solemn and slow,   15
One by one, row after row,
Up and up the pine-trees go,
So, like black priests up, and so
Down the other side again
    To another greater, wilder country,   20
That's one vast red drear burnt-up plain,
Branched through and through with many a vein
Whence iron's dug, and copper's dealt;
    Look right, look left, look straight before,—

4 *1849–88S* So, here's   11 *1884S–8S* cattle-track,   12 *1872S–88S* And
cattle-track   14 *1872S–88S* O' the mountain   16 *Hood* One after one, row
upon row,   18 *Hood* So like   24 *Hood,1845* before,

   12 *open-chase*: 'chase' here means 'Open ground stored with such beasts as are hunted':
Johnson.
   23 *dealt*: distributed; produced.

Beneath they mine, above they smelt,   25
    Copper-ore and iron-ore,
And forge and furnace mould and melt,
    And so on, more and ever more,
Till at the last, for a bounding belt,
    Comes the salt sand hoar of the great sea-shore,   30
—And the whole is our Duke's country.

III.

I was born the day this present Duke was—
    (And O, says the song, ere I was old!)
In the castle where the other Duke was—
    (When I was happy and young, not old!)   35
I in the kennel, he in the bower:
We are of like age to an hour.
My father was huntsman in that day;
Who has not heard my father say
That, when a boar was brought to bay,   40
Three times, four times out of five,
With his huntspear he'd contrive
To get the killing-place transfixed,
And pin him true, both eyes betwixt?
And that's why the old Duke would rather   45
He lost a salt-pit than my father,

29 *1845–63* Till, at the last,   31*Hood–1863* country!   35 *1849* was hopeful
and   36 *1845–63* Kennel, he .... Bower: 38 *1845–65* Huntsman
40 *Hood* That when   41 *Hood,1845* Three, four times   44 *Hood,1845* true
both   45 *Hood,1845* That's why .... Duke had rather *1849* And that's why ....
Duke had rather   46 *Hood,1845* Lost a salt-pit *1849* Have lost a salt-pit

    30 *the great sea-shore*: that of the Black Sea.
    33 *And O, says the song*: cf. Coleridge, 'Youth and Age', 22, and below, 727 n.
    36 *the kennel*: hovel.
        the bower: the inner apartment of a mansion, used by the lady. The word is common
in ballads. The two words are capitalized in *1845*, for emphasis.
    42 *huntspear*: the only example in OED is from Marlowe and Nashe, *Dido Queen of
Carthage*, III. iii. 33: 'Bearing his huntspeare bravely in his hand' (*Complete Works of Christo-
pher Marlowe*, ed. Fredson Bowers, 2 vols., Cambridge, 1973, vol. ii). Cf. *Paracelsus*, i. 481 n.
    43 *killing-place*: not in OED.

And loved to have him ever in call;
That's why my father stood in the hall
When the old Duke brought his infant out
    To show the people, and while they passed   50
The wondrous bantling round about,
    Was first to start at the outside blast
As the Kaiser's courier blew his horn
Just a month after the babe was born.
"And," quoth the Kaiser's courier, "since   55
"The Duke has got an heir, our Prince
    "Needs the Duke's self at his side:"
The Duke looked down and seemed to wince,
    But he thought of wars o'er the world wide,
Castles a-fire, men on their march,   60
The toppling tower, the crashing arch;
    And up he looked, and awhile he eyed
The row of crests and shields and banners
Of all achievements after all manners,
    And "ay," said the Duke with a surly pride.   65
    The more was his comfort when he died
At next year's end, in a velvet suit,
With a gilt glove on his hand, his foot
In a silken shoe for a leather boot,
Petticoated like a herald,   70
    In a chamber next to an ante-room,
    Where he breathed the breath of page and groom,
    What he called stink, and they, perfume:

47 *Hood* lov'd .... call: 48 *1845* the Hall   54 *Hood* Just one month ....
born: *1845* Just a month .... born: 56 *1845–65* Heir,   63 *Hood* crests, and
shields, and banners, *1845–63* crests and shields and banners,   65 *Hood,1845* pride:
68 *Hood–1875* hand, and his foot   69 *Hood,1845* In a silk shoe   71–3 {in-
dented in *1888–9* only}   *72 {reading of *1845–88S,DC,1889*} *Hood* breath'd ....
groom, *1888* breathed .... groom   73 *Hood* call'd stink, and they *1845* called stink
and they,

51 *bantling*: baby.
64 *achievements*: cf. Johnson's second meaning, 'the escutcheon, or ensigns armorial,
granted to any man for the performance of great actions'.
69 *for*: instead of.
73 *stink . . . perfume*: cf. *Sordello*, vi. 878–9.

—They should have set him on red Berold
Mad with pride, like fire to manage!   75
They should have got his cheek fresh tannage
Such a day as to-day in the merry sunshine!
Had they stuck on his fist a rough-foot merlin!
(Hark, the wind's on the heath at its game!
Oh for a noble falcon-lanner   80
To flap each broad wing like a banner,
And turn in the wind, and dance like flame!)
Had they broached a white-beer cask from Berlin
—Or if you incline to prescribe mere wine
Put to his lips, when they saw him pine,   85
A cup of our own Moldavia fine,
Cotnar for instance, green as May sorrel
And ropy with sweet,—we shall not quarrel.

IV.

So, at home, the sick tall yellow Duchess
Was left with the infant in her clutches,   90
She being the daughter of God knows who:
   And now was the time to revisit her tribe.

---

79 *Hood* —Hark, ... game— *1845,1849* —Hark, ... game!   80 *Hood* Oh!
82 *Hood,1845* flame!   83 *Hood* broach'd a cask of white beer from Berlin *1845* {as
Hood except 'Berlin!'} *1849–88S* broached a cask of white beer from Berlin!   84 *1849*
wine—   85 *Hood–1888S* lips   87 *Hood–1863* Cotnar, for .... sorrel,
89 *Hood,1845* So at home   92 *Hood–1863* tribe,

74 *Berold*: according to the *Biographie universelle*, xl (1825), 523 n., Berold was the name
of the father of the founder of the House of Savoy. Browning probably came on him when
he worked on *King Victor and King Charles*, and gave his name to the Old Duke's horse.

76 *tannage*: probably a nonce-word: no other example in OED.

78 *merlin*: a European species of falcon, small but fierce as a bird of prey: 'rough-foot':
having feathered legs.

79 *the wind's on the heath*: the conditions are good for hawking. George Borrow was twice
to use the phrase in ch. xxv of *Lavengro* (1851).

80 *falcon-lanner*: a falcon, similar to the peregrine, but smaller: *Falco lanarius*.

83 *white-beer*: pale ale.

87 *Cotnar*: a wine from Moldavia, a principality of SE Europe which was to become part
of Romania in 1859.

88 *ropy*: 'Forming or developing viscid, glutinous, or slimy threads; sticky and stringy':
OED.

Abroad and afar they went, the two,
   And let our people rail and gibe
At the empty hall and extinguished fire,   95
   As loud as we liked, but ever in vain,
Till after long years we had our desire,
   And back came the Duke and his mother again.

                              v.

And he came back the pertest little ape
That ever affronted human shape;   100
Full of his travel, struck at himself.
   You'd say, he despised our bluff old ways?
—Not he! For in Paris they told the elf
   Our rough North land was the Land of Lays,
   The one good thing left in evil days;   105
Since the Mid-Age was the Heroic Time,
   And only in wild nooks like ours
Could you taste of it yet as in its prime,
   And see true castles, with proper towers,
Young-hearted women, old-minded men,   110
And manners now as manners were then.
So, all that the old Dukes had been, without knowing it,
This Duke would fain know he was, without being it;
'T was not for the joy's self, but the joy of his showing it,
Nor for the pride's self, but the pride of our seeing it,   115
He revived all usages thoroughly worn-out,
The souls of them fumed-forth, the hearts of them torn-out:

93 *Hood,1845* So abroad and *1849,1863* So, abroad and   94 *Hood,1845* people curse
and   95 *Hood* hall and extinguish'd *1845–63* Hall and extinguished   96 *Hood*
Loud as we lik'd, ... vain; *1845* Loud as we liked, ... vain,   99 *Hood,1845* pertest
ape   101 *Hood–1849* himself—   102 *Hood* despis'd . . . . ways *1845,1849*
despised . . . . ways *1884S,1886S* depised . . . . ways?   104 *Hood–1888S* That our
rough North land   106 *Hood,1845* For the   109 *Hood* True castles, ...
towers, *1845* True Castles, ... Towers,   112 *Hood* all the old dukes *1845* all the old
Dukes   115 *Hood,1845* seeing it.

101 *struck at himself*: taken with himself.

106 *the Mid-Age*: neither OED nor OED² has this form, in the historical sense. OED² has
several examples of 'Middle Age', however.

116 *He revived all usages*: cf. Introduction, p. 98.

117 *fumed-forth*: having dispersed in vapour, passed away.

And chief in the chase his neck he perilled
On a lathy horse, all legs and length,
With blood for bone, all speed, no strength;   120
—They should have set him on red Berold
With the red eye slow consuming in fire,
And the thin stiff ear like an abbey-spire!

VI.

Well, such as he was, he must marry, we heard:
And out of a convent, at the word,   125
Came the lady, in time of spring.
—Oh, old thoughts they cling, they cling!
That day, I know, with a dozen oaths
I clad myself in thick hunting-clothes
Fit for the chase of urochs or buffle   130
In winter-time when you need to muffle.
But the Duke had a mind we should cut a figure,
     And so we saw the lady arrive:
My friend, I have seen a white crane bigger!
     She was the smallest lady alive,   135
Made in a piece of nature's madness,
Too small, almost, for the life and gladness
     That over-filled her, as some hive
Out of the bears' reach on the high trees
Is crowded with its safe merry bees: 140
In truth, she was not hard to please!
Up she looked, down she looked, round at the mead,
Straight at the castle, that's best indeed

---

121 *Hood* They .... Berold *1845–63* —They .... Berold,   130 *Hood–1888S* urox
or   131 *Hood* In winter-time, ... muffle; *1845,1849* In winter-time .... muffle;
136 *Hood* Made, in .... nature's *1845–63* Made, in .... Nature's *1865* Made in ....
Nature's   140 *Hood,1845* bees—   143 *1845* Castle,

119 *lathy*: thin as a lath. Cf. Scott, *The Fair Maid of Perth*, ch. ii: 'his figure was thin and
lathy'.

130 *urochs*: 'urox' (*Hood's* to *1888S*) is the Anglicized form of 'urochs', the Lithuanian
bison.

     buffle: an obsolete form of 'buffalo'.

To look at from outside the walls:
As for us, styled the "serfs and thralls,"   145
She as much thanked me as if she had said it,
    (With her eyes, do you understand?)
Because I patted her horse while I led it;
    And Max, who rode on her other hand,
Said, no bird flew past but she inquired   150
What its true name was, nor ever seemed tired—
    If that was an eagle she saw hover,
And the green and grey bird on the field was the plover.
When suddenly appeared the Duke:
    And as down she sprung, the small foot pointed   155
On to my hand,—as with a rebuke,
    And as if his backbone were not jointed,
The Duke stepped rather aside than forward,
    And welcomed her with his grandest smile;
And, mind you, his mother all the while   160
Chilled in the rear, like a wind to Nor'ward;
    And up, like a weary yawn, with its pullies
Went, in a shriek, the rusty portcullis;
    And, like a glad sky the north-wind sullies,
The lady's face stopped its play,   165
As if her first hair had grown grey;
For such things must begin some one day.

VII.

In a day or two she was well again;
As who should say, "You labour in vain!
"This is all a jest against God, who meant   170
"I should ever be, as I am, content

---

147 *Hood,1845* her eye, do   149 *Hood* who went on   152 *1849* hover,—
153 *Hood,1845* And the green and gray bird .... plover? *1849* If the green and gray bird
.... plover.   154 *Hood* appear'd .... Duke, *1845,1849* appeared .... Duke,
163 *Hood,1845* portcullis,   166 *Hood–1863* grey—   167 *Hood–1863* day!

145 *"serfs and thralls"*: bond-servants, in old legal terminology.
161 *chilled*: intransitive.

"And glad in his sight; therefore, glad I will be."
So, smiling as at first went she.

VIII.

She was active, stirring, all fire—
Could not rest, could not tire—   175
To a stone she might have given life!
   (I myself loved once, in my day)
—For a shepherd's, miner's, huntsman's wife,
   (I had a wife, I know what I say)
Never in all the world such an one!   180
And here was plenty to be done,
And she that could do it, great or small,
She was to do nothing at all.
There was already this man in his post,
   This in his station, and that in his office,   185
And the Duke's plan admitted a wife, at most,
   To meet his eye, with the other trophies,
Now outside the hall, now in it,
   To sit thus, stand thus, see and be seen,
At the proper place in the proper minute,   190
   And die away the life between.
And it was amusing enough, each infraction
   Of rule—(but for after-sadness that came)
To hear the consummate self-satisfaction
   With which the young Duke and the old dame   195
Would let her advise, and criticise,
And, being a fool, instruct the wise,
   And, child-like, parcel out praise or blame:
They bore it all in complacent guise,

---

172 *Hood–1849* his sight; .... be!" *1863* His sight; .... be!" *1865* His sight; .... be.
173 *Hood,1845* So smiling   176 *Hood,1845* she had given   178 *1845–65*
Shepherd's, Miner's, Huntsman's   188 *1845–63* Hall,   191 *Hood,1845*
between: 197 *Hood* wise;   198 *Hood,1884S–8S* blame.

   172 *And glad in his sight*: cf. Ps. 21:6.
   191 *die away*: rare as a transitive verb, but cf. Richardson, *Clarissa* (7 vols., 1748), vii. 179:
'God dies away in us, as I may say, all human satisfactions.'
   197 *a fool, instruct the wise*: cf. the proverbial 'A fool may give a wise man counsel.'

As though an artificer, after contriving   200
A wheel-work image as if it were living,
Should find with delight it could motion to strike him!
So found the Duke, and his mother like him:
The lady hardly got a rebuff—
That had not been contemptuous enough,   205
With his cursed smirk, as he nodded applause,
And kept off the old mother-cat's claws.

IX.

So, the little lady grew silent and thin,
    Paling and ever paling,
As the way is with a hid chagrin;   210
    And the Duke perceived that she was ailing,
And said in his heart, "'Tis done to spite me,
"But I shall find in my power to right me!"
Don't swear, friend! The old one, many a year,
Is in hell, and the Duke's self . . . you shall hear.   215

X.

Well, early in autumn, at first winter-warning,
When the stag had to break with his foot, of a morning,
A drinking-hole out of the fresh tender ice
That covered the pond till the sun, in a trice,
Loosening it, let out a ripple of gold,   220
    And another and another, and faster and faster,
Till, dimpling to blindness, the wide water rolled:
Then it so chanced that the Duke our master

200 *Hood* As tho' an artificer, having contriv'd *1845,1849* {as *1888* except 'tho"}
201 *Hood* as if it liv'd,   202 *1884S–8S* strike him   203 *Hood* like him—
1845,1849 like him,—   208 *Hood* So . . . . lady *1845* So . . . . Lady *1849–65* So, ...
Lady   213 *Hood* right me."   214 *Hood* friend,—the old one, *1845–63*
friend—the Old One, *1865* friend—the old one,   215 *1845–63* Hell, {Line 215 is
the last in the poem as printed in *Hood*; after it is printed, 'END OF PART THE FIRST.'}
222 *1884S–8S* rolled,—

    201 *A wheel-work image*: cf. *Sordello*, v. 447, and 'A Death in the Desert', 448–9.
    205 *had not been*: would not have been.
    217 *When the stag*: 'The stag—& sun melting the water—beautiful description like the
morning itself': EBB. Cf. Introduction, above.
    222 *dimpling to blindness*: until one could not look at it.

Asked himself what were the pleasures in season,
　　And found, since the calendar bade him be hearty,　225
He should do the Middle Age no treason
　　In resolving on a hunting-party.
Always provided, old books showed the way of it!
　　What meant old poets by their strictures?
And when old poets had said their say of it,　230
　　How taught old painters in their pictures?
We must revert to the proper channels,
Workings in tapestry, paintings on panels,
And gather up woodcraft's authentic traditions:
Here was food for our various ambitions,　235
As on each case, exactly stated—
　　To encourage your dog, now, the properest chirrup,
　　Or best prayer to Saint Hubert on mounting your stirrup—
We of the household took thought and debated.
Blessed was he whose back ached with the jerkin　240
His sire was wont to do forest-work in;

233 *1845,1849* pannels,　　234 *1845–63* Woodcraft's .... traditions: *1884S–8S*
woodcraft's .... traditions.　　236 *1845–63* stated,　237 *1845–63* —To
encourage　　238 *1845–75,1872S* St. Hubert

225 *And found*: EBB quotes as 'Finding the calender bade him be hearty, / Did resolve on a hunting party—', and comments: 'Does not that first line seem as if it were meditating a rhyme for the second?—I suppose the meaning is that the time of year reminded him of the need of festivity; but there is something forced in the expression, or appears to *me* to be so. And then the second line . . is it not too short to the ear?'

226 *the Middle Age*: cf. above, 106 n.

228 *Always provided*: EBB quotes as '"Oh, and old books they knew the way of it"—&c—', with the comment: 'All this is quite clear to *me*—& I like the "brightness". Still people are sure to say, from the break in the narrative that it's obscure—& *so* little a change (of a word or two) would allow them to read on without thinking!! You had written "they *taught* the way of it"—which is clearer as far as the word goes,—only "taught", I see, comes afterwards. Would "showed" do? But then the next line "what meant old poets by their strictures?" makes the meaning questionable till the reader can take the context of before & *after* . . which is too long to wait, for readers in general.'

229 *strictures*: comments.

233 *Workings in tapestry*: cf. *Sordello*, ii. 517 ff.

234 *woodcraft's authentic traditions*: with reference to hunting.

238 *Saint Hubert*: Hubert, who died in 727, 'Apostle of the Ardennes', was the patron saint of hunters and trappers in that area. His emblem is a stag.

239 *the household*: in the extended sense, including the retainers and servants.

Blesseder he who nobly sunk "ohs"
And "ahs" while he tugged on his grandsire's trunk-hose;
What signified hats if they had no rims on,
    Each slouching before and behind like the scallop,   245
    And able to serve at sea for a shallop,
Loaded with lacquer and looped with crimson?
So that the deer now, to make a short rhyme on 't,
    What with our Venerers, Prickers and Verderers,
    Might hope for real hunters at length and not murderers,   250
And oh the Duke's tailor, he had a hot time on 't!

XI.

Now you must know that when the first dizziness
    Of flap-hats and buff-coats and jack-boots subsided,
    The Duke put this question, "The Duke's part provided,
"Had not the Duchess some share in the business?"   255

---

249 *1845–63* Prickers,   250 *1845–63* at length,   251 *1845* oh . . . . tailor—
1849,1863 oh, ... tailor—

242 *sunk*: suppressed.

243 *trunk-hose*: 'Large breeches formerly worn': Johnson.

244 *What signified hats*: EBB quotes as 'What meant a hat if it had no rims on', commenting: 'Do you like "*what meant*"? I do not quite—& the connection is broken. And then, "the rims"—a hat has only one rim ever—except for the rhyme of "crimson". So why not write . . 'a hat where never a rim's on". *That* w.ᵈ do—wouldn't it? You are not to think that I have not a proper respect & admiration for all these new live rhymes & that I would not make every sacrifice in reason for them.'

246 *a shallop*: a sloop, a type of sailing boat.

249 *Venerers, Prickers and Verderers*: OED has no earlier example of 'venerer', huntsman. A pricker is 'a mounted attendant at a hunt', a verderer an official of the King's forest with responsibility for the game.

251 *And oh*: EBB quotes as '"And the Duke's tailor to have" &c', with the comment: 'A slip of the pen for "might have" or "should have". Otherwise "the deer" are made to hope this of the tailor. *Quære*, if . . "And *so*, the Duke's tailor might have" &c would not assist the rhythm. I am doubtful though.'

252 *Now you must know*: EBB quotes the line as printed, with 'that' underlined and the query: 'Why erase "that"? Is not the rhythm better with it?'
    dizziness: fancy, folly.

253 *flap-hats*: Browning was to admire the 'great black flap hats' in Brittany in 1866 (*Life*, p. 265). Here he is describing archaic attire. Buff is 'a sort of leather . . . used for waist belts, pouches, and military accoutrements' (Johnson). Cf. Scott, *The Fair Maid of Perth*, ch. ii.

For out of the mouth of two or three witnesses
Did he establish all fit-or-unfitnesses:
And, after much laying of heads together,
Somebody's cap got a notable feather
By the announcement with proper unction   260
That he had discovered the lady's function;
Since ancient authors gave this tenet,
    "When horns wind a mort and the deer is at siege,
"Let the dame of the castle prick forth on her jennet,
    "And, with water to wash the hands of her liege   265
"In a clean ewer with a fair toweling,
"Let her preside at the disemboweling."
Now, my friend, if you had so little religion
    As to catch a hawk, some falcon-lanner,
    And thrust her broad wings like a banner   270
Into a coop for a vulgar pigeon;
And if day by day and week by week
    You cut her claws, and sealed her eyes,
And clipped her wings, and tied her beak,
    Would it cause you any great surprise   275
If, when you decided to give her an airing,
You found she needed a little preparing?

---

262 *1845,1849* authors held this   264 *1845–63* Castle   267 *1845* "Let her
superintend the   276 *1845,1849* If when . . . . airing

    257 *Did he establish*: EBB quotes as 'He established all fit & unfitnesses', commenting
that it 'seems *short* too—& also the next line—And does the lady "pace" forth or "*prick*"
forth on her jinnet? [264]'
    259 *Somebody's cap*: i.e. someone gained credit.
    263 *a mort*: 'the peculiar blast of a bugle-horn, such as her father used to wind on the fall
of the stag, and which huntsmen then called a *mort*': Scott, *Kenilworth*, ch. xxxiii, para. 9. Cf.
The Winter's Tale, I. ii. 118, and 'Chevy Chase', 31.
    264 *prick forth*: ride out on her little Spanish horse. Cf. *The Faerie Queene*, I. i. 1.
    269 *As to catch a hawk*: EBB quotes: 'As catch', asking: 'Is not "to" left out?'
      falcon-lanner: see 80 n.
    272 *And if day by day*: EBB quotes as 'And if day by day, week by week—', asking: 'Should
it not be "*and* week by week"—? Also I do wish those following "*ands*", written by your
hand & erased, in the next lines, both back again. Your ear's first impulse led you to them,
& rightly according to mine.' She concludes: 'This is a beautiful image, the hawk's—& so
new, & so true!'
    273 *sealed*: to seal or seel means 'To close the eyes (of a hawk or other bird) by stitching
up the eyelids with a thread tied behind the head' (OED). It is part of the training.

—I say, should you be such a curmudgeon,
If she clung to the perch, as to take it in dudgeon?
Yet when the Duke to his lady signified,   280
Just a day before, as he judged most dignified,
In what a pleasure she was to participate,—
    And, instead of leaping wide in flashes,
    Her eyes just lifted their long lashes,
As if pressed by fatigue even he could not dissipate,   285
And duly acknowledged the Duke's forethought,
But spoke of her health, if her health were worth aught,
Of the weight by day and the watch by night,
And much wrong now that used to be right,
So, thanking him, declined the hunting,—   290
Was conduct ever more affronting?
With all the ceremony settled—
    With the towel ready, and the sewer
    Polishing up his oldest ewer,
    And the jennet pitched upon, a piebald,   295
    Black-barred, cream-coated and pink eye-balled,—
No wonder if the Duke was nettled!
And when she persisted nevertheless,—
Well, I suppose here's the time to confess
That there ran half round our lady's chamber   300

---

281 *1875* dignified   295 *1872S–88S* a pieballed,

284 *Her eyes*: 'It is beautiful too just afterwards', EBB wrote after her note on 272, 'about the "eyes."'

287 *if her health were worth aught*: EBB quotes as 'if that were worth aught', repeats 'were worth aught', and comments: 'there is something clogged in the sound. And, in the next line, why not read .. for clearness .. "Of the weight by day & the watch by night?" But I go back to observe that you make your Duchess'es [*sic*] eyes acknowledge the Duke's forethought & speak of her health &c—as if such a Duke could be likely to understand that sort of speaking. The personal pronoun has been forgotten somehow—Just see if it has not.'

291 *Was conduct*: EBB quotes as 'Could conduct be more affronting? / All the ceremony settled—', with the comment: 'I like these short lines sometimes .. when anything is to be expressed by abruptness—but not here, I think. Not in the second, at least—.'

293 *sewer*: 'An officer who serves up a feast': Johnson.

296 *eye-balled*: probably a nonce compound. Cf. 'Through the Metidja', 30.

300 *That there ran*: EBB quotes the line as printed, italicizing 'That' and commenting that that was what he had 'written first—& why not? The ear was right at first, I am nearly sure .. I *feel* so, I mean. And again in the next couplet "And that Jacynth the tirewoman

A balcony none of the hardest to clamber;
And that Jacynth the tire-woman, ready in waiting,
Stayed in call outside, what need of relating?
And since Jacynth was like a June rose, why, a fervent
Adorer of Jacynth of course was your servant;   305
And if she had the habit to peep through the casement,
   How could I keep at any vast distance?
  And so, as I say, on the lady's persistence,
The Duke, dumb-stricken with amazement,
Stood for a while in a sultry smother,   310
  And then, with a smile that partook of the awful,
Turned her over to his yellow mother
   To learn what was held decorous and lawful;
And the mother smelt blood with a cat-like instinct,
As her cheek quick whitened thro' all its quince-tinct.   315
Oh, but the lady heard the whole truth at once!
  What meant she?—Who was she?—Her duty and station,
The wisdom of age and the folly of youth, at once,
   Its decent regard and its fitting relation—

---

301 *1845* clamber,   305 *1845–63* Jacynth, of course,   313 *1845–70,1872S–*
88S was decorous   315 *1845,1849* quince-tinct—   317 *1884S–8S* station.

ready in waiting". Why not leave it so? Only I should be inclined to write "But" for "And"—
He "confesses" that the balcony went round the chamber,—the rest . . the listening . . was
all matter of course . . "what need of relating?" And instead of "Would stay in call outside",
might not "Stayed in call outside" do better, & with less clogging?'

  302 *tire-woman*: lady's maid.

  307 *How could I keep*: EBB quotes as 'How could I be &c / So as I say &c', and comments:
'Is there not a sameness in the fall of the accents which you w^d choose to avoid. Suppose it
were written, "*And so*" (in the true idiom of storytellers) in the latter line?'

  309 *dumb-stricken*: antedates the one example in OED.

  310 *smother*: cf. Johnson: 'A state of suppression. Not in use.'

  315 *quince-tinct*: yellowish colour. No other example in OED[2].

  316—17 *Oh, but the lady*: EBB writes: '"Oh but the lady heard the whole truth for
once"–!', and then (without quotation marks) What meant she?' what was she? duty &
station–Quære . . "*her* duty & station".

  318 *at once*: EBB quotes the line with 'for once' and asks: '*Would* the Dowager Duchess
talk of the folly of youth *for once*—& not always? Yet the *rhymes*! Which sh^d not be hurt for
the world!—Then why not save rhyme & reason by writing "at once" in both places?
Would'nt it answer every purpose?'

In brief, my friend, set all the devils in hell free   320
And turn them out to carouse in a belfry
And treat the priests to a fifty-part canon,
And then you may guess how that tongue of hers ran on!
Well, somehow or other it ended at last
And, licking her whiskers, out she passed;   325
And after her,—making (he hoped) a face
    Like Emperor Nero or Sultan Saladin,
Stalked the Duke's self with the austere grace
    Of ancient hero or modern paladin,
From door to staircase—oh such a solemn   330
Unbending of the vertebral column!

XII.

However, at sunrise our company mustered;
    And here was the huntsman bidding unkennel,

320 *1870–88S* my friends,   328 *1845* with all the grace   329 *1845,1849*
paladin,—   330 *1845–63* oh, such   332 *1845,1849* mustered,

320 *my friend*: 'my friends' (*1870*) is no doubt one of the 'nonsensical' readings Browning
complained of in that edition. Cf. textual notes to 408, 567, 655, 729, and 891.

321 *And turn them out*: EBB quotes without 'out', and asks: 'Did you not miss "out" in the
transcribing? "And turn them out" &c.'

322 *canon*: '"A canon", in music, is a piece wherein the subject is repeated—in various
keys—and being strictly obeyed in the repetition, becomes the "Canon"—the imperative
law—in what follows. Fifty of such parts would be indeed a notable peal: to manage three is
enough of an achievement for a good musician': Browning to Hiram Corson, in a letter
dated 28 December 1886, reproduced in facsimile in the latter's *An Introduction to the Study
of Robert Browning's Poetry* (ed. of 1899, Boston).

323 *And then you may guess*: EBB quotes as 'And you may fancy how her tongue ran on',
commenting: 'I do *not* like the rhythm—though harmony is not required—to be sure. You
felt a need, by that erasure. I like the "well" too, which vanishes in a blot, in the next line.'

326 *And after her*: EBB quotes as 'And after her, making a face', and asks: 'Could'nt it be
made a little longer? And I am not sure that I like the fall down the staircase, & what
follows about the towel. Perhaps I do not clearly understand what Jacynth means—I
promised to tell all my impressions.' Browning obviously revised 326–31.

327 *Nero . . . Saladin*: Nero, tyrannical Roman Emperor, AD 54–68. Saladin became
Sultan of Egypt about 1174, and captured Jerusalem. The Crusaders brought him to a truce.
He is prominent in Scott's *The Talisman*, which may slightly have influenced this poem.

329 *paladin*: one of the twelve Peers or famous warriors of Charlemagne's court; hence a
knightly hero.

And there 'neath his bonnet the pricker blustered,
 With feather dank as a bough of wet fennel;   335
For the court-yard walls were filled with fog
You might have cut as an axe chops a log—
Like so much wool for colour and bulkiness;
And out rode the Duke in a perfect sulkiness,
Since, before breakfast, a man feels but queasily,   340
 And a sinking at the lower abdomen
 Begins the day with indifferent omen.
And lo, as he looked around uneasily,
The sun ploughed the fog up and drove it asunder
This way and that from the valley under;   345
 And, looking through the court-yard arch,
Down in the valley, what should meet him
 But a troop of Gipsies on their march?
No doubt with the annual gifts to greet him.

XIII.

Now, in your land, Gipsies reach you, only   350
 After reaching all lands beside;
North they go, South they go, trooping or lonely,
 And still, as they travel far and wide,

---

336 *1845–65* court-yard's four walls 337 *1845* might cut . . . . log, *1849,1863*
might cut . . . . log. *1865–88S* might cut . . . . log— 340 *1845,1849* Since
341 *1845* sinking of the 342 *1845,1849* omen: 343 *1845* around,
344–5 *1872S–88S* asunder, | . . . . and that, 346 *1845,1849* thro' 348 *1845,*
1849 Gipsies . . . . march, *1863,1884S–8S* Gipsies . . . . march, 350 *1845* Now in
this land, Gipsies reach you only *1849* {as *1888* except 'Gypsies'}

---

335 *wet fennel*: 'This "bough of wet fennel" wont turn to hemlock—will it? I like it very
much—see it, through the fog, close to my eyes': EBB. (She refers to Browning's having
mistaken hemlock for fennel when he was in Rome: Kintner, i. 110–11).

350 *in your land*: EBB quotes as 'In *this* land, gypsies reach you only', and comments: 'I
am not sure—but is not a word wanted? such as "can" before reach. Do read the line in con-
nection with the following ones & see. Certainly I miss something in—"Still as they travel
the world wide" perhaps "the world *so* wide". Left out by a slip of the pen?'

Gypsies are prominent in Scott, whose work Browning knew well; while interest in
them had been further stimulated by two books by George Borrow: *The Zincali: or an
Account of the Gypsies of Spain* (1841), and *The Bible in Spain* (1843). Gypsies were very
numerous in Moldavia, and were renowned metal-workers.

Catch they and keep now a trace here, a trace there,
That puts you in mind of a place here, a place there.   355
But with us, I believe they rise out of the ground,
And nowhere else, I take it, are found
With the earth-tint yet so freshly embrowned:
Born, no doubt, like insects which breed on
The very fruit they are meant to feed on.   360
For the earth—not a use to which they don't turn it,
   The ore that grows in the mountain's womb,
   Or the sand in the pits like a honeycomb,
They sift and soften it, bake it and burn it—
Whether they weld you, for instance, a snaffle   365
With side-bars never a brute can baffle;
Or a lock that's a puzzle of wards within wards;
Or, if your colt's fore-foot inclines to curve inwards,
Horseshoes they hammer which turn on a swivel
And won't allow the hoof to shrivel.   370
Then they cast bells like the shell of the winkle
That keep a stout heart in the ram with their tinkle;
But the sand—they pinch and pound it like otters;
Commend me to Gipsy glass-makers and potters!
Glasses they'll blow you, crystal-clear,   375
Where just a faint cloud of rose shall appear,
As if in pure water you dropped and let die
A bruised black-blooded mulberry;
And that other sort, their crowning pride,
With long white threads distinct inside,   380
Like the lake-flower's fibrous roots which dangle
Loose such a length and never tangle,

---

355 *1845,1849* place there: 356 *1845* But with us   358 *1845–72S*
embrowned;   360 *1845,1849* feed on: 362 *1845* mountains'
369 *1845–65* they'll hammer   370 *1845,1849* shrivel;   372 *1845,1849*
tinkle: 377 *1845* in water one dropped   378 *1863* A bruise black-blooded

  365 *snaffle*: 'A simple form of bridle-bit': OED.

  374 *Commend me*: colloquial, 'give me for choice'. EBB quotes as 'Commend me to them
for glass potters', commenting: 'Another short line, which, here again, I cant quite like—
But all this is so characteristic & strong & fresh,—& the glass with the mulberry-tinge is so
beautiful, that it is shameful to talk of "not liking" in any relation.'

Where the bold sword-lily cuts the clear waters,
And the cup-lily couches with all the white daughters:
Such are the works they put their hand to,   385
The uses they turn and twist iron and sand to.
And these made the troop, which our Duke saw sally
Toward his castle from out of the valley,
Men and women, like new-hatched spiders,
Come out with the morning to greet our riders.   390
And up they wound till they reached the ditch,
Whereat all stopped save one, a witch
That I knew, as she hobbled from the group,
By her gait directly and her stoop,
I, whom Jacynth was used to importune   395
To let that same witch tell us our fortune,
The oldest Gipsy then above ground;
And, sure as the autumn season came round,
She paid us a visit for profit or pastime,
And every time, as she swore, for the last time.   400
And presently she was seen to sidle
Up to the Duke till she touched his bridle,
So that the horse of a sudden reared up
As under its nose the old witch peered up
With her worn-out eyes, or rather eye-holes   405
    Of no use now but to gather brine,
    And began a kind of level whine
Such as they use to sing to their viols
When their ditties they go grinding
Up and down with nobody minding: 410

386 *1845,1849* And the uses   387 *1845,1849* troop   388 *1845–65* Towards
his   390 *1845,1849* riders;   391 *1889* ditch. {imperfect comma?}
392 *1845–63* witch,   394 *1845–63* gait, directly,   *396 {reading of *1845*}
1849–89,1872S–88S fortune.   398 *1845–63* And, so sure   *408 {reading of
1845,1865,1868,1884S–8S} *1849,1863,1870–89,1872S* they used to   410 *1884S,*
1886S minding.

  383 *sword-lily*: strictly 'the genus *Gladiolus*', but here used of some other plant: OED.
  384 *cup-lily*: also used imprecisely.
  403 *So that the horse*: EBB quotes as 'So that his *foolish* horse well nigh reared up', with the
comment: 'Foolish, put in afterwards—& do you like that clogging rhythm?'

And then, as of old, at the end of the humming
Her usual presents were forthcoming
—A dog-whistle blowing the fiercest of trebles,
(Just a sea-shore stone holding a dozen fine pebbles,)
Or a porcelain mouth-piece to screw on a pipe-end,—   415
And so she awaited her annual stipend.
But this time, the Duke would scarcely vouchsafe
   A word in reply; and in vain she felt
   With twitching fingers at her belt
   For the purse of sleek pine-martin pelt,   420
Ready to put what he gave in her pouch safe,—
Till, either to quicken his apprehension,
Or possibly with an after-intention,
She was come, she said, to pay her duty
To the new Duchess, the youthful beauty.   425
No sooner had she named his lady,
Than a shine lit up the face so shady,
And its smirk returned with a novel meaning—
For it struck him, the babe just wanted weaning;
If one gave her a taste of what life was and sorrow,   430
She, foolish to-day, would be wiser to-morrow;
And who so fit a teacher of trouble
As this sordid crone bent well-nigh double?
So, glancing at her wolf-skin vesture,
   (If such it was, for they grow so hirsute   435
   That their own fleece serves for natural fur-suit)
He was contrasting, 't was plain from his gesture,
The life of the lady so flower-like and delicate
With the loathsome squalor of this helicat.

---

411 *1845–65* And, then   425 *1845* beauty: 428 *1884S–8S* meaning:
430 *1845* life is and sorrow, *1884S–8S* life was and sorrow   437 *1845* He con-
trasted, 'twas *1849* He was contrasting, 'twas

   420 *pine-martin*: a marten or martin is an animal yielding valuable fur.

   430 *If one gave her a taste*: EBB quotes as 'Give her a taste of what &c' and asks: 'Does this
connect itself aright with what precedes it? Or is something missed? I dont see the connec-
tion.'

   439 *helicat*: Pettigrew states that this is not in OED, but 'hellicat' is, with three quota-
tions from Scott. Cf. *The Black Dwarf*, ch. ix: 'get puir Grace out o' that auld hellicat's
clutches'.

I, in brief, was the man the Duke beckoned 440
   From out of the throng, and while I drew near
He told the crone—as I since have reckoned
   By the way he bent and spoke into her ear
With circumspection and mystery—
The main of the lady's history, 445
Her frowardness and ingratitude:
And for all the crone's submissive attitude
I could see round her mouth the loose plaits tightening,
And her brow with assenting intelligence brightening,
   As though she engaged with hearty goodwill 450
   Whatever he now might enjoin to fulfil,
And promised the lady a thorough frightening.
And so, just giving her a glimpse
Of a purse, with the air of a man who imps
The wing of the hawk that shall fetch the hernshaw, 455
   He bade me take the Gipsy mother
   And set her telling some story or other
Of hill or dale, oak-wood or fernshaw,
To wile away a weary hour
For the lady left alone in her bower, 460
Whose mind and body craved exertion
And yet shrank from all better diversion.

---

441 *1884S–8S* throng: 442 *1845–63* crone,   444 *1845–63* mystery,
446 *1845–70,1872S–88S* ingratitude; *1875* {as *1888*}   449 *1845* brightening *1863*
brightening.   450 *1845,1849* As tho' . . . . good will *1863* As though, ... goodwill
453 *1845* so just   459 *1849–65* To while away

  445 *main*: main part.
  446 *frowardness*: perversity.
  448 *plaits*: wrinkles.
  450 *As though*: EBB quotes as "As though she engaged with a hearty goodwill / All he now enjoined to fulfil', asking: 'Does not the meaning & rhythm enjoin rather "To all he engaged her to fulfil"—You are so fond of elisions—are you not?'
  454 *imps*: to imp is to engraft feathers in the wing of a bird, to restore or improve its flight.
  455 *hernshaw*: more often 'heronshaw', a young heron.
  458 *fernshaw*: 'A brake or thicket of fern': OED, which gives no other example.

XIV.

Then clapping heel to his horse, the mere curveter,
    Out rode the Duke, and after his hollo
Horses and hounds swept, huntsman and servitor,   465
    And back I turned and bade the crone follow.
And what makes me confident what's to be told you
    Had all along been of this crone's devising,
Is, that, on looking round sharply, behold you,
    There was a novelty quick as surprising: 470
For first, she had shot up a full head in stature,
    And her step kept pace with mine nor faltered,
As if age had foregone its usurpature,
    And the ignoble mien was wholly altered,
And the face looked quite of another nature,   475
And the change reached too, whatever the change meant,
    Her shaggy wolf-skin cloak's arrangement:
For where its tatters hung loose like sedges,
    Gold coins were glittering on the edges,
Like the band-roll strung with tomans   480
    Which proves the veil a Persian woman's:
And under her brow, like a snail's horns newly
    Come out as after the rain he paces,

---

463 *1845,1849* curvetter,   472 *1845,1849* faultered,   475 *1845* looked of
quite another   477 *1845,1849* arrangement,

    463 *curveter*: a horse which 'curvets', raising its rear legs before its forelegs are back on
the ground. Browning may have found the word in Charles Lever's *Charles O'Malley*
(1841), ch. xxxiii, the source of the only example in OED.
    468 *Had all along*: EBB quotes as 'Had all along been of her devising', with the query:
'Why not "her own devising"—for the rhythm?'
    473 *usurpature*: EBB quotes as 'As if age forwent its usurpature—', with the suggestion:
'"As if age had forgone" . . quære! for rhythm & meaning. Also in the two next lines there
seems to me an effort necessary on the part of the reader to keep the tune . . on account of a
want of a word here & there.'
    480 *band-roll*: a banderole or bandrol is a streamer or ribbon. Here the reference may be
to the band which a Persian woman often wears across her forehead, on the outside of her
all-enveloping chador.
        tomans: Persian gold coins.
    483 *Come out*: EBB quotes as 'Come out after the rain *he traces*', and asks: 'What is quite the
significance here of "traces"? You want it for "places" afterwards,—but for nothing else I
fancy. It seems forced. But all this "description" is very vivid, & I delight in this snail-figure.'

Two unmistakeable eye-points duly
　　Live and aware looked out of their places.   485
So, we went and found Jacynth at the entry
Of the lady's chamber standing sentry;
I told the command and produced my companion,
And Jacynth rejoiced to admit any one,
For since last night, by the same token,   490
Not a single word had the lady spoken:
They went in both to the presence together,
While I in the balcony watched the weather.

XV.

And now, what took place at the very first of all,
I cannot tell, as I never could learn it: 495
Jacynth constantly wished a curse to fall
On that little head of hers and burn it
If she knew how she came to drop so soundly
　　Asleep of a sudden and there continue
The whole time sleeping as profoundly   500
　　As one of the boars my father would pin you
'Twixt the eyes where life holds garrison,
—Jacynth forgive me the comparison!
But where I begin my own narration
Is a little after I took my station   505
To breathe the fresh air from the balcony,
And, having in those days a falcon eye,

---

486 *1845,1849* So we   487 *1845–65* Lady's . . . . sentry; *1884S–8S* lady's . . . . sentry.
489 *1884S–8S* rejoiced, she said, to admit   491 *1845–65* Lady spoken: *1884S–8S*
lady spoken.   492 *1845,1849* So they went in   499–500 *1884S–8S* sudden,
. . . . whole time,   502 *1845–63* where the life   503 *1884S–8S* —Jacynth,
504 *1845* own relation

486 *So, we went*: EBB quotes as 'So we went up the steps where our master', commenting:
'Another short line.'
488 *I told the command*: EBB quotes as 'Told the Duke's command', and asks: 'Should it
not be "And told his command" . . for the clearness. The next line "Jacynth said", is difficult
to read in tune—And lower still [492], "So they went in", I sh.ᵈ be inclined to write "So they
went along", or "And so they went in" . . for a like reason.'
502 *'Twixt the eyes*: cf. above, 43–4.

To follow the hunt thro' the open country,
From where the bushes thinlier crested
The hillocks, to a plain where's not one tree.   510
When, in a moment, my ear was arrested
By—was it singing, or was it saying,
Or a strange musical instrument playing
In the chamber?—and to be certain
I pushed the lattice, pulled the curtain,   515
And there lay Jacynth asleep,
Yet as if a watch she tried to keep,
In a rosy sleep along the floor
With her head against the door;
While in the midst, on the seat of state,   520
Was a queen—the Gipsy woman late,
With head and face downbent
On the lady's head and face intent:
For, coiled at her feet like a child at ease,
The lady sat between her knees   525

---

510 *1845,1849* tree:—   514 *1884S–8S* —and, to be certain,   518 *1845* sleep
on the   520 *1845* And in the   521 *1845* Like a queen the gypsy woman sate,
1849 {as *1845* except 'Gipsy'}   523 *1845,1849* Lady's . . . . intent, *1863,1865* Lady's
. . . . intent: 525 *1845* lady sate . . . . knees *1849* Lady sate . . . . knees *1863,1865*
Lady sat . . . . knees *1868–88S* lady sat . . . . knees,

508 *To follow the hunt*: EBB quotes as 'Follow the hunt', and comments: 'quære "To
follow"—for clearness'.
512 *By—was it singing*: EBB quotes as 'By .. was it singing, was it saying ..', and
comments: 'I doubt rather .. just doubt .. whether an "*or*" might not with advantage
precede the "was it saying"—but this *is* very musical, (*I* dont ask "was it singing, was it say-
ing") & a worthy beginning to a passage of extreme beauty, & power too—The whole
expression & picture of it, quite exquisite, & one of the worthiest things you have done I
think.' Embarrassed by Browning's unbounded gratitude for her suggestions, EBB wrote,
on 26 July *1845*, that she no longer agreed with her own suggestion here: 'Thinking of it at
a distance, it grows clear to me that you were right, & that there should be and must be no
'or' to disturb the listening pause. Now *sh^d* there?' (Kintner, i. 137). Browning persisted in
taking her initial advice, however.
518 *In a rosy sleep*: EBB quotes the line with 'along the floor', asking: 'Would not "on the
floor" improve the general rhythm? And "along" in one line is echoed too closely by
"against" in the following—is it not? for another motive.' Browning adopted 'on the floor'
in *1845*, but restored 'along the floor' in *1849*. EBB adds: 'I doubt whether the "hers" in
some following lines do not by their distribution confuse the image a little.' Browning
clearly put this right.

And o'er them the lady's clasped hands met,
And on those hands her chin was set,
And her upturned face met the face of the crone
Wherein the eyes had grown and grown
As if she could double and quadruple   530
At pleasure the play of either pupil
   —Very like, by her hands' slow fanning,
As up and down like a gor-crow's flappers
They moved to measure, or bell-clappers.
   I said "Is it blessing, is it banning,   535
"Do they applaud you or burlesque you—
   "Those hands and fingers with no flesh on?"
But, just as I thought to spring in to the rescue,
   At once I was stopped by the lady's expression:
For it was life her eyes were drinking   540
From the crone's wide pair above unwinking,
   —Life's pure fire received without shrinking,
Into the heart and breast whose heaving
Told you no single drop they were leaving,
   —Life, that filling her, passed redundant   545
   Into her very hair, back swerving
Over each shoulder, loose and abundant,
   As her head thrown back showed the white throat curving;

---

532 *1845,1849* like by her hands *1863* like, by her hands,   534 *1845,1849* measure
like bell clappers *1863–75,1872S* measure, or bell clappers. *1884S–8S* measure, or like bell-
clappers.   535 *1845,1849* —I said, is *1863–75* I said, is *1872S–88S* I said, "Is
536 *1845,1849* Do. . . .burlesque you? *1863–75* Do. . . .burlesque you—   537 *1845–
75* Those . . . . on?   538 *1845,1849* When, just   541 *1845* crones' wide pair
unwinking,   542 *1845,1849* Life's pure fire *1872S–88S* —Life's pure fire,
544 *1845,1849* leaving—   545 *1845,1849* Life, that . . . . past   548 *1845–75*
curving,

   529 *the eyes had grown*: 'The description of the eyes growing larger with the fanning of
the hands, is wonderful—I admire it all very much': EBB.
   532 *like*: likely.
   533 *gor-crow*: carrion crow.
   535 *banning*: cursing. Cf. Scott, *Rob Roy*, ch. xxxix: 'Ower bad for blessing, and ower
gude for banning.'
   545 *—Life, that filling her*: EBB quotes as 'For filling her it past redundant', and com-
ments: 'I sh^d be half inclined to repeat, "Life, that filling her passed redundant", something
for rhythm, something for clearness. It is full of beauty & expression.'

And the very tresses shared in the pleasure,
Moving to the mystic measure,   550
Bounding as the bosom bounded.
I stopped short, more and more confounded,
As still her cheeks burned and eyes glistened,
As she listened and she listened:
When all at once a hand detained me,   555
The selfsame contagion gained me,
And I kept time to the wondrous chime,
Making out word and prose and rhyme,
Till it seemed that the music furled
        Its wings like a task fulfilled, and dropped   560
        From under the words it first had propped,
And left them midway in the world:
Word took word as hand takes hand,
I could hear at last, and understand,
And when I held the unbroken thread,   565
The Gipsy said:—

        "And so at last we find my tribe,
        "And so I set thee in the midst,

552 *1845* I stopped, more   554 *1845,1849* and she listened,— *1884S–8S* and she
listened.   556 *1845–65* And the selfsame contagion   562 *1845–75,1872S*
world, *1884S–8S* world.   563 *1845–65* And word took   564 *1884S–8S*
understand;   *567 (reading of *1849–68*) *1845* And .... tribe, *1870–89,1872S–88S*
"And .... tribe.

550 *mystic measure*: as in Shelley, *Prometheus Unbound*, IV. 77 and 129.
556 *The selfsame contagion*: 'when the narrator says that the "contagion" gained him, the
hearer feels something of the same—and when the music furled its wings .. with all that
follows—it's very beautiful, & mystical in effect—Yet in the line "From under the words it
propped" I think there sh.^d be .. "it first had propped" .. or a like modification, for the
meaning's sake. I like *so* much .. the word took word as hand took hand! *all*, in fact!—You
have wrought the charm with power.'
559–60 *furled / Its wings*: cf. Shelley, *Queen Mab*, ii. 20.
567 "*And so at last*: 'In the incantation .. a little attention to the rhythm seems neces-
sary—and another word here & there, especially in the early part of it. It ought to be
musical—ought it not?—"And art ready to say & do". Should it not be "And all thou art
ready to say & do". Also "And I bid my people probe"–Is not *that* more broken than, in this
place, should be? Perhaps I sh.^d like better "And I speak to my people & bid them probe"—
but this & ever so much before, is such impertinence that I am quite & really ashamed of
it—& should be still more, if it did not come of obedience rather than want of reverence.'

"And to one and all of them describe
    "What thou saidst and what thou didst,   570
"Our long and terrible journey through,
"And all thou art ready to say and do
"In the trials that remain:
"I trace them the vein and the other vein
"That meet on thy brow and part again,   575
"Making our rapid mystic mark;
    "And I bid my people prove and probe
    "Each eye's profound and glorious globe
"Till they detect the kindred spark
"In those depths so dear and dark,   580
"Like the spots that snap and burst and flee,
"Circling over the midnight sea.
"And on that round young cheek of thine
    "I make them recognize the tinge,
"As when of the costly scarlet wine   585
    "They drip so much as will impinge
"And spread in a thinnest scale afloat
"One thick gold drop from the olive's coat
"Over a silver plate whose sheen
"Still thro' the mixture shall be seen.   590
"For so I prove thee, to one and all,
    "Fit, when my people ope their breast,
"To see the sign, and hear the call,
    "And take the vow, and stand the test
    "Which adds one more child to the rest—   595
"When the breast is bare and the arms are wide,
"And the world is left outside.

---

571 *1845,1849* thro',   573 *1884S–8S* remain.   575 *1884S–8S* again
581 *1845,1849* snap, and burst,   583 *1845,1849* that young round cheek
591 *1845,1849* For,

   581 *Like the spots*: on reading the proof, EBB quoted this line without the first 'and',
apparently preferring an earlier version, which Browning therefore restored. She wrote:
'Your "and burst"?' The reference is probably to 'St Elmo's fire', the electrical charges
sometimes seen at the masthead of ships: 'snap' here means 'wink': OED 'Snap', vb. III. 10b.
   596 *When the breast*: on reading the proof, EBB quoted this line with 'ope wide' and
asked: 'Why not "*are* wide"? You have "ope their breast" just before—& besides . .'.

"For there is probation to decree,
"And many and long must the trials be
"Thou shalt victoriously endure,   600
"If that brow is true and those eyes are sure;
"Like a jewel-finder's fierce assay
    "Of the prize he dug from its mountain-tomb—
"Let once the vindicating ray
    "Leap out amid the anxious gloom,   605
"And steel and fire have done their part
"And the prize falls on its finder's heart;
"So, trial after trial past,
"Wilt thou fall at the very last
"Breathless, half in trance   610
"With the thrill of the great deliverance,
    "Into our arms for evermore;
"And thou shalt know, those arms once curled
    "About thee, what we knew before,
"How love is the only good in the world.   615
"Henceforth be loved as heart can love,
"Or brain devise, or hand approve!

601 *1884S–8S* sure.   606–7 *1884S–8S* part, | . . . . heart:

  599 *And many and long*: on reading the proof, EBB copied out 599–601 (to 'true'), 600
reading 'All of which thou shalt endure', and commented: 'But the "true brow" &c are not
necessary for the trial so much as for the successful issue of it', suggesting what became the
wording of 600 and remarking 'but you will set it right'.
  601 *If that brow is true*: EBB has "With the fortitude those eyes assure" and the comment:
'The meaning is apparent—but "eyes assuring fortitude" is forced in the mode of expres-
sion perhaps, & looks as if the rhyme were troubling you. And then, if it is not hyper-
criticism, there is a rather objectionable sameness in the form of ending those three lines . .
with the words "endure" . . "assure" . . & "essay" . . to my ear—all dissyllables & similarly
accented.'
  602 *assay*: testing.
  606 *And steel and fire*: EBB quotes without the first word, and comments: 'You had writ-
ten "and steel & fire &" and why not?'
  610 *Breathless*: EBB quotes this line, and the beginning of the next, and observes: 'Just to
prove how I can like the short lines sometimes, let me instance this "Breathless" . . & the one
beneath, . . "Stand up, look below," [618] where the effect is so good & startling. But all this
passage is quite exquisite . . I mean down this page and the next & the next to the end of the
prophecy—the figure "Shall some one deck thee &c" [636 ff.] a most beautiful, infinitely
beautiful, revivification of what is old in the seed of it.'
  615 *in the world*: on reading the proof, EBB quotes as 'in this world', and suggests 'in *the*
world, 'because "this" catches the voice. I just ask.'

"Stand up, look below,
"It is our life at thy feet we throw
"To step with into light and joy;   620
"Not a power of life but we employ
"To satisfy thy nature's want;
"Art thou the tree that props the plant,
"Or the climbing plant that seeks the tree—
"Canst thou help us, must we help thee?   625
"If any two creatures grew into one,
"They would do more than the world has done:
"Though each apart were never so weak,
"Ye vainly through the world should seek
"For the knowledge and the might   630
"Which in such union grew their right:
"So, to approach at least that end,
"And blend,—as much as may be, blend
"Thee with us or us with thee,—
"As climbing plant or propping tree,   635
"Shall some one deck thee, over and down
    "Up and about, with blossoms and leaves?
"Fix his heart's fruit for thy garland-crown,
    "Cling with his soul as the gourd-vine cleaves,
"Die on thy boughs and disappear   640
"While not a leaf of thine is sere?
"Or is the other fate in store,
"And art thou fitted to adore,

---

621 *1845–65* but we'll employ   622 *1884S–8S* want.   624 *1845* that takes
the tree—   *627 (reading of DC,*1889*) *1845–88S* done; *1888* done   628 *1845,*
1849 Tho' each   629 *1845,1849* Yet vainly thro' the world should ye seek *1863,1865*
(as *1845,1849* except 'through') *1884S–8S* "Yet through the world should we vainly seek
630 *1884S–8S* "For the sum of knowledge and the might   632 *1845–63* approach,
at least,   634 *1845–65* with thee,   636 *1845–75* thee,....down, *1872S–88S*
thee .... down,

626 *If any two creatures*: cf. the notion that man is only half a complete creature, so that
each half goes about with a passionate longing to find its complement and coalesce again.
This may be found in Aristophanes' speech in Plato, *Symposium* (189A–193D), where it is
intended to be humorous and dramatic. It often occurs, much more seriously, in Shelley.

639 *gourd-vine*: the plant which bears the gourd (an American usage, according to OED).

"To give thy wondrous self away,
"And take a stronger nature's sway?   645
"I foresee and could foretell
"Thy future portion, sure and well:
"But those passionate eyes speak true, speak true,
"Let them say what thou shalt do!
"Only be sure thy daily life,   650
"In its peace or in its strife,
"Never shall be unobserved;
     "We pursue thy whole career,
     "And hope for it, or doubt, or fear,—
"Lo, hast thou kept thy path or swerved,   655
"We are beside thee in all thy ways,
"With our blame, with our praise,
"Our shame to feel, our pride to show,
"Glad, angry—but indifferent, no!
"Whether it be thy lot to go,   660
"For the good of us all, where the haters meet
"In the crowded city's horrible street;
"Or thou step alone through the morass
"Where never sound yet was

---

646 *1845–65,1884S–8S* and I could   647 *1845–63* well—   648–9 *1845–63*
eyes speak true, speak true, | And let *1865* eyes speak true, | Let   650–1 *1845–63*
Only, be .... peace,   654 *1845* fear, *1884S–8S* fear.   655 *1870,1875* has
thou   656 *1845–63* thee,   659 *1845,1849* Glad, sorry—but
660 *1845–65* it is thy   663 *1845,1849* thro' the morass *1884S–8S* through the lone
morass

644 *To give thy wondrous self*: 'I doubt whether it w^d not be better & clearer to interpose
"To", & write "*To* give thy wondrous self away",' EBB commented. 'You sometimes make a
dust, a dark dust, by sweeping away your little words. And so, lower down [658], "Shame to
feel & pride to show" Why not write it "With our shame to feel" &c? for rhythm &
clearness. And I go back to ask if what you have written "Never shall be unobserved" [652]
w^d not be better written, for the general rhythm, "Shall never be unobserved"—It is just a
doubt.'

645 *And take a stronger nature's sway*: like Palma in *Sordello*, iii. 358–9.

649 *Let them say*: on reading the proof, EBB quotes the line as printed above, and
suggests that it should open with '*And* let'. It did, in *1845*, but Browning reverted to the
original wording in *1865*.

656 *in all thy ways*: cf. Ps. 91:11.

"Save the dry quick clap of the stork's bill,   665
"For the air is still, and the water still,
"When the blue breast of the dipping coot
"Dives under, and all is mute.
"So, at the last shall come old age,
"Decrepit as befits that stage;   670
"How else wouldst thou retire apart
"With the hoarded memories of thy heart,
"And gather all to the very least
"Of the fragments of life's earlier feast,
"Let fall through eagerness to find   675
"The crowning dainties yet behind?
"Ponder on the entire past
"Laid together thus at last,
"When the twilight helps to fuse
"The first fresh with the faded hues,   680
"And the outline of the whole,
"As round eve's shades their framework roll,
"Grandly fronts for once thy soul.
"And then as, 'mid the dark, a gleam
"Of yet another morning breaks,   685
"And like the hand which ends a dream,
"Death, with the might of his sunbeam,
"Touches the flesh and the soul awakes,
"Then——"
　　　　　　Ay, then indeed something would happen!

---

665 *1845* dry clap of the stork's quick bill,　　　667 *1884S–8S* the dripping coot
668 *1849* all again is　　　669 *1845–63,1872S* So at　　　677 *1863,1865* Past
680 *1845–63* fresh,　　　682 *1845* eve-shades . . . . roll, *1889* (some copies) eve's shades
. . . . roll. (faulty type)　　　683 *1845,1849* soul: *1884S–8S* soul!　　　689 *1845–63*
Ay, then, indeed,

　　665 *the dry clap* (*1845*): 'The "dry clap of the stork's bill" I like very very much, with all
the silence of the morass round it', EBB commented. 'But "With the memories of thy
heart" [672] seems to me a too short line for the place . . and I am fastidious enough besides
to wish your "pick up" changed to "gather" or perhaps "gathering". "Pick up" seems a little
too mean for the association, altogether. How I like it all . . with that grand fronting of the
soul [683] . . to the end!' On reading the proof, however, she queried 665: 'Is not this line
out of time? wanting a syllable?' In *1845*, accordingly, Browning inserted 'quick' before
'bill', moving it to its present position in *1849*.

But what? For here her voice changed like a bird's;   690
    There grew more of the music and less of the words;
Had Jacynth only been by me to clap pen
To paper and put you down every syllable
    With those clever clerkly fingers,
    All I've forgotten as well as what lingers   695
In this old brain of mine that's but ill able
To give you even this poor version
    Of the speech I spoil, as it were, with stammering
    —More fault of those who had the hammering
    Of prosody into me and syntax,   700
    And did it, not with hobnails but tintacks!
But to return from this excursion,—
Just, do you mark, when the song was sweetest,
The peace most deep and the charm completest,
There came, shall I say, a snap—   705
    And the charm vanished!
    And my sense returned, so strangely banished,
And, starting as from a nap,
I knew the crone was bewitching my lady,
With Jacynth asleep; and but one spring made I   710
Down from the casement, round to the portal,
    Another minute and I had entered,—
When the door opened, and more than mortal
    Stood, with a face where to my mind centred

---

690 *1875* bird's,   691 *1884S–8S* words.   695 *1845* What I've *1849,1863* All
that I've   697 *1884–8S* even the poorest version   698 *1872S–88S* stammer-
ing!   704 *1884S–8S* The piece most   711 *1845* casement, round . . . . portal,
1884S–8S casement, round . . . . portal,—   712 *1845,1849* entered,

702 *But to return*: EBB quotes as 'To return from this excursion—' with a comment
which reminds us of the numerous revisions there clearly were in Browning's manuscript:
'Really I could almost make a general & unexcepting remark of it, that whenever you erase
a word, you should immediately put it back again. Now see how short this line is—& how
one just below it "Peace most deep & the charm completest" *requires* for every reason, a
"The" (erased) before Peace. Do see if it is not so.'

706 *And the charm*: EBB quotes as 'And sudden the charm vanished', with the query:
'And do you see any reason for dismissing this word *sudden*, which hinders to my mind &
ear the effect of suddenness.'

All beauties I ever saw or shall see,   715
The Duchess: I stopped as if struck by palsy.
She was so different, happy and beautiful,
    I felt at once that all was best,
    And that I had nothing to do, for the rest,
But wait her commands, obey and be dutiful.   720
Not that, in fact, there was any commanding;
    I saw the glory of her eye,
And the brow's height and the breast's expanding,
    And I was hers to live or to die.
As for finding what she wanted,   725
You know God Almighty granted
Such little signs should serve wild creatures
    To tell one another all their desires,
    So that each knows what its friend requires,
And does its bidding without teachers.   730
I preceded her; the crone
Followed silent and alone;
I spoke to her, but she merely jabbered
    In the old style; both her eyes had slunk
    Back to their pits; her stature shrunk;   735
In short, the soul in its body sunk
Like a blade sent home to its scabbard.

---

716 *1845–63* Duchess—   720 *1845* dutiful: 721–2 *1845–63* commanding,
| —I saw   724 *1845* die: 727 *1845–63* serve his wild   *729 (reading
of *1845–68*) *1870–88S,1888,1889* what his friend   737 *1845* scabbard;

715 *All beauties*: EBB quotes as 'All the beauties I ever saw or shall see', with the query:
'Would it not be better, if "the" were left out before "beauties". The omission helps the
reader to the right accentuation of the line, I fancy—taken with context.' She or Browning
added a stress-mark above 'shall'.

727 *Such little signs*: 'I like the "little sign" given to the "wild creatures"—though that line
does appear rather clogged, to be sure. And the description of the crone with her eyes slink-
ing back to their pits .. & the soul sinking in the body like a sword sent home to its
scabbard!—it is very striking & powerful,—& does not remind one of parts of Christobel
[*sic*] to its own disadvantage as to originality—which you always have, you know, by the
right divine'. Cf. Coleridge, *Christabel*, ii. 583 ff.

We descended, I preceding;
Crossed the court with nobody heeding;
All the world was at the chase,   740
The courtyard like a desert-place,
The stable emptied of its small fry;
I saddled myself the very palfrey
I remember patting while it carried her,
The day she arrived and the Duke married her.   745
And, do you know, though it's easy deceiving
Oneself in such matters, I can't help believing
The lady had not forgotten it either,
And knew the poor devil so much beneath her
Would have been only too glad for her service   750
To dance on hot ploughshares like a Turk dervise,
But, unable to pay proper duty where owing it,
Was reduced to that pitiful method of showing it:
For though the moment I began setting
His saddle on my own nag of Berold's begetting,   755
(Not that I meant to be obtrusive)
     She stopped me, while his rug was shifting,
     By a single rapid finger's lifting,
And, with a gesture kind but conclusive,
And a little shake of the head, refused me,—   760
I say, although she never used me,
Yet when she was mounted, the Gipsy behind her,
And I ventured to remind her,

738 *1845* preceding,   739 *1845* heeding,   742 *1884S–8S* fry.
745 *1845* married her;   750 *1872S–88S* glad, ... service,   752 *1845–65*
But unable....it   753 *1868–88S* showing it.   754 *1845* For tho' *1872S–88S*
For though,

   743 *palfrey*: a light horse suitable for a lady.
   751 *To dance on hot ploughshares*: cf. Southey, *Joan of Arc*, iii. 540. Cf. *Christmas-Eve*, 113.
     dervise: dervish: Johnson has 'dervis'.
   757 *She stopped me*: 'And where the lady prepares for her flight & flies, I like it all
much—the very irregularity & looseness of the measure having a charm of music—falling
like a golden chain, with links fastened though loose. And the nature, the beauty
altogether!—Only why put in "straight" before "home", in the line "Such a reward,—I
should have gone home again" [776]. Why not leave it so?'

I suppose with a voice of less steadiness
   Than usual, for my feeling exceeded me,   765
—Something to the effect that I was in readiness
   Whenever God should please she needed me,—
Then, do you know, her face looked down on me
With a look that placed a crown on me,
And she felt in her bosom,—mark, her bosom—   770
And, as a flower-tree drops its blossom,
Dropped me . . . ah, had it been a purse
Of silver, my friend, or gold that's worse,
Why, you see, as soon as I found myself
   So understood,—that a true heart so may gain   775
   Such a reward,—I should have gone home again,
Kissed Jacynth, and soberly drowned myself!
It was a little plait of hair
   Such as friends in a convent make
   To wear, each for the other's sake,—   780
This, see, which at my breast I wear,
Ever did (rather to Jacynth's grudgment),
And ever shall, till the Day of Judgment.
And then,—and then,—to cut short,—this is idle,
   These are feelings it is not good to foster,—   785
I pushed the gate wide, she shook the bridle,
   And the palfrey bounded,—and so we lost her.

---

769 *1884S–8S* With a look, a look that   772 *1845,1849* Dropped me—
787 *1845,1849* lost her!

   765 *exceeded*: was too much for.

   780 *To wear*: EBB has 'And wear' as the beginning of the line, and asks 'Why not "wearing each"?—it is just a *quære*.'

   782 *grudgment*: resentment. Perhaps a nonce-word: OED spells as 'grudgement', but has no other example.

   785 *These are feelings*: on reading the proof, EBB quotes the line as 'These are feelings 'tis no good to foster', and comments: '"it is not good" . . I ask—for the rhythm & to escape the jingle of "no" . . "so".'

XVI.

When the liquor's out why clink the cannikin?
I did think to describe you the panic in
The redoubtable breast of our master the mannikin,   790
And what was the pitch of his mother's yellowness,
    How she turned as a shark to snap the spare-rib
    Clean off, sailors say, from a pearl-diving Carib,
When she heard, what she called the flight of the feloness
—But it seems such child's play,   795
What they said and did with the lady away!
And to dance on, when we've lost the music,
Always made me—and no doubt makes you—sick.
Nay, to my mind, the world's face looked so stern
As that sweet form disappeared through the postern,   800
She that kept it in constant good humour,
It ought to have stopped; there seemed nothing to do more.
But the world thought otherwise and went on,
And my head's one that its spite was spent on:
Thirty years are fled since that morning,   805
And with them all my head's adorning.
Nor did the old Duchess die outright,
As you expect, of suppressed spite,
The natural end of every adder
Not suffered to empty its poison-bladder: 810
But she and her son agreed, I take it,
That no one should touch on the story to wake it,

---

788 *1845–63* out, why .... cannikin? *1865* out why .... cannikin?   794 *1845,*
heard what she called .... feloness— *1849* heard, what she called, ... feloness—
1863,1865 heard, what she called, ... feloness   795 *1845* But .... play
796 *1845* lady away, *1849* lady away! *1863,1865* Lady away!   798 *1884S–8S* you—
sick   799 *1845* And, to   800 *1845,1849* thro'

    788 *why clink the cannikin?*: Pettigrew cites *Othello*, II. iii. 64: 'And let me the canakin
clink, clink.' A cannikin or canakin is a small can.

    790 *the mannikin*: cf. 99–100.

    793 *Carib*: 'One of the native race which occupied the southern islands of the West
Indies at their discovery: in earlier times often used with the connotation of *cannibal*': OED.

    794 *feloness*: OED has no other example. Cf. French, *la félonne*.

    806 *adorning*: ornament, i.e. hair. Cf. 1 Pet. 3:3.

For the wound in the Duke's pride rankled fiery,
So, they made no search and small inquiry—
And when fresh Gipsies have paid us a visit, I've   815
Noticed the couple were never inquisitive,
But told them they're folks the Duke don't want here,
And bade them make haste and cross the frontier.
Brief, the Duchess was gone and the Duke was glad of it,
    And the old one was in the young one's stead,   820
    And took, in her place, the household's head,
And a blessed time the household had of it!
And were I not, as a man may say, cautious
How I trench, more than needs, on the nauseous,
I could favour you with sundry touches   825
Of the paint-smutches with which the Duchess
Heightened the mellowness of her cheek's yellowness
(To get on faster) until at last her
Cheek grew to be one master-plaster
Of mucus and fucus from mere use of ceruse: 830
In short, she grew from scalp to udder
Just the object to make you shudder.

XVII.

You're my friend—
What a thing friendship is, world without end!
How it gives the heart and soul a stir-up   835
    As if somebody broached you a glorious runlet,
    And poured out, all lovelily, sparklingly, sunlit,

---

813 *1872S–88S* fiery;   814 *1845,1849* So they . . . . inquiry— *1872S–88S* So, they
. . . . inquiry: 819 *1845* The Duchess . . . . of it, *1849,1865,1868* Brief, the Duchess
. . . . of it   830–1 *1845,1849* ceruse | Till in short   832 *1845,1849* shudder!
{In *1845* Section XVI continues without a break to the end of the poem. Section XVII was
first so marked in *1849*.}   837 *1845,1849* out all lovelily, sparkling, and sunlit,

818 *Brief*: adverbial. Cf. *As You Like It*, iv. iii. 149, and 'Fra Lippo Lippi', 97.

824 *How I trench*: 'Does he trench a little more than is needful "on the nauseous" in the
description of the yellow Duchess? I *doubt*, I confess . . but you can judge better': EBB.

829 *master-plaster*: a nonce formation.

830 *fucus*: 'Paint for the face. Not in use': Johnson.

834 *world without end!*: a phrase common in the *Book of Common Prayer*.

Our green Moldavia, the streaky syrup,
Cotnar as old as the time of the Druids—
Friendship may match with that monarch of fluids;   840
Each supples a dry brain, fills you its ins-and-outs,
Gives your life's hour-glass a shake when the thin sand doubts
Whether to run on or stop short, and guarantees
Age is not all made of stark sloth and arrant ease.
I have seen my little lady once more,   845
    Jacynth, the Gipsy, Berold, and the rest of it,
For to me spoke the Duke, as I told you before;
    I always wanted to make a clean breast of it:
And now it is made—why, my heart's blood, that went trickle,
    Trickle, but anon, in such muddy driblets,   850
Is pumped up brisk now, through the main ventricle,
    And genially floats me about the giblets.
I'll tell you what I intend to do:
I must see this fellow his sad life through—
He is our Duke, after all,   855
And I, as he says, but a serf and thrall.
My father was born here, and I inherit
    His fame, a chain he bound his son with;

840–1 *1845,1849* Friendship's as good as that monarch of fluids | To supple a dry brain, fill
you its ins-and-outs,—   842 *1845,1849* Life's   844 *1845,1849* ease!
845 *1845* my Lady *1849–65* my little Lady   847 *1865* before   848 *1845,*
1849 of it,   849 *1845* why the heart's-blood, *1849–65* why, my heart's-blood,
850 *1845–68* dribblets,   851 *1845,1849* thro'   852 *1845,1849* giblets!
853 *1845* what I shall do: 854 *1845,1849* thro'   855 *1845,1849* —He is our
Duke   856 *1845,1849* thrall;   857 *1845,1849* here   858 *1845,1849*
with,— *1863* with:

---

838 *Moldavia*: cf. 87 n.

842 *Gives your life's hour-glass*: on reading the proof, EBB quotes as 'Give Life's hourglass
a shake when the thin sand doubts' and asks: 'Would not "*And* give Life's hourglass" &c . .
be useful to throw the accent in the right place for securing the rhyme without an effort to
the reader?'

843 *Whether to run on*: EBB quotes the line without 'guarantees' and asks: 'Where's the
rhyme to *that*? I have looked in vain for it.'

850 *Trickle*: on reading the proof, EBB quotes the line with 'but now', and asks: 'Should
it not be "but *anon*"? Because you have "now" in the next line—see.'

852 *floats me*: 'floats about my giblets'.

856 *serf and thrall*: cf. 145.

Could I pay in a lump I should prefer it,
    But there's no mine to blow up and get done with: 860
So, I must stay till the end of the chapter.
For, as to our middle-age-manners-adapter,
Be it a thing to be glad on or sorry on,
Some day or other, his head in a morion
And breast in a hauberk, his heels he'll kick up,   865
Slain by an onslaught fierce of hiccup.
And then, when red doth the sword of our Duke rust,
And its leathern sheath lie o'ergrown with a blue crust,
Then I shall scrape together my earnings;
    For, you see, in the churchyard Jacynth reposes,   870
    And our children all went the way of the roses:
It's a long lane that knows no turnings.
One needs but little tackle to travel in;
    So, just one stout cloak shall I indue:
And for a staff, what beats the javelin   875
    With which his boars my father pinned you?
And then, for a purpose you shall hear presently,
    Taking some Cotnar, a tight plump skinful,
I shall go journeying, who but I, pleasantly!

---

860 *1845–63* done with,   861 *1845,1849* So I must .... chapter: 864 *1845,*
1849 One day .... morion, *1863,1865* Some day .... morion,   866 *1845* by some
onslaught .... hiccup: *1849* by some onslaught .... hiccup.   868 *1845* sheath is
o'ergrown .... crust, *1849* sheath lies o'ergrown .... crust, *1865* sheath lie o'ergrown ....
crust   869 *1849,1863* Then, I   870–1 *1845,1849* Churchyard .... roses—
872–3 *1845,1849* turnings— | One .... travel in,   874 *1845* one cloak .... indue,
1849 one stout cloak .... indue,   879 *1845,1849* pleasantly?

    862 *our middle-age-manners-adapter*: EBB quotes as 'Of middle-age manners: I hereby
vaticinate .. that is innate . .', commenting: 'The rhyme does seem to me & persist in seem-
ing to me, to be overstrained. You cant get a rhyme without distraining the accents too!—
Now judge!'

    864 *morion*: 'A helmet; armour for the head; a casque': Johnson. Cf. Scott, *Marmion*, I. ix. 4.
    865 *hauberk*: 'A coat of mail; a breastplate': Johnson.
    872 *It's a long lane*: proverbial: ODEP, p. 480a.
    873 *tackle*: equipment, 'gear'.
    874 *indue*: cf. Scott, *Waverley*, ch. xii: 'The Baron ... had indued a pair of jack-boots'
(p. 55 in the ed. of C. Lamont, 1981).
    876 *pinned you*: transfixed for you.

Sorrow is vain and despondency sinful.   880
What's a man's age? He must hurry more, that's all;
   Cram in a day, what his youth took a year to hold:
   When we mind labour, then only, we're too old—
What age had Methusalem when he begat Saul?
And at last, as its haven some buffeted ship sees,   885
   (Come all the way from the north-parts with sperm oil)
   I hope to get safely out of the turmoil
And arrive one day at the land of the Gipsies,
And find my lady, or hear the last news of her
From some old thief and son of Lucifer,   890
His forehead chapleted green with wreathy hop,
Sunburned all over like an Æthiop.
And when my Cotnar begins to operate
And the tongue of the rogue to run at a proper rate,
And our wine-skin, tight once, shows each flaccid dent,   895
I shall drop in with—as if by accident—
"You never knew, then, how it all ended,
"What fortune good or bad attended
"The little lady your Queen befriended?"
—And when that's told me, what's remaining?   900
This world's too hard for my explaining.
The same wise judge of matters equine
Who still preferred some slim four-year-old

880 *1845* sinful: 882 *1845* what youth takes a .... hold; *1849* {as *1888* except
'hold;'}   883 *1884S–8S* labour, then, then only, we're   887 *1845,1849* I shall
get   891 *1845,1849* chapletted .... hop, *1870,1875* chapleted .... hop
892 *1845,1849* Æthiop: 897 *1845* knew then how *1849* knew then, how
898 *1845–63* "What fortunes good   901 *1845,1849* explaining—   903 *1845*
some hot four-year-old

   880 *Sorrow is vain*: proverbial. Cf. ODEP, p. 754a.
   883 *When we mind labour*: on reading the proof, EBB quotes as 'When we mind labour
then, only then, we're too old' and asks: 'Should it not be "When we mind labour, then
only, we're too old"', commenting: 'I mean .. does not the rhythm prove the *rhyme* better,
by the throwing of the accent?'
   884 *What age had Methusalem*: Saul's father was Kish (I Sam. 14:51): a clear example of a
'dramatic' error on Browning's part.
   891 *His forehead chapleted*: EBB quotes as 'With his forehead chapletted with wreathy
hop', and asks: 'Why not (looking at the context) write instead "His forehead chapletted
green with wreathy hop"—for the two "withs", and other reasons.'
      wreathy: as in Pope, *Odyssey*, vi. 152.

To the big-boned stock of mighty Berold,
And, for strong Cotnar, drank French weak wine,   905
He also must be such a lady's scorner!
    Smooth Jacob still robs homely Esau:
    Now up, now down, the world's one see-saw.
—So, I shall find out some snug corner
Under a hedge, like Orson the wood-knight,   910
Turn myself round and bid the world good night;
And sleep a sound sleep till the trumpet's blowing
    Wakes me (unless priests cheat us laymen)
To a world where will be no further throwing
    Pearls before swine that can't value them. Amen!   915

905 *1845,1849* And for strong Cotnar   907 *1845,1849* Esau,   908 *1845*
Now up .... see-saw! *1849* Now up, ... see-saw!   909 *1845* —So I
911 *1845* good night,   912 *1845* blowing,   914 *1845,1849* where's to be
915 *1845* them: Amen.

907 *Smooth Jacob*: Gen. 27:11: 'And Jacob said ... Behold, Esau my brother is a hairy
man, and I am a smooth man.' Gen. 25 describes how Jacob persuaded Esau to sell him his
birthright.
908 *Now up, now down*: cf. Pope, *An Epistle to Dr Arbuthnot*, 323–4.
909 *—So, I shall find out*: about here EBB found a line which appears to have read: 'Jove,
if in spirit they went a cow shares'. She commented: 'Do you like that? *I* do not—I confess.
And I fancy that some of the next lines might be clarified & *raised* a little to advantage. It is a
very singular & striking poem, full of power . . remarkable for it even among your average
works, & quite wonderful for the mechanism & rhyming power of it—Also what strikes
me in it is the purely beautiful manner in which the beauty reveals itself from the gro-
tesqueness . . taking & giving effect . . & keeping such true measure with nature.'
910 *Orson*: In an early French romance the infant Orson (French *ourson*, 'bearcub') is
carried away by a bear, and reared as a wild man. Browning will have known the ballad
'Valentine and Ursin' in Percy's *Reliques of Ancient English Poetry*.
915 *Pearls before swine*: Matt. 7:6.

EARTH'S IMMORTALITIES

MRS ORR aptly describes this pair of poems, which originally appeared without the sub-titles, as 'A sad and subtle little satire on the vaunted permanence of love and fame.'[1] Each is dramatic: there is no point in trying to identify the grave or the lover. When Browning was asked whether the refrain of the second poem was 'cynical, or sad, or trustful?', he replied: 'A mournful comment on the short duration of the conventional "For Ever!"'[2]

About 29 October 1845 Elizabeth Barrett referred to these as among the 'new poems'—'full of beauty'—which she had first seen in the proof.[3]

1849 Dramatic Romances and Lyrics; 1863 Lyrics; 1868– Dramatic Lyrics.

EARTH'S IMMORTALITIES.

FAME.

SEE, as the prettiest graves will do in time,
Our poet's wants the freshness of its prime;
Spite of the sexton's browsing horse, the sods
Have struggled through its binding osier rods;
Headstone and half-sunk footstone lean awry,   5
Wanting the brick-work promised by-and-by;
How the minute grey lichens, plate o'er plate,
Have softened down the crisp-cut name and date!

sub-title {*1845* has 'I.' at the head of the first section instead of 'FAME.'}   4 *1845,1849*
thro' . . . . osier-rods; *1863–5S* through . . . . osier-rods;

5 *footstone*: the only example of the word, in this sense, in OED is from Browning's 'St Martin's Summer', 27: 'Headstone, footstone moss may drape'.

[1] *Handbook*, p. 293.   [2] *New Poems*, p. 176.   [3] Kintner, i. 252.

LOVE.

So, the year's done with!
 (*Love me for ever!*)   10
All March begun with,
 April's endeavour;
May-wreaths that bound me
 June needs must sever;
Now snows fall round me,   15
 Quenching June's fever—
 (*Love me for ever!*)

second sub-title {*1845* has 'II.' instead of 'LOVE.'}   9 *1845* So the   13 *1845*
May-wreathes   14 *1845,1849* sever!

SONG

This is one of the 'new poems' which Elizabeth Barrett first saw on 28 or 29 October 1845, in a proof. It may refer to her. A month later she sent Browning a ring containing a lover's knot of her hair (Kintner, i. 299–300).

1849 Dramatic Romances and Lyrics; 1863 Lyrics; 1868– Dramatic Lyrics.

SONG.

I.

Nay but you, who do not love her,
   Is she not pure gold, my mistress?
Holds earth aught—speak truth—above her?
   Aught like this tress, see, and this tress,
And this last fairest tress of all,   5
So fair, see, ere I let it fall?

II.

Because, you spend your lives in praising;
   To praise, you search the wide world over:
Then why not witness, calmly gazing,
   If earth holds aught—speak truth—above her?   10
Above this tress, and this, I touch
But cannot praise, I love so much!

5 *1845* this one last tress *1865S* this, last fairest tress   6 *1845,1849* fall!
7 *1845* Because   8 *1845,1849,1872S–88S* over;   9 *1845* So why *1849,1863,*
1865S So, why   11 *1845–63* and this

THE BOY AND THE ANGEL

THIS poem was published in *Hood's Magazine* for August 1844, the month of Browning's departure on his second journey to Italy. It had no doubt been written at some time after the publication of *Dramatic Lyrics* in late November 1842. In its original form, in 66 lines, it presented something of an enigma to its readers.

Elizabeth Barrett's criticisms of the *Hood's* text show that she understood Browning's meaning, and feared that few others would. Her comments (printed in our notes) are perceptive and helpful, and led to notable revisions. In particular Browning heeded her remark that 'a little dilation of the latter stanzas of this simple noble ballad, would ... increase the significance ... of the whole'. In *1845*, accordingly, he added five new couplets (two after the present l. 54 and one each after ll. 62, 66, and 70). Several of the short abrupt lines became longer and more musical, the story became clearer, while the contrast between the human and the angelic was stressed. The symmetry of the poem's structure helped to throw into relief its moral message. On reading the proof Elizabeth wrote, about 29 October, that the poem 'overtakes that wish of mine which ran on so fast' (Kintner, i. 252). In *1849* Browning added one further couplet (37–8), of which he had already added a preliminary version in manuscript to Domett's copy.

Elizabeth's use of the word 'ballad' is apt. There is nothing obviously 'dramatic' in this poem which Mrs Orr termed 'an imaginary legend which presents one of Mr Browning's deepest convictions in a popular form'. The parallel with *Pippa Passes* is striking.

1849 Dramatic Romances and Lyrics; 1863 Romances; 1868– Dramatic Romances.

THE BOY AND THE ANGEL.

MORNING, evening, noon and night,
"Praise God!" sang Theocrite.

Then to his poor trade he turned,
Whereby the daily meal was earned.

Hard he laboured, long and well;   5
O'er his work the boy's curls fell.

But ever, at each period,
He stopped and sang, "Praise God!"

Then back again his curls he threw,
And cheerful turned to work anew.   10

Said Blaise, the listening monk, "Well done;
"I doubt not thou art heard, my son:

"As well as if thy voice to-day
"Were praising God, the Pope's great way.

"This Easter Day, the Pope at Rome   15
"Praises God from Peter's dome."

1 *Hood* Morning, noon, eve, and night, *1845,1849* Morning, evening, noon, and night,
2 *Hood* "Praise God," sang Theocrite; *1845–65* "Praise God," sang Theocrite.   4 *Hood*
By which the . . . . earn'd. *1845–65* By which the . . . . earned.   5 *Hood* labour'd, ...
well,   6 *Hood,1845* O'er the work his boy's curls fell; *1849–65* O'er his work the
boy's curls fell: 8 *Hood* stopp'd . . . . God;" *1845* stopped . . . . God:" *1849–65*
stopped . . . . God." *1884S–8S* stopped . . . . God!   12 *Hood* son;   13 *Hood*
"As if thy   14 *Hood* God . . . . way; *1845* God . . . . way.

1 *Morning, evening*: EBB asked if Browning preferred the *Hood's* reading to the line as
printed from *1845* onwards, which was her suggestion, 'for rhythm'.

2 *Theocrite*: the name means 'Chosen by God'.

6 *the boy's curls*: Domett found the *1845* reading a 'stumbling block'. '*I* thought & others
that it was *Theocrite's boy*, and that the worthy workman was the "happy father thereof"—
Had you written "*the*" boy's curls—or "his boy-curls" making boy an adjective—that bog
would have been avoided': PK 46:378.

11 *Blaise*: the monk is called after a bishop and martyr of unknown date.

13 *As well*: EBB quotes the *Hood's* version of the line, and comments: 'I think you must
have meant to write "As well as if thy voice today". Not that the short lines are not good in
this place.'

Said Theocrite, "Would God that I
"Might praise him, that great way, and die!"

Night passed, day shone,
And Theocrite was gone.   20

With God a day endures alway,
A thousand years are but a day.

God said in heaven, "Nor day nor night
"Now brings the voice of my delight."

Then Gabriel, like a rainbow's birth,   25
Spread his wings and sank to earth;

Entered, in flesh, the empty cell,
Lived there, and played the craftsman well;

And morning, evening, noon and night,
Praised God in place of Theocrite.   30

And from a boy, to youth he grew:
The man put off the stripling's hue:

The man matured and fell away
Into the season of decay:

18 *Hood–1865,1880S–8S* Him,   22 *Hood* years are as a day: *1880S–8S* years are but a day,   23 *Hood* In Heaven God said, "Nor *1845–65* God said in Heaven, "Nor 24 *Hood* "Brings one voice   26 *Hood* earth,   27 *Hood* Enter'd the *1845–65* Entered in flesh, the   28 *Hood* And play'd the craftsman well, *1845,1849* {as *1888* except 'well:'} *1889* {as *1888* except 'well,': faulty type}   29 *Hood* And morn, noon, eve, and night, *1845,1849* {as *1888* except 'noon,'}   31 *Hood* boy .... grew; 32 *Hood* man .... stripling's hue; *1845* Man .... Stripling's hue: 33–4 *Hood* matured, ... decay;

23–4 *God said*: EBB quotes the *Hood's* version of these lines, and comments: 'Taking this verse with the context, will you consider if, "God said in heaven" is not of a simpler & rather solemner entonation—The next line, I do not like much. It might be more definite in meaning, I think.'

25 *Gabriel*: in Dan. 8:16 ff. Gabriel is ordered to explain Daniel's vision to him. In Luke 1:19 ff. he is again sent as a messenger.

like a rainbow's birth: cf. Rev. 10:1.

27–8 *Entered*: EBB quotes the *Hood's* version, asking: 'Do you prefer to have short lines in this place, & why?

And ever o'er the trade he bent,   35
And ever lived on earth content.

(He did God's will; to him, all one
If on the earth or in the sun.)

God said, "A praise is in mine ear;
"There is no doubt in it, no fear: 40

"So sing old worlds, and so
"New worlds that from my footstool go.

"Clearer loves sound other ways:
"I miss my little human praise."

Then forth sprang Gabriel's wings, off fell   45
The flesh disguise, remained the cell.

'T was Easter Day: he flew to Rome,
And paused above Saint Peter's dome.

In the tiring-room close by
The great outer gallery,   50

With his holy vestments dight,
Stood the new Pope, Theocrite:

And all his past career
Came back upon him clear,

---

35 *Hood* Yet ever . . . . bent, *1845* And ever . . . . bent   36 *Hood* And ever lived con-
tent.   37–8 {no equivalent in *Hood* or *1845*, but RB added in pencil in *Domett
1845*:} He did God's will—to him all one | If on the Earth—or in the Sun *1849* as *1888*
42 *Hood* go;   43 *Hood* ways;   46 *Hood* The flesh, remain'd   48 *Hood*
And paused above the dome.   49 *Hood* tiring-room,   *52 {reading of *1845–
88S*,DC,*1889*} *Hood* Theocrite, *1888* Theocrite   54 *Hood* clear— *1845* clear.

37–8 *He did God's will*: these are the lines which were added in *1849* to clarify the meaning.
39 *a praise*: this antedates 'praise' meaning 'a laudatory utterance' in OED², where most
examples relate to African poems of praise.
45–6 *Then forth*: EBB quotes the *Hood's* version and comments: 'Is not something wrong
here? If you mean that the flesh remained in the cell, (named before) you do not say it: &
what else is said?'
49 *tiring-room*: vestry.
51 *dight*: adorned, dressed.
52 *the new Pope*: there has been no pope with this name.

Since when, a boy, he plied his trade,   55
Till on his life the sickness weighed;

And in his cell, when death drew near,
An angel in a dream brought cheer:

And rising from the sickness drear
He grew a priest, and now stood here.   60

To the East with praise he turned,
And on his sight the angel burned.

"I bore thee from thy craftsman's cell
"And set thee here; I did not well.

"Vainly I left my angel-sphere,   65
"Vain was thy dream of many a year.

"Thy voice's praise seemed weak; it dropped—
"Creation's chorus stopped!

"Go back and praise again
"The early way, while I remain.   70

"With that weak voice of our disdain,
"Take up creation's pausing strain.

55–8 {no equivalent in *Hood*} *1845* Since when, a boy, he plied his trade | Till on his life the sickness weighed: | And in his cell when death drew near | An angel in a dream brought cheer: 59 *Hood* How rising .... drear *1884S–8S* And, rising .... drear, 60 *Hood* priest   61 *Hood* east .... turn'd, *1845* East .... turned   62 *Hood* And in the Angel burn'd:—   63 {no equivalent in *Hood*} *1845–88S* {as *1888* except 'cell,'}   *64 {reading of *1845–88S*} {no equivalent in *Hood*} *1888,1889* 'And set 65 *Hood* "Vainly I left my sphere, *1845* "Vainly I left my angel's sphere, *1849* "Vainly I left my angel's-sphere,   *66 {reading of *1845–88S,1889*} *Hood* "Vainly hast thou lived many a year; *1888* "Vain was thy dream of many a year   67–8 {no equivalent in *Hood*}   69 *Hood* "Go back,   70 *Hood* way, while I remain; *1845,1849* way— while I remain.   71–2 {no equivalent in *Hood*} *1845–65* {as *1888* except 'Creation's'}

61–2 *To the East*: EBB quotes the *Hood's* text and comments: 'I like & see plainly this burning in of the Angel upon Theocrite as he looks to the east: but I doubt whether it will be as clear to all readers, you suggest it so very barely. Would not a touch or two improve the revelation? Do think.'
71 *of our disdain*: which we disdained.

"Back to the cell and poor employ:
"Resume the craftsman and the boy!"

Theocrite grew old at home;   75
A new Pope dwelt in Peter's dome.

One vanished as the other died:
They sought God side by side.

73 *Hood* "Be again the boy all curl'd;   74 *Hood* "I will finish with the world." *1845–*
65 "Become the craftsman and the boy!"   75 *Hood* home,   76 *Hood* Gabriel
dwelt in Peter's dome: *1845–65* {as *1888* except 'Dome.'}   77 *Hood* vanish'd ....
died;

73 *Back to the cell*: EBB quotes the *Hood's* line—'Be again the boy all curled'—and com-
ments: 'At any rate you will write "Be thou again" .. will you not? but I doubt about the
curled boy—Anyone "*becurled*" may be right .. but a curled boy "tout rond" does strike me
as of questionable correctness. Think, yourself. And I do ask you to think besides, whether a
little dilation of the latter stanzas of this simple noble ballad, would not increase the sig-
nificance & effect of the whole. Readers will not see at a glance all you have cast into it,
unless you make more *surface*—It is my impression at least.'
    employ: employment.
74 *Resume*: become again.

MEETING AT NIGHT

IN *1845* this and the following piece have the common title 'Night and Morning'. The first twelve lines are headed 'I.—Night', and the last four 'II.—Morning'. From *1849* the common title disappears, in favour of the two titles printed here; and the pieces have a rule between them. There is no evidence to enable us to date the composition of the poems.

1849 Dramatic Romances and Lyrics; 1863 Lyrics; 1868– Dramatic Lyrics.

MEETING AT NIGHT.

I.

THE grey sea and the long black land;
And the yellow half-moon large and low;
And the startled little waves that leap
In fiery ringlets from their sleep,
As I gain the cove with pushing prow,   5
And quench its speed i' the slushy sand.

II.

Then a mile of warm sea-scented beach;
Three fields to cross till a farm appears;
A tap at the pane, the quick sharp scratch
And blue spurt of a lighted match,   10
And a voice less loud, thro' its joys and fears,
Than the two hearts beating each to each!

6 *1845–68* speed in the   11 *1872S–88S* through joys

PARTING AT MORNING

MANY readers have been misled by the word 'him' in l. 3, which refers to the sun. When Browning was asked whether the last line is 'an expression by her of her sense of loss of him, or the despairing cry of a ruined woman?', he replied: 'Neither: it is *his* confession of how fleeting is the belief (implied in the first part) that such raptures are self-sufficient and enduring—as for the time they appear': *New Poems*, p. 176. Cf. the second part of 'Earth's Immortalities' ('Love'), which immediately precedes this pair of poems from *1863*.

'Parting at Morning' is akin to the *aubade* or *alba*, on which type of poem we may consult *EOS: An Enquiry into the Theme of Lovers' Meetings and Partings at Dawn in Poetry*, ed. Arthur T. Hatto (Mouton: The Hague, 1965), and ch. v of *The Medieval Lyric*, by Peter Dronke (1968). As Dronke observes on p. 167, 'The *alba* shows a secret meeting: the lovers meet by night . . ., they know that the coming of day will cut short their joys, and that the very quality and poignancy of their love is conditioned by this. Daylight brings back the claims of the real, waking world, which both lovers must acknowledge.'

1849 Dramatic Romances and Lyrics; 1863 Lyrics; 1868– Dramatic Lyrics.

PARTING AT MORNING.

ROUND the cape of a sudden came the sea,
And the sun looked over the mountain's rim:
And straight was a path of gold for him,
And the need of a world of men for me.

2 *1845,1849* rim—

NATIONALITY IN DRINKS

(CLARET AND TOKAY)

THESE poems were first published in *Hood's Magazine* for June 1844, as a pair, with the single title 'Claret and Tokay'. They were reprinted in the same form in *1845*. In *1849* they were dropped, probably because Elizabeth Barrett did not greatly like them: she told Browning that she considered 'the "Tokay" . . . inferior to all' the other *Hood's* poems.[1] Both reappeared in *1863*, however, when 'Here's to Nelson's memory!' (which had been printed in *1845* as the second of three 'Home-Thoughts, from Abroad') became the third of a trio of poems with the general title 'Nationality in Drinks'. 'Claret and Tokay' were no doubt written after the publication of *Dramatic Lyrics* in November 1842.

1863 Lyrics; 1868– Dramatic Lyrics.

NATIONALITY IN DRINKS.

I.

My heart sank with our Claret-flask,
    Just now, beneath the heavy sedges
That serve this pond's black face for mask;
    And still at yonder broken edges
O' the hole, where up the bubbles glisten,   5
After my heart I look and listen.

II.

Our laughing little flask, compelled
    Thro' depth to depth more bleak and shady;

---

1 *Hood* sunk . . . . claret-flask, *1845* sunk . . . . Claret-flask,   5 *Hood–1868* Of the hole,   8 *Hood* Through

[1] Kintner, i. 131.

As when, both arms beside her held,
    Feet straightened out, some gay French lady   10
Is caught up from life's light and motion,
And dropped into death's silent ocean!

Up jumped Tokay on our table,
Like a pygmy castle-warder,
Dwarfish to see, but stout and able,
Arms and accoutrements all in order;
And fierce he looked North, then, wheeling South,   5
Blew with his bugle a challenge to Drouth,
Cocked his flap-hat with the tosspot-feather,
Twisted his thumb in his red moustache,
Jingled his huge brass spurs together,
Tightened his waist with its Buda sash,   10
And then, with an impudence nought could abash,
Shrugged his hump-shoulder, to tell the beholder,
For twenty such knaves he should laugh but the bolder:
And so, with his sword-hilt gallantly jutting,
And dexter-hand on his haunch abutting,   15
Went the little man, Sir Ausbruch, strutting!

11–12 *1845* Life's . . . . Death's

5 *Hood* north; then, ... south, *1845* north, then, ... south,   9 *Hood,1845* Gingled
11 *Hood* then with . . . . naught *1845* then with . . . . nought   12 *Hood,1845*
Shrugged his hump-shoulder, | To tell the beholder,   13 *Hood* bolder; *1845* bolder,
14 *1845* so with   16 *Hood,1845* man from Ausbruch,

  1 *Tokay*: a rich sweet Hungarian wine.
  6 *Drouth*: thirst, the desire for alcohol.
  7 *tosspot-feather*: no doubt a nonce-compound: 'tosspot', a heavy drinker.
  10 *Buda*: from Buda, on the right bank of the Danube, the medieval capital of Hungary.
In 1873 it was to be formally joined with Pest, on the opposite bank, to become the city of
Budapest.
  15 *dexter-hand*: right hand (particularly in heraldry).
  16 *Sir Ausbruch*: Ausbruch is the type of Tokay which is exported. The early readings
betray Browning's misconception that there was a place of this name.

SAUL
[being 'Part the First', as published in *1845*]

ON 3 May 1845 Browning mentioned to Elizabeth Barrett 'a certain "Saul" I should like to show you one day', describing it as 'one of my Dramatic Romances'.[1] On the twenty-third she enquired about 'something I read for [i.e. as] "Saul"', but it was not until three months later that he took her the manuscript of the uncompleted poem. He was obviously uncertain about it, but she replied at once:

your 'Saul' is unobjectionable as far as I can see ... He was tormented by an evil spirit—but how, we are not told .. & the consolation is not obliged to be definite .. is it? A singer was sent for as a singer—& all that you are called upon to be true to, are the general characteristics of David the chosen, standing between his sheep & his dawning hereafter, between innocence & holiness, & with what you speak of as the 'gracious gold locks' besides the chrism of the prophet, on his own head—and surely you have been happy in the tone & spirit of these lyrics .. broken as you have left them. Where is the wrong in all this? For the right & beauty, they are more obvious—& I cannot tell you how the poem holds me & will not let me go until it blesses me .. & so, where are the 'sixty lines' thrown away? I do beseech you .. you who forget nothing, .. to remember them directly, & to go on with the rest .. *as* directly (be it understood) as is not injurious to your health. The whole conception of the poem, I like .. & the execution is exquisite up to this point—& the sight of Saul in the tent, just struck out of the dark by that sunbeam, "a thing to see," .. not to say that afterwards when he is visibly 'caught in his pangs' like the king serpent, .. the sight is grander still. How could you doubt about this poem.[2]

Browning commented that she had been 'lenient' to it. A few days later, anxious about his health, she suggested that he might publish, in his next *Bell*, only the poems which were complete and required no retouching: he could put 'Saul' aside, meanwhile. From a letter she wrote about 29 October, however, we learn that he had decided to publish it: she commented that 'Saul' was 'noble & must have his full royalty some day', with the suggestion that it might be well 'to print it in the meanwhile as a

[1] Kintner, i. 55.
[2] Kintner, i. 73, 173: Kintner suggests that the 'sixty lines' which Browning had discarded were to become Section X of the poem as printed in *1855*.

fragment confessed .. sowing asterisks at the end. Because as a poem of yours it stands there & wants unity, and people can't be expected to understand the difference between incompleteness & defect, unless you make a sign.'[1] It was an important suggestion, on which he acted.

On 9 December, a month after the publication of the pamphlet, Elizabeth told Browning of the profound impression which the poem had made on John Kenyon, and insisted that 'the next parts must certainly follow & complete what will be a great lyrical work—now remember'. On 2 March 1846 she told him of Kenyon's earnest hope that he would finish 'Saul', 'which you ought to do, . . must do—*only not now*',[2] the final words being due to her continuing worry about his health. In fact Browning did not return to the poem until the early 1850s; he published the completed version in *Men and Women* in 1855.

The main source of the poem is the passage in 1 Sam. 16, in which we are told how when 'the Spirit of the LORD departed from Saul, and an evil spirit from the LORD troubled him', he commanded his servants 'to seek out a man, who is a cunning player on an harp', who should play to him and so restore his spirits. So David son of Jesse was sent for, 'And it came to pass, when the evil spirit from God was upon Saul, that David took an harp, and played with his hand: so Saul was refreshed, and was well, and the evil spirit departed from him.'

These verses will have been familiar to Browning from a very early age, and must have assumed a particular importance for him because of the passion for music which once led him to say that 'when I was nine years old I should have been very indignant if you had told me that I was going to be anything else than a musician'.[3] In *Pauline* he had described music as 'earnest of a heaven, / Seeing we know emotions strange by it, / Not else to be revealed'. It is not surprising that several of his most remarkable poems should deal with the power which music exerts over our minds and passions, or that the last of his *Parleyings* should be with Charles Avison, the composer whose once-celebrated Grand March he remembered his mother playing when he was a small boy.

Apart from the passage in 1 Samuel, a number of other possible influences have been suggested. As DeVane points out, it is likely that Smart's preface to his *Ode for Musick on Saint Cecilia's Day* had remained in Browning's mind:

It would not be right to conclude, without taking notice of a fine subject for an Ode on S. Cecilia's Day, which was suggested to the Author by his friend the

---

[1] Kintner, i. 177, 185, 252.   [2] Kintner, i. 315, 508.
[3] Maynard, p. 140; *Pauline*, 365–6.

learned and ingenious Mr. Comber . . . that is David's playing to King Saul when he was troubled with the evil Spirit. He was much pleased with the hint at first, but at length was deterred from improving it by the greatness of the subject.[1]

While there is no evidence that Browning knew *The Spirit of Hebrew Poetry*, James Marsh's translation of the work by Johann Gottfried von Herder, the following passage is tantalizingly suggestive:

If we look at the incidents of these early periods of Hebrew history, what themes do most of them furnish for the simplest poetical effusions, combined with the most natural musick, in short for the pictures of lyric poetry! . . . take *David in the presence of Saul*. More than one poet has availed himself of the beauty of this situation, but no one to my knowledge has yet stolen the harp of David, and produced a poem, such even as Dryden's ode . . . where Timotheus plays before Alexander.[2]

Any consideration of such further possible influences as the *Seven Penitential Psalms* of Sir Thomas Wyatt,[3] John Brown's 'The Cure of Saul. A Sacred Ode' (in *A Dissertation on . . . Poetry and Music*, 1763), Alfieri's *Saulle*, and one or two passages in *Daphnis and Chloe*, by Longus, must be left to Volume V.

In *1845* 'Saul' is printed in short verse, perhaps (as DeVane conjectures) because of the double-column format of the pamphlet. In *1849* the short verse remains. From *1855* the poem is printed in long verse, but we notice that the long (primarily anapaestic) pentameters look slightly awkward, since most lines have a word or two left over, which have to be printed below them.

The completed poem will appear in Volume V. Here we give the text of *1845* only, collated with that of *1849*.

1849 Dramatic Romances and Lyrics; 1863 Lyrics; 1868– Dramatic Lyrics.

[1] *The Poems* (2 vols., Reading, 1791), i. 40.
[2] Vol. ii, p. 197. Herder's *Vom Geist der ebräischen Poesie* had appeared in two volumes in 1782–3 (trans. Marsh, 2 vols., 1833).
[3] On Wyatt and 'Saul' see James A. S. McPeek, 'The Shaping of *Saul*', JEGP 44 (1945), 360–6: DeVane points out that the Brownings owned the 1831 edition of Wyatt (Kelley and Coley, A 2504). Brown's *Dissertation* was mentioned by W. L. Phelps, 'Dr. John Brown, *The Cure for Saul*', MLN 24 (June 1909), 162.

SAUL.

SAID Abner, "At last thou art come!
    "Ere I tell, ere thou speak,—
"Kiss my cheek, wish me well!" Then I wished it,
    And did kiss his cheek:
And he, "Since the King, oh my friend,   5
    "For thy countenance sent,
Nor drunken nor eaten have we;
    Nor, until from his tent
Thou return with the joyful assurance
    The king liveth yet,   10
Shall our lip with the honey be brightened,
    —The water, be wet.

"For out of the black mid-tent's silence,
    A space of three days,
No sound hath escaped to thy servants,   15
    Of prayer nor of praise,

1 *Abner*: the captain of Saul's host: 1 Sam. 14:50. Here he is addressing David.

6 *countenance*: cf. Acts 2:28: 'thou shalt make me full of joy with thy countenance'. David was 'of a beautiful countenance, and goodly to look to': 1 Sam. 16:12.

8 *Nor*: EBB quotes an earlier reading, 'Nor till from his tent', and asks: 'Would you not rather write "until," here? to break the course of monosyllables, with another reason.'

13 *For out of*: EBB quotes an earlier reading, 'For in the black midtent silence / Three drear days', and remarks: 'A word seems omitted before silence—& the short line is too short to the ear—not to say that "drear days" conspires against "dread ways" found afterwards. And the solemn flow of these six lines sh^d be uninterrupted, I think.'

14 *three days*: 'Saul here suggests Christ in the tomb, in the same way, for example, that Jonah was thought to prefigure Christ: "For as Jonas was three days and three nights in the whale's belly; so shall the Son of man be three days and three nights in the heart of the earth" (Mat. 12:40). Such a suggestion is reinforced when we learn that during Saul's absence the faithful have fasted as the Christian does during the Lenten season. Also, while in the tent Saul has wrestled with the evil spirit as Christ during his entombment descended to Hell and defeated the devil. Saul remains Saul, but he typifies Christ': Ward Hellstrom, 'Time and Type in Browning's Saul', ELH 33 (1966), 376.

To betoken that Saul and the Spirit
     Have gone their dread ways.

"Yet now my heart leaps, O beloved!
     God's child, with his dew   20
On thy gracious gold hair, and those lilies
     Still living and blue
As thou brak'st them to twine round thy harp-strings,
     As if no wild heat
Were raging to torture the desert!"   25
     Then I, as was meet,
Knelt down to the God of my fathers,
     And rose on my feet,
And ran o'er the sand burnt to powder.
     The tent was unlooped;   30
I pulled up the spear that obstructed,
     And under I stooped;
Hands and knees o'er the slippery grass-patch—
     All withered and gone—

---

18 {revised and followed by two new lines in *1849*}: Have ended their strife, | And that faint
in his triumph the monarch | Sinks back upon life.

20 *God's child*: in the Bible good men are sometimes called the children of God. In
1 Sam. 16:13 we hear how Samuel anointed David, 'and the Spirit of the Lord came upon
[him] from that day forward'.

   his dew: cf. Ps. 110:3: 'thou hast the dew of thy youth'.
21 *gold hair*: probably 'gold locks' earlier: see EBB, quoted above, p. 153.
21–2 *lilies / Still living and blue*: Mrs Sara Coleridge wrote to John Kenyon 'to enquire
whether [Browning] had authority for the "blue lilies" .. rather than white': Kintner,
i. 508. When EBB passed on the enquiry to Browning, he replied: 'lilies are of all colours
in Palestine—one sort is particularized as *white* with a dark blue spot and streak—the
water lily, lotos, which I think I meant, is *blue* altogether': 539. EBB reassured Kenyon.
Cf. Moore's note to a line in *Lalla Rookh*, where he glosses 'Blue water-lillies' as 'The
blue lotos, which grows in Cashmere and in Persia': *Poetical Works* (10 vols., 1840–1), vi.
81 n.
24 *As if no wild heat*: cf. 65–7.
27 *God of my fathers*: Deut. 1:21 etc.
32 *And under I stooped*: 'The entrance of David into the tent is very visible & character-
istic—& you see his youthfulness in the activity of it—and the repetition of the word
"foldskirts" [37, 39] has an Hebraic effect': EBB.

That leads to the second enclosure,   35
  I groped my way on,
Till I felt where the foldskirts fly open;
  Then once more I prayed,
And opened the foldskirts and entered,
  And was not afraid;   40
And spoke, "Here is David, thy servant!"
  And no voice replied;
And first I saw nought but the blackness;
  But soon I descried
A something more black than the blackness   45
  —The vast, the upright
Main-prop which sustains the pavilion,—
  And slow into sight
Grew a figure, gigantic, against it,
  And blackest of all;—   50
Then a sunbeam, that burst thro' the tent-roof,
  Showed Saul.

35 *the second enclosure*: Hellstrom (cf. 14 n.) points out that before the building of the temple by David's son Solomon, the tabernacle of the Israelites was a tent (Exod. 40:2), tripartite in structure.

37 *foldskirts*: OED², which quotes from the 1855 version of the poem, has no other example.

45 *A something*: EBB quotes as 'Something', and asks: 'Should it not be "A something"? more definitely? And the rhythm cries aloud for it, it seems to me.'

46 *—The vast, the upright*: EBB quotes as 'The vast, upright', and comments: '*quære*— '*the* upright'' .. for rhythm?'

49 *gigantic*: for Saul's stature, see 1 Sam. 9:2.

51 *Then a sunbeam*: EBB quotes an earlier version of the line, 'Then a sunbeam burst thro' the blind tent-roof', and comments: 'Now, will you think whether to enforce the admirable effect of your sudden sunbeam, this first line should not be rendered more rapid by the removal of the clogging epithet "blind"—which you repeat, too, I believe, farther on in the next page [64]. What if you tried the line thus "Then a sunbeam that burst through the tent roof— / Showed Saul." The manifestation in the short line appears to me completer, from the rapidity being increased in the long one. I only *ask*—It is simply an impression. I have told you how very fine I do think all this showing of Saul by the sunbeam—& how the more you come to see him, the finer it is. The "All heavily hangs" as applied to the King-serpent, you quite feel in your own muscles.'

He stood as erect as that tent-prop;
　　Both arms stretched out wide
On the great cross-support in the centre   55
　　That goes to each side:
So he bent not a muscle but hung there
　　As, caught in his pangs
And waiting his change the king-serpent
　　All heavily hangs,   60
Far away from his kind, in the Pine,
　　Till deliverance come
With the Spring-time,—so agonized Saul,
　　Drear and black, blind and dumb.

Then I tuned my harp,—took off the lilies   65
　　We twine round its chords
Lest they snap 'neath the stress of the noontide
　　—Those sunbeams like swords!
And I first played the tune all our sheep know,
　　As, one after one,   70
So docile they come to the pen-door
　　Till folding be done

57 *1849* muscle,　　　　59 *1849* change,　　　　64 *1849* and stark, blind　　　　72 *1849*
done;

54 *Both arms*: a type of the Crucifixion. Hellstrom remarks that it is significant that the
cruciform figure 'should be in the Holy of Holies, for the Ark of the Covenant, which was
a type of the cross, was kept in the Holy of Holies': art. cit., p. 378.

59 *the king-serpent*: a serpent may be an emblem of good (as in *Queen Mab*), or of Christ
crucified. Cf. John 3:14: 'And as Moses lifted up the serpent in the wilderness, even so must
the Son of man be lifted up.' There was a widespread belief that a serpent could renew itself
(as it renews its skin).

63 *With the Spring-time*: we know that 'the' was added in proof, on EBB's tentative sug-
gestion: '"with *the* springtime" . . I ask'.

65 *took off the lilies*: 'The breaking of the band of lilies round the harp is a relief &
refreshment in itself after that dreadful sight—and then how beautifully true it is that the
song sh.ᵈ begin so . . with the sheep!—"As one after one / Docile they come to the pen-
door"! [70–1] But the rhythm sh.ᵈ not interrupt itself where the sheep come docilely—& is
not a word wanted . . a syllable rather . . before that "Docile"? Will you consider?': EBB.

66 *chords*: 'The string[s] of a musical instrument': Johnson.

69 *our sheep*: cf. 1 Sam. 16:11.

72 *folding*: as in 'Love among the Ruins', st. v.

—They are white and untorn by the bushes,
  For lo, they have fed
Where the long grasses stifle the water   75
  Within the stream's bed;
How one after one seeks its lodging,
  As star follows star
Into eve and the blue far above us,
  —So blue and so far!   80

Then the tune for which quails on the cornland
  Will leave each his mate
To follow the player; then, what makes
  The crickets elate
Till for boldness they fight one another: 85
  And then, what has weight
To set the quick jerboa a-musing
  Outside his sand house
—There are none such as he for a wonder—
  Half bird and half mouse!   90
—God made all the creatures and gave them
  Our love and our fear,
To show, we and they are his children,
  One family here.

Then I played the help-tune of our Reapers,   95
  Their wine-song, when hand

76 *1849* bed: 95 *1849* reapers,

  75 *Where the long grasses*: 'The long grasses stifling the water!.. how beautiful, *that* is!—
"One after one seeks its lodging / As star follows star / Into the blue far above us / —So blue
& so far!—" [77–80]. It appears to me that the two long lines require a syllable each at the
beginning, to keep the procession of sheep uninterrupted. The ear expects to read every
long & short line in the sequences of this metre, as one long line—& where it cannot do so,
a loss .. an abruption .. is felt—& there sh^d be nothing abrupt in the movement of these
pastoral, starry images—do you think so? Is it not Göthe who compares the stars to sheep?
which you reverse here': EBB.
  81 *the tune*: Browning was interested in the methods by which quails were captured: cf.
'The Englishman in Italy', 35.
  87 *jerboa*: a small rodent, found in the deserts of Africa, which looks somewhat like a
bird, and is a great jumper.
  95 *help-tune*: not in OED.

Grasps hand, eye lights eye in good friendship,
   And great hearts expand,
And grow one in the sense of this world's life;
   And then, the low song   100
When the dead man is praised on his journey—
   "Bear, bear him along
"With his few faults shut up like dead flowrets;
   "Are balm-seeds not here
"To console us? The land has got none such   105
   "As he on the bier—
"Oh, would we might keep thee, my brother!"
   And then, the glad chaunt
Of the marriage,—first go the young maidens—
   Next, she whom we vaunt   110
As the beauty, the pride of our dwelling:
   And then, the great march
When man runs to man to assist him
   And buttress an arch
Nought can break .. who shall harm them, our brothers? 115
   Then, the chorus intoned
As the Levites go up to the altar
   In glory enthroned—
But I stopped here—for here, in the darkness,
   Saul groaned: 120

105 *1849* land is left none such   109 *1849* maidens,   113 *1849* assist him,
115 *1849* them, our friends?   120 *1849* Saul groaned.

100 *the low song*: cf. the funeral procession of Eglamor, in *Sordello*, ii. 169 ff., and 'A Grammarian's Funeral'.

102 *Bear*: reading the proof, EBB quotes as 'Bear him along', commenting: 'It does seem as a break in the chant. Why not repeat "Bear, bear him along"? Only a question.'

104 *balm-seeds*: seeds of comfort.

107 *Oh, would we might keep thee, my brother!*: EBB quotes this without the initial exclamation, commenting: 'Why not "Oh, would &c"—It throws a wail into the line, & swells the rhythm rightly I think.'

111 *As the beauty*: EBB quotes without the first word, with the comment: 'Why not "For the beauty"—or "As the beauty"—?'

117 *Levites*: priests' assistants.

119 *But I stopped here*: EBB quotes as 'But I stopped—for here, in the darkness / Saul groaned', commenting: 'Very fine—& the preceding images full of beauty & characteristic life!—but in this long line, I just ask if the rhythm would gain by repeating here .. thus .. "But I stopped here—for here in the darkness". I just ask, being doubtful.'

And I paused, held my breath in such silence!
　　And listened apart—
And the tent shook, for mighty Saul shuddered,—
　　And sparkles 'gan dart
From the jewels that woke in his turban   125
　　—At once with a start
All the lordly male-sapphires, and rubies
　　Courageous at heart;
So the head, but the body still moved not,—
　　Still hung there erect.   130
And I bent once again to my playing,
　　Pursued it unchecked,
As I sang, "Oh, our manhood's prime vigour!
　　—No spirit feels waste,
No muscle is stopped in its playing   135
　　No sinew unbraced,—
And the wild joys of living! The leaping
　　From rock up to rock—
The rending their boughs from the palm-trees,—
　　The cool silver shock   140
Of a plunge in the pool's living water—
　　The hunt of the bear,
And the sultriness showing the lion
　　Is couched in his lair:
And the meal—the rich dates—yellowed over   145
　　With gold dust divine,
And the locust's-flesh steeped in the pitcher—

122 *1849* apart;　　127 *1849* All its lordly　　129 *1849* head—but .... not,
135 *1849* playing,　　136 *1849* unbraced;—　　142 *1849* The haunt of
147 *1849* pitcher,

123 *And the tent shook*: 'And the shaking of the tent from the shudder of the King .. what effect it all has!—and I like the jewels *waking* in his turban!': EBB. Cf. Shelley, *Adonais*, 256.

127 *male-sapphires*: 'male' is applied to precious stones 'on account of depth, brilliance or other accident of colour': OED.

129 *So the head*: EBB quotes as 'So the head—but the body stirred not', observing: 'If you wrote "So the head—but the body .. *that* stirred not—" Just see the context!'

141 *living water*: as in John 4:10 (where it is metaphorical, however); cf. Song of Solomon 4:15.

147 *locust's flesh*: probably the fruit of the carob-tree. See OED 'locust', 4, and 'carob', with notes on the use of 'locust' in the Bible to mean this fruit.

The full draught of wine,
And the sleep in the dried river channel
  Where tall rushes tell 150
The water was wont to go warbling
  So softly and well,—
How good is man's life here, mere living!
  How fit to employ
The heart and the soul and the senses 155
  For ever in joy!
Hast thou loved the white locks of thy father
  Whose sword thou didst guard
When he trusted thee forth to the wolf hunt
  For glorious reward? 160
Didst thou see the thin hands of thy mother
  Held up, as men sung
The song of the nearly-departed,
  And heard her faint tongue
Joining in while it could to the witness 165
  "Let one more attest,
"I have lived, seen God's hand thro' that life-time,
  "And all was for best . . ."
Then they sung thro' their tears, in strong triumph,
  Not much,—but the rest! 170
And thy brothers—the help and the contest,
  The working whence grew
Such result, as from seething grape-bundles
  The spirit so true—
And the friends of thy boyhood—that boyhood 175
  With wonder and hope,
And the promise and wealth in the future,—

174 *1849* true: 177 *1849* Present promise, and wealth

152 *So softly and well*: EBB quotes without 'So', asking: '*Is* not a syllable wanted at the beginning of the short line, to make the water warble softly .. right softly?'

165 *Joining in*: EBB quotes as 'Join in, while it could, to the witness', and comments: 'Would "Joining in" be better to the ear?'

177 *And the promise*: EBB quotes as 'And promise & wealth for the future', and comments: 'I think you meant to write "the" before promise.'

The eye's eagle scope,—
Till lo, thou art grown to a monarch,
    A people is thine!   180
Oh all, all the world offers singly,
    On one head combine,
On one head the joy and the pride,
    Even rage like the throe
That opes the rock, helps its glad labour,   185
    And lets the gold go—
And ambition that sees a sun lead it
    Oh, all of these—all
Combine to unite in one creature
    —Saul!   190

(End of Part the First.)

---

181 *1849* Oh all gifts the world offers singly,   187 *1849* lead it—

    184 *the throe*: cf. *Colombe's Birthday*, v. 111: 'an earthquake's throe'.

    187 *And ambition*: EBB quotes the line, from the proof, without 'it', and asks: 'Is there not a misprint?'

    190 *Saul!*: 'All I said about this poem in my note, I think more & more. Full of power & beauty it is,—& the conception, very striking': EBB.

TIME'S REVENGES

On 11 February 1845 Browning told Elizabeth Barrett that he would rather hear from her than see any of his other friends: even 'dear noble Carlyle', 'my own friend Alfred over the sea', or other 'true lovers' of his. This poem may have been written by then, since Domett was no doubt in Browning's mind as he wrote it. For Domett's intelligent enthusiasm for Browning's poetry cf. the introduction to 'Waring' in Volume III.

'It seems to me while I appreciate the conception of this poem fully, & much admire some things in it, that it requires more finishing than the other poems,' EBB wrote on reading the MS: '—I mean particularly the first part, but may be as wrong as possible notwithstanding.' She added a caution repeated on other occasions: 'I do beseech you in regard to all these notes, to separate the right from the wrong as carefully as possible—& in the hope of your doing so, I have ventured to put down everything that came into my head.'

In *1845* this piece consisted of 68 lines. DeVane is misleading when he says that two lines were replaced by new material: our lines 54*a* and 54*b* were omitted from *1849*, in deference to EBB. This and later editions show further smaller revisions. A proof, corrected in Browning's hand for the *Selection* of 1865, is in Princeton University Library.

1849 Dramatic Romances and Lyrics; 1863 Romances; 1868– Dramatic Romances.

TIME'S REVENGES.

I'VE a Friend, over the sea;
I like him, but he loves me.
It all grew out of the books I write;
They find such favour in his sight

---

2 *1845,1849* loves me;

Title: *Twelfth Night*, v. i. 362–3: 'And thus the whirligig of time brings in his revenges.'

That he slaughters you with savage looks   5
Because you don't admire my books.
He does himself though,—and if some vein
Were to snap to-night in this heavy brain,
To-morrow month, if I lived to try,
Round should I just turn quietly,   10
Or out of the bedclothes stretch my hand
Till I found him, come from his foreign land
To be my nurse in this poor place,
And make my broth and wash my face
And light my fire and, all the while,   15
Bear with his old good-humoured smile
That I told him "Better have kept away
"Than come and kill me, night and day,
"With, worse than fever throbs and shoots,
'The creaking of his clumsy boots."   20
I am as sure that this he would do,
As that Saint Paul's is striking two:
And I think I rather ... woe is me!
—Yes, rather would see him than not see,
If lifting a hand could seat him there   25
Before me in the empty chair
To-night, when my head aches indeed,
And I can neither think nor read

6 *1845,1849,1865S* don't .... books: *1863,1865* do n't .... books: *1868* do n't .... books.
14 *1845,1849* make me broth, and .... face,   15 *1845–63* fire,   19 *1845,*
1849 "With worse than fever's throbs *1863–8,1865S* "With, worse than fever's throbs
20 *1845,1849* "At the creaking   21 *1845* would do   *22 {Emendation based
on} *1845–63* Two: *1865,1865S* Two. *1868–89* two.   23 *1845–63* I had rather .. *1865*
I had rather ... *1865S* and *proof* I would rather ...   24 *1845–65S* rather see .... not
see, *1868–75,1872S* rather should see .... not see, *1884S–8S* rather would see .... not see
25 *1845–75,1872S* hand would seat *1865S* and *proof* as *1888* | 28–9 *1845,1849*
think, nor read, | And these blue fingers will not hold

7 *He does*: EBB quotes as '*He* does though; and if some vein', and asks: 'Will you con-
sider, taking the context, whether "He does himself" would not be better?'
10 *Round should I*: EBB quotes as 'I should just turn round nor ope an eye', enquiring:
'Do you like .. "nor ope an eye"? I cannot, much. Nor do I like the "living to *try*"— —You
see how I tell you the truth .. *my* truth .. as I fancy I see the truth.'
22 *Saint Paul's*: the clock on St Paul's cathedral, Wren's masterpiece in the centre of
London.

Nor make these purple fingers hold
The pen; this garret's freezing cold! 30

And I've a Lady—there he wakes,
The laughing fiend and prince of snakes
Within me, at her name, to pray
Fate send some creature in the way
Of my love for her, to be down-torn, 35
Upthrust and outward-borne,
So I might prove myself that sea
Of passion which I needs must be!
Call my thoughts false and my fancies quaint
And my style infirm and its figures faint, 40
All the critics say, and more blame yet,
And not one angry word you get.
But, please you, wonder I would put
My cheek beneath that lady's foot
Rather than trample under mine 45
The laurels of the Florentine,
And you shall see how the devil spends
A fire God gave for other ends!
I tell you, I stride up and down
This garret, crowned with love's best crown, 50
And feasted with love's perfect feast,
To think I kill for her, at least,
Body and soul and peace and fame,
Alike youth's end and manhood's aim,
—So is my spirit, as flesh with sin, 55

31 *1845–63* Lady—There he wakes, *1868–88S* Lady—there he wakes   35 *1845–*
65S down-torn   36 *1845,1849* and onward borne *1863* and outward-borne
39–40 *1845,1849* quaint, | . . . . infirm,   42 *1845–65S* get!   44 *1845–65S*
Lady's   47 *1845–65* Devil   48 *1845* The fire   50,51 *1845* Love's
54–5 [*1845* has two extra lines, as follows:] manhood's aim, | [54*a*] As all my genius, all my
learning | [54*b*] Leave me, where there's no returning, | —So is

32 *The laughing fiend*: the devil.
46 *The laurels*: I would rather fawn on the lady than excel Dante as a poet.
54a–b *As all my genius* (*1845*): quoting these two lines, EBB asked: 'Is not that . . the last
line . . somewhat weak & indefinite, for *you*?' Surprisingly, Browning left the lines, drop-
ping them in *1849*.

Filled full, eaten out and in
With the face of her, the eyes of her,
The lips, the little chin, the stir
Of shadow round her mouth; and she
—I'll tell you,—calmly would decree   60
That I should roast at a slow fire,
If that would compass her desire
And make her one whom they invite
To the famous ball to-morrow night.

There may be heaven; there must be hell;   65
Meantime, there is our earth here—well!

---

58 *1845,1849* lips and little   61 *1845* fire   65 *1845* be a Heaven; there must
be a Hell; *1849–65S* be Heaven; there must be Hell;   66 *1845–65S* Earth

58–9 *the stir / Of shadow*: cf. Keats, 'Hyperion', i. 7 ('no stir of air').

63 *And make her one*: EBB quotes as 'And purchase her the dear *invite*', commenting: 'I
protest zealously against that word—Now is'nt it a vulgarism, & out of place altogether
here?' OED describes the use of 'invite' as a noun as colloquial, and cites Theodore Hook as
censuring it as in bad taste in 1825. It is very possible that Browning intended it to suit his
speaker, however, or the woman of whom he is enamoured.

THE GLOVE

THIS poem is a further retelling, with a different moral or *significatio*, of an old story which had recently been retold by Leigh Hunt in 'The Glove and the Lions', published in the *New Monthly Magazine* for May 1836.[1] In twenty-four lines (which would look better printed as a ballad of forty-eight) Hunt describes how the lady loved by De Lorge challenges him to recover her glove: he does so and then throws it, 'but not with love, right in the lady's face': an act approved of by King Francis.

In a footnote Hunt tells his readers to 'See the story in St. Foix's History of Paris,[2] who quotes it from Brantome.' In the seventh essay of Brantôme's voluminous memoirs, later known as *Vies des dames galantes*, the story has the same moral. It became a celebrated tale. Schiller wrote a ballad on the subject, 'Der Handschuh', published in 1798 and translated into English in 1844.[3] Scott told the anecdote in his *Essay on Chivalry* in 1818, while Letitia Elizabeth Landon included it in her poem *The Troubadour*.[4]

We do not know when Browning wrote his poem, but it is of interest that Bulwer Lytton's translation of Schiller and a new edition of Leigh Hunt's *Poetical Works*, published by Moxon, both appeared in March 1844.[5] 'The Glove' may have been written before Browning left for Italy in August.

This is one of the pieces which Elizabeth Barrett seems not to have seen until she had a proof of *Dramatic Romances and Lyrics*. Her suggestions are included in our notes.[6] 'And for your "Glove"', she wrote about 29 October 1845, 'all women should be grateful,—& Ronsard, honoured, in this fresh shower of music on his old grave . . though the chivalry of the interpretation, as well as much beside, is so plainly yours, . . could only be yours perhaps. And even *you* are forced to let in a third person . . close to

---

[1] Griffin and Minchin, p. 127; *New Monthly Magazine*, 1836, Part II, p. 40.

[2] *Historical Essays upon Paris. Translated from the French of M. de Saintfoix* (3 vols., 1767), i. 149–50. 'Brantome' was Pierre de Bourdeilles, seigneur de Brantôme (c. 1540–1614).

[3] See *The Poems and Ballads of Schiller, translated by Sir Edward Bulwer Lytton* (2 vols., 1844), i. 9–11.

[4] *The Troubadour* (1825), pp. 102 ff. We see no reason to associate the *Mémoires* of the Marquis de Lassay with 'The Glove', as DeVane does.

[5] *The Athenæum*, pp. 208a and 252c.

[6] But for five illegible lines which she deleted, with the note: '(All wrong of me!)'.

the doorway . . before you can do any good. What a noble lion you give us too, with the "flash on his forehead", & "leagues in the desert already" as we look on him!—And then, with what a "curious felicity" you turn the subject "glove" to another use & strike De Lorge's blow back on him with it, in the last paragraph of your story!—And the versification! And the lady's speech—(to return!) so calm, & proud—yet a little bitter!' In another letter she called it 'that delightful "Glove"'.[1] On 14 November she alluded to it again.

We doubt DeVane's claim that 'a great deal of Browning's own experi-ence' went into the poem, and his conjecture that this is why he did not show it to Elizabeth earlier. Lines 121–2, however, in which Ronsard defines his poetic concerns as against those of the older school represented by Marot, have an obvious relevance to Browning's own work.

DeVane erroneously states that two lines were added to the poem between *1845* and *1849*.

1849 Dramatic Romances and Lyrics; 1863 Romances; 1868– Dramatic Romances.

THE GLOVE.

(PETER RONSARD *loquitur*.)

"HEIGHO!" yawned one day King Francis,
"Distance all value enhances!
"When a man's busy, why, leisure
"Strikes him as wonderful pleasure:
"'Faith, and at leisure once is he?   5
"Straightway he wants to be busy.

1 *1845–88S* "HEIGHO,"   3 *1845* why   4 *1845,1849* pleasure,—
5 *1845* is he—

Title: *Peter Ronsard*: Pierre de Ronsard (1524–85), the central figure of the French poeti-cal Renaissance. As a youth he was a page at court.

1 *King Francis*: François I (1494–1547), King of France from 1515 and a notable patron of the arts, with a keen interest in literature.

2 *Distance*: proverbial. The best-known English version is by Thomas Campbell: ''Tis distance lends enchantment to the view': *The Pleasures of Hope*, i. 7.

3 *leisure*: cf. *I Henry IV*, i. ii. 197 ff.

[1] Kintner, i. 252, 268.

"Here we've got peace; and aghast I'm
"Caught thinking war the true pastime.
"Is there a reason in metre?
"Give us your speech, master Peter!"   10
I who, if mortal dare say so,
Ne'er am at loss with my Naso,
"Sire," I replied, "joys prove cloudlets:
"Men are the merest Ixions"—
Here the King whistled aloud, "Let's   15
"—Heigho—go look at our lions!"
Such are the sorrowful chances
If you talk fine to King Francis.

And so, to the courtyard proceeding,
Our company, Francis was leading,   20
Increased by new followers tenfold
Before he arrived at the penfold;
Lords, ladies, like clouds which bedizen
At sunset the western horizon.
And Sir De Lorge pressed 'mid the foremost   25
With the dame he professed to adore most.
Oh, what a face! One by fits eyed
Her, and the horrible pitside;
For the penfold surrounded a hollow
Which led where the eye scarce dared follow,   30

8 *1845–65* pastime!   20 *1845* company .... leading *1868* company, ... leading.
1870,1875 company, ... leading;   24 *1845* horizon,   26 *1845* Dame ....
most— *1849–88S* dame .... most—

7 *Here we've got peace*: Pettigrew suggests a reference to the period 1538–43.

8 *war the true pastime*: cf. Cowper, *The Task*, v. 187–8: 'But war's a game, which, were
their subjects wise, / Kings would not play at.'

12 *my Naso*: Publius Ovidius Naso (43 BC–AD ?17), the Latin poet, whose work greatly
influenced Ronsard, above all in providing him with mythological allusions.

13 *joys prove cloudlets*: when Ixion presumed to attempt to seduce Juno, Jupiter made a
cloud in her shape, and carried it to the place where they had arranged to meet: Ixion was
caught in the snare. See Ovid, *Metamorphoses*, xii. 504 ff.

23 *bedizen*: 'To dress out; a low word': Johnson.

25 *Sir De Lorge*: the son of a Scotsman who went to France at the beginning of the reign
of François I, Jacques de Montgo(m)mery, better known by the name de Lorges, was one of
the most valiant soldiers of the period. *The Biographie universelle* has an article on him: xxix.
571–2.

And shelved to the chamber secluded
Where Bluebeard, the great lion, brooded.
The King hailed his keeper, an Arab
As glossy and black as a scarab,
And bade him make sport and at once stir   35
Up and out of his den the old monster.
They opened a hole in the wire-work
Across it, and dropped there a firework,
And fled: one's heart's beating redoubled;
A pause, while the pit's mouth was troubled,   40
The blackness and silence so utter,
By the firework's slow sparkling and sputter;
Then earth in a sudden contortion
Gave out to our gaze her abortion.
Such a brute! Were I friend Clement Marot   45
(Whose experience of nature's but narrow,
And whose faculties move in no small mist
When he versifies David the Psalmist)
I should study the brute to describe you
Illum Juda Leonem de Tribu.   50
One's whole blood grew curdling and creepy
To see the black mane, vast and heapy,
The tail in the air stiff and straining,
The wide eyes, nor waxing nor waning,
As over the barrier which bounded   55
His platform, and us who surrounded

---

32 *1845* Bluebeard .... lion   39 *1845,1849* fled;   42 *1889* {some copies}
sputter: {faulty semi-colon}   44 *1845–65* abortion!   45 *1845* .. Such
50 *1845–65* Tribu!

32 *Bluebeard*: 'La Barbe-bleue' is one of the fairy-tales published by Charles Perrault in
1697. Bluebeard was in the habit of murdering his wives.

    the great lion: according to Griffin and Minchin, p. 38, Browning is remembering a
lion in a menagerie he loved to visit as a boy. Cf. Maynard, p. 81.

    34 *scarab*: the glossy black scarab-beetle, *scarabaeus*. ('Arab' is loosely used for 'black'.)

    45 *Clement Marot*: Clément Marot (1496–1544) succeeded his father in the service of the
King. He was a transitional figure between the medieval tradition of allegorical verse and
the new spirit of the sixteenth century. He versified many of the Psalms. His fame was
eclipsed by that of Ronsard and the Pléiade.

    50 *Illum . . . Leonem*: from the Vulgate text of Rev. 5:5: 'ecce vicit leo de tribu Juda'.

    52 *heapy*: as in Pope's translation of the *Odyssey*, xix. 515.

The barrier, they reached and they rested
On space that might stand him in best stead:
For who knew, he thought, what the amazement,
The eruption of clatter and blaze meant,   60
And if, in this minute of wonder,
No outlet, 'mid lightning and thunder,
Lay broad, and, his shackles all shivered,
The lion at last was delivered?
Ay, that was the open sky o'erhead!   65
And you saw by the flash on his forehead,
By the hope in those eyes wide and steady,
He was leagues in the desert already,
Driving the flocks up the mountain,
Or catlike couched hard by the fountain   70
To waylay the date-gathering negress:
So guarded he entrance or egress.
"How he stands!" quoth the King: "we may well swear,
("No novice, we've won our spurs elsewhere
"And so can afford the confession,)   75
"We exercise wholesome discretion
"In keeping aloof from his threshold,
"Once hold you, those jaws want no fresh hold,
"Their first would too pleasantly purloin
"The visitor's brisket or surloin: 80
"But who's he would prove so fool-hardy?
"Not the best man of Marignan, pardie!"

---

58 *1845–68* On the space *1870,1875* O' the space   59 *1889* (some copies) amaze-
ment. (faulty type)   65 *1845* o'erhead;   73 *1889* (some copies) swear. (faulty
type)   74 *1845,1849* "No .... elsewhere, *1863,1865* ("No .... elsewhere,
75 *1845* confession *1849* confession,   77 *1845–88S* threshold;   80 *1884S–*
8S sirloin:

   69 *Driving the flocks*: when she saw the poem in proof, EBB queried the line: 'Should it
not be '*Or* driving'—no, perhaps not.'
   70 *Or catlike couched*: cf. *As You Like It*, IV. iii. 113 ff.: 'A lioness ... Lay couching, head on
ground, with catlike watch, / When that the sleeping man should stir.'
   82 *Marignan*: It. Melegnano, near Milan, where François I defeated the Swiss in 1515.
   pardie: Fr. *pardieu!*, 'by God!'

The sentence no sooner was uttered,
Than over the rails a glove fluttered,
Fell close to the lion, and rested: 85
The dame 't was, who flung it and jested
With life so, De Lorge had been wooing
For months past; he sat there pursuing
His suit, weighing out with nonchalance
Fine speeches like gold from a balance.   90

Sound the trumpet, no true knight's a tarrier!
De Lorge made one leap at the barrier,
Walked straight to the glove,—while the lion
Ne'er moved, kept his far-reaching eye on
The palm-tree-edged desert-spring's sapphire,   95
And the musky oiled skin of the Kaffir,—
Picked it up, and as calmly retreated,
Leaped back where the lady was seated,
And full in the face of its owner
Flung the glove.

            "Your heart's queen, you dethrone her?   100
"So should I!"—cried the King—"'t was mere vanity,
"Not love, set that task to humanity!"
Lords and ladies alike turned with loathing
From such a proved wolf in sheep's clothing.

Not so, I; for I caught an expression   105
In her brow's undisturbed self-possession
Amid the Court's scoffing and merriment,—
As if from no pleasing experiment

---

88 *1845,1849* sate   92 *1845* one spring at   96 *1845* Caffre,—
98 *1845* Sprang back .... seated, *1884S–8S* Leaped back .... seated   100 *1845,*
1849 glove—   101 *1845,1849* should I"—   102 *1845* set the task
107 *1845* merriment,

  91 *Sound the trumpet*: i.e. this is a challenge.
  96 *Kaffir*: from the Arabic *kāfir*, 'unbeliever', applied to the black animists of Africa.
  101 *'t was mere vanity*: cf. Leigh Hunt, 'The Glove and the Lions', last line: '"No love,"
quoth he, "but vanity, sets love a task like that"' (Pettigrew).
  104 *wolf in sheep's clothing*: proverbial: see ODEP.

She rose, yet of pain not much heedful
So long as the process was needful,—   110
As if she had tried in a crucible,
To what "speeches like gold" were reducible,
And, finding the finest prove copper,
Felt the smoke in her face was but proper;
To know what she had *not* to trust to,   115
Was worth all the ashes and dust too.
She went out 'mid hooting and laughter;
Clement Marot stayed; I followed after,
And asked, as a grace, what it all meant?
If she wished not the rash deed's recalment?   120
"For I"—so I spoke—"am a poet:
"Human nature,—behoves that I know it!"

She told me, "Too long had I heard
"Of the deed proved alone by the word:
"For my love—what De Lorge would not dare!   125
"With my scorn—what De Lorge could compare!
"And the endless descriptions of death
"He would brave when my lip formed a breath,
"I must reckon as braved, or, of course,
"Doubt his word—and moreover, perforce,   130
"For such gifts as no lady could spurn,
"Must offer my love in return.
"When I looked on your lion, it brought
"All the dangers at once to my thought,

110 *1845,1849* needful—   111 *1845* tried in a crucible *1872S–88S* tried, in a cru-
cible, 114 *1872S–88S* Felt smoke   116 *1845,1849* ashes,   119 *1845,1849*
meant—   121 *1845–65* Poet: *125 {reading of *1863,65,70,75,72S–88S*}
1845,1849 love,—what .... not dare! *1868* love—what .... nor dare! *1888,1889* love—
what .... not dare: {faulty exclamation mark}   133 *1845* on the lion,

124 *the deed proved alone by the word*: proverbial, Cf. Plautus, *Pseudolus*, 108: 'Utinam quae
dicis dictis facta suppetant' (I only wish the things you do would come up to the things you
say). EBB quotes from the proof as 'Of the deed—only proved by the word', and com-
ments: 'Should it not be rather "proved alone by the word". Because she did not mean "only
proved" but "not proved at all".'
126 *With my scorn*: EBB quotes (from the proof) as 'With my scorn found he woe to
compare', and comments: 'Do you mean it to stand *so*? & is it not a doubtful sense? I do not
like it much .. this line.'

"Encountered by all sorts of men,   135
"Before he was lodged in his den,—
"From the poor slave whose club or bare hands
"Dug the trap, set the snare on the sands,
"With no King and no Court to applaud,
"By no shame, should he shrink, overawed,   140
"Yet to capture the creature made shift,
"That his rude boys might laugh at the gift,
"—To the page who last leaped o'er the fence
"Of the pit, on no greater pretence
"Than to get back the bonnet he dropped,   145
"Lest his pay for a week should be stopped.
"So, wiser I judged it to make
"One trial what 'death for my sake'
"Really meant, while the power was yet mine,
"Than to wait until time should define   150
"Such a phrase not so simply as I,
"Who took it to mean just 'to die.'
"The blow a glove gives is but weak:
"Does the mark yet discolour my cheek?
"But when the heart suffers a blow,   155
"Will the pain pass so soon, do you know?"

I looked, as away she was sweeping,
And saw a youth eagerly keeping
As close as he dared to the doorway.
No doubt that a noble should more weigh   160

---

142 *1845* gift,—   143 *1845,1849* "To the   145 *1845* "Than recover the . . . .
dropped   146 *1845,1849* stopped—   150 *1845* "Than defer it till time
153 *1845,1849* weak—   159 *1845,1849* doorway: *1863,1865* doorway;

144 *pretence*: intention or purpose, as in Shakespeare.

149 *the power was yet mine*: EBB quotes 'while yet power was mine' from the proof, ask-
ing 'Why not "Really meant, while the power yet was mine—" it seems less strained in the
rhythm.'

155–6 *But when the heart*: EBB quotes from the proof these two lines as printed, but with
'hurt' in 156, and the comment: 'Heart & hurt . . observe—Would "pain" do in the last
line—or another word.'

158 *a youth*: cf. *Paracelsus*, i. 816 ff., and *Pippa Passes*, ii. 282 ff.

His life than befits a plebeian;
And yet, had our brute been Nemean—
(I judge by a certain calm fervour
The youth stepped with, forward to serve her)
—He'd have scarce thought you did him the worst turn   165
If you whispered "Friend, what you'd get, first earn!"
And when, shortly after, she carried
Her shame from the Court, and they married,
To that marriage some happiness, maugre
The voice of the Court, I dared augur.   170

For De Lorge, he made women with men vie,
Those in wonder and praise, these in envy;
And in short stood so plain a head taller
That he wooed and won . . . how do you call her?
The beauty, that rose in the sequel   175
To the King's love, who loved her a week well.
And 't was noticed he never would honour
De Lorge (who looked daggers upon her)
With the easy commission of stretching
His legs in the service, and fetching   180
His wife, from her chamber, those straying
Sad gloves she was always mislaying,
While the King took the closet to chat in,—
But of course this adventure came pat in.

---

172 *1845* These in wonder . . . . those in   173 *1872S–88S* And, in short, 175 *1863,*
1865 Beauty,   176*1845,1849* well;   180–1 *1845* service . . . . wife . . . .
chamber   184 *1845,1849* pat in;

---

162 *Nemean*: the killing of the Nemean lion, which had terrorized the neighbourhood, was the first of the labours of Hercules. DeVane points out that Daniel Bartoli often refers to the story in his *Dei simboli trasportati al morale*, a book very well known to Browning: see his *Parleyings*, p. 58.

167 *And when*: EBB quotes the line from the proof with 'speedily after', asking: 'Why not "quickly" or "shortly" instead of "speedily"—the reason being the rhythm in *reference to the previous line*—will you consider?'

169 *maugre*: in spite of, Fr. *malgré*. The rhyme indicates the required pronunciation.

182 *gloves*: cf. *Strafford*, i. ii. 94, where Wentworth complains that he is not regarded as a trustworthy courtier, having 'saved the throne' but never 'picked up the Queen's glove prettily.'

And never the King told the story,   185
How bringing a glove brought such glory,
But the wife smiled—"His nerves are grown firmer:
"Mine he brings now and utters no murmur."

Venienti occurrite morbo!
With which moral I drop my theorbo.   190

185 *1845* And never he finished the story,   186 *1845* bringing the glove . . . . glory,
1875 bringing a glove . . . . glory   187 *1845,1849* firmer—   188 *1845–65*
murmur!"

189 *Venienti*: 'meet the disease while it is (still) on its way': Persius, *Satires*, iii. 64. The
poet means that the lady who threw down her glove had acted wisely.

190 *theorbo*: a large lute, much used in the seventeenth century. Quarles mentions the
instrument in the Invocation to his *Emblems*, a favourite book of Browning's.

INTRODUCTION TO *LURIA*

We know more about the composition of *Luria* than about that of any other of Browning's works. He mentioned it in the fourth of his letters to Elizabeth Barrett, and their subsequent correspondence enables us to trace it from a point close to its conception to the arrival of the proofs and its eventual publication, with *A Soul's Tragedy*, on 13 April 1846.

The first reference occurs in a letter in which Browning told Elizabeth that what he had printed so far gave '*no* knowledge' of him, and that he had 'never . . . begun, even, what [he hoped he] was born to begin and end,—"R. B. a poem"'. He hoped sometimes that he was 'doing better with this darling "Luria"—so safe in my head, & a tiny slip of paper I cover with my thumb!'[1] We have only a hint of what he had jotted down,[2] but we may conjecture that he conceived the work when he visited Italy for the second time in 1844: it is likely that he reflected on the influence of Moorish art and architecture on that occasion, as he may well have begun to do when he first found himself in Venice in 1838.

'And what is *Luria*?', Elizabeth asked in her reply. 'A poem and not a drama? I mean, a poem not in the dramatic form? Well! I have wondered at you sometimes, not for daring, but for bearing to trust your noble works into the great mill of the "rank, popular" play-house, to be ground to pieces between the teeth of vulgar actors and actresses.' He immediately responded: 'That "Luria" you enquire about, shall be my last play . . for it is but a play, woe's me! I have one done here, "A Soul's Tragedy," as it is properly enough called, but *that* would not do to end with—(end I will).' He goes on to give a brief account of it:

Luria is a Moor, of Othello's country, and devotes himself to something he thinks Florence, and the old fortune follows—all in my brain, yet, but the bright weather helps and I will soon loosen my Braccio and Puccio (a pale discontented man), and Tiburzio (the Pisan, good true fellow, this

---

[1] Kintner, i. 17–18.   [2] See below, p. 185.

one), and Domizia the Lady .. loosen all these on dear foolish (ravishing must his folly be) golden-hearted Luria, all these with their worldly-wisdom and Tuscan shrewd ways,—and, for me, the misfortune is, I sympathise just as much with these as with him.[1]

From about the end of February until May Browning's work on *Luria* was held up by severe headaches[2] and by a crisis in his relations with Elizabeth. On 26 May she asked to hear more of it, however,[3] and within three weeks he was looking forward to printing, during the autumn, the 'last four "Bells", Lyrics, Romances, The Tragedy [*A Soul's Tragedy*], & Luria'. He was profoundly encouraged by having at last found an understanding reader—a reader whose first anxiety (none the less) was that he should not overtax his strength.

It is not until 27 October that we hear of his taking out *Luria*, reading it through—'the skeleton'—and hoping 'to finish it soon now'. He adds: 'It is for a purely imaginary Stage,—very simple and straightforward. Would you .. no, Act by Act, as I was about to propose that you should read it,—that process would affect the oneness I most wish to preserve.' Of course Elizabeth asked to see Act I. On 12 November she wrote:

I read Luria's first act twice through before I slept last night, & feel just as a bullet might feel . . . shot into the air and suddenly arrested & suspended. It . . . is all life, & we know (that is, the reader knows) that there must be results here & there. How fine that sight of Luria is upon the lynx hides—how you see the Moor in him just in the glimpse you have by the eyes of another—& that laugh when the horse drops the forage, what wonderful truth & character you have in *that*!—And then, when *he* is in the scene—! "Golden-hearted Luria" you called him once to me, & his heart shines already .. wide open to the morning sun. The construction seems to me very clear everywhere—and the rhythm, even over-smooth in a few verses, where you invert a little artificially—but *that* shall be set down on a separate strip of paper: & in the meantime I am snatched up into "Luria" & feel myself driven on to the ends of the poet, just as a reader should.

Browning was delighted: 'does it so interest you? Better is to come of it. How you lift me up!' She wrote about it again on 3 December:

---

[1] Kintner, i. 22, 26.　　[2] Kintner, i. 55.　　[3] Kintner, i. 82, 95.

Luria is very great. You will avenge him with the sympathies of the world,—that, I foresee .. And for the rest, it is a magnanimity which grows & grows, & which will, of a worldly necessity, fall by its own weight at last; nothing less being possible. The scene with Tiburzio & the end of the [second] act with its great effects, are more pathetic than professed pathos—When I come to criticize, it will be chiefly on what I take to be a little occasional flatness in the versification, which you may remove if you please, by knotting up a few lines here & there. But I shall write more of Luria,—& well remember in the meanwhile, that you wanted smoothness, you said.[1]

A few days later she told him that she had 'written about "Luria" in another place', adding that he would have 'the papers' when she had 'read through the play'. She added: 'How different this living poetry is from the polished rhetoric of *Ion*. The man & the statue are not more different.'[2]

'This week I have done nothing to "Luria",' he wrote on 9 December, but within a few days Act III was completed, and by the 24th Sarianna had copied it and it was in the hands of Elizabeth. She read it swiftly, and wrote at once:

I have been reading your third act which is perfectly noble & worthy of you both in the conception & expression, & carries the reader on triumphantly .. to speak for one reader. It seems to me too that the language is freer— there is less inversion & more breadth of rhythm. It just strikes me so for the first impression: at any rate the interest grows & grows. You have a secret about Domizia, I guess—which will not be told till the last perhaps. And that poor, noble Luria, who will be equal to the leap .. as it is easy to see. It is full, altogether, of magnanimities:—noble, & nobly put. I will go on with my notes, & those, you shall have at once .. I mean together .. presently. And don't hurry & chafe yourself for the fourth act—now that you are better! . . . Luria will be great now whatever you do.[3]

On the twenty-seventh she praised 'the exquisite analysis . . . of the worth of a woman's sympathy' in Act III:

indeed of the exquisite double-analysis of unlearned & learned sympathies. Nothing could be better, I think, than this:—

[1] Kintner, i. 251, 266–7 (for the comments on the 'separate strip of paper', see below, pp. 186 ff.), 273, 304.
[2] Kintner, i. 311.   [3] Kintner, i. 313, 341–2.

> To the motive, the endeavour, the heart's self
> Your quick sense looks; you crown and call aright
> The soul of the purpose ere 'tis shaped as act,
> Takes flesh i' the world, and clothes itself a king—

except the characterizing of the 'learned praise,' which comes afterwards in its fine subtle truth. What would these critics do to you ... who would deprive you of the exercise of the discriminative faculty of the metaphysicians? As if a poet could be great without it!

She continued by telling him that *Luria* grew on her the more she read it:

how fine he is when the doubt breaks on him—I mean, where he begins . . 'Why then, all is very well'—It is most affecting, I think, all that process of doubt . . & that reference to the friends at home (which at once proves him a stranger, & intimates, by just a stroke, that he will not look home for comfort out of the new foreign treason) is managed by you with singular dramatic dexterity . . . .

> . . . 'so slight, so slight,
> And yet it tells you they are dead & gone'—

And then, the direct approach . .

> You now, so kind here, all you Florentines,
> What is it in your eyes?—

Do you not feel it to be success, . . '*you* now'?—*I* do, from my low ground as reader. The whole breaking round him of the cloud, & the manner in which he *stands*, facing it, . . I admire it all thoroughly. Braccio's vindication of Florence strikes me as almost too *poetically* subtle for the man—but nobody could have the heart to wish a line of it away—*that* would be too much for critical virtue![1]

On 10 January 1846 Browning told her that Act IV was 'done—but too roughly this time!' The next day he was in two minds about taking it to her, but was inclined to do so:

the roughness matters little in this stage—Chorley says very truly that a tragedy implies as much power *kept back* as brought out—very true that is—I do not, on the whole, feel dissatisfied . . as was to be but expected . . with the effect of this last [Act]—the *shelve* of the hill, whence the end is seen, you continuing to go down to it . . so that at the very last you may

---

[1] Kintner, i. 346–7 (quoting *Luria*, III. 68–71, 101, 110–11, 114–15).

pass off into a plain and so away . . . It is all in long speeches—the *action*, *proper*, is in them—they are no descriptions, or amplifications—but here . . in a drama of this kind, all the *events*, (and interest), take place in the *minds* of the actors . . somewhat like Paracelsus in that respect.

Six days later he told her that the act was completed, and had been copied by his sister. Four days after that Elizabeth had read it, and wrote about it at length:

the new act is powerful & subtle, & very affecting, it seems to me, after a grave, suggested pathos; the reasoning is done on every hand with admirable directness & adroitness, & poor Luria's iron baptism under such a bright crossing of swords, most miserably complete. Still . . is he to die *so*? can you mean it? Oh—indeed I foresaw *that*—not a guess of mine ever touched such an end—and I can scarcely resign myself to it as a necessity, even now . . I mean, to the act, as Luria's act, whether it is final or not—the act of suicide being so unheroical. But you are a dramatic poet & right perhaps, where, as a didactic poet, you would have been wrong, . . & after the first shock, I begin to see that your Luria is the man Luria & that his "sun" lights him so far & not farther than so, & to understand the natural reaction of all that generous trust & hopefulness, what naturally it would be. Also, it is satisfactory that Domizia, having put her woman's part off to the last, should be too late with it—it will be a righteous retribution. I had fancied that her object was to isolate him, . . to make his military glory & national recompense ring hollowly to his ears, & so, commend herself, drawing back the veil.

She goes on to consider the other principal characters:

Puccio's scornful working out of the low work, is very finely given, I think, . . & you have 'a cunning right hand', to lift up Luria higher in the mind of your readers, by the very means used to pull down his fortunes—you show what a man he is by the very talk of his rivals . . by his "natural god"ship over Puccio. Then Husain is nobly characteristic—I like those streaks of Moorish fire in his speeches. "Why 'twas all fighting" &c. . . *that* passage perhaps is over-subtle for a Husain—but too nobly right in the abstract to be altered, if it is so or not. Domizia talks philosophically besides, & how eloquently; . . . I agree with yourself a little when you say . . (did you *not* say? . .) that some of the speeches . . Domizia's for instance . . are too lengthy. I think I should like them to coil up their strength, here & there, in a few passages. Luria . . poor

Luria .. is great & pathetic when he stands alone at last, & 'all his waves have gone over him'—Poor Luria![1]

Browning replied that her reaction to Domizia, and to the death of Luria, were what he would have wished, adding: 'the last act throws light back on all, I hope':

Observe only, that Luria *would* stand, if I have plied him effectually with adverse influences, in such a position as to render any other end impossible without the hurt to Florence which his religion is, to avoid inflicting—passively awaiting, for instance, the sentence and punishment to come at night, would as surely inflict it as taking part with her foes: his aim is to prevent the harm she will do herself by striking him—so he moves aside from the blow.[2]

He adds that he knows that 'there is very much to . . . improve and heighten in this fourth act, as in the others—but the right aspect of things seems obtained and the rest of the work is plain and easy'.

A few days later he told her that he had written about half of the last act, and in ten days the completed play was in her hands. On 10 February she told him that she was 'possessed' by it, and that it had 'moved & affected' her

without the ordinary means & dialect of pathos, by that calm attitude of moral grandeur . . . it is very fine. For the execution, *that* too is worthily done . . . although I agree with you, that a little quickening & drawing in closer here & there, especially toward the close where there is no time to lose, the reader feels, would make the effect stronger—but you will look to it yourself—and such a conception *must* come in thunder & lightning, as a chief god would—*must* make its own way .. & will not let its poet go until he speaks it out to the ultimate syllable.

She continues:

Domizia disappoints me rather. You might throw a flash more of light on her face—might you not? But what am I talking? I think it a magnificent work—a noble exposition of the ingratitude of men against their "heroes," & (what is peculiar) an *humane* exposition .. not misanthropical, after the usual fashion of such things: for the return, the remorse, saves it—& the "Too late" of the repentance & compensation covers with its solemn toll

[1] Kintner, i. 377, 381, 406–7 (cf. IV. 196 n.).
[2] Kintner, i. 411.

the fate of persecutors & victim—We feel that Husain himself could only say afterward .. "*That is done*." And now .. surely you think well of the work as a whole? You cannot doubt, I fancy, of the grandeur of it—& of the *subtilty* too, for it is subtle—too subtle perhaps for stage purposes, though as clear, .. as to expression .. as to medium .. as "bricks and mortar" .. shall I say?

> "A people is but the attempt of many
> To rise to the completer life of one."

There is one of the fine thoughts. And how fine *he* is, your Luria, when he looks back to his East, through the halfpardon and halfdisdain of Domizia—Ah—Domizia! would it hurt her to make her more a woman .. a little? .. I wonder!

She has read Act V twice, and is now sitting down to read the whole play '*through*'.[1]

Browning himself believed that 'so long as the parts cohere and the whole is discernible, all will be well yet', adding:

I shall not look at it, nor think of it, for a week or two, and then see what I have forgotten. Domizia is all wrong—I told you I knew that her special colour had faded,—it was but a bright line, and the more distinctly deep that it was so narrow—One of my half dozen words on my scrap of paper "pro memoriâ" was, under the "Act V," "*she loves*"—to which I could not bring it, you see! Yet the play requires it still,—something may yet be effected, though: I meant that she should propose to go to Pisa with him, and begin a new life. But there is no hurry—I suppose it is no use publishing much before Easter—I will try and remember what my whole character *did* mean—it was, in two words, understood at the time by "panther's-beauty"—on which hint I ought to have spoken! But the work grew cold, and you came between, and the sun put out the fire on the hearth "nec vult panthera domari!"[2]

'The more I read & read your Luria, the grander it looks', she wrote the next day: '—and it will make its own road with all understanding men, you need not doubt .. & still less need you try to make me uneasy about the harm I have done in "coming between," & all the rest of it.'[3] She insisted that 'the fifth act *rises*!', but agreed that his hand had 'vacillated' in the portrayal of Domizia:

---

[1] Kintner, i. 445–6. [2] Kintner, i. 451. [3] Kintner, i. 452–3.

We do not know her with as full a light on her face, as the other persons—
we do not see the *panther*, . . no, certainly we do not—but you will do a
very little for her which will be everything, after a time . . & I assure you
that if you were to ask for the manuscript before you should not have a
page of it—*now*, you are only to rest. What a work to rest upon! Do
consider what a triumph it is!—The more I read, the more I think of it,
the greater it grows—and as to "faded lines", you never cut a pomegranate
that was redder in the deep of it—Also, no one can say 'This is not clearly
written.' . . . Subtle thoughts you always must have, in & out of Sordello.

On 13 February we find Browning uncertain whether to publish
A Soul's Tragedy meanwhile, somewhat better pleased (as it seems)
with *Luria*, yet confessing that he has 'lost, of late, interest in
dramatic writing'. Elizabeth, for her part, was worried that he was
overstraining himself. Two days later she told him that she was
pushing 'poor "Luria" out of sight', refusing to finish her notes on
the play 'till the harm he has done shall have passed away'. On the
25th, however, he had come to see things differently and thought
that *A Soul's Tragedy* would 'do after all': he would

bring one part at least next time,—and 'Luria' take away, if you let me, so
all will be off my mind . . . Don't think I am going to take any extra-
ordinary pains—there are some things in the 'Tragedy' I should like to
preserve and print now, leaving the future to spring as it likes, in any
direction,—and these half-dead, half-alive works fetter it, if left behind.

Elizabeth was worried, because he had promised to rest for three
days, and she feared that he would over-exert himself. On 1 March
she was pleased that he had not asked for *Luria*, and insisted that she
would not have returned it to him, even if he had. Nine days later
she had been rereading *A Soul's Tragedy*, and had difficulty in know-
ing which of the two works to prefer, though judging that 'for pure
nobleness, "Luria" is unapproachable'.[1]

On 18 March he asked her to give *Luria* back to him when he
visited her the next day, 'So shall printing begin, and headache end'.
It seems that she gave him her voluminous comments at the same
time, since the day after his visit we find her begging him to let
Luria go to the printer as it is, '& above all things not to care for my

---

[1] Kintner, i. 455, 472, 493, 525.

infinite foolishnesses as you see them in those notes'. Her sense of his impulsiveness comes out in her plea (a day later) that he should 'try not to suffer through Luria. Let Mr. Moxon wait a week rather. There is time enough.' He replied:

I am unwell and entirely irritated with this sad Luria—I thought it a failure at first, I find it infinitely worse than I thought—it is a pure exercise of *cleverness*, even where most successful,—clever attempted reproduction of what was conceived by another faculty, and foolishly let pass away. If I go on, even hurry the more to get on, with the printing,—it is to throw out and away from me the irritating obstruction once & forever. I have corrected it, cut it down, and it may stand and pledge me to doing better hereafter.[1]

Her careful and detailed comments, printed in full in our notes, were of great assistance to Browning and remain of interest to us. Except for her doubts about the character of Domizia, they relate always to details of expression and rhythm. She points out that his fondness for 'that *absolute* construction' sometimes 'makes the meaning a little doubtful', and sometimes objects to his inversions. Occasionally she finds the rhythm of a line unsatisfactory, and suggests an improvement. Her criticisms are invariably accompanied by the most generous praise. Browning realized that he was now being read by a woman (herself a famous poet) who understood him, and was not disposed to heed her urging 'above all things not . . . [to] care for [her] infinite foolishnesses . . . in those notes'. 'The "good" you do me, I see *you* cannot see nor understand *yet*', he wrote: '—there is my answer! Here, in this instance, I corrected everything,—altered, improved. Did you notice the alterations (curtailments) . . .?'[2]

Her numerous comments on the manuscript were supplemented by a few on the proofs. Taken together they provide us with a great many early readings for which we have no other evidence.

On 24 March she had assured him that 'Luria will have his triumph presently', writing in her next letter:

You will take heart again about Luria . . which I agree with you, is more diffuse . . that is, less close, than any of your works . . not diffuse in any

[1] Kintner, i. 546, 548, 550, 551. Cf. *Browning and Domett*, p. 124.
[2] Kintner, ii. 579.

bad sense, .. but round, copious, & another proof of that wonderful variety of faculty which is so striking in you, & which signalizes itself both in the thought & in the medium of the thought. You will appreciate 'Luria' in time—or others will do it for you. It is a noble work under every aspect.[1]

In the three weeks before the publication of the last of the *Bells and Pomegranates* Browning's view of the two works which it contains went up and down. On 25 March he told Elizabeth that they were both 'failures—the life-incidents ought to have been acted over again, experienced afresh'. Four days later he sent her a proof of the last three Acts (as it seems), commenting: 'I like Luria better now,—it may do, now,—probably because it *must*.' The next day she returned the proof, telling him that it had 'more than pleased' her. 'It is noble & admirable; & grows greater, the closer seen. The most exceptionable part, it seems to me, is Domizia's retraction at the last, for which one looks round for the sufficient motive. But the impression of the whole work goes straight to the soul—it is heroic in the best sense.' On the first of April he asked whether she had noticed how he had followed her suggestions, but admitted that he '*could not* bring [Domizia] to [his] purpose':

I left the neck stiff that was to have bowed of its own accord—for nothing graceful could be accomplished by pressing with both hands on the head above! I meant to make her leave off her own projects thro' love of Luria: as it is, they in a manner fulfil themselves, so far as she has any power over them, and then, she being left unemployed, sees Luria, begins to see him,—having hitherto seen only her own ends which he was to further.— Oh, enough of it! I have told you . . . that you have been "helping" me to cover a defeat, not gain a triumph.

Six days later he complained that he had received '*one* proof, only', apparently a revise so unsatisfactory that he considered it not 'fit to send' her, since it was 'just as bad as if I had let it alone in the first instance'. 'All your corrections are golden', he adds.[2]

Elizabeth received her copy on the day of publication, 13 April 1846, John Forster having somehow 'waylaid the first copy'. 'How "Luria" takes possession of me more & more!', she wrote on the

---

[1] Kintner, i. 554, 557.
[2] Kintner, i. 558–9, 568, ii. 573, 579–80, 597–8 (see v. 329 n.).

16th. '*Such* a noble work!—of a fulness, a moral grandeur!—& the language everywhere worthy. Tell me what you hear the people say.' The following day Kenyon visited her and praised it 'properly': 'And when he tried to find out a few darknesses, I proved to him that they were all clear noonday blazes instead, & that his eyes were just dazzled.'[1] The high praise of Landor,[2] the 'Great Dramatic Poet' to whom 'these last attempts for the present at dramatic poetry' were dedicated, was of particular importance to Browning. But for a handful of close friends, however, there were few to praise *Luria*. Describing Browning as 'a great poet', an anonymous reviewer in *Douglas Jerrold's Shilling Magazine* remarked that while he might pay too little attention to the taste of his readers, he understood 'character and human emotion profoundly, and delineate[d] it powerfully': in this play 'he has a great idea, which ... he nobly realises'. Two years later John Russell Lowell was to rate *Luria* among the best of Browning's plays 'in its clearness of purpose, the energetic rapidity of its movement, the harmony of its details, the natural attraction with which they all tend toward and at last end in the consummation, and in the simplicity of its tragic element'.[3]

There is so little history in *Luria* that it is pointless to search for specific sources. From his first visit to Pisa and Florence in 1844 these cities played an important part in Browning's life and in his poetry. The background of the drama, the defeat of Pisa by Florence in 1406 (without which the commerce of Florence could not have developed as it did in the following years), was known to him from a great many books, ranging from Sismondi's *Histoire des républiques italiennes du Moyen Âge* and Machiavelli's *Historie fiorentine* to the chronicles which he had consulted when he was at work on *Sordello*.[4]

---

[1] Kintner, ii. 619, 628, 633–4.

[2] In PK 46:155 (published in A. J. Armstrong, *Baylor Browning Interests Series Five* (Waco, Texas, 1932).

[3] John Forster praised it, with reservations, in the *Examiner* for 25 April 1846. For the quotations from *Jerrold's Magazine* see the issue for June 1846, pp. 573–4, and for Lowell's praise, the *North American Review* for April 1848 (p. 386).

[4] See the Introduction to *Sordello* in Vol. II. Machiavelli is mentioned on several occasions in the letters. On 2 June 1846 EBB was afraid that Browning might be causing his head to ache by reading him: Kintner, ii. 749.

No 'source' for the play has provided so much amusement as a *Florentine History* alleged to have been written by a certain 'Sapio Amminato'. DeVane, who states that the reference

We note that the final event which gave Florence the control of Pisa and its ports, the opening of the Pisan gates by Giovanni Gambacorti on the night of 8–9 October 1406, has no place in Browning's work.

The action of *Luria* takes place on a single day (like *Colombe's Birthday* it has five Acts, 'Morning', 'Noon', 'Afternoon', 'Evening', and 'Night', so adding another time of day to the pattern of *Pippa Passes*), shortly before the epoch of the Medici when 'the arts, sciences, and literature adopted Florence as their native country'.[1] It is to that future that Luria looks forward in a speech in Act I:

> Florence at peace, and the calm studious heads
> Come out again, the penetrating eyes;
> As if a spell broke, all's resumed, each art
> You boast, more vivid that it slept awhile.
> 'Gainst the glad heaven, o'er the white palace-front
> The interrupted scaffold climbs anew;
> The walls are peopled by the painter's brush;
> The statue to its niche ascends to dwell.
> The present noise and trouble have retired
> And left the eternal past to rule once more.

The central theme is the contrast between the Florentines, ruled by the intellect, and the generosity and 'simple Moorish instinct' of Luria: the contrast between ice and fire. Although Husain warns Luria that

> . . . There stands a wall
> 'Twixt our expansive and explosive race
> And those absorbing, concentrating men,

Luria remains true to the memory of the change which had come over him when he arrived in Florence, and felt 'a soul' growing within him which controlled 'The boundless unrest of the savage heart!' As Jacopo remarks, 'That man believes in Florence, as the

to this in Cooke's *Guide-Book* derives from one 'H. S. Pancoast', doubted the importance of this supposed source, but it was left to the Ohio editor to point out that the writer in question must have been Scipio Ammirato, who published *Dell'Istorie Fiorentine . . . libri venti* in 1600. There is no reason to suppose Browning indebted to Ammirato.

[1] P. 224 in the one-volume abridgement of Sismondi's *History of the Italian Republics* (1832).

saint / Tied to the wheel believes in God'. For Luria Florence 'stands for mankind': he believes himself 'nearer Florence than her sons'.[1] The Moorish front which he sketches for the Duomo is a symbol of his belief that he and his people have something of importance to give to the Florentines. He is a heroic failure.

While the *dramatis personae* have no historical originals, the debt of *Luria* to *Othello* has escaped no one.[2] In Browning's play, as in Shakespeare's, the meaning of the word 'Moor' is vague.[3] It is clear that he is black, but what matters most is that he is as different from the Florentines as Count Gismond is from the speaker of 'My Last Duchess'. It is a reminder of Browning's intensely dramatic genius that he could tell Elizabeth Barrett that he sympathized 'just as much' with the Florentines as with Luria.[4]

The Text

There seems to be no manuscript of *Luria* extant. In his copy of the one-volume *Bells and Pomegranates* (now at Brigham Young University) Browning altered 'wind' to 'mind' at v. 173, though the change was not made in *1849* or any subsequent edition. Four lines were cut in *1849* (III. 269a; IV. 215a and b, 238a), and eighteen added. The potentially ambiguous inverted structure of I. 140 was normalized in *1849*. Because IV. 267 was printed at the foot of the page in *1849* the gap in the first edition between ll. 267 and 268 was lost; Luria's soliloquy was printed without a break in subsequent editions.

Browning made a number of changes in each edition; in particular he revised parts of Act III in *1868*. In the Gordon N. Ray copy of vol. v of *1870* (Pierpont Morgan Library) he made more than a hundred changes, most of which were adopted in *1888*, though not in *1875*. Twelve occur on just one page of Act V, in the final speeches of Tiburzio and Braccio (between ll. 307 and 334 in the present edition). Although these were all incorporated into *1888*,

---

[1] I. 293–302, II. 351, II. 81–3, I. 323–4, I. 108–9, II. 242, II. 166.
[2] See, in particular, G. R. Elliot, 'Shakespeare's Significance for Browning': *Anglia* 32:90–162.
[3] See G. K. Hunter, 'Othello and Colour Prejudice': *Proceedings of the British Academy*, 53 (1968 for 1967), 139–63.
[4] Cf. above, p. 180.

Browning's alteration of the previous line to 'Your rectitude, and duly crown the same,' (v. 306) never appeared in print. Browning also made an unusually large number of alterations (twenty-one) in the Dykes Campbell and Brown University copies of *1888*; all are recorded in our textual notes.

LURIA:
A TRAGEDY

title *1846* BELLS AND POMEGRANATES. No. VIII. AND LAST. LURIA; AND A SOUL'S TRAGEDY. BY ROBERT BROWNING, Author of "Paracelsus." LONDON: EDWARD MOXON, DOVER STREET. MDCCCXLVI.

I DEDICATE

THIS LAST ATTEMPT FOR THE PRESENT AT DRAMATIC POETRY

TO A GREAT DRAMATIC POET;

"WISHING WHAT I WRITE MAY BE READ BY HIS LIGHT:"

IF A PHRASE ORIGINALLY ADDRESSED, BY NOT THE LEAST

WORTHY OF HIS CONTEMPORARIES,

TO SHAKESPEARE,

MAY BE APPLIED HERE, BY ONE WHOSE SOLE PRIVILEGE IS IN

A GRATEFUL ADMIRATION,

TO WALTER SAVAGE LANDOR.

LONDON: 1846.

---

dedication *1846* THESE LAST ATTEMPTS ... TO A ... POET {black letter in *1846*} ... *March 29, 1846. 1849* {no dateline} *1863–75 London*,

I DEDICATE: on 29 March 1846 Browning told EBB that he was 'vexed, foolishly vexed perhaps', that he could not dedicate to her 'without attracting undesirable notice' (Kintner, i. 568). 'As to dedications', she replied, '. . . believe me that I would not have them if I could . . that is, *even if there were no dangers*. I could not bear to have words from you which the world might listen to . . I mean, that to be commended of you in *that* way . . on *that* ground, would make me feel cold to the heart. Oh no, no, no!—It is better to have the proofsheet as I had it this morning' (Kintner, ii. 574).

Page-references given by EBB for her additional notes show that the dedication was added in proof. In 1846 it covers both works: after that, it refers only to *Luria*.

The quotation is from 'To the Reader' in John Webster's play, *The White Divel* (1612), but Webster has 'their light', since he gives seven names, those of Chapman, Jonson, Beaumont and Fletcher, Shakespeare, Dekker, and Heywood. Browning admired Landor's *Imaginary Conversations* and Dramatic Scenes, but the dedication was no doubt inspired above all by the lines which Landor had addressed to him the previous year: see our frontispiece, and pp. 9–10 above. EBB praised the dedication as 'most graceful & complete', commenting: 'Landor will be gratified & grateful' (Kintner, ii. 599).

PERSONS.

LURIA, *a Moor, Commander of the Florentine Forces.*

HUSAIN, *a Moor, his friend.*

PUCCIO, *the old Florentine Commander, now* LURIA'S *chief officer.*

BRACCIO, *Commissary of the Republic of Florence.*

JACOPO (LAPO), *his secretary.*

TIBURZIO, *Commander of the Pisans.*

DOMIZIA, *a noble Florentine lady.*

SCENE.—LURIA'S *Camp between Florence and Pisa.*

TIME, 14—.

part title *1846* LURIA. A TRAGEDY IN FIVE ACTS. *1849–75* LURIA. A TRAGEDY. persons ('SCENE' and 'Time' in reverse order in *1846–75*)

Commissary: a (powerful) official representative or commissioner.

LURIA.

ACT I.

MORNING.

BRACCIO, *as dictating to his* Secretary; PUCCIO *standing by.*

Braccio [*to* PUCCIO]. Then, you join battle in an hour?

Puccio.   Not I;
Luria, the captain.

Braccio [*to the* Secretary]. "In an hour, the battle."
[*To* PUCCIO.] Sir, let your eye run o'er this loose digest,
And see if very much of your report
Have slipped away through my civilian phrase.   5
Does this instruct the Signory aright
How army stands with army?

Puccio [*taking the paper*].   All seems here:
—That Luria, seizing with our city's force
The several points of vantage, hill and plain,
Shuts Pisa safe from help on every side,   10
And, baffling the Lucchese arrived too late,
Must, in the battle he delivers now,
Beat her best troops and first of chiefs.

Braccio.   So sure?
Tiburzio's a consummate captain too!

---

*5 {reading of *1846–75*,DC,BrU,*1889*} *1888* phrase

6 *Signory*: 'A governing body, *esp.* that of Venice or other mediaeval Italian republic':
OED. Cf. *Othello*, I. ii. 18.

10 *Pisa*: Pisa occupied an important strategic position. It is 8 miles from the mouth of
the Arno, on which Florence is built.

11 *the Lucchese*: the forces of Lucca, a province of Italy with its capital, of the same
name, 13 miles NE of Pisa. As Porter and Clarke point out, Lucca 'was attached to the cause
of Pisa at this time, because hopeful of regaining its independence from the dominance of
Florence, and also because it had been united a century earlier with Pisa under Castruccio'.

12 *delivers*: 'to deliver battle' means to give battle.

 Puccio. Luria holds Pisa's fortune in his hand.   15
 Braccio [*to the* Secretary]. "The Signory hold Pisa in their hand."
Your own proved soldiership's our warrant, sir:
So, while my secretary ends his task,
Have out two horsemen, by the open roads,
To post with it to Florence!
 Puccio [*returning the paper*]. All seems here;   20
Unless . . . Ser Braccio, 't is my last report!
Since Pisa's outbreak, and my overthrow,
And Luria's hastening at the city's call
To save her, as he only could, no doubt;
Till now that she is saved or sure to be,—   25
Whatever you tell Florence, I tell you:
Each day's note you, her Commissary, make
Of Luria's movements, I myself supply.
No youngster am I longer, to my cost;
Therefore while Florence gloried in her choice   30
And vaunted Luria, whom but Luria, still,
As if zeal, courage, prudence, conduct, faith,
Had never met in any man before,
I saw no pressing need to swell the cry.
But now, this last report and I have done: 35
So, ere to-night comes with its roar of praise,
'T were not amiss if some one old i' the trade
Subscribed with, "True, for once rash counsel's best.

---

16 *1846* hand:" *1849* hand!   17 *1846* sir.   18 *1846* You, while
32 *1846* As courage, prudence, conduct, zeal and faith   34 *1846* cry:
38 *1846,1849* best;

 18 *So, while my secretary*: reading the proof, EBB quotes this line as 'And while my
secretary ends his task—', commenting: 'See if to write . . You, while my secretary ends his
task . . would be directer & more animated. It just strikes me.'
 20 *post*: travel rapidly.
 21 *Ser*: Master. Cf. 'In A Gondola', 192.
 28 *I myself supply*: EBB commented on the proof: '"Myself supply" . . Is that quite
correct? *I myself supply*—Myself supplies . . I doubt a little. Then a slight shadow seems to
fall over the meaning—one thinks twice. Why not "Of Luria's movements, I myself supply
. ." It is better perhaps than the "move".'
 31 *And vaunted*: EBB gives an earlier version of this line, 'And vaunted Luria Luria, who
but he?' and comments: '—*whom* but *him?* is it not?'

"This Moor of the bad faith and doubtful race,
"This boy to whose untried sagacity,   40
"Raw valour, Florence trusts without reserve
"The charge to save her,—justifies her choice;
"In no point has this stranger failed his friends.
"Now praise!" I say this, and it is not here.
    Braccio [*to the* Secretary]. Write, "Puccio, superseded in the
        charge,   45
"By Luria, bears full witness to his worth,
"And no reward our Signory can give
"Their champion but he'll back it cheerfully."
Aught more? Five minutes hence, both messengers!
                                    [Puccio *goes.*
    Braccio [*after a pause, and while he slowly tears the paper into shreds*].
I think ... (pray God, I hold in fit contempt   50
This warfare's noble art and ordering,
And,—once the brace of prizers fairly matched,
Poleaxe with poleaxe, knife with knife as good,—
Spit properly at what men term their skill!—)
Yet here I think our fighter has the odds.   55
With Pisa's strength diminished thus and thus,
Such points of vantage in our hands and such,
Lucca still off the stage, too,—all's assured:
Luria must win this battle. Write the Court,
That Luria's trial end and sentence pass!   60
    Secretary. Patron,—
    Braccio.   Ay, Lapo?
    Secretary.   If you trip, I fall;
'T is in self-interest I speak—
    Braccio.   Nay, nay,

43 *1846,1849* friends; *1863–75* friends: 44 *1846* praise"!   *48 [reading of
1846–75} *1888,1889* 'Their   49 s.d. *1846* †[*Exit* Puccio   50 *1846,1849* ...
pray   54 *1846,1849* skill ...   55 *1846,1849* odds;   58 *1846,1849*
With Lucca off   59 *1846* battle

    39 *This Moor of the bad faith*: EBB quotes these words and comments: 'You say afterwards
"The boy" & "the stranger" .. Why not "This boy" & "this stranger" to carry forward the
emphasis?'

    52 *prizers*: prize-fighters, as in *As You Like It*, II. iii. 8, and *Sordello*, v. 168.

    61 *Lapo*: an alternative name for Jacopo: see the list of 'Persons'.

You overshoot the mark, my Lapo! Nay!
When did I say pure love's impossible?
I make you daily write those red cheeks thin,   65
Load your young brow with what concerns it least,
And, when we visit Florence, let you pace
The Piazza by my side as if we talked,
Where all your old acquaintances may see:
You'd die for me, I should not be surprised.   70
Now then!
      Secretary. Sir, look about and love yourself!
Step after step, the Signory and you
Tread gay till this tremendous point's to pass;
Which pass not, pass not, ere you ask yourself,—
Bears the brain steadily such draughts of fire,   75
Or too delicious may not prove the pride
Of this long secret trial you dared plan,
Dare execute, you solitary here,
With the grey-headed toothless fools at home,
Who think themselves your lords, such slaves are they?   80
If they pronounce this sentence as you bid,
Declare the treason, claim its penalty,—
And sudden out of all the blaze of life,
On the best minute of his brightest day,

---

63 *1865* You overshot the   70 *1846–65* surprised!   74 *1846* yourself
80 *1846–65* lords, they are such slaves?

68 *The Piazza*: the Piazza della Signoria, in front of the building now known as the Palazzo Vecchio.

74 *Which pass not*: EBB quotes as 'Which pass not, to yourself no question put—', with an important and perceptive comment: 'You are fond of that *absolute* construction—but I think that sometimes it makes the meaning a little doubtful,—& here there is some weakness from the inversion—You simply mean to say . . "Which, do not pass without consideration". Then, the "*put*" is a bad word at all times to my ear.'

80 *Who think*: EBB quotes this line and asks: 'Do you gain anything by the inversion? If you write "they are such slaves", do you not on the contrary gain, in force of opposition, propriety of accent & directness—?' Browning took her advice from *1846* to *1865*, but reverted to his original word-order from *1868*.

81 *If they pronounce*: EBB quotes as 'If as you bid this sentence they pronounce', commenting 'I lean to protest against the frequent inversions', asking why he does not simply give the line as it is now printed: 'Is there an objection? And it gives the effect, I think, of more impulse, to these noble lines.'

From that adoring army at his back,   85
Thro' Florence' joyous crowds before his face,
Into the dark you beckon Luria. . . .
    Braccio.   Then—
Why, Lapo, when the fighting-people vaunt,
We of the other craft and mystery,
May we not smile demure, the danger past?   90
    Secretary. Sir, no, no, no,—the danger, and your spirit
At watch and ward? Where's danger on your part,
With that thin flitting instantaneous steel
'Gainst the blind bull-front of a brute-force world?
If Luria, that's to perish sure as fate,   95
Should have been really guiltless after all?
    Braccio. Ah, you have thought that?
    Secretary.   Here I sit, your scribe,
And in and out goes Luria, days and nights;
This Puccio comes; the Moor his other friend,
Husain; they talk—that's all feigned easily;   100
He speaks (I would not listen if I could),
Reads, orders, counsels:—but he rests sometimes,—
I see him stand and eat, sleep stretched an hour
On the lynx-skins yonder; hold his bared black arms
Into the sun from the tent-opening; laugh   105
When his horse drops the forage from his teeth
And neighs to hear him hum his Moorish songs.
That man believes in Florence, as the saint
Tied to the wheel believes in God.

---

*100 (reading of DC,BrU,*1889*) *1846–88* talk—all that's feigned   *104 (reading of
DC,BrU,*1889*) *1846–88* lynx-skins,   107 *1846* songs: *1849* songs,

    85 *From that adoring army*: EBB quotes with 'the adoring' and writes: 'Query . . From *that*
adoring . .'.

    89 *mystery*: trade.

    93 *that thin flitting*: EBB quotes these five words, and the next line (with 'Against'), com-
menting: 'How I like [this]': she underlines 94: 'It is a noble, expressive figure.'

    103 *I see him stand*: EBB comments: 'The description of Luria, too, admirable, or more.
The "bared black arms held out into the sun from the tent opening"—what a picture! And
the laugh when the horse drops the forage—one *knows* Luria from henceforth.' Cf. another
comment by EBB, quoted on p. 180 above.

    108–9 *the saint / Tied to the wheel*: possibly an allusion to St Catherine of Alexandria.

Braccio.   How strange!
You too have thought that!
       Secretary.   Do but you think too,   110
And all is saved! I only have to write,
"The man seemed false awhile, proves true at last,
"Bury it"—so I write the Signory—
"Bury this trial in your breast for ever,
"Blot it from things or done or dreamed about!   115
"So Luria shall receive his meed to-day
"With no suspicion what reverse was near,—
"As if no meteoric finger hushed
"The doom-word just on the destroyer's lip,
"Motioned him off, and let life's sun fall straight."   120
       Braccio [*looks to the wall of the tent*]. Did he draw that?
       Secretary.   With charcoal, when the watch
Made the report at midnight; Lady Domizia
Spoke of the unfinished Duomo, you remember;
That is his fancy how a Moorish front
Might join to, and complete, the body,—a sketch,—   125
And again where the cloak hangs, yonder in the shadow.
       Braccio. He loves that woman.
       Secretary.   She is sent the spy

---

109 *1846–65* God! .... strange—   112–13,114–20 {no quotation marks in *1846*,
1849}   112 *1846–75* last;   113 *1846–65* write to the   114 *1846–65*
your breasts for   115 *1846,1849* about, *1863,1865* about:

    110 *You too have thought that!*: 'Finely characteristic': EBB.
    113 *"Bury it"*: EBB quotes as 'Bury it .. so I write to Signory', and comments: 'I think you
ought to have the preposition, either by .. "Bury it ... write I to the Signory" .. or by
putting the "to" into the text as it is, which would not ruffle the line too much.'
    119 *doom-word*: given by OED[2] without any example.
    121 *Did he draw that?*: on reading the proof EBB quotes these words and comments: 'It
struck me before & does now again—why not .. for the sake of the myopic readers, (the
majority) .. put a direction here *"Looks to the wall of the tent"*—?' Browning did.
    124 *a Moorish front*: 'I return Mr. Radford's letter with many thanks', Browning wrote to
Furnivall in 1882: 'I never heard nor dreamed there had been any such notion at any time of
a Moorish Front for the Duomo—it was altogether a fancy of my own illustrative of the
feelings natural to Luria and Braccio each after his kind': *Trumpeter*, p. 48, which has a note
about such a suggestion which had been made in 1822. The Duomo is the cathedral of
Santa Maria del Fiore, at the centre of Florence.

Of Florence,—spies on you as you on him:
Florence, if only for Domizia's sake,
Is surely safe. What shall I write?
   Braccio.   I see—   130
A Moorish front, nor of such ill design!
Lapo, there's one thing plain and positive;
Man seeks his own good at the whole world's cost.
What? If to lead our troops, stand forth our chiefs,
And hold our fate, and see us at their beck,   135
Yet render up the charge when peace return,
Have ever proved too much for Florentines,
Even for the best and bravest of ourselves—
If in the struggle when the soldier's sword
Should sink its point before the statist's pen,   140
And the calm head replace the violent hand,
Virtue on virtue still have fallen away
Before ambition with unvarying fate,
Till Florence' self at last in bitterness
Be forced to own such falls the natural end,   145
And, sparing further to expose her sons
To a vain strife and profitless disgrace,
Declare, "The foreigner, one not my child,
"Shall henceforth lead my troops, reach height by height
"The glory, then descend into the shame;   150

---

130 *1846* Were surely   134 *1846* our chief,   136 *1846–65* peace returned,
140 *1846* Before the statist's pen should sink its point,   141 *1846* And to the calm
head yield the violent hand,   143 *1846* unvarying fortune,   145 *1846* own
defeat the natural end,   148 *1846* Have said, "The Foreigner, no child of mine,

  136 *Yet render up*: EBB quotes as 'And yet Renounce the same, its hour gone by', and
comments: 'This eloquence of Braccio should be quite uninvolved . . now should it not?—
the connection of the different sentences, seen clearly? Why not without the inversion?'

  137 *Have ever proved*: EBB writes out 137–42 and the first two words of 143, with the
comment: 'By shifting a few of the unimportant words so, you make it clear to run & read.
And then by this shifting, you escape a rather questionable-looking opposition of "after" &
"before", in "If virtue *after* virtue still have fallen *before* ambition".' She gives '*If*' at the
beginning of 139, and 140–3 as follows: 'Before the statist's pen should sink its point, /
And to the calm head, yield, the violent hand, / Virtue on virtue still have fallen away / Before
ambition.'

  140 *statist's*: 'statist' in the obsolete sense of statesman, politician.

"So shall rebellion be less guilt in him,
"And punishment the easier task for me:"
—If on the best of us such brand she set,
Can I suppose an utter alien here,
This Luria, our inevitable foe,   155
Confessed a mercenary and a Moor,
Born free from many ties that bind the rest
Of common faith in Heaven or hope on earth,
No past with us, no future,—such a spirit
Shall hold the path from which our staunchest broke,   160
Stand firm where every famed precursor fell?
My Lapo, I will frankly say, these proofs
So duly noted of the man's intent,
Are for the doting fools at home, not me.
The charges here, they may be true or false: 165
—What is set down? Errors and oversights,
A dallying interchange of courtesies
With Pisa's General,—all that, hour by hour,
Puccio's pale discontent has furnished us,
Of petulant speeches, inconsiderate acts,   170
Now overhazard, overcaution now;
Even that he loves this lady who believes
She outwits Florence, and whom Florence posted
By my procurement here, to spy on me,
Lest I one minute lose her from my sight—   175
She who remembering her whole House's fall,
That nest of traitors strangled in the birth,
Now labours to make Luria (poor device
As plain) the instrument of her revenge

152 *1846,1849* me"   153 *1846,1849* us this brand   *1846* she sets,
157 *1846–65* from any ties   *164 {reading of *1863–75*,DC,BrU,*1889*} *1846,1849*
me; *1888* me   165 *1846–65* false,   167 *1846,1849* This dallying
178 *1846–65* ... poor   179 *1846–65* plain ...   *1846–75* revenge!

   151 *So shall rebellion*: EBB quotes as 'So shall in him rebellion be less guilt, / And
punishment for me the easier task', adding: 'I propose still without the inversion', and then
writes the lines as printed. 'Is not the emphasis marked better so?', she asks, underlining the
last word of each line.
   171 *overhazard*: not in OED.

—That she is ever at his ear to prompt   180
Inordinate conceptions of his worth,
Exorbitant belief in worth's reward,
And after, when sure disappointment follows,
Proportionable rage at such a wrong—
Why, all these reasons, while I urge them most,   185
Weigh with me less than least—as nothing weigh.
Upon that broad man's-heart of his, I go:
On what I know must be, yet, while I live,
Shall never be, because I live and know.
Brute-force shall not rule Florence! Intellect   190
May rule her, bad or good as chance supplies:
But intellect it shall be, pure if bad,
And intellect's tradition so kept up
Till the good come—'t was intellect that ruled,
Not brute-force bringing from the battle-field   195
The attributes of wisdom, foresight's graces
We lent it there to lure its grossness on;
All which it took for earnest and kept safe
To show against us in our market-place,
Just as the plumes and tags and swordsman's-gear   200
(Fetched from the camp where, at their foolish best,
When all was done they frightened nobody)
Perk in our faces in the street, forsooth,
With our own warrant and allowance. No!

---

182 *1846–68* in its reward,   186 *1846–65* weigh!   187 *1846–65* go!
*188 {reading of DC,BrU,*1889*} *1846–88* yet while I live   189 *1846,1849* Will
never   *1846–65* know!   *193 {reading of *1846–65* and of RB's emendation in
the Pierpont Morgan copy of *1870*} *1868–75* up! *1888,1889* up.   194 *1846–65* good
comes—'twas

   185 *Why, all these reasons*: EBB quotes as 'Even these reasons while I urge them most' and
comments: 'This sounds to my ear *numerically* [i.e. metrically] a weak line—this setting of
"Even" as a dissyllable to open a line. "Why, even these reasons while I urge them most"
would seem to give more freedom—will you ring it, & listen?'
   187 *go*: proceed, rely.
   198 *All which*: EBB quotes with 'And which', asking: 'Did you mean to write "All
which"? a slip of the pen perhaps?'
   203 *Perk*: Johnson defines the verb as meaning "To hold up the head with an affected
briskness'. Cf. 'The Pied Piper', 153.

The whole procedure's overcharged,—its end   205
In too strict keeping with the bad first step.
To conquer Pisa was sheer inspiration?
Well then, to perish for a single fault,
Let that be simple justice! There, my Lapo!
A Moorish front ill suits our Duomo's body: 210
Blot it out—and bid Luria's sentence come!

> [LURIA, *who, with* DOMIZIA, *has entered unobserved at the close*
> *of the last phrase, now advances.*

    Luria. And Luria, Luria, what of Luria now?
    Braccio. Ah, you so close, sir? Lady Domizia too?
I said it needs must be a busy moment
For one like you: that you were now i' the thick   215
Of your duties, doubtless, while we idlers sat . . .
    Luria. No—in that paper,—it was in that paper
What you were saying!
    Braccio.   Oh—my day's despatch!
I censure you to Florence: will you see?
    Luria. See your despatch, your last, for the first time?   220
Well, if I should, now? For in truth, Domizia,
He would be forced to set about another,
In his sly cool way, the true Florentine,
To mention that important circumstance.
So, while he wrote I should gain time, such time!   225
Do not send this!
    Braccio.   And wherefore?
    Luria.   These Lucchese
Are not arrived—they never will arrive!
And I must fight to-day, arrived or not,
And I shall beat Tiburzio, that is sure:
And then will be arriving his Lucchese,   230
But slowly, oh so slowly, just in time

---

207 *1846* inspiration!   210 *1846* The Moorish   211 s.d. *1846–75 now
advancing.*   221 *1846* Why, if   224 *1846–65* circumstance;
228 *1849–68* not; *1870* not   229 *1846* sure,   230 *1846,1849* arriving my
Lucchese,

   219 *I censure you*: meant to sound like a joke, but in fact true.

To look upon my battle from the hills,
Like a late moon, of use to nobody!
And I must break my battle up, send forth,
Surround on this side, hold in check on that.   235
Then comes to-morrow, we negotiate,
You make me send for fresh instructions home,
—Incompleteness, incompleteness!
   Braccio.   Ah, we scribes!
Why, I had registered that very point,
The non-appearance of our foes' ally,   240
As a most happy fortune; both at once
Were formidable: single faced, each falls.
   Luria. So, no great battle for my Florentines!
No crowning deed, decisive and complete,
For all of them, the simple as the wise,   245
Old, young, alike, that do not understand
Our wearisome pedantic art of war,
By which we prove retreat may be success,
Delay—best speed,—half loss, at times,—whole gain:
They want results: as if it were their fault!   250
And you, with warmest wish to be my friend,
Will not be able now to simply say
"Your servant has performed his task—enough!
"You ordered, he has executed: good!
"Now walk the streets in holiday attire,   255
"Congratulate your friends, till noon strikes fierce,
"Then form bright groups beneath the Duomo's shade!"
No, you will have to argue and explain,
Persuade them, all is not so ill in the end,
Tease, tire them out! Arrive, arrive, Lucchese!   260
   Domizia. Well, you will triumph for the past enough,
Whatever be the present chance; no service
Falls to the ground with Florence: she awaits
Her saviour, will receive him fittingly.

233 *1846* nobody,—   235 *1846* that!   243 *1846* And so no battle
258 *1846–65* No!   262 *1846–1865* Present's chance—

Luria. Ah Braccio, you know Florence! Will she, think
    you,   265
Receive one . . . what means "fittingly receive"?
—Receive compatriots, doubtless—I am none:
And yet Domizia promises so much!
    Braccio. Kind women still give men a woman's prize.
I know not o'er which gate most boughs will arch,   270
Nor if the Square will wave red flags or blue.
I should have judged, the fullest of rewards
Our state gave Luria, when she made him chief
Of her whole force, in her best captain's place.
    Luria. That, my reward? Florence on my account   275
Relieved Ser Puccio?—mark you, my reward!
And Puccio's having all the fight's true joy—
Goes here and there, gets close, may fight, himself,
While I must order, stand aloof, o'ersee.
That was my calling, there was my true place!   280
I should have felt, in some one over me,
Florence impersonate, my visible head,
As I am over Puccio,—taking life
Directly from her eye! They give me you:
But do you cross me, set me half to work?   285
I enjoy nothing—though I will, for once!
Decide, shall we join battle? may I wait?
    Braccio. Let us compound the matter; wait till noon:
Then, no arrival,—
    Luria.   Ah, noon comes too fast!

---

265 *1846,1849* Florence . .   266 *1846,1849* receive?"   271 *1846,1849* blue—
1863,1865 blue: 278 *1846,1849* there, directs, may   279 *1846–65* o'ersee!
284 *1846,1849* you!   286 *1846–63* nothing—but I

276 *Ser Puccio*: cf. above, 21 n.

282 *Florence impersonate*: EBB quotes as 'Florence, to feel, in some one over me', and
comments: 'I quite understand . . but the construction is not clear notwithstanding. A word
will do it—And how fine & joyous & generous all this is of Luria!—And his turning (after-
wards) from the east's "drear vastness" [317], & the acclimating of his soul to the west . .
noble it is, as he speaks it.'

Cf. Keats, *Isabella*, 398: 'Love impersonate'.

285 *cross*: thwart.

I wonder, do you guess why I delay   290
Involuntarily the final blow
As long as possible? Peace follows it!
Florence at peace, and the calm studious heads
Come out again, the penetrating eyes;
As if a spell broke, all's resumed, each art   295
You boast, more vivid that it slept awhile.
'Gainst the glad heaven, o'er the white palace-front
The interrupted scaffold climbs anew;
The walls are peopled by the painter's brush;
The statue to its niche ascends to dwell.   300
The present noise and trouble have retired
And left the eternal past to rule once more;
You speak its speech and read its records plain,
Greece lives with you, each Roman breathes your friend:
But Luria—where will then be Luria's place?   305
    Domizia. Highest in honour, for that past's own sake,
Of which his actions, sealing up the sum
By saving all that went before from wreck,
Will range as part, with which be worshipped too.
    Luria. Then I may walk and watch you in your streets,   310
Lead the smooth life my rough life helps no more,
So different, so new, so beautiful—
Nor fear that you will tire to see parade
The club that slew the lion, now that crooks
And shepherd-pipes come into use again?   315
For very lone and silent seems my East
In its drear vastness: still it spreads, and still
No Braccios, no Domizias anywhere—
Not ever more! Well, well, to-day is ours!
    Domizia [*to* Braccio]. Should he not have been one of us?
    Luria.   Oh, no!   320
Not one of you, and so escape the thrill

295 *1865–75* all resumed,   296 *1863* that lept awhile. *1846,1849* awhile!
300 *1846,1849* dwell;   301 *1846–65* The Present's noise   302 *1846,1849*
more.——   304 *1846,1849* friend,   311 *1846–65* Leading the life

   298 *scaffold*: scaffolding.

Of coming into you, of changing thus,—
Feeling a soul grow on me that restricts
The boundless unrest of the savage heart!
The sea heaves up, hangs loaded o'er the land,   325
Breaks there and buries its tumultuous strength;
Horror, and silence, and a pause awhile:
Lo, inland glides the gulf-stream, miles away,
In rapture of assent, subdued and still,
'Neath those strange banks, those unimagined skies.   330
Well, 't is not sure the quiet lasts for ever!
Your placid heads still find rough hands new work;
Some minute's chance—there comes the need of mine:
And, all resolved on, I too hear at last.
Oh, you must find some use for me, Ser Braccio!   335
You hold my strength; 't were best dispose of it:
What you created, see that you find food for—
I shall be dangerous else!
    Braccio.   How dangerous, sir?
    Luria. There are so many ways, Domizia warns me,
And one with half the power that I possess,   340
—Grows very formidable. Do you doubt?
Why, first, who holds the army . . .
    Domizia.   While we talk,
Morn wears; we keep you from your proper place,
The field.
    Luria. Nay, to the field I move no more;
My part is done, and Puccio's may begin: 345
I cannot trench upon his province longer
With any face.—You think yourselves so safe?
Why, see—in concert with Tiburzio, now—
One could . . .
    Domizia.   A trumpet!

322 *1846,1849* you, and changing   330 *1846–65* skies!   332 *1846,1849* find
our hands   333 *1846–75* minutes'   336 *1846–63* it!   339 *1846–63*
Oh, there are many   341 *1846–75* formidable!   343 *1846,1849* wears,
344 *1846,1849* In the field!— *1863,1865* In the field.   *1846,1849* more!   345 *1846,
1849* begin! *1863,1865* begin.

Luria.   My Lucchese at last!
Arrived, as sure as Florence stands! Your leave!   350

                                        [*Springs out*.

    Domizia. How plainly is true greatness charactered
By such unconscious sport as Luria's here,
Strength sharing least the secret of itself!
Be it with head that schemes or hand that acts,
Such save the world which none but they could save,   355
Yet think whate'er they did, that world could do.
    Braccio. Yes: and how worthy note, that these same great ones
In hand or head, with such unconsciousness
And all its due entailed humility,
Should never shrink, so far as I perceive,   360
From taking up whatever tool there be
Effects the whole world's safety or mishap,
Into their mild hands as a thing of course!
The statist finds it natural to lead
The mob who might as easily lead him—   365
The captain marshals troops born skilled in war—
Statist and captain verily believe!
While we poor scribes . . . you catch me thinking now,
That I shall in this very letter write
What none of you are able! To it, Lapo!   370

                                        [DOMIZIA *goes*.

---

352 *1846–63* such unconsciousness as   353 *1846,1849* And sharing
357 *1846,1849* that those same   361 *1846–63* whatever offices | 362 *1846–*
63 Involve the   366 *1846,1849* The Soldier marshals men who know as much—
1863 The soldier marshals   367 *1846–63* and Soldier verily   370 s.d. *1846*
†[*Exit* DOMIZIA.

    351 *charactered*: portrayed, shown.
    357 *Yes*: EBB quotes this line with 'the truly great ones' at the end, and the comment: 'If
you put "*that* those same great ones", you make it clearer. To apprehend the construction at
once, the reader seeks a "that", it seems to me. The thought is excellent.'
    358 *unconsciousness*: having read the proof, EBB quotes as '*in*consciousness' and com-
ments: 'You always write inconsciousness—The word in general use is "*un*consciousness"—
English use! apart from your reasons.' Cf. 'A Bean-Stripe', 116 (in *Ferishtah's Fancies*).
'Inconsciously' remains at IV. 199, but in *Sordello*, VI. 148 it is revised to 'unconsciously' after
1865.
    362 *Effects*: which effects.

This last worst all-affected childish fit
Of Luria's, this be-praised unconsciousness,
Convinces me; the past was no child's play:
It was a man beat Pisa,—not a child.
All's mere dissimulation—to remove   375
The fear, he best knows we should entertain.
The utmost danger was at hand. Is 't written?
Now make a duplicate, lest this should fail,
And speak your fullest on the other side.

    Secretary. I noticed he was busily repairing   380
My half-effacement of his Duomo sketch,
And, while he spoke of Florence, turned to it,
As the Mage Negro king to Christ the babe.
I judge his childishness the mere relapse
To boyhood of a man who has worked lately,   385
And presently will work, so, meantime, plays:
Whence, more than ever I believe in him.

    Braccio [*after a pause*]. The sword! At best, the soldier, as he says,
In Florence—the black face, the barbarous name,
For Italy to boast her show of the age,   390
Her man of men! To Florence with each letter!

---

372 {no equivalent in *1846*}   375 *1846* 'Tis mere   377 *1846* hand. 'Tis writ-
ten?   378 *1846* make the duplicate,   382 *1846* And to it, while he spoke of
Florence, turned   383 *1863* Negro turns to   384 *1846,1849* the true relapse

    372 *be-praised*: as in Goldsmith, 'Retaliation', 118.

    373 *Convinces me*: EBB quotes as 'Convinces me . . no child's play was the Past', and com-
ments: 'Now if you wrote straightforwardly "Convinces me the past was no child's play . ."
is there an objection. Because there is a "most say" in the next line which occupies the
precisely corresponding place to "child's play" &, so, jingles . . or is it a mere fancy of mine?
And then, where nothing is gained by an inversion, the simpler form seems better.'

    378 *Now make*: EBB quotes the line as 'Now make the duplicate, if this should fail,' and
comments: 'quy. . . *lest* this should fail?'

    383 *the Mage Negro king*: one of the Magi, or wise men: Matt. 2. In Renaissance paintings
one of the Magi is commonly black. See the article by G. K. Hunter mentioned above,
p. 191 n. 3.

    386 *so, meantime, plays*: EBB quotes '—so plays—', and asks: 'Is the connection clear?—or
the meaning "even." Do you mean "so in plays" . . "it is so in plays". But then you set your
readers thinking . . or rather looking to the dictionary.'

    391 *Her man of men*: cf. *Sordello*, v. 766.

ACT II.

NOON.

Domizia. Well, Florence, shall I reach thee, pierce thy heart
Thro' all its safeguards? Hate is said to help—
Quicken the eye, invigorate the arm;
And this my hate, made up of many hates,
Might stand in scorn of visible instrument,   5
And will thee dead: yet do I trust it not.
Nor man's devices nor Heaven's memory
Of wickedness forgot on earth so soon,
But thy own nature,—hell and thee I trust,
To keep thee constant in that wickedness,   10
Where my revenge may meet thee. Turn aside
A single step, for gratitude or shame,—
Grace but this Luria,—this wild mass of rage

---

3 *1846,1849* arm,   4 *1846* made of so many   6 *1846* not;   11 *1846,*
1849 thee: 12 *1846* For gratitude a single step, or shame,—   13 *1846*
Grace thou this

  2 *Hate is said to help*: EBB quotes 2–3 as 'Thro' all its safeguards, pass 'twixt all the play / Of
arrowy wiles', and comments: 'Does it not look, at least, like a confusion of metaphor—
though a person may be defended from a dagger for instance, by a shower of arrows prevent-
ing the approach of an assassin—Still it would simplify it, if you made the means of defence
the seven folds of a shield, or the subtle linkings of a mail—Is it worth a consideration.'

  7 *Nor man's devices*: EBB quotes as 'Nor man's device, nor Heaven to keep in mind / The
wickedness forgot on earth too soon', asking: 'Might it be written "Nor man's devices, nor
Heaven's pure memory / Of wickedness forgot on earth too soon, / But thy own heart; 'tis
Hell, I trust, & thee / That firm thou keep &c".' She comments: 'I do not understand
exactly . . 'tis Hell & thee[.] If you wrote "it is for Hell & thee / To keep thy first course
firmly to the end" *that* would be clear,—but would it be as you desire?' From the revised
text as given in the proof she quoted 'Nor man's device nor Heaven's memory', and asked:
'Do you like "Heaven" as a disyllable? It always seems to make a weak line. Would not an
"S" to "device" remedy it unobjectionably?'

  13 *Grace . . . rage*: EBB quotes an earlier version, 'And this wild mass of rage that I prepare /
Luria, To launch against thee', and comments: 'Do observe that this line and a half seem to
have fallen down from the height of the argument into a strange place. It is a distracted con-
struction . . a little. Would it be straighter . . lie more coherently, if you wrote it somehow
thus . . "turn aside / For gratitude a single step, or shame . . / Grace thou this Luria, . . this wild
mass of rage / I now prepare to launch against thyself, ... / With other payment.'

I have prepared to launch against thee now,—
With other payment than thy noblest found,—   15
Give his desert for once its due reward,—
And past thee would my sure destruction roll.
But thou, who mad'st our House thy sacrifice,
It cannot be thou wilt except this Moor
From the accustomed fate of zeal and truth: 20
Thou wilt deny his looked-for recompense,
And then—I reach thee. Old and trained, my sire
Could bow down on his quiet broken heart,
Die awe-struck and submissive, when at last
The strange blow came for the expected wreath;   25
And Porzio passed in blind bewilderment
To exile, never to return,—they say,
Perplexed in his frank simple honest soul,
As if some natural law had changed,—how else
Could Florence, on plain fact pronouncing thus,   30
Judge Porzio's actions worthy such reward?
But Berto, with the ever-passionate pulse,
—Oh that long night, its dreadful hour on hour,
In which no way of getting his fair fame
From their inexplicable charges free,   35
Was found, save pouring forth the impatient blood
To show its colour whether false or no!
My brothers never had a friend like me

14 _1846–63_ That I prepare to   19 _1846_ thou dost except   22 _1846,1849_
thee!   31 _1846–65_ such an end?   36 _1846_ save to pour forth   37 _1846_
And show
___

25 _The strange blow_: EBB quotes as 'For the expected wreath the strange blow came', and
suggests the version printed.

30 _Could Florence_: EBB quotes as 'When Florence on plain fact pronouncing so / Could to
such actions such an end decree' and comments: 'You invert. . invert! Tell me if an air of stiff-
ness is not given by such unnecessary inversions. You throw important words too at arm's
length from their emphasis by it in this instance.'

31 _Judge Porzio's actions_: EBB suggests 'Could judge such actions worthy of such an end',
with a laconic 'quy.'

32 _Berto_: her other brother: cf. III. 292.

34 _In which no way_: EBB quotes 'not one / Possible way of getting his fair fame', and com-
ments: 'If you repeat "one", "not one / _One_ possible way of getting his fair fame" you
strengthen the line, do you not. It seems a willowy line otherwise.'

Close in their need to watch the time, then speak,
—Burst with a wakening laughter on their dream,   40
Cry, "Florence was all falseness, so, false here!"
And show them what a simple task remained—
To leave dreams, rise, and punish in God's name
The city wedded to the wickedness.
None stood by them as I by Luria stand.   45
So, when the stranger cheated of his due
Turns on thee as his rapid nature bids,
Then, Florence, think, a hireling at thy throat
For the first outrage, think who bore thy last,
Yet mutely in forlorn obedience died!   50
He comes—his friend—black faces in the camp
Where moved those peerless brows and eyes of old.

Enter LURIA *and* HUSAIN.

Domizia. Well, and the movement—is it as you hope?
'T is Lucca?
    Luria.   Ah, the Pisan trumpet merely!
Tiburzio's envoy, I must needs receive.   55
    Domizia. Whom I withdraw before; tho' if I lingered
You could not wonder, for my time fleets fast.
The overtaking night brings such reward!
And where will then be room for me? Yet, praised,
Remember who was first to promise praise,   60
And envy those who also can perform!   [*Goes.*
    Luria. This trumpet from the Pisans?—
    Husain.   In the camp;
A very noble presence—Braccio's visage

41 *1846,1849* Say, Florence   *1846* was one falsehood, so *1846–65* here,— {no quotation marks in *1846–65*}   44 *1846,1849* to its wickedness— *1863,1865* to its wickedness.
45 *1846–65* stand!   52 *1846–75* old!   56 *1846,1849* before; yet if
57 *1846,1849* fast;   58 *1846* brings Florence' praise   59 *1846* for mine? Yet
still *1849–65* Yet still   60 *1846–65* promise it,   61 *1846,1849* And envies
those *1863,1865* And envied those   s.d. *1846* †[*Exit.*

50 *Yet mutely*: EBB comments (on an earlier version which she saw in the proof): 'Observe the three concluding lines of Domizia's soliloquy—There is a rhyme between the last & the third from the bottom .. "died" .. "pride".'

On Puccio's body—calm and fixed and good;
A man I seem as I had seen before: 65
Most like, it was some statue had the face.
    Luria. Admit him! This will prove the last delay.
    Husain. Ay, friend, go on, and die thou going on!
Thou heardst what the grave woman said but now:
To-night rewards thee. That is well to hear;   70
But stop not therefore: hear it, and go on!
    Luria. Oh, their reward and triumph and the rest
They round me in the ears with, all day long?
All that, I never take for earnest, friend!
Well would it suit us,—their triumphal arch   75
Or storied pillar,—thee and me, the Moors!
But gratitude in those Italian eyes—
That, we shall get?
    Husain.   It is too cold an air.
Our sun rose out of yonder mound of mist:
Where is he now? So, I trust none of them.   80
    Luria. Truly?
    Husain.   I doubt and fear. There stands a wall
'Twixt our expansive and explosive race
And those absorbing, concentrating men.
They use thee.
    Luria.   And I feel it, Husain! yes,
And care not—yes, an alien force like mine   85
Is only called to play its part outside
Their different nature; where its sole use seems
To fight with and keep off an adverse force,
As alien,—which repelled, mine too withdraws:
Inside, they know not what to do with me.   90
Thus I have told them laughingly and oft,

---

67 *1846,1849* delay!   70 *1846,1849* thee! .... hear!   74 *1846* But that, I
never took for   77 *1846* Just gratitude   80 *1846–65* them!   83 *1846–*
65 men!   84 *1846–65* thee! .... Husain;   89 *1846* repelled, ours too
90 *1846–63* me;   91 *1846,1849* So I

    73 *They round me in the ears with*: whisper to me. Cf. *King John*, II. i. 566, and *The Ring and*
the Book, iv. 600.

But long since am prepared to learn the worst.

    Husain. What is the worst?

    Luria.   I will forestall them, Husain,

Will speak the destiny they dare not speak—

Banish myself before they find the heart.   95

I will be first to say, "The work rewards!

"I know, for all your praise, my use is over,

"So may it prove!—meanwhile 't is best I go,

"Go carry safe my memories of you all

"To other scenes of action, newer lands."—   100

Thus leaving them confirmed in their belief

They would not easily have tired of me.

You think this hard to say?

    Husain.   Say or not say,

So thou but go, so they but let thee go!

This hating people, that hate each the other,   105

And in one blandness to us Moors unite—

Locked each to each like slippery snakes, I say,

Which still in all their tangles, hissing tongue

And threatening tail, ne'er do each other harm;

While any creature of a better blood,   110

They seem to fight for, while they circle safe

And never touch it,—pines without a wound,

Withers away beside their eyes and breath.

See thou, if Puccio come not safely out

Of Braccio's grasp, this Braccio sworn his foe,   115

As Braccio safely from Domizia's toils

Who hates him most! But thou, the friend of all,

. . . Come out of them!

---

92 *1846,1849* since I prepared *1863,1865* since has prepared   94 *1846–65* And speak my destiny   95 *1846,1849* heart!   98 *1846,1849* it be!—meanwhile 99 *1846–1865* "And carry   100 *1846,1849* lands,"—   102 *1846,1849* me! 103 *1846–65* Say it or not,   109 *1846* At threatening   113 *1846,1849* away before their   115 *1846* grasp, the Braccio   116 *1846* And Braccio

    96 *I will be first to say*: about here there occurred two lines quoted by EBB: 'Devoted brows are to be crowned no longer / Whom the smile paid, or word of praise, so well—'. She comments: 'It is not clear . . will not be to the reader, I think—& a word or two more will answer the desired purpose.' The lines were cut.

Luria.   The Pisan trumpet now!
Husain. Breathe free—it is an enemy, no friend!   [*Goes.*
Luria. He keeps his instincts, no new culture mars   120
Their perfect use in him; just so the brutes
Rest not, are anxious without visible cause,
When change is in the elements at work,
Which man's trained senses fail to apprehend.
But here,—he takes the distant chariot wheel   125
For thunder, festal flame for lightning's flash,
The finer traits of cultivated life
For treachery and malevolence: I see!

Enter TIBURZIO.

Luria. Quick, sir, your message! I but wait your message
To sound the charge. You bring no overture   130
For truce? I would not, for your General's sake,
You spoke of truce: a time to fight is come,
And, whatsoe'er the fight's event, he keeps
His honest soldier's-name to beat me with,
Or leaves me all himself to beat, I trust!   135
Tiburzio. I am Tiburzio.
Luria.   You? 'T is—yes ... Tiburzio!
You were the last to keep the ford i' the valley
From Puccio, when I threw in succours there!
Why, I was on the heights—through the defile
Ten minutes after, when the prey was lost!   140
You wore an open skull-cap with a twist
Of water-reeds—the plume being hewn away;

119 s.d. *1846* †[*Exit.*   121 *1846* him; and so   125 *1846–63* chariot-wheels
126 *1846–63* festal fire for   128 *1846* see.   129 *1846,1849* message.
130 *1846–63* bring not overtures   *133 {reading of *1846–75*} *1888,1889* whatso'er
136 *1846* You? Ah, yes . .   140 *1849* lost;   141 *1846,1849* open scull-cap

133 *And, whatsoe'er the fight's event*: EBB quotes as 'And either way the fight's event, he
keeps', and comments: 'It would be clearer & more unquestionable if you wrote it, perhaps,
"And, let the fight end either way, he keeps . ." This is the pettiest, paltriest criticism of
straws! but just these straws hide the path, with you, sometimes.'

While I drove down my battle from the heights,
I saw with my own eyes!
   Tiburzio.   And you are Luria
Who sent my cohort, that laid down its arms   145
In error of the battle-signal's sense,
Back safely to me at the critical time—
One of a hundred deeds. I know you. Therefore
To none but you could I . . .
   Luria.   No truce, Tiburzio!
   Tiburzio. Luria, you know the peril imminent   150
On Pisa,—that you have us in the toils,
Us her last safeguard, all that intercepts
The rage of her implacablest of foes
From Pisa: if we fall to-day, she falls.
Tho' Lucca will arrive, yet, 't is too late.   155
You have so plainly here the best of it,
That you must feel, brave soldier as you are,
How dangerous we grow in this extreme,
How truly formidable by despair.
Still, probabilities should have their weight: 160
The extreme chance is ours, but, that chance failing,
You win this battle. Wherefore say I this?
To be well apprehended when I add,
This danger absolutely comes from you.
Were you, who threaten thus, a Florentine . . .   165
   Luria. Sir, I am nearer Florence than her sons.
I can, and have perhaps obliged the State,
Nor paid a mere son's duty.

---

148 *1846–75* you!   150 *1846,1849* peril's imminent   *152 (reading of *1846–75*,DC,BrU,*1889*) *1888* safeguard all   157 *1846* soldier that you   159 *1846* despair: 161 *1846–65* The extremest chance   *1846* ours;   162 *1846* battle:

146 *In error of*: misunderstanding.

152 *Us her last safeguard*: EBB quotes as 'Pisa's last safeguard, all to intercept / The rage of her implacablest of foes / From Pisa', and asks: 'Does the construction seem clear to yourself? Give us a little light.'

161 *extreme*: stressed on the first syllable, as usual in Browning.

167 *obliged the State*: cf. *Othello*, v. ii. 342: 'I have done the state some service'.

Tiburzio.   Even so.
Were you the son of Florence, yet endued
With all your present nobleness of soul,   170
No question, what I must communicate
Would not detach you from her.
        Luria.   Me, detach?
        Tiburzio. Time urges. You will ruin presently
Pisa, you never knew, for Florence' sake
You think you know. I have from time to time   175
Made prize of certain secret missives sent
From Braccio here, the Commissary, home:
And knowing Florence otherwise, I piece
The entire chain out, from these its scattered links.
Your trial occupies the Signory;   180
They sit in judgment on your conduct now.
When men at home inquire into the acts
Which in the field e'en foes appreciate . . .
Brief, they are Florentines! You, saving them,
Seek but the sure destruction saviours find.   185
        Luria. Tiburzio!
        Tiburzio.   All the wonder is of course.
I am not here to teach you, nor direct,
Only to loyally apprise—scarce that.
This is the latest letter, sealed and safe,
As it left here an hour ago. One way   190
Of two thought free to Florence, I command.
The duplicate is on its road; but this,—
Read it, and then I shall have more to say.

---

168 *1846–65* so!   173 *1846–65* urges: 178 *1846* otherwise, can piece
*179 [reading of *1846–75*,DC,BrU] *1888,1889* links   *1846* these scattered
181 *1846,1849* now!   185 *1846–65* Will seek the   186 *1846–65* Tiburzio—
1846,1849 course!   187 *1846* you, or direct,

    176 *Made prize of*: seized.
    179 *The entire chain*: EBB, having read the proof, suggested: 'The entire chain out from
these scattered links', commenting: 'Why not so—instead of the "his" or proposed "*its*"?
The meaning is clear.'
    186 *of course*: natural, to be expected.

Luria. Florence!
    Tiburzio.   Now, were yourself a Florentine,
This letter, let it hold the worst it can,   195
Would be no reason you should fall away.
The mother city is the mother still,
And recognition of the children's service
Her own affair; reward—there's no reward!
But you are bound by quite another tie.   200
Nor nature shows, nor reason, why at first
A foreigner, born friend to all alike,
Should give himself to any special State
More than another, stand by Florence' side
Rather than Pisa's; 't is as fair a city   205
You war against as that you fight for—famed
As well as she in story, graced no less
With noble heads and patriotic hearts:
Nor to a stranger's eye would either cause,
Stripped of the cumulative loves and hates   210
Which take importance from familiar view,
Stand as the right and sole to be upheld.
Therefore, should the preponderating gift
Of love and trust, Florence was first to throw,
Which made you hers, not Pisa's, void the scale,—   215
Old ties dissolving, things resume their place
And all begins again. Break seal and read!
At least let Pisa offer for you now!
And I, as a good Pisan, shall rejoice—
Though for myself I lose, in gaining you,   220
This last fight and its opportunity;
The chance it brings of saving Pisa yet,

---

200 *1846–65* tie;   *204 {reading of *1846–75*,BrU} *1888,1889* Florence
*205 {reading of *1846–65*} *1868–89* Pisa; 'tis   *206 {reading of DC,BrU,*1889*}
1846–88 against, as

  215 *Which made you hers*: quoting 213–14 as printed, and an earlier version of 215—
'Made you her own not Pisa's, void the scale'—she commented: 'I dare to propose "Which
made you her own not Pisa's, void the scale," because without it, the thread of meaning gets
entangled.'

Or in the turn of battle dying so
That shame should want its extreme bitterness.

    Luria. Tiburzio, you that fight for Pisa now   225
As I for Florence . . . say my chance were yours!
You read this letter, and you find . . . no, no!
Too mad!

    Tiburzio. I read the letter, find they purpose
When I have crushed their foe, to crush me: well?

    Luria. You, being their captain, what is it you do?   230

    Tiburzio. Why, as it is, all cities are alike;
As Florence pays you, Pisa will pay me.
I shall be as belied, whate'er the event,
As you, or more: my weak head, they will say,
Prompted this last expedient, my faint heart   235
Entailed on them indelible disgrace,
Both which defects ask proper punishment.
Another tenure of obedience, mine!
You are no son of Pisa's: break and read!

    Luria. And act on what I read? What act were fit?   240
If the firm-fixed foundation of my faith
In Florence, who to me stands for mankind,
—If that break up and, disimprisoning
From the abyss . . . Ah friend, it cannot be!
You may be very sage, yet—all the world   245
Having to fail, or your sagacity,
You do not wish to find yourself alone!
What would the world be worth? Whose love be sure?
The world remains: you are deceived!

    Tiburzio.   Your hand!
I lead the vanguard.—If you fall, beside,   250
The better: I am left to speak! For me,
This was my duty, nor would I rejoice

230 *1846* And you, their   232 {no equivalent in *1846*} *1849,1863* Pisa will pay me
much as Florence you;   242 *1849,1863* Florence, which to   243 *1846–63*
<u>that breaks up</u>   247 *1849* alone

    242 *stands for mankind*: cf. *Sordello*, iv. 1023.

If I could help, it misses its effect;
And after all you will look gallantly
Found dead here with that letter in your breast.   255
   Luria. Tiburzio—I would see these people once
And test them ere I answer finally!
At your arrival let the trumpet sound:
If mine return not then the wonted cry
It means that I believe—am Pisa's!
   Tiburzio.   Well!   [*Goes*.
   Luria. My heart will have it he speaks true! My blood   261
Beats close to this Tiburzio as a friend.
If he had stept into my watch-tent, night
And the wild desert full of foes around,
I should have broke the bread and given the salt   265
Secure, and, when my hour of watch was done,
Taken my turn to sleep between his knees,
Safe in the untroubled brow and honest cheek.
Oh world, where all things pass and nought abides,
Oh life, the long mutation—is it so?   270
Is it with life as with the body's change?
—Where, e'en tho' better follow, good must pass,
Nor manhood's strength can mate with boyhood's grace,
Nor age's wisdom, in its turn, find strength,
But silently the first gift dies away,   275
And though the new stays, never both at once.
Life's time of savage instinct o'er with me,
It fades and dies away, past trusting more,
As if to punish the ingratitude

---

255 *1846,1849* breast!   259 *1846–63* mine returns not   260 s.d. *1846* †[*Exit*.
262 *1846* friend;   264 *1846* the wide desert   268 *1846* the unclouded brow
*273 (reading of *1846–75*,DC,BrU,*1889*) *1888* grace   276 *1846–65* once!
277 *1846,1849* instinct's o'er

   254–5 *And after all*: EBB quotes the two lines and comments: 'Very fine all this is. I infinitely admire the whole interview between Luria & Tiburzio. Nothing can be nobler. And the suppressed emotion *tells*.'
   265 *broke the bread and given the salt*: in token of friendship.
   270 *Oh life, the long mutation*: cf. *King Lear*, iv. i. 10–12: 'World, world, O world! / But that thy strange mutations make us hate thee, / Life would not yield to age.'

With which I turned to grow in these new lights,   280
And learned to look with European eyes.
Yet it is better, this cold certain way,
Where Braccio's brow tells nothing, Puccio's mouth,
Domizia's eyes reject the searcher: yes!
For on their calm sagacity I lean,   285
Their sense of right, deliberate choice of good,
Sure, as they know my deeds, they deal with me.
Yes, that is better—that is best of all!
Such faith stays when mere wild belief would go.
Yes—when the desert creature's heart, at fault   290
Amid the scattering tempest's pillared sands,
Betrays its step into the pathless drift—
The calm instructed eye of man holds fast
By the sole bearing of the visible star,
Sure that when slow the whirling wreck subside,   295
The boundaries, lost now, shall be found again,—
The palm-trees and the pyramid over all.
Yes: I trust Florence: Pisa is deceived.

Enter BRACCIO, PUCCIO, *and* DOMIZIA.

Braccio. Noon's at an end: no Lucca? You must fight.
Luria. Do you remember ever, gentle friends,   300
I am no Florentine?
Domizia.   It is yourself
Who still are forcing us, importunately,

---

284 *1846* yes .. *1849* yes—   287 *1846* That as   289 *1846* when the wild
1846–65 go!   291 *1846* tempest and its sands,   292 *1846–63* its steps into
295 *1846–63* wreck subsides,   297 *1846* all!   298 *1849* deceived!
299 *1846* Lucca!

287 *Sure, as they know my deeds*: EBB quotes as 'That as they know my deeds, with me they
deal', and asks: 'Why not "That as they know my deeds, they deal with *me*"?', adding: 'Oh
this Luria! how great he is.'

290 *at fault*: having lost its way.

295 *the whirling wreck*: storm, or the mass of cloud driven by the storm. Cf. OED 'rack',
sb.[1] 2–3, and 'wrack', sb.5.b. Confusion in the spelling of the word is not uncommon.

297 *The palm-trees*: EBB quotes the line with 'o'er' and the comment: 'Dont coop up such
a wide desert-line by the contracted 'o'er', jangling with "all" too. There is room for "over
all" surely, said out broadly.'

To bear in mind what else we should forget.
    Luria. For loss!—for what I lose in being none!
No shrewd man, such as you yourselves respect,   305
But would remind you of the stranger's loss
In natural friends and advocates at home,
Hereditary loves, even rivalships
With precedent for honour and reward.
Still, there's a gain, too! If you take it so,   310
The stranger's lot has special gain as well.
Do you forget there was my own far East
I might have given away myself to, once,
As now to Florence, and for such a gift,
Stood there like a descended deity?   315
There, worship waits us: what is it waits here?

                              [Shows the letter.

See! Chance has put into my hand the means
Of knowing what I earn, before I work.
Should I fight better, should I fight the worse,
With payment palpably before me? See!   320
Here lies my whole reward! Best learn it now
Or keep it for the end's entire delight?
    Braccio. If you serve Florence as the vulgar serve,
For swordsman's-pay alone,—break seal and read!
In that case, you will find your full desert.   325
    Luria. Give me my one last happy moment, friends!
You need me now, and all the graciousness
This letter can contain will hardly balance
The after-feeling that you need no more.
This moment . . . oh, the East has use with you!   330

*303 {reading of *1846–75*} *1888,1889* forget   308 *1846* loves, or rivalships,
309 *1846–63* With precedents for   310 *1846* you recollect,   311 *1846–63*
well! *1865* well   316 *1846–63* worship greets us! what do I get here? *1865* us!
318 *1846–65* work!   320 *1846* With the crown palpably *1849,1863* With your
crown palpably   321 *1846–63* Best know it   *1846* now?   325 *1846–65*
desert! 327 *1846–63* the gratitude   328 *1846* letter may contain would never
balance *1849,1863* will never balance   329 *1846–65* that your need's at end!

   308 *rivalships*: cf. Jonson, *The Magnetic Lady*, II. iv. 21.
   312 *my own far East*: cf. Introduction, p. 190.
   330 *has use with you*: is of use to you.

Its sword still flashes—is not flung aside
With the past praise, in a dark corner yet!
How say you? 'T is not so with Florentines,
Captains of yours: for them, the ended war
Is but a first step to the peace begun: 335
He who did well in war, just earns the right
To begin doing well in peace, you know:
And certain my precursors,—would not such
Look to themselves in such a chance as mine,
Secure the ground they trod upon, perhaps?   340
For I have heard, by fits, or seemed to hear,
Of strange mishap, mistake, ingratitude,
Treachery even. Say that one of you
Surmised this letter carried what might turn
To harm hereafter, cause him prejudice: 345
What would he do?
    Domizia [*hastily*]. Thank God and take revenge!
Hurl her own force against the city straight!
And, even at the moment when the foe
Sounded defiance . . .
                [TIBURZIO's *trumpet sounds in the distance.*
    Luria.   Ah, you Florentines!
So would you do? Wisely for you, no doubt.   350
My simple Moorish instinct bids me clench
The obligation you relieve me from,
Still deeper! [*To* PUCCIO.] Sound our answer, I should say,
And thus:—[*tearing the paper.*]—The battle! That solves every
    doubt.

335 *1846–65* begun   337 *1846–65* know!   338 *1846* Now, certain
339 *1846–63* as this,   342 *1846–63* strange occurrences, ingratitude,
347 *1846–63* Turn her   *1846–65* straight,   350 *1846–75* doubt!
351 *1846* instinct leads to sink *1849,1863* me sink   352 *1846* you relieved me
353 *1846–65* say!   *354 (reading of *1868–75*,DC,BrU,*1889*) *1846–65* doubt! *1888*
doubt   *1846* thus! s.d. *1846* (*As the Trumpet answers, the scene shuts.*)

343 *Treachery even*: EBB quotes the line as ending '—Say that such an one', and com-
ments: 'The line seems to want strengthening by another syllable—"Of treachery even . ."? I
only ask.'

351 *clench*: clinch. Johnson gives the two spellings. OED notes the differentiation of
meaning as later.

ACT III.

Puccio, *as making a report to* Jacopo.

Puccio. And here, your captain must report the rest;
For, as I say, the main engagement over
And Luria's special part in it performed,
How could a subaltern like me expect
Leisure or leave to occupy the field   5
And glean what dropped from his wide harvesting?
I thought, when Lucca at the battle's end
Came up, just as the Pisan centre broke,
That Luria would detach me and prevent
The flying Pisans seeking what they found,   10
Friends in the rear, a point to rally by.
But no, more honourable proved my post!
I had the august captive to escort
Safe to our camp; some other could pursue,
Fight, and be famous; gentler chance was mine—   15
Tiburzio's wounded spirit must be soothed!
He's in the tent there.
    Jacopo.   Is the substance down?
I write—"The vanguard beaten and both wings
"In full retreat, Tiburzio prisoner"—
And now,—"That they fell back and formed again   20
"On Lucca's coming." Why then, after all,
'T is half a victory, no conclusive one?
    Puccio. Two operations where a sole had served.
    Jacopo. And Luria's fault was—?
    Puccio.   Oh, for fault—not much!
He led the attack, a thought impetuously,   25

4 *1846–63* could subalterns like myself expect *1865–75* could subaltern like myself expect
11 *1846,1849* by: 20 *1846* they fall back and form again

—There's commonly more prudence; now, he seemed
To hurry measures, otherwise well judged.
By over-concentrating strength at first
Against the enemy's van, both wings escaped:
That's reparable, yet it is a fault.   30

                    Enter BRACCIO.

   Jacopo. As good as a full victory to Florence,
With the advantage of a fault beside—
What is it, Puccio?—that by pressing forward
With too impetuous . . .
   Braccio.   The report anon!
Thanks, sir—you have elsewhere a charge, I know.   35
                             [PUCCIO *goes*.

There's nothing done but I would do again;
Yet, Lapo, it may be the past proves nothing,
And Luria has kept faithful to the close.
   Jacopo. I was for waiting.
   Braccio.   Yes: so was not I.
He could not choose but tear that letter—true!   40
Still, certain of his tones, I mind, and looks:—
You saw, too, with a fresher soul than I.
So, Porzio seemed an injured man, they say!
Well, I have gone upon the broad, sure ground.

                    Enter LURIA, PUCCIO, *and* DOMIZIA.

   Luria [*to* PUCCIO]. Say, at his pleasure I will see Tiburzio!   45
All's at his pleasure.
   Domizia [*to* LURIA]. Were I not forewarned
You would reject, as you do constantly,
Praise,—I might tell you how you have deserved
Of Florence by this last and crowning feat:

---

35 *1846* know s.d. *1846* †[*Exit* PUCCIO.   38 *1846,1849* the end! *1863* the end.
39 *1846,1849* I!   45 *1846–65* Tiburzio: 46 *1846–63* not so sure
48 *1846–63* you what you
   35 *charge*: duty.

But words offend.

    Luria.   Nay, you may praise me now.   50
I want instruction every hour, I find,
On points where once I saw least need of it;
And praise, I have been used to slight perhaps,
Seems scarce so easily dispensed with now.
After a battle half one's strength is gone;   55
The glorious passion in us once appeased,
Our reason's calm cold dreadful voice begins.
All justice, power and beauty scarce appear
Monopolized by Florence, as of late,
To me, the stranger: you, no doubt, may know   60
Why Pisa needs must bear her rival's yoke.
And peradventure I grow nearer you,
For I, too, want to know and be assured.
When a cause ceases to reward itself,
Its friend seeks fresh sustainments; praise is one,   65
And here stand you—you, lady, praise me well.
But yours—(your pardon)—is unlearned praise.
To the motive, the endeavour, the heart's self,
Your quick sense looks: you crown and call aright
The soul o' the purpose, ere 't is shaped as act,   70
Takes flesh i' the world, and clothes itself a king.
But when the act comes, stands for what 't is worth,
—Here's Puccio, the skilled soldier, he's my judge!
Was all well, Puccio?

    Puccio.   All was ... must be well:
If we beat Lucca presently, as doubtless ...   75
—No, there's no doubt, we must—all was well done.

50 *1846,1849* words are vain! *Lur.* Nay, *1863* words are vain. *Lur.* Nay,   *1846–65* now!
53 *1846–65* to do without,   54 *1846–63* Seems not so easy to dispense with
1846,1863,1865 now: *1849* now,   56–7 {no equivalent in *1846*}   56 *1849–65*
And glorious   61 *1846,1849* must give her rival place; *1863* must give her rival
place.   62 *1846–63* And I am growing nearer you, perhaps,   63 *1846*
assured: *1849* assured,   64 *1846* So, when a cause does not reward   65 *1846–*
63 friend needs fresh   66 *1846,1849* well!   67 *1846* —your pardon—
1846–65 praise: 70 *1846–68* of the   71 *1846,1849* king;   73 *1846,*
1849 soldier;

    68 *To the motive*: see EBB's praise of this passage quoted above, pp. 181–2.

   Luria. In truth? Still you are of the trade, my Puccio!
You have the fellow-craftsman's sympathy.
There's none cares, like a fellow of the craft,
For the all-unestimated sum of pains   80
That go to a success the world can see:
They praise then, but the best they never know
—While you know! So, if envy mix with it,
Hate even, still the bottom-praise of all,
Whatever be the dregs, that drop's pure gold!   85
—For nothing's like it; nothing else records
Those daily, nightly drippings in the dark
Of the heart's blood, the world lets drop away
For ever—so, pure gold that praise must be!
And I have yours, my soldier! yet the best   90
Is still to come. There's one looks on apart
Whom all refers to, failure or success;
What's done might be our best, our utmost work,
And yet inadequate to serve his need.
Here's Braccio now, for Florence—here's our service—   95
Well done for us, seems it well done for him?
His chosen engine, tasked to its full strength
Answers the end? Should he have chosen higher?
Do we help Florence, now our best is wrought?
   Braccio. This battle, with the foregone services,   100
Saves Florence.
   Luria.   Why then, all is very well!
Here am I in the middle of my friends,
Who know me and who love me, one and all.
And yet . . . 't is like . . . this instant while I speak
Is like the turning-moment of a dream   105

77 *1846–63* truth? But you   78 *1846,1849* sympathy!   79 *1846–63* none
knows like   80 *1846–63* | The all   82 *1846,1849* know: 83 *1846,*
1849 —But you   *1846–65* know!—Oh, if   90 *1846* soldier; *1849* soldier:
94 *1846,1849,1865* need: 96 *1846–63* us, is it   97 *1846* The chosen
98 *1849–65* Answers his end?   99 *1846–63* is done?   103 *1846–75* all!

   80 *all-unestimated*: a type of compound familiar in Shakespeare, e.g. in *King Lear*,
I. iv. 199.

   101 *Why then*: for EBB's praise of this passage, see Introduction, p. 182.

When ... Ah, you are not foreigners like me!
Well then, one always dreams of friends at home;
And always comes, I say, the turning-point
When something changes in the friendly eyes
That love and look on you ... so slight, so slight ...   110
And yet it tells you they are dead and gone,
Or changed and enemies, for all their words,
And all is mockery and a maddening show.
You now, so kind here, all you Florentines,
What is it in your eyes ... those lips, those brows ...   115
Nobody spoke it, yet I know it well!
Come now—this battle saves you, all's at end,
Your use of me is o'er, for good, for ill,—
Come now, what's done against me, while I speak,
In Florence? Come! I feel it in my blood,   120
My eyes, my hair, a voice is in my ears
That spite of all this smiling and soft speech
You are betraying me. What is it you do?
Have it your way, and think my use is over—
Think you are saved and may throw off the mask—   125
Have it my way, and think more work remains
Which I could do,—so, show you fear me not!
Or prudent be, or daring, as you choose,
But tell me—tell what I refused to know
At noon, lest heart should fail me! Well? That letter?   130
My fate is sealed at Florence! What is it?
    Braccio. Sir, I shall not deny what you divine.
It is no novelty for innocence
To be suspected, but a privilege:
Thereafter certain compensation comes.   135
Charges, I say not whether false or true,
Have been preferred against you some time since,

107 *1846,1849* home,   113 *1846,1849* show!   118 *1846–63* for evil,—
121 *1846–63* my ear   122 *1846–63* and kind speech   123 *1846–75* me!
125 *1846–63* That you   128 *1846–63* or generous, as   130 *1846* heart might
fail   131 *1846–63* is known at   132 *1846–63* not conceal what   *1846*
divine; *1849* divine: *135 {editors' emendation: all editions have 'The after'}

Which Florence was bound, plainly, to receive,
And which are therefore undergoing now
The due investigation. That is all.   140
I doubt not but your innocence will prove
Apparent and illustrious, as to me,
To them this evening, when the trial ends.
    Luria. My trial?
    Domizia.   Florence, Florence to the end,
My whole heart thanks thee!
    Puccio [*to* BRACCIO].   What is "trial," sir?   145
It was not for a trial—surely, no—
I furnished you those notes from time to time?
I held myself aggrieved—I am a man—
And I might speak,—ay, and speak mere truth, too,
And yet not mean at bottom of my heart   150
What should assist a—trial, do you say?
You should have told me!
    Domizia.   Nay, go on, go on!
His sentence! Do they sentence him? What is it?
The block—wheel?
    Braccio.   Sentence there is none as yet,
Nor shall I give my own opinion now   155
Of what it should be, or is like to be.
When it is passed, applaud or disapprove!
Up to that point, what is there to impugn?
    Luria. They are right, then, to try me?
    Braccio.   I assert,
Maintain and justify the absolute right   160
Of Florence to do all she can have done
In this procedure,—standing on her guard,
Receiving even services like yours
With utmost fit suspicious wariness.

141 *1846,1849* will shine   143 *1849* ends   148 *1846,1849* I hold myself
149 *1846* and the mere   153 *1846* sentence? What   154 *1846–63* block?
155 *1846–63* opinion here   156 *1846* be: *1849* be,

    142 *illustrious*: with a reminiscence of the obsolete sense, 'clearly manifest'.

In other matters, keep the mummery up!   165
Take all the experiences of all the world,
Each knowledge that broke through a heart to life,
Each reasoning which, to reach, burnt out a brain,
—In other cases, know these, warrant these,
And then dispense with these—'t is very well!   170
Let friend trust friend, and love demand love's like,
And gratitude be claimed for benefits,—
There's grace in that,—and when the fresh heart breaks,
The new brain proves a ruin, what of them?
Where is the matter of one moth the more   175
Singed in the candle, at a summer's end?
But Florence is no simple John or James
To have his toy, his fancy, his conceit
That he's the one excepted man by fate,
And, when fate shows him he's mistaken there,   180
Die with all good men's praise, and yield his place
To Paul and George intent to try their chance!
Florence exists because these pass away.
She's a contrivance to supply a type
Of man, which men's deficiencies refuse;   185

---

166 *1846–63* of the whole world,   168 *1846–63* to work out, cost a
170 *1846–63* with them—'tis   171 *1846–63* demand its like,   174 *1846–63*
a martyr, what   *1846,1849* of it?   182 *1846,1849* chance: 183 *1846–63*
away; *1865* away: 185 *1846* mens'

166 *Take all*: commenting on the proof, EBB quotes as 'Let all the experiences of the
whole world', and asks: '*do what? be what?* How is the construction here? Know these—
warrant these—. Still I think that you might by a word make it clearer. The noble passage
deserves all possible lights along it.'
    Somewhere before this occurred the line 'Nor did this urge me, that if judge I must'.
EBB commented: 'You will wonder when I complain of darkness here—but certainly it is
doubtfully worded.—"Nor did this urge me".' Browning deleted the line.
    167 *Each knowledge*: EBB, on reading the MS, wrote out this line, as we have it, with the
next as 'Each reasoning it cost a brain to yield', and commented: 'A noble first line &
thought! and should you not interpose a word in the second . . "Each reasoning *that* it cost"
&c or if you wrote . . Each reasoning which to work out, cost a brain. Oh . . it is only that the
second line appears to sound feebly in comparison with the great thing it has to say, & also
with the great line preceding it in utterance—And then I write down what comes into my
head. Braccio's fortification of Florence is (for the rest) very subtle & noble—One half for-
gives Braccio in it.'
    170 *'t is very well*: an echo of the last line of *The Cenci*.

She binds so many, that she grows out of them—
Stands steady o'er their numbers, though they change
And pass away—there's always what upholds,
Always enough to fashion the great show.
As see, yon hanging city, in the sun,   190
Of shapely cloud substantially the same!
A thousand vapours rise and sink again,
Are interfused, and live their life and die,—
Yet ever hangs the steady show i' the air,
Under the sun's straight influence: that is well,   195
That is worth heaven should hold, and God should bless!
And so is Florence,—the unseen sun above,
Which draws and holds suspended all of us,
Binds transient vapours into a single cloud
Differing from each and better than they all.   200
And shall she dare to stake this permanence
On any one man's faith? Man's heart is weak,
And its temptations many: let her prove
Each servant to the very uttermost
Before she grant him her reward, I say!   205
    Domizia. And as for hearts she chances to mistake,
Wronged hearts, not destined to receive reward,
Though they deserve it, did she only know,
—What should she do for these?
    Braccio.   What does she not?
Say, that she gives them but herself to serve!   210
Here's Luria—what had profited his strength,
When half an hour of sober fancying
Had shown him step by step the uselessness
Of strength exerted for strength's proper sake?
But the truth is, she did create that strength,   215

186 *1846* many, she   189 *1846,1849* show!   195 *1846–63* well!
196 *1846–70* Heaven to hold, and God to bless!   198 *1846* That draws
199 *1846–63* transient mists and vapours into one   207 *1846,1849* That are not
208 {no equivalent in *1846*} *1849–75* know!   214 *1846–65* for its proper

    193 *interfused*: cf. *Paradise Lost*, vii. 89, as well as Wordsworth, 'Tintern Abbey', 96.
    214 *proper*: own.

Draw to the end the corresponding means.
The world is wide—are we the only men?
Oh, for the time, the social purpose' sake,
Use words agreed on, bandy epithets,
Call any man the sole great wise and good!   220
But shall we therefore, standing by ourselves,
Insult our souls and God with the same speech?
There, swarm the ignoble thousands under him:
What marks us from the hundreds and the tens?
Florence took up, turned all one way the soul   225
Of Luria with its fires, and here he glows!
She takes me out of all the world as him,
Fixing my coldness till like ice it checks
The fire! So, Braccio, Luria, which is best?

    Luria. Ah, brave me? And is this indeed the way   230
To gain your good word and sincere esteem?
Am I the baited animal that must turn
And fight his baiters to deserve their praise?
Obedience is mistake then? Be it so!
Do you indeed remember I stand here   235
The captain of the conquering army,—mine—
With all your tokens, praise and promise, ready
To show for what their names meant when you gave,
Not what you style them now you take away?
If I call in my troops to arbitrate,   240
And dash the first enthusiastic thrill
Of victory with this you menace now—
Commend to the instinctive popular sense,

216 *1846–65* Drew to   220 *1846–63* man, sole Great and Wise   226 *1846–*
63 he stands!   228 *1846,1849* it stays   232 *1846–65* baited tiger that
234 *1846–65* Obedience has no fruit then?   238 *1846–65* names were when
241 *1846–65* And in their first   242 *1846–63* victory, tell them how you menace
me— *1865* victory, tell them this   243 *1846–65* Commending to their plain
instinctive sense,

    230 *brave*: defy.

    238 *To show*: about here there was a line, quoted by EBB: 'Who did the several acts your-
selves gave names'. She comments: 'you mean "gave names to". Then why not say "your-
selves have named"—for clearness.' The line disappeared.

My story first, your comment afterward,—
Will they take, think you, part with you or me?　　　　　245
If I say—I, the labourer they saw work,
Ending my work, ask pay, and find my lords
Have all this while provided silently
Against the day of pay and proving faith,
By what you call my sentence that's to come—　　　　　250
Will friends advise I wait complacently?
If I meet Florence half way at their head,
What will you do, my mild antagonist?

　　　Braccio. I will rise up like fire, proud and triumphant
That Florence knew you thoroughly and by me,　　　　　255
And so was saved. "See, Italy," I'll say,
"The crown of our precautions! Here's a man
"Was far advanced, just touched on the belief
"Less subtle cities had accorded long;
"But we were wiser: at the end comes this!"　　　　　260
And from that minute, where is Luria? Lost!
The very stones of Florence cry against
The all-exacting, nought-enduring fool
Who thus resents her first probation, flouts
As if he, only, shone and cast no shade,　　　　　265
He, only, walked the earth with privilege
Against suspicion, free where angels fear:
He, for the first inquisitive mother's-word,

---

246 *1846–63* When I say simply, I, the man they know, *1865* When I say, I, the labourer they know,　　　247 *1846–65* ask payment, and find Florence　　　248 *1846–65* Has all　　　249 *1846–65* proving words,　　　251 *1846–65* Will they sit waiting it complacently?　　　252 *1846–65* When I resist that sentence at　　　254 *1846* Then I will rise like　　　256 *1846,1849* saved:　　　257 *1846–65* "The need of *1846,1849* precautions—　　　258 *1846–65* the reward　　　259 *1846–65* accorded him—　　　261 *1846–63* minute all your strength will go— *1865* minute all your strength expires.　　　263 *1846–63* all-exacting, unenduring Luria, *1865* all-exacting, unenduring fool,　　　264 *1846–65* Resenting her first slight probation thus {*1849* thus, *1863,1865* thus;}　　　267 *1846–65* free from causing fear—　　　268 *1846–65* So, for

　　262 *The very stones*: cf. *Julius Caesar*, III. ii. 230, *Macbeth*, II. i. 57–8, and Luke 19:40.

　　267 *where angels fear*: cf. Pope, *An Essay on Criticism*, 625.

Must turn, and stand on his defence, forsooth!
Reward? You will not be worth punishment!   270
    Luria. And Florence knew me thus! Thus I have lived,—
And thus you, with the clear fine intellect,
Braccio, the cold acute instructed mind,
Out of the stir, so calm and unconfused,
Reported me—how could you otherwise!   275
Ay?—and what dropped from you, just now, moreover?
Your information, Puccio?—Did your skill,
Your understanding sympathy approve
Such a report of me? Was this the end?
Or is even this the end? Can I stop here?   280
You, lady, with the woman's stand apart,
The heart to see with, past man's brain and eyes,
. . . I cannot fathom why you should destroy
The unoffending one, you call your friend—
Still, lessoned by the good examples here   285
Of friendship, 't is but natural I ask—
Had you a further aim, in aught you urged,
Than your friend's profit—in all those instances
Of perfidy, all Florence wrought of wrong—
All I remember now for the first time?   290
    Domizia. I am a daughter of the Traversari,
Sister of Porzio and of Berto both,
So, have foreseen all that has come to pass.

---

269 *1846* Turned round and stood on *1849–65* He turned, and stood on   269a *1846*
 And you will sink into the savage back.   276 *1846–65 you*,   278 *1846–65*
And understanding   280 *1846* is this the end even? Can I stop?   *1849,1863* here—
282 *1846,1849* with, not those learned eyes, *1863* with, not man's learned eyes, *1865* with,
not man's brain and eyes,   283 *1846* you would destroy me,—   284–5 {no
equivalent in *1846*}   284 *1849* unoffending man, you   285 *1849–65* So,
looking at the   286 *1846* It is but natural, therefore, I should ask   287 *1846–*
63 further end, in all you spoke, *1865* you spoke,   288–9 {no equivalent in *1846*}
288 *1849,1863* Than profit to me, in those *1865* Than profit to me,— all   289 *1849,*
1863 perfidy from Florence to her chiefs—   292 *1846–63* both. *1865–70* both:
293 *1846–63* I have   *1846* pass:

   291 *the Traversari*: in the early thirteenth century the Traversari were a wealthy and
powerful family in Ravenna. On the death of Paolo Traversari in 1240, however, the glory
of the 'domus Traversariorum' became a thing of the past.

I knew the Florence that could doubt their faith,
Must needs mistrust a stranger's—dealing them   295
Punishment, would deny him his reward.
And I believed, the shame they bore and died,
He would not bear, but live and fight against—
Seeing he was of other stuff than they.
    Luria. Hear them! All these against one foreigner!   300
And all this while, where is, in the whole world,
To his good faith a single witness?
    Tiburzio [*who has entered unseen during the preceding dialogue*].
                         Here!
Thus I bear witness, not in word but deed.
I live for Pisa; she's not lost to-day
By many chances—much prevents from that!   305
Her army has been beaten, I am here,
But Lucca comes at last, one happy chance!
I rather would see Pisa three times lost
Than saved by any traitor, even by you;
The example of a traitor's happy fortune   310
Would bring more evil in the end than good;—
Pisa rejects the traitor, craves yourself!
I, in her name, resign forthwith to you
My charge,—the highest office, sword and shield!
You shall not, by my counsel, turn on Florence   315
Your army, give her calumny that ground—
Nor bring one soldier: be you all we gain!
And all she'll lose,—a head to deck some bridge,
And save the cost o' the crown should deck the head.
Leave her to perish in her perfidy,   320

295 *1846–65* stranger's—holding back   296 *1846–65* Reward from them, must hold back his reward.   297 *1846* believed, that shame   302 s.d. *1846–65 entered during*   303 *1846–65* witness to it, not in word | 304 *1846–65* But deed. I live for Pisa; she's not lost   307 *1846–65* one chance exists.   308 *1846, 1849* rather had see   309 *1846* even you. *1849* you.   311 *1846,1849* good.   312 *1846–65* rejects such: save yourself and her!   314 *1846–65* highest of her offices.   316 *1846–65* Her army,   317 *1846* bring it with you: you are all   *1849–65* bring it with you: be   *1846,1849* gain,   319 *1846–63* the crown's cost that should

Plague-stricken and stripped naked to all eyes,
A proverb and a by-word in all mouths!
Go you to Pisa! Florence is my place—
Leave me to tell her of the rectitude,
I, from the first, told Pisa, knowing it.   325
To Pisa!
    Domizia. Ah my Braccio, are you caught?
    Braccio. Puccio, good soldier and good citizen,
Whom I have ever kept beneath my eye,
Ready as fit, to serve in this event
Florence, who clear foretold it from the first—   330
Through me, she gives you the command and charge
She takes, through me, from him who held it late!
A painful trial, very sore, was yours:
All that could draw out, marshal in array
The selfish passions 'gainst the public good—   335
Slights, scorns, neglects, were heaped on you to bear:
And ever you did bear and bow the head!
It had been sorry trial, to precede
Your feet, hold up the promise of reward
For luring gleam; your footsteps kept the track   340
Thro' dark and doubt: take all the light at once!
Trial is over, consummation shines;
Well have you served, as well henceforth command!
    Puccio. No, no . . . I dare not! I am grateful, glad;
But Luria—you shall understand he's wronged: 345
And he's my captain: this is not the way
We soldiers climb to fortune: think again!
The sentence is not even passed, beside!
I dare not: where's the soldier could?
    Luria.   Now, Florence—
Is it to be? You will know all the strength   350

---

*322 {editors' emendation} *1846,1849* a bye word *1863–75* a bye-word *1888,1889* and by-
word   *1846* in men's mouths!   323 *1846,1849* Pisa—   327 *1846–65* and
selected man,   343 *1846* Well you have served,   344 *1846* No. no . .
1846,1849 not . .

    322 *A proverb and a by-word*: cf. 1 Kgs. 9:7.

O' the savage—to your neck the proof must go?
You will prove the brute nature? Ah, I see!
The savage plainly is impassible:
He keeps his calm way through insulting words,
Sarcastic looks, sharp gestures—one of which   355
Would stop you, fatal to your finer sense,
But if he stolidly advance, march mute
Without a mark upon his callous hide,
Through the mere brushwood you grow angry with,
And leave the tatters of your flesh upon,   360
—You have to learn that when the true bar comes,
The murk mid-forest, the grand obstacle,
Which when you reach, you give the labour up,
Nor dash on, but lie down composed before,
—He goes against it, like the brute he is: 365
It falls before him, or he dies in his course.
I kept my course through past ingratitude:
I saw—it does seem, now, as if I saw,
Could not but see, those insults as they fell,
—Ay, let them glance from off me, very like,   370
Laughing, perhaps, to think the quality
You grew so bold on, while you so despised
The Moor's dull mute inapprehensive mood,
Was saving you: I bore and kept my course.
Now real wrong fronts me: see if I succumb!   375
Florence withstands me? I will punish her.

351 *1846–68* Of the   355 *1846* Cold looks, sharp gestures—any one
356 *1846* you and offend your   *1846–65* sense: *1868–75* sense.   357 *1846* he
steadily pursues the path *1849,1863* he steadily advances, still *1865* he steadily advance, still
march   *359 {reading of *1846–75*,DC; comma missing or imperfectly printed in
some copies of *1888,1889*}   *361 {reading of *1846–75*,DC,*1889*} *1888* {some copies}
comes   362 *1846–63* The thick mid forest, the real obstacle, *1863* {as *1846,1849* but
'mid-forest'} *1865* The thick mid-forest,   365 *1846–65* is!   366 *1846–65*
course!   374 *1846,1849* you; *1863* you.   *1846,1849* course: 376 *1846–65*
her!

353 *impassible*: 'Incapable of suffering; . . . exempt from pain': Johnson.
365 *He goes against it*: EBB quotes as 'He goes on like the brute he is *against*', and asks:
'Did you mean to write "against", & not rather "until"?' She adds: 'The interest is carried
nobly on through this act—Poor Luria!—'
376 This line ends the verse-paragraph.

At night my sentence will arrive, you say.
Till then I cannot, if I would, rebel
—Unauthorized to lay my office down,
Retaining my full power to will and do: 380
After—it is to see. Tiburzio, thanks!
Go; you are free: join Lucca! I suspend
All further operations till to-night.
Thank you, and for the silence most of all!
[*To* BRACCIO.] Let my complacent bland accuser go   385
Carry his self-approving head and heart
Safe through the army which would trample him
Dead in a moment at my word or sign!
Go, sir, to Florence; tell friends what I say—
That while I wait my sentence, theirs waits them!   390
[*To* DOMIZIA.] You, lady,—you have black Italian eyes!
I would be generous if I might: oh, yes—
For I remember how so oft you seemed
Inclined at heart to break the barrier down
Which Florence finds God built between us both.   395
Alas, for generosity! this hour
Asks retribution: bear it as you may,
I must—the Moor—the savage,—pardon you!
Puccio, my trusty soldier, see them forth!

377 *1846–65* say!   379 {no equivalent in *1846*}   382 *1846–65* Lucca.
383 *1846* till the night.   385 *1846* my self-justified accuser   386 {no equi-
valent in *1846*} *1849,1863* And carry   390 *1846–63* wait their sentence,   *1846*
them.   391 *1846* have dark Italian   393 *1846* When I .... oft it seemed
394 *1846* You were inclined to   395 *1846* And lift me to you .. all that praise of
old! *1849* Florence makes God build between   396 *1846* generosity—
397 *1846–63* Demands strict justice—bear   *1846–65* may!   398 *1863,1865* you.
399 *1846–63* (*To Puc.*) Puccio,

ACT IV.

Enter Puccio *and* Jacopo.

Puccio. What Luria will do? Ah, 't is yours, fair sir,
Your and your subtle-witted master's part,
To tell me that; I tell you what he can.
    Jacopo. Friend, you mistake my station: I observe
The game, watch how my betters play, no more.   5
    Puccio. But mankind are not pieces—there's your fault!
You cannot push them, and, the first move made,
Lean back and study what the next shall be,
In confidence that, when 't is fixed upon,
You find just where you left them, blacks and whites: 10
Men go on moving when your hand's away.
You build, I notice, firm on Luria's faith
This whole time,—firmlier than I choose to build,
Who never doubted it—of old, that is—
With Luria in his ordinary mind.   15
But now, oppression makes the wise man mad:
How do I know he will not turn and stand
And hold his own against you, as he may?
Suppose he but withdraw to Pisa—well,—
Then, even if all happen to your wish,   20
Which is a chance . . .

---

1 *1849–65 will*   2 *1865–75* You and   4 *1846,1849* station!   8 *1846–*
63 back to study   *1846–65* next should be,   9 *1846* fixed at length,
10 *1846–65* You'll find   15 *1846–65* mind: 16 *1846,1849* mad—
1863,1865 mad.   19 *1846* But say that he withdraws to *1849* Suppose that he with-
draws to *1863* but withdraws to   20 *1846–63* all happens to

    2 *subtle-witted*: as in *Hudibras*, II. iii. 470, and Shelley's translation of the Homeric 'Hymn
to Mercury', 518.

    10 *You find*: EBB quotes as 'Just where you left them blacks & whites you'll find' and,
quoting the line as printed (but for 'You'll find' at the beginning), demands: 'Why not, O
you inverter'. She adds: 'I like the thought very much.'

Jacopo.   Nay—'t was an oversight,
Not waiting till the proper warrant came:
You could not take what was not ours to give.
But when at night the sentence really comes,
Our city authorizes past dispute   25
Luria's removal and transfers the charge,
You will perceive your duty and accept?
    Puccio. Accept what? muster-rolls of soldiers' names?
An army upon paper? I want men,
The hearts as well as hands—and where's a heart   30
But beats with Luria, in the multitude
I come from walking through by Luria's side?
You gave them Luria, set him thus to grow,
Head-like, upon their trunk; one heart feeds both,
They feel him there, live twice, and well know why.   35
—For they do know, if you are ignorant,
Who kept his own place and respected theirs,
Managed their sweat, yet never spared his blood.
All was your act: another might have served—
There's peradventure no such dearth of heads—   40
But you chose Luria: so, they grew one flesh,
And now, for nothing they can understand,
Luria removed, off is to roll the head;
The body's mine—much I shall do with it!
    Jacopo. That's at the worst.
    Puccio.   No—at the best, it is!   45
Best, do you hear? I saw them by his side.

25 *1846–65* And Florence authorizes   26 *1846–65* and your own advance,
30 *1846–65* Their hearts   31 *1846–63* That's not with   33 *1846,1849* gave
him to them, set   *1846–63* him on to   34 *1846* A head upon   *1846–65* trunk,
1846–63 one blood feeds   35 *1846–65* there and live and   *1846* why *1849–65*
why!   37 *1846* and kept theirs alike,—   38 *1846–63* their ease, yet
1846 his own: *1849,1863* his own.   39 *1846–63* your deed: another   40 *1846–
65* of men—   41 *1865–70* you choose Luria—   *1846,1849* grew to him:
1863,1865 grew to him.   43 *1846–63* Luria's removed,   45 *1846,1849* worst!
46 *1846* side: *1849* side;

34 *upon their trunk*: by grafting. Cf. *Sordello*, iii. 477, and *A Blot in the 'Scutcheon*, i. iii. 51.
41 *one flesh*: cf. Gen. 2:24.

Only we two with Luria in the camp
Are left that keep the secret? You think that?
Hear what I know: from rear to van, no heart
But felt the quiet patient hero there   50
Was wronged, nor in the moveless ranks an eye
But glancing told its fellow the whole story
Of that convicted silent knot of spies
Who passed thro' them to Florence; they might pass—
No breast but gladlier beat when free of such!   55
Our troops will catch up Luria, close him round,
Bear him to Florence as their natural lord,
Partake his fortune, live or die with him.

    Jacopo. And by mistake catch up along with him
Puccio, no doubt, compelled in self despite   60
To still continue second in command!

    Puccio. No, sir, no second nor so fortunate!
Your tricks succeed with me too well for that!
I am as you have made me, live and die
To serve your end—a mere trained fighting-hack,   65
With words, you laugh at while they leave your mouth,
For my life's rule and ordinance of God!
I have to do my duty, keep my faith,
And earn my praise, and guard against my blame,
As I was trained. I shall accept your charge,   70
And fight against one better than myself,

---

48 *1846–65* that know the *1846* secret? That you think?   49 *1846–65* I saw: from
55 *1846,1849* of them!   57 *1846–63* Lead him   58 *1846–63* his fortunes,
live   *1846,1849* him!   64 *1846–65* me, and shall die   65 *1846–65* A mere
trained fighting hack to serve your end;   *66 {reading of *1846–75*,DC,BrU,*1889*}
1888 mouth   67 *1846–63* life's rules and   68 *1846* Duty have I to do, and
faith to keep,   69 *1846* And praise to earn, and blame to guard against,

    51 *moveless*: a favourite word with Shelley: e.g. *The Revolt of Islam*, v. 2287.

    63 *Your tricks*: EBB queries an earlier reading, 'Your tricks with me too well succeed for
that', and suggests that which Browning here adopts. 'Is there an objection', she asks.
    About here there was a line, 'Set for your heart on stoutness ne'er so firm', 'Which line',
EBB commented, 'I do *not* very much like. I dont like a firm stoutness, or a heart set firmly
on stoutness . . read it any way, & I set about objecting.'
    68 *I have to do my duty*: EBB quotes as 'Duty to do have I, & faith to keep', and queries a
change to 'Duty have I to do'. Browning goes further from inversion. 'Puccio speaks admir-
ably yet like a soldier', EBB comments.

Spite of my heart's conviction of his worth—
That, you may count on!—just as hitherto
I have gone on, persuaded I was wronged,
Slighted, insulted, terms we learn by rote,—   75
All because Luria superseded me—
Because the better nature, fresh-inspired,
Mounted above me to its proper place!
What mattered all the kindly graciousness,
The cordial brother's-bearing? This was clear—   80
I, once the captain, now was subaltern,
And so must keep complaining like a fool!
Go, take the curse of a lost soul, I say!
You neither play your puppets to the end,
Nor treat the real man,—for his realness' sake   85
Thrust rudely in their place,—with such regard
As might console them for their altered rank.
Me, the mere steady soldier, you depose
For Luria, and here's all your pet deserves!
Of what account, then, is your laughing-stock?   90
One word for all: whatever Luria does,
—If backed by his indignant troops he turn,
Revenge himself, and Florence go to ground,—
Or, for a signal everlasting shame,
He pardon you, simply seek better friends,   95
Side with the Pisans and Lucchese for change
—And if I, pledged to ingrates past belief,

72 *1846,1849* And my own heart's conviction   *1846* his wrongs—   74 *1846*
Have I gone . . . . was slighted,   75 *1846* Degraded, all the terms *1849* Slighted, and
all the terms *1863,1865* Slighted, and moody, terms   76 {no equivalent in *1846*}
78 *1846* place: 80 *1846–63* And cordial   81 *1846* I was once captain, am
subaltern now, *1849–75* captain, was subaltern now,   83 *1846* So take   *1846–63*
lost man, I   88 *1865* you deposed   89 *1846,1849* all that he deserves!
90 *1846–65* then, are my services?   92 *1846–63* he turns   93 *1846–65* In
self-defence and   *1846–63* Florence goes to   95 *1846,1849* He pardons you, and
simply seeks his friends *1863* He pardons you, simply seeks better   96 *1846–63* And
heads the   *1846–65* Pisan and the Lucchese troops   97 *1846–65* I, for you
ingrates

   80 *brother's-bearing*: cf. 'brother's speech': *Sordello*, v. 635.

   93 *go to ground*: is destroyed. Cf. German *zugrunde gehen*, and examples in OED,
'ground', *sb*. III. 8b.

Dare fight against a man such fools call false,
Who, inasmuch as he was true, fights me,—
Whichever way he win, he wins for worth,   100
For every soldier, for all true and good!
Sir, chronicling the rest, omit not this!

As they go, enter LURIA *and* HUSAIN.

Husain. Saw'st thou?—For they are gone! The world lies bare
Before thee, to be tasted, felt and seen
Like what it is, now Florence goes away!   105
Thou livest now, with men art man again!
Those Florentines were all to thee of old;
But Braccio, but Domizia, gone is each,
There lie beneath thee thine own multitudes!
Saw'st thou?
    Luria.   I saw.
    Husain.   Then, hold thy course, my king!   110
The years return. Let thy heart have its way:
Ah, they would play with thee as with all else,
Turn thee to use, and fashion thee anew,
Find out God's fault in thee as in the rest?
Oh watch, oh listen only to these fiends   115
Once at their occupation! Ere we know,
The free great heaven is shut, their stifling pall
Drops till it frets the very tingling hair,

98 *1846* Resolve to fight against one false to us, *1849–65* Resolve to fight against a man
called false,   99 *1846,1849* he is true   *1846–65* fights there—   100 *1846,
1849* he wins, he wins for me, *1863,1865* he wins for me, *1868,1870* way we win,
101 *1846,1849* for the common good! *1863,1865* for the true   102 s.d. *1846*
†[*Exeunt. Enter*   107 *1846–65* were eyes to   108 *1846,1849* each—
1863,1865 each: 109 *1846,1849* multitudes— *1863,1865* multitudes.
110 *1846,1849* Sawest   *1846* saw. *Hus.* So hold   111 *1846–68* way!
112 *1846–63* else?   115 *1846–65* watch but, listen only to these men *1868* watch,
but listen   116 *1846–75* Ere ye know,

116 *Ere we know*: about here, probably in this speech of Husain's or in his next, there
occurred the words 'Far too plain / Souls show themselves for men to choose & read.' EBB
comments: 'It seems to me too that the whole of this passage is somewhat diffusely given, &
not distinctly. If this soul-reading is so easy & achievable by boys, is it a *consequence* that
Luria should be read wrong? Will you look & wave your wand once?'
    118 *frets*: agitates. Cf. *The Merchant of Venice*, IV. i. 77.

So weighs it on our head,—and, for the earth,
Our common earth is tethered up and down,   120
Over and across—"here shalt thou move," they cry!
    Luria. Ay, Husain?
    Husain.   So have they spoiled all beside!
So stands a man girt round with Florentines,
Priests, greybeards, Braccios, women, boys and spies,
All in one tale, all singing the same song,   125
How thou must house, and live at bed and board,
Take pledge and give it, go their every way,
Breathe to their measure, make thy blood beat time
With theirs—or, all is nothing—thou art lost—
A savage, how shouldst thou perceive as they?   130
Feel glad to stand 'neath God's close naked hand!
Look up to it! Why, down they pull thy neck,
Lest it crush thee, who feel'st it and wouldst kiss,
Without their priests that needs must glove it first,
Lest peradventure flesh offend thy lip.   135
Love woman! Why, a very beast thou art!
Thou must . . .
    Luria.   Peace, Husain!
    Husain.   Ay but, spoiling all,
For all else true things substituting false,
That they should dare spoil, of all instincts, thine!
Should dare to take thee with thine instincts up,   140
Thy battle-ardours, like a ball of fire,
And class them and allow them place and play
So far, no farther—unabashed the while!
Thou with the soul that never can take rest—

120 *1846* The common   121 *1846,1849* here . . . . move,   *1846–63* they say!
125 *1846–63* tale, each singing   130 *1846* how should such perceive
133 *1846* feel it and would kiss,   135 *1846* In mercy to thy lip it else will wound!
1849 peradventure it should wound thy *1863,1865* peradventure it offend   *1849,1863*
lip!   136 *1846* Woman—   *138 {reading of *1846*} *1849* For all, else true,
things substituting *1863–89* For all, else true things, substituting

    125 *All in one tale*: the same phrase occurs in *Pippa Passes*, I. 311, and elsewhere in
Browning.
    134 *glove*: for the verb, cf. *2 Henry IV*, I. i. 147.
    142 *play*: freedom of movement.

Thou born to do, undo, and do again,   145
And never to be still,—wouldst thou make war?
Oh, that is commendable, just and right!
"Come over," say they, "have the honour due
"In living out thy nature! Fight thy best:
"It is to be for Florence, not thyself!   150
"For thee, it were a horror and a plague;
"For us, when war is made for Florence, see,
"How all is changed: the fire that fed on earth
"Now towers to heaven!"—

    Luria.   And what sealed up so long
My Husain's mouth?

    Husain.   Oh friend, oh lord—for me,   155
What am I?—I was silent at thy side,
Who am a part of thee. It is thy hand,
Thy foot that glows when in the heart fresh blood
Boils up, thou heart of me! Now, live again,
Again love as thou likest, hate as free!   160
Turn to no Braccios nor Domizias now,
To ask, before thy very limbs dare move,
If Florence' welfare be concerned thereby!

    Luria. So clear what Florence must expect of me?

    Husain. Both armies against Florence! Take revenge!   165
Wide, deep—to live upon, in feeling now,—
And, after live, in memory, year by year—
And, with the dear conviction, die at last!
She lies now at thy pleasure: pleasure have!
Their vaunted intellect that gilds our sense,   170
And blends with life, to show it better by,
—How think'st thou?—I have turned that light on them!

146 *1846* But never . . . . still,—thou wouldst make   148–54 {no quotation marks in
1846,1849}   157 *1846,1849* That am   159 *1846* up as thine does! Thou wilt
live again, *1849–68* again!   160 *1846* as freely,   162 *1846* limbs may move,
163 *1846* be not touched therein!   167 *1846–63* after, in remembrance, year
168 *1846* And, in the   171 *1846* They blend with

    172 *How think'st thou?*: EBB quotes the line with 'I have turned on them their arm' as its
second part, and asks: 'Is there an objection to making this clear by repeating the word
"light". "I have turned their light on *them*". Then in the next line "A transient thing was this
our thirst of war" if you wrote "They called our thirst of war a transient thing" you allow

They called our thirst of war a transient thing;
"The battle-element must pass away
"From life," they said, "And leave a tranquil world."   175
—Master, I took their light and turned it full
On that dull turgid vein they said would burst
And pass away; and as I looked on life,
Still everywhere I tracked this, though it hid
And shifted, lay so silent as it thought,   180
Changed shape and hue yet ever was the same.
Why, 't was all fighting, all their nobler life!
All work was fighting, every harm—defeat,
And every joy obtained—a victory!
Be not their dupe!

           —Their dupe? That hour is past!   185
Here stand'st thou in the glory and the calm:
All is determined. Silence for me now!

                                 [HUSAIN *goes.*

    Luria. Have I heard all?
    Domizia [*advancing from the background*]. No, Luria, I remain!
Not from the motives these have urged on thee,
Ignoble, insufficient, incomplete,   190
And pregnant each with sure seeds of decay,
As failing of sustainment from thyself,
—Neither from low revenge, nor selfishness,
Nor savage lust of power, nor one, nor all,
Shalt thou abolish Florence! I proclaim   195
The angel in thee, and reject the sprites

174–5 {no quotation marks in *1846,1849*}   175 *1846,1849* world: 181 *1846–*
63 Changed oft the hue   *1846,1849* same: 186 *1846–75* calm!   187 *1846–*
75 determined! s.d. *1846* †[*Exit* HUSAIN.   188 *1846* I am here. *1849* I am here!
196 *1846,1849* the spirits

the reader to see at a glance what otherwise he will seek studiously. And so worthy of all admiration it is, this discourse of Husain's, with his true doctrine that "all work is fighting".'

   196 *sprites*: in a letter of 21 January 1846 EBB quotes 196–8 (with 'rejects' in 196 and 'That' in 197) and asks: 'why not "spirits" rather than "sprites", which has a different association by custom? "Spirits" is quite short enough, it seems to me, for a last word—it sounds like a monosyllable that trembles . . or thrills, rather': Kintner, i. 407. In her notes she made the same point: 'A fine expression the first ['I proclaim / The angel in thee']—but why not write "spirits" at length?' Browning made the revision, but reverted to 'sprites' after *1849.*

Which ineffectual crowd about his strength,
And mingle with his work and claim a share!
Inconsciously to the augustest end
Thou has arisen: second not in rank   200
So much as time, to him who first ordained
That Florence, thou art to destroy, should be.
Yet him a star, too, guided, who broke first
The pride of lonely power, the life apart,
And made the eminences, each to each,   205
Lean o'er the level world and let it lie
Safe from the thunder henceforth 'neath their tops;
So the few famous men of old combined,
And let the multitude rise underneath,
And reach them and unite—so Florence grew: 210
Braccio speaks true, it was well worth the price.
But when the sheltered many grew in pride
And grudged the station of the elected ones,
Who, greater than their kind, are truly great
Only in voluntary servitude—   215
Time was for thee to rise, and thou art here.
Such plague possessed this Florence: who can tell
The mighty girth and greatness at the heart
Of those so perfect pillars of the grove
She pulled down in her envy? Who as I,   220
The light weak parasite born but to twine

---

200 *1846* not to him   201 *1846* In rank so much as time, who   202 *1846*
The Florence   207 *1846,1849* their arms—   210 *1849* grew!
211 *1846,1849* speaks well, it   213 *1846* grudged their station to the glorious ones,
1849 the glorious ones,   215*a 1846* Which they who, being less, would fain be
more,   215*b 1846* And so accept not, then are least of all—

  199 *Inconsciously*: cf. above, l. 358 n.
  201 *him who first ordained*: Porter and Clarke take this to refer to Dante (1265–1321),
who took a prominent part in the politics of his city. The Ohio editor suggests Julius
Caesar, sometimes mentioned as the mythical founder of Florence. It is not clear, however,
that any identifiable man is intended.
  213 *the elected ones*: the governing body of the city.
  221–2 *born . . . live?*: in her notes on the proof, EBB quotes as printed, but comments:
'or—"and measuring them, so live"—Is there an objection? Because the trisyllabic "measur-

Round each of them and, measuring them, live?
My light love keeps the matchless circle safe,
My slender life proves what has passed away.
I lived when they departed; lived to cling   225
To thee, the mighty stranger; thou wouldst rise
And burst the thraldom, and avenge, I knew.
I have done nothing; all was thy strong bole.
But a bird's weight can break the infant tree
Which after holds an aery in its arms,   230
And 't was my care that nought should warp thy spire
From rising to the height; the roof is reached
O' the forest, break through, see extend the sky!
Go on to Florence, Luria! 'T is man's cause!
Fail thou, and thine own fall were least to dread: 235
Thou keepest Florence in her evil way,
Encouragest her sin so much the more—
And while the ignoble past is justified,
Thou all the surelier warp'st the future growth,
The chiefs to come, the Lurias yet unborn,   240

---

222 *1846,1849* them, so live?   224 *1846,1849* away!   228 *1846* strong
heart— *1849* strong heart: *1863,1865* strong heart.   229 *1846* But as a bird's weight
breaks the   231 *1846* So did I care   232 *1846,1849* reached— *1863,1865*
reached: 233 *1846,1849* Break through and there is all the sky above! *1863* Break
through and there extends the sky above! *1865* Break through and see extend the sky above!
235 *1846* But fail thou, and thy fall is least *1849,1863* fall is least   *1846–65* dread!
238 *1846–65* the bloody past   238a *1846* The murder of those gone before
approved.   239 *1846,1849* surelier dost work against *1863,1865* surelier dost the
Future wrong,   240 *1846,1849* The men to

ing" weakens the line.' Browning inserted 'so', but dropped it after *1849*.
    About here EBB found 'Above them which still safelier bids them live'. 'Not a very
favorite line perhaps of mine', she commented, '—but the "*weaklier*" must not stand so near
it anywise. See below. [Browning must have revised or cut the passage.] The word "break"
too ends several lines. My belief is that the whole passage will strike you as diffuse, & that
you will teach it to coil up gathering strength. Domizia speaks her speech, for the rest, elo-
quently & well—she has her side of truth like the rest—& one feels for poor Luria so much
the more. "'Tis well for them to see—but him!" Poor Luria, how great & benignant he is in
circumstances which make misanthropes of other men. It is very fine . . all to the end.'

    228 *bole*: trunk. A favourite word of Browning's. Cf. the unpublished poem, 'A Forest
Thought', 9 ff.: Vol. I, p. 542.
    230 *aery*: an eagle's nest.
    234 *'T is man's cause*: cf. *Sordello*, iv. 1012.

That, greater than thyself are reached o'er thee
Who giv'st the vantage-ground their foes require
As o'er my prostrate House thyself wast reached.
Man calls thee, God requites thee! All is said,
The mission of my House fulfilled at last: 245
And the mere woman, speaking for herself,
Reserves speech—it is now no woman's time.

                                                    [DOMIZIA *goes.*

   Luria. Thus at the last must figure Luria, then!
Doing the various work of all his friends,
And answering every purpose save his own.   250
No doubt, 't is well for them to wish; but him—
After the exploit what were left? Perchance
A little pride upon the swarthy brow
At having brought successfully to bear
'Gainst Florence' self her own especial arms,—   255
Her craftiness, impelled by fiercer strength
From Moorish blood than feeds the northern wit:
But after!—once the easy vengeance willed,
Beautiful Forence at a word laid low
—(Not in her domes and towers and palaces,   260
Not even in a dream, that outrage!)—low,
As shamed in her own eyes henceforth for ever,
Low, for the rival cities round to laugh,
Conquered and pardoned by a hireling Moor!
—For him, who did the irreparable wrong,   265
What would be left, his life's illusion fled,—

241 *1849* Who, greater   242 *1849* That giv'st   *243 (reading of DC,
BrU,*1889*) *1846–75* reached! *1888* reached *1865* thyself was reached!   244 *1846,
1849* God shall judge thee: *1863* thee. *1865* thee,   245 *1846,1849* last!
247 s.d. *1846* †[*Exit* DOMIZIA.   248 s.d. *1846* Lur. (*sol.*)   *1846,1849* So at
251 *1846* to see; but *1849* wish; for him—   252 *1846* what remains? Perchance
1849 what is left?   *253 (reading of *1846*,DC,BrU,*1889*) *1849–88* brow,
*257 (reading of DC,BrU) *1846–63* wit— *1865–75* wit. *1888,1889* wit   261 *1846*
Not in a dream that outrage!)—but laid low   263 *1846* And for   *1846–63* to see,
266 *1846* left, the life's

   242 *giv'st*: on reading the proof, EBB quotes as 'give', and suggests the printed reading.
   250 *every purpose save his own*: cf. Taurello Salinguerra in *Sordello*.
   260 *her domes and towers*: cf. Wordsworth, 'Composed upon Westminster Bridge', 6.

What hope or trust in the forlorn wide world?
How strange that Florence should mistake me so!
Whence grew this? What withdrew her faith from me?
Some cause! These fretful-blooded children talk 270
Against their mother,—they are wronged, they say—
Notable wrongs her smile makes up again!
So, taking fire at each supposed offence,
They may speak rashly, suffer for their speech:
But what could it have been in word or deed 275
Thus injured me? Some one word spoken more
Out of my heart, and all had changed perhaps.
My fault, it must have been,—for, what gain they?
Why risk the danger? See, what I could do!
And my fault, wherefore visit upon them, 280
My Florentines? The notable revenge
I meditated! To stay passively,
Attend their summons, be as they dispose!
Why, if my very soldiers keep the rank,
And if my chieftains acquiesce, what then? 285
I ruin Florence, teach her friends mistrust,
Confirm her enemies in harsh belief,
And when she finds one day, as find she must,
The strange mistake, and how my heart was hers,
Shall it console me, that my Florentines 290
Walk with a sadder step, in graver guise,
Who took me with such frankness, praised me so,
At the glad outset? Had they loved me less,
They had less feared what seemed a change in me.
And after all, who did the harm? Not they! 295

269 *1846,1849* How grew   272 *1846,1849* wrongs a smile   274 *1846* These may   *1846,1849* for rash speech—   276 *1846–63* That injured   277 *1846–63* perhaps! *1865–70* perhaps   281 *1846–63* The generous revenge 282 *1846–65* I meditate! To stay here passively,   283 *1846–63* Go at their *1846–65* dispose—   284 *1846* soldiers stop not that, *1849–65* keep their ranks, 285 *1846* if I moderate my chiefs, what *1849,1863* if I pacify my chiefs, what 288 *1846–65* as she must find,   290 *1846* This shall console   291 *1846–63* step, a graver face,   293 *1846* outset! Had they been less sure *1849* outset! 295 *1846* And is it they who will have done the harm?

How could they interpose with those old fools
I' the council? Suffer for those old fools' sake—
They, who made pictures of me, sang the songs
About my battles? Ah, we Moors get blind
Out of our proper world, where we can see!   300
The sun that guides is closer to us! There—
There, my own orb! He sinks from out the sky.
Why, there! a whole day has he blessed the land,
My land, our Florence all about the hills,
The fields and gardens, vineyards, olive-grounds,   305
All have been blest: and yet we Florentines
With souls intent upon our battle here,
Found that he rose too soon, or set too late,
Gave us no vantage, or gave Pisa much—
Therefore we wronged him! Does he turn in ire   310
To burn the earth that cannot understand?
Or drop out quietly, and leave the sky,
His task once ended? Night wipes blame away.
Another morning from my East shall spring
And find all eyes at leisure, all disposed   315
To watch and understand its work, no doubt.
So, praise the new sun, the successor praise,
Praise the new Luria and forget the old!

                              [*Taking a phial from his breast.*

Strange! This is all I brought from my own land
To help me: Europe would supply the rest,   320
All needs beside, all other helps save one!
I thought of adverse fortune, battle lost,
The natural upbraiding of the loser,

297 *1846–68* In the   *1846–63,1870* fools' sakes—   *1865,1868* fools' sakes
298 *1846* me, turned the   300 *1846* we are right!   301 *1846* us! See—
302 *1846* See, my   *1846–75* sky!   307 *1846–63* With minds intent
308 *1846* or rose too late, *1849,1863* or else too late,   309 *1846–65* Pisa more—
310 *1846–63* And so we   *1865* Therefore so we   313 *1846,1849* away:
314 *1846,1849* shall rise   315 *1849,1863* leisure, more disposed   316 *1846*
watch it and approve its every work. *1849* watch it and approve its   317 *1846,1849*
praise!   321 *1846–63* save this!   322 *1846–75* fortune, battles lost,
323 *1846–63* natural upbraidings of

And then this quiet remedy to seek
At end of the disastrous day.   [*He drinks.*
              'T is sought!   325
This was my happy triumph-morning: Florence
Is saved: I drink this, and ere night,—die! Strange!

326 *triumph-morning*: cf. *Richard II*, v. ii. 66: 'triumph-day'.

ACT V.

NIGHT.

LURIA *and* PUCCIO.

Luria. I thought to do this, not to talk this: well,
Such were my projects for the city's good,
To help her in attack or by defence.
Time, here as elsewhere, soon or late may take
Our foresight by surprise thro' chance and change;   5
But not a little we provide against
—If you see clear on every point.
    Puccio.   Most clear.
    Luria. Then all is said—not much, if you count words,
Yet to an understanding ear enough;
And all that my brief stay permits, beside.   10
Nor must you blame me, as I sought to teach
My elder in command, or threw a doubt
Upon the very skill, it comforts me
To know I leave,—your steady soldiership
Which never failed me: yet, because it seemed   15
A stranger's eye might haply note defect
That skill, through use and custom, overlooks—
I have gone into the old cares once more,
As if I had to come and save again
Florence—that May—that morning! 'T is night now.   20
Well—I broke off with? . . .
    Puccio.   Of the past campaign
You spoke—of measures to be kept in mind
For future use.

---

s.d. *1846,1849* LURIA. PUCCIO.   1 *1846,1849* well!   3 *1846* To save her
1849 To save her from attack   5 *1846* With chance and change our foresight by
surprise; *1849* surprise with chance   8 *1846* much, to count the words,
9 *1846–63* Yet for an   *1846,1849* enough,   14 *1846* leave,—that steady
15 *1849* That never   17 *1846,1849* Which skill

Luria.   True, so ... but, time—no time!
As well end here: remember this, and me!
Farewell now!
   Puccio.   Dare I speak?
   Luria.   South o' the river—   25
How is the second stream called ... no,—the third?
   Puccio. Pesa.
   Luria.   And a stone's cast from the fording-place,
To the east,—the little mount's name?
   Puccio.   Lupo.
   Luria.   Ay!
Ay—there the tower, and all that side is safe!
With San Romano, west of Evola,   30
San Miniato, Scala, Empoli,
Five towers in all,—forget not!
   Puccio.   Fear not me!
   Luria. —Nor to memorialize the Council now,
I' the easy hour, on those battalions' claim,
Who forced a pass by Staggia on the hills,   35
And kept the Sienese at check!
   Puccio.   One word—
Sir, I must speak! That you submit yourself
To Florence' bidding, howsoe'er it prove,
And give up the command to me—is much,
Too much, perhaps: but what you tell me now,   40
Even will affect the other course you choose—

---

25 *1846–65* speak? *Lur.*—The south   35 *1846–75* On the other side, by
36 *1846,1849* That kept the Siennese at   *1863–75* Who kept   41 *1846* Even affects
the other course to choose—

   27 *Pesa*: this small river, like Montelupo and the other places mentioned, are all within
35 miles or so of Florence, and are important for the defence of the vital road from Flor-
ence to Pisa on the coast. The Ohio editor suggests that 'Evola' may be an error for the River
Egola, between San Romano and San Miniato.
   41 *Even will affect*: EBB quotes as 'Even affects the other course to choose', and com-
ments: 'I do not like the lines which begin "Even" making a disyllable of it: they sound weak
to me. But there is an objection here besides, because .. observe the meaning .. you do not
mean to say "it even *affects* the other course" &c but that "it affects even the other *course*"
&c—Do you see? I am always making that mistake myself, & everybody else makes it .. but

Poor as it may be, perils even that!
Refuge you seek at Pisa: yet these plans
All militate for Florence, all conclude
Your formidable work to make her queen   45
O' the country,—which her rivals rose against
When you began it,—which to interrupt,
Pisa would buy you off at any price!
You cannot mean to sue for Pisa's help,
With this made perfect and on record?
   Luria.   I—   50
At Pisa, and for refuge, do you say?
   Puccio. Where are you going, then? You must decide
On leaving us, a silent fugitive,
Alone, at night—you, stealing through our lines,
Who were this morning's Luria,—you escape   55
To painfully begin the world once more,
With such a past, as it had never been!
Where are you going?
   Luria.   Not so far, my Puccio,
But that I hope to hear, enjoy and praise
(If you mind praise from your old captain yet)   60
Each happy blow you strike for Florence.
   Puccio.   Ay,—
But ere you gain your shelter, what may come?
For see—though nothing's surely known as yet,
Still—truth must out—I apprehend the worst.
If mere suspicion stood for certainty   65
Before, there's nothing can arrest the step
Of Florence toward your ruin, once on foot.

42 *1849–65* be, peril even   45 *1846* The formidable   46 *1846–68* Of the
48 *1846* off in any case!   52 *1846* going? Then   53 *1846* To leave the camp
a   55 *1846* you, escaped   59 *1846* But I shall get to hear and know and *1849*
hear, and know, and   61 *1846–75* Florence!   62 *1846* come!
66 *1846–63* the steps

there is a right & a wrong way after all. If you wrote "Affects the other course even, left to
choose" or "Affects even the other course we have to choose"— .. see!—I admire the
dialogue here—it is suggestive & full besides.'

   64 *truth must out*: proverbial. Cf. *The Merchant of Venice*, II. ii. 73, and ODEP, p. 845a.

Forgive her fifty times, it matters not!
And having disbelieved your innocence,
How can she trust your magnanimity?   70
You may do harm to her—why then, you will!
And Florence is sagacious in pursuit.
Have you a friend to count on?
    Luria.   One sure friend.
    Puccio. Potent?
    Luria.   All-potent.
    Puccio.   And he is apprised?
    Luria. He waits me.
    Puccio.   So!—Then I, put in your place,   75
Making my profit of all done by you,
Calling your labours mine, reaping their fruit,
To this, the State's gift, now add yours beside—
That I may take as my peculiar store
These your instructions to work Florence good.   80
And if, by putting some few happily
In practice, I should both advantage her
And draw down honour on myself,—what then?
    Luria. Do it, my Puccio! I shall know and praise.
    Puccio. Though so, men say, "mark what we gain by
        change   85
"—A Puccio for a Luria!"
    Luria.   Even so.
    Puccio. Then, not for fifty hundred Florences,
Would I accept one office save my own,

---

78 *1849–65* To these, the   *1846* add this from you— *1849,1863* add this of yours—
1865 add this beside—   79 *1846–63* take to my   80 *1846* All these instruc-
tions to do Florence *1849,1863* All your instructions to do Florence *1865* All your instruc-
tions   *1846* good, *1849* good;   84 *1846,1849,1865–75* praise! *1863* praise
86 *1849–75* so!

69–70 *And having . . . magnanimity?*: EBB quotes these two lines and comments: 'True &
overcoming . . & put so excellently well—The suggested pathos of this situation . . how
deep it is. Poor great Luria! I feel that I ought not to be able to count the trefoil when lifted
to the summit of a mountain . . but I do not like that little ending word to Puccio's speech . .
"you bid"—"*Bid*!" the accent on "bid"—Wont you say "You bid me" at least—'. Browning
revised.

79 *store*: treasure.

Fill any other than my rightful post
Here at your feet, my captain and my lord! 90
That such a cloud should break, such trouble be,
Ere a man settle, soul and body, down
Into his true place and take rest for ever!
Here were my wise eyes fixed on your right-hand,
And so the bad thoughts came and the worse words, 95
And all went wrong and painfully enough,—
No wonder,—till, the right spot stumbled on,
All the jar stops, and there is peace at once!
I am yours now,—a tool your right-hand wields!
God's love, that I should live, the man I am, 100
On orders, warrants, patents, and the like,
As if there were no glowing eye i' the world
To glance straight inspiration to my brain,
No glorious heart to give mine twice the beats!
For, see—my doubt, where is it?—fear? 't is flown! 105
And Florence and her anger are a tale
To scare a child. Why, half-a-dozen words
Will tell her, spoken as I now can speak,
Her error, my past folly—and all's right,
And you are Luria, our great chief again! 110
Or at the worst—which worst were best of all—
To exile or to death I follow you.
    Luria. Thanks, Puccio! Let me use the privilege
You grant me: if I still command you,—stay!
Remain here—my vicegerent, it shall be, 115
And not successor: let me, as of old,
Still serve the State, my spirit prompting yours—
Still triumph, one for both. There! Leave me now!
You cannot disobey my first command?
Remember what I spoke of Jacopo, 120

---

92 *1846* man settles soul   93 *1846* and takes rest   94 *1846* There were
99 *1846* wields.   105 *1846* see,—the doubt   107 *1846* child— *1849–75*
child!   110 *1846* Luria, the great   112 *1849–75* you!
    98 *jar*: discord, trouble.

And what you promised to concert with him!
Send him to speak with me—nay, no farewell!
You shall be by me when the sentence comes.

[PUCCIO goes.

So, there's one Florentine returns again!
Out of the genial morning-company   125
One face is left to take into the night.

Enter JACOPO.

  Jacopo. I wait for your command, sir.
    Luria.   What, so soon?
I thank your ready presence and fair word.
I used to notice you in early days
As of the other species, so to speak,   130
Those watchers of the lives of us who act—
That weigh our motives, scrutinize our thoughts.
So, I propound this to your faculty
As you would tell me, were a town to take
. . . That is, of old. I am departing hence   135
Under these imputations; that is nought—
I leave no friend on whom they may rebound,
Hardly a name behind me in the land,
Being a stranger: all the more behoves
That I regard how altered were the case   140
With natives of the country, Florentines
On whom the like mischance should fall: the roots
O' the tree survive the ruin of the trunk—
No root of mine will throb, you understand.
But I had predecessors, Florentines,   145
Accused as I am now, and punished so—
The Traversari: you know more than I
How stigmatized they are and lost in shame.

121 *1846,1849* to observe with   *1846* him: 122 *1846–63* farewell—
123 *1846* You will be   s.d. †[*Exit* PUCCIO.   *125 {reading of
1846,DC,BrU,*1889*} *1849–88* company,   127 *1846–63* your commands, Sir.
131 *1846* The watchers   132 *1846,1849* thoughts;   144 *1846* understand:
*148 {reading of *1846*,DC,BrU,*1889*} *1849–88* are, and

  147 *the Traversari*: see III. 291 and n.

Now Puccio, who succeeds me in command,
Both served them and succeeded, in due time;   150
He knows the way, holds proper documents,
And has the power to lay the simple truth
Before an active spirit, as I count yours:
And also there's Tiburzio, my new friend,
Will, at a word, confirm such evidence,   155
He being the great chivalric soul we know.
I put it to your tact, sir—were't not well,
—A grace, though but for contrast's sake, no more,—
If you who witness, and have borne a share
Involuntarily in my mischance,   160
Should, of your proper motion, set your skill
To indicate—that is, investigate
The right or wrong of what mischance befell
Those famous citizens, your countrymen?
Nay, you shall promise nothing: but reflect,   165
And if your sense of justice prompt you—good!

    Jacopo. And if, the trial past, their fame stand clear
To all men's eyes, as yours, my lord, to mine—
Their ghosts may sleep in quiet satisfied!
For me, a straw thrown up into the air,   170
My testimony goes for a straw's worth.
I used to hold by the instructed brain,
And move with Braccio as my master-mind;
The heart leads surelier: I must move with you—
As greatest now, who ever were the best.   175

---

151 *1846* way, and holds the documents,   153 *1846–63* I know yours:
156 *1846–63* the chivalric   157 *1846–63* your instinct—were't   163 *1846,*
1849 The reason or the wrong of what befel {*1863* as *1846,1849* but 'befell'}
167 *1846* fame stands white   171 *1846* worth: *173 {RB's correction in
Brigham Young copy of *1846* adopted; all printed versions have 'master-wind'} *1846–63* as
the master-wind;

  156 *He being*: EBB quotes this line as 'Being the thrice chivalric soul we know', and asks:
'Is there an objection to saying .. "He being the &c" .. because there seems a weakness
otherwise .. to the *ear* I mean.'

  175 *As greatest now*: EBB quotes an earlier version, 'As greater now who better still have
been', asking 'Why not .. "As greater now who have been better still"—it is more natural,
more clear, less stiff perhaps.'

So, let the last and humblest of your servants
Accept your charge, as Braccio's heretofore,
And tender homage by obeying you!

> [JACOPO *goes.*

Luria. Another! Luria goes not poorly forth.
If we could wait! The only fault's with time;   180
All men become good creatures: but so slow!

Enter DOMIZIA.

Luria. Ah, you once more?
Domizia.   Domizia, whom you knew,
Performed her task, and died with it. 'T is I,
Another woman, you have never known.
Let the past sleep now!
Luria.   I have done with it.   185
Domizia. How inexhaustibly the spirit grows!
One object, she seemed erewhile born to reach
With her whole energies and die content,—
So like a wall at the world's edge it stood,
With nought beyond to live for,—is that reached?   190
Already are new undreamed energies
Outgrowing under, and extending farther
To a new object; there's another world.
See! I have told the purpose of my life;
'T is gained: you are decided, well or ill—   195
You march on Florence, or submit to her—
My work is done with you, your brow declares.
But—leave you? More of you seems yet to reach:
I stay for what I just begin to see.
Luria. So that you turn not to the past!
Domizia.   You trace   200

177 *1846* heretofore. s.d. †[*Exit* JACOPO.   178 {no equivalent in *1846*} *1849,1863*
And offer homage,   179 *1846-65* forth!   180 *1846* If one could
181 *1865* slow   182 *1846-63* Domizia, that you   183 *1846,1849* I!
184 {no equivalent in *1846*}   185 *1846-63* now.   189 *1846-65* world's end
it   190 *1846* is it reached, . . *1849,1863* is it reached?   192 *1846-63* extend-
ing further   193 *1846-75* world!   194 *1846* See: 196 {no equivalent
in *1846*}   197 *1846,1849* declares: 198 *1846-68* reach! *1870,1875* reach.

Nothing but ill in it—my selfish impulse,
Which sought its end and disregarded yours?
   Luria. Speak not against your nature: best, each keep
His own—you, yours—most, now that I keep mine,
—At least, fall by it, having too weakly stood.   205
God's finger marks distinctions, all so fine,
We would confound: the lesser has its use,
Which, when it apes the greater, is forgone.
I, born a Moor, lived half a Florentine;
But, punished properly, can end, a Moor.   210
Beside, there's something makes me understand
Your nature: I have seen it.
   Domizia.   Aught like mine?
   Luria. In my own East . . . if you would stoop and help
My barbarous illustration! It sounds ill;
Yet there's no wrong at bottom: rather, praise.   215
   Domizia. Well?
   Luria.   We have creatures there, which if you saw
The first time, you would doubtless marvel at
For their surpassing beauty, craft and strength.
And though it were a lively moment's shock
When you first found the purpose of forked tongues   220
That seem innocuous in their lambent play,
Yet, once made know such grace requires such guard,
Your reason soon would acquiesce, I think,
In wisdom which made all things for the best—

202 *1846–63* its ends and   204 *1846–65* now when I   205 *1846* having
weakly   *208 {reading of *1865*,DC,BrU,*1889*} *1846–63*,*1868–88* is foregone.
210 *1846,1849* can die a   211 *1846–63* there is what makes   212 *1846,1849*
it—*Dom.* One like   214 *1846,1849* illustration . .   *1846* ill *1849,1863* ill—
220 *1846–75* Wherein you found   *1846* of their tongues *1849,1863* of those tongues
1865 purpose out of tongues   221 *1846–63* That seemed innocuous
222 *1846,1849* grace required such   224 *1846–65* In the Wisdom   *1846* best,
1849 best;

   206 *God's finger*: 'I admire this excellent true thought, which cannot be said better—no,
nor clearer': EBB. Cf. *Paracelsus*, iii. 117 and n.
   221 *That seem innocuous*: EBB quotes as 'Whose lambent play so all innocuous seemed',
commenting: 'Or . . "Whose lambent play seemed so innocuous" . . why object to natural
sequency of the words.'
   224 *all things for the best*: cf. *Samson Agonistes*, 1745.

So, take them, good with ill, contentedly,   225
The prominent beauty with the latent sting.
I am glad to have seen you wondrous Florentines:
Yet...
   Domizia. I am here to listen.
   Luria.   My own East!
How nearer God we were! He glows above
With scarce an intervention, presses close   230
And palpitatingly, his soul o'er ours:
We feel him, nor by painful reason know!
The everlasting minute of creation
Is felt there; now it is, as it was then;
All changes at his instantaneous will,   235
Not by the operation of a law
Whose maker is elsewhere at other work.
His hand is still engaged upon his world—
Man's praise can forward it, man's prayer suspend,
For is not God all-mighty? To recast   240
The world, erase old things and make them new,
What costs it Him? So, man breathes nobly there.
And inasmuch as feeling, the East's gift,
Is quick and transient—comes, and lo, is gone—
While Northern thought is slow and durable,   245

226 *1846–63* the secret sting.   227 *1846* Florentines *1849* Florentines,
231 *1846–75* ours!   234 *1846,1849 Now*   237 *1846–65* work!
238 *1846,1849* His soul is   242 *1846–75* there!

228 *My own East!*: cf. *The Return of the Druses*, v. 264 ff.

233 *The everlasting minute*: EBB quotes this line, followed by the word 'Arrested', and comments: 'Fine, that is—but I do not see what business that word "arrested" has—it *darkens*, I fancy. "Suspended" might convey the thought .. might it not? .. but perhaps neither word is needed.'

On Browning's attitude to the science of his day, see his important letter to Furnivall, 11 October 1881, in which, after referring to *Paracelsus*, he remarks that 'time and space [are] purely conceptions of our own, wholly inapplicable to intelligence of another kind— with whom, as I made Luria say, there is an "everlasting moment of creation," if one at all—past, present, and future, one and the same state': *Trumpeter*, p. 34. In Georg Roppen's words (*Evolution and Poetic Belief*, Oslo, 1956: Oxford, Basil Blackwell, p. 126), 'In the "everlasting minute of creation" he has discovered a formula which defines the wonder of organic growth and change as he first came face to face with it in *Paracelsus*, and which aptly expresses his theistic and neo-Platonic attitude.'

Surely a mission was reserved for me,
Who, born with a perception of the power
And use of the North's thought for us of the East,
Should have remained, turned knowledge to account,
Giving thought's character and permanence   250
To the too transitory feeling there—
Writing God's message plain in mortal words.
Instead of which, I leave my fated field
For this where such a task is needed least,
Where all are born consummate in the art   255
I just perceive a chance of making mine,—
And then, deserting thus my early post,
I wonder that the men I come among
Mistake me! There, how all had understood,
Still brought fresh stuff for me to stamp and keep,   260
Fresh instinct to translate them into law!
Me, who . . .
    Domizia. Who here the greater task achieve,
More needful even: who have brought fresh stuff
For us to mould, interpret and prove right,—
New feeling fresh from God, which, could we know   265
O' the instant, where had been our need of it?
—Whose life re-teaches us what life should be,
What faith is, loyalty and simpleness,
All, once revealed but taught us so long since
That, having mere tradition of the fact,—   270
Truth copied falteringly from copies faint,
The early traits all dropped away,—we said
On sight of faith like yours, "So looks not faith
"We understand, described and praised before."

246 *1846,1849* Oh, what a   249 *1846–63* have stayed there and turned it to *1865–*
75 remained and turned it to   251 *1846,1849* too-transitory Feelings there—
252 *1846–63* God's messages in   *1846–65* words!   265 *1849–65* New feelings
fresh   266 *1849–65* of them?   269 *1846* All their revealment, taught *1849,*
1863 All, their revealment taught   273–4 {no quotation marks in *1846*}
273 *1846,1849* faith of yours,   274 *1846* and taught before. *1849,1863* and taught
before."

———

    267 *re-teaches*: a rare compound, like 're-known' (278): in each case OED knows of only
one earlier example.

But still, the feat was dared; and though at first   275
It suffered from our haste, yet trace by trace
Old memories reappear, old truth returns,
Our slow thought does its work, and all's re-known.
Oh noble Luria! What you have decreed
I see not, but no animal revenge,   280
No brute-like punishment of bad by worse—
It cannot be, the gross and vulgar way
Traced for me by convention and mistake,
Has gained that calm approving eye and brow!
Spare Florence, after all! Let Luria trust   285
To his own soul, he whom I trust with mine!
    Luria. In time!
    Domizia.   How, Luria?
    Luria.   It is midnight now,
And they arrive from Florence with my fate.
    Domizia. I hear no step.
    Luria.   I feel one, as you say.

             Enter HUSAIN.

    Husain. The man returned from Florence!
    Luria.   As I knew.   290
    Husain. He seeks thee.
    Luria.   And I only wait for him.
Aught else?
    Husain. A movement of the Lucchese troops
Southward—
    Luria.   Toward Florence? Have out instantly . . .
Ah, old use clings! Puccio must care henceforth.
In—quick—'t is nearly midnight! Bid him come!   295

275 *1846–63* the truth was shown; and   276 *1846–65* It suffer from
277 *1846–63* reappear, the likeness grows,   278 *1846* all is known   281 {no
equivalent in *1846*}   284 *1846* brow.   286 *1846–65* soul, and I will trust to
him! *1868–75* soul, and I will trust him mine!   289 *1846,1849* step . . *1846–63* feel
it, as   *1849* say!   *293 {reading of *1846–75*} *1888,1889* instantly . .
294 *1846–63* henceforth!

Enter TIBURZIO, BRACCIO, *and* PUCCIO.

Tiburzio?—not at Pisa?

   Tiburzio.   I return
From Florence: I serve Pisa, and must think
By such procedure I have served her best.
A people is but the attempt of many
To rise to the completer life of one;   300
And those who live as models for the mass
Are singly of more value than they all.
Such man are you, and such a time is this,
That your sole fate concerns a nation more
Than much apparent welfare: that to prove   305
Your rectitude, and duly crown the same,
Imports us far beyond to-day's event,
A battle's loss or gain: man's mass remains,—
Keep but God's model safe, new men will rise
To take its mould, and other days to prove   310
How great a good was Luria's glory. True—
I might go try my fortune as you urged,
And, joining Lucca, helped by your disgrace,
Repair our harm—so were to-day's work done;
But where leave Luria for our sons to see?   315
No, I look farther. I have testified
(Declaring my submission to your arms)
Her full success to Florence, making clear
Your probity, as none else could: I spoke,
And out it shone!

   Luria.   Ah—until Braccio spoke!   320

---

296 *1846* Tiburzio,—   305 *1846* Than its immediate welfare; and to prove *1849–75* Than its apparent welfare; and to prove   306 {RB's alteration in the Pierpont Morgan copy of *1870*} ⟨duly crown the same,⟩ [recognize its worth,]   307 *1846* Of consequence beyond the day's event. *1849,1863* Imports it far *1849–75* beyond the day's event,   308 {no equivalent in *1846*} *1849,1863* Its battle's   *1849–75* gain—the mass remains,   309 *1846–75* but the model   310 *1846* To study it, and many another day. *1849,1863* To study it, and   311 {no equivalent in *1846*} *1849–75* Luria's having lived.   312 *1846–75* you bade,   315 {no equivalent in *1846*} *1849* where were Luria *1863–75* where find Luria   316 *1846* But I 318 *1846,1849* Your full   320 *1846–63* And it shone clearly! *Lur.* Ah—till Braccio

299 *A people*: see EBB's comment, on p. 185 above. Cf., too, *Sordello*, vi. 120.

Braccio. Till Braccio told in just a word the whole—
His lapse to error, his return to knowledge:
Which told . . . Nay, Luria, *I* should droop the head,
I whom shame rests with! Yet I dare look up,
Sure of your pardon now I sue for it,   325
Knowing you wholly. Let the midnight end!
'T is morn approaches! Still you answer not?
Sunshine succeeds the shadow past away;
Our faces, which phantasmal grew and false,
Are all that felt it: they change round you, turn   330
Truly themselves now in its vanishing.
Speak, Luria! Here begins your true career:
Look up, advance! All now is possible,
Fact's grandeur, no false dreaming! Dare and do!
And every prophecy shall be fulfilled   335
Save one—(nay, now your word must come at last)
—That you would punish Florence!
      Husain [*pointing to* LURIA's *dead body*]. That is done.

---

322 *1846–63* His old great error, and return *1865* error, and return   324 *1846*
Whom all shame rests with, yet *1849* with,   325 *1863–75* pardon when I
326 *1846–63* wholly—so let midnight   327 *1846,1849* Sunrise will come next! Still
1863 Sunrise approaches! *1865* Morning approaches!   328 *1846–63* The shadow of
the night is past away: 329 *1846* The circling faces here 'mid which it rose *1849*
Our circling faces here 'mid which it rose *1863* Our circling faces here 'mid which it grew
330 *1846–75* they close round   *1846–65* you now   331 *1846–63* To witness its
completest vanishing. *1865* Themselves in its completest vanishing. *1868–75* Themselves
now in its complete vanishing.   333 *1846–75* up to it!—All   334 *1846–75*
The glory and the grandeur of each dream—   337 *1846,1849* done!—   s.d. *1846*
Curtain falls.

   328 *the shadow past away*: perhaps revised in *1865* because Browning considered the
original line too Shelleyan: cf. *Adonais*, 352, in particular.
   329 *Our faces*: this line gave Browning trouble. 'I alter "little circle" to "circling faces"—
which is more like what I meant', he wrote to EBB on 7 April 1846 (Kintner, ii. 598). He
revised again later.
   334 *The glory and the grandeur* (*1846–75*): perhaps revised after *1875* because Browning
noticed the near-repetition of l. 5 of Wordsworth's 'Ode: Intimations of Immortality':
'The glory and the freshness of a dream'.
   337 *That is done*: 'The play ends nobly', EBB wrote at the end of her detailed comments,
'bearing itself up to its own height to the last . . & leaving an impression which must be an
emotion with all readers. Do think that just my first thoughts have been set down in these
notes, & take them at their worth—or no-worth.'

INTRODUCTION TO *A SOUL'S TRAGEDY*

ON 22 May 1842, in an account of what he hoped to accomplish in the course of that year, Browning told Domett that he intended to 'finish a wise metaphysical play (about a great mind and soul turning to ill)'.[1] He was almost certainly referring to *A Soul's Tragedy*,[2] though no more was to be heard of it for almost three years. On 26 February 1845, writing to Elizabeth Barrett about *Luria*, he mentioned that he had by him, 'done', a play called 'A Soul's Tragedy', which would not make a fitting end to his series of plays. He told her that it dealt with 'the other sadder ruin of one Chiappino'—sadder, that is, than the ruin of Luria. She was immediately interested, replying that the title 'sounds . . like the step of a ghost of an old Drama!' On 13 June she made it clear that she would like to see something of it, 'act or scene'.[3] He immediately responded that it was to be published as one of the last four *Bells*,[4] and promised to have it transcribed for her. We next hear of the work on 3 August, when he told her that it 'could go to press next week', though he had been advised to wait for 'November at earliest'.[5]

---

[1] *Correspondence*, v. 356. (Since *Luria* and *A Soul's Tragedy* are frequently mentioned together in the letters of Browning and EBB, the Introduction to *Luria* should be read in association with this. Some repetition has been inevitable.)

[2] This has been questioned by Clyde de L. Ryals, in his *Becoming Browning* (Columbus, Ohio, 1983), p. 276 n. 8. While the questioning is useful, we accept the usual identification: there is no mention elsewhere of anything else that could be described as 'a wise metaphysical play'. We know that the play had been 'written two or three years ago', as Browning told EBB in February 1846; but in what form it had been 'written', or to what extent he was now revising it, we do not know. In *A Soul's Tragedy* as we have it Chiappino is far from being 'a great mind and soul', nor is his name (which derives from It. *chiappare* ('entrap'), and seems to mean a scoundrel or opportunist) one that could be given to a hero. Whereas Luria reminds us of Othello, Chiappino has a good deal of Iago about him. The development of the argument of the play reminds us of Browning's remark that he sympathized 'just as much' with the Florentines as with Luria. We notice that Act I gives us '*what was called* the poetry of Chiappino's life' (italics added), not true poetry. Perhaps Chiappino is called 'another sadder ruin' because his ruin is spiritual.

A Soul's Tragedy is the work of a dedicated reader of Mandeville and of Machiavelli. Browning's skill as a casuist, already evident in many passages in *Sordello* and in other of his early poems, is brilliantly exemplified here.

[3] Kintner, i. 26, 29, 94.   [4] See above, p. 180.   [5] Kintner, i. 143.

Elizabeth was worried about his health. 'Dont let the tragedy or aught else do you harm', she wrote on 22 August, and repeated this warning about 'the tragedies' on 9 September. On 24 October, however, she looked forward to their publication after that of *Dramatic Romances and Lyrics*.[1]

The next important reference occurs on 10 February 1846, when she warns him that she will soon 'dun' him for *A Soul's Tragedy*: 'you told me it was finished .. otherwise I would not speak a word, .. feeling that you want rest'.[2] In his reply Browning told her about the 'slip of paper' on which he had jotted down his original idea for *Luria*,[3] and continued:

For the Soul's Tragedy—*that* will surprise you, I think—There is no trace of you there,—you have not put out the black face of *it*—it is all sneering and *disillusion*—and shall not be printed but burned if you say the word— now wait and see and then say! I will bring the first of the two parts next Saturday.[4]

That same evening he reread *A Soul's Tragedy*, however, and changed his mind:

though there were not a few points which still struck me as successful in design & execution, yet on the whole I came to a decided opinion—that it will be better to postpone the publication of it for the present: it is not a good ending,—an auspicious wind-up of this series,—subject-matter & style are alike unpopular even for the literary *grex* [crowd] that stands aloof from the purer *plebs* [common people], and uses that privilege to display & parade an ignorance which the other is altogether unconscious of—so that, if Luria is *clearish*, the Tragedy would be an unnecessary troubling the waters: whereas, if I printed it first in order, my readers . . . would make the (comparatively) little they did not see into, a full excuse for shutting their eyes at the rest . . . at bottom, I believe the proper objec- tion is to the immediate, *first* effect of the whole—its moral effect,— which is dependent on the contrary supposition of its being really understood, in the main drift of it—yet I don't know; for I wrote it with the intention of producing the best of all effects—perhaps the truth is, that I am tired, rather, and desirous of getting done, and Luria will answer my purpose so far: will not the best way be to reserve this unlucky play and, in

---

[1] Kintner, i. 171, 185, 248.   [2] Kintner, i. 446.
[3] See above, p. 179.   [4] Kintner, i. 451–2.

the event of a second edition,—as Moxon seems to think such an appari-
tion possible,—might not this be quietly inserted?—in its place, too, for it
was written two or three years ago.[1]

In reply Elizabeth suggested that if the first part had been tran-
scribed she could 'read *that* perhaps, without drawing [him] in to
think of the second'—though it might be better for him 'to keep off
altogether for the present'. A few days later she told him that if she
had *A Soul's Tragedy* in her possession, he would not be allowed to
see it again 'for a month at least'.[2]

Meanwhile he was coming to the conclusion that it would 'do
after all':

I will bring one part at least next time,—and 'Luria' take away, if you let
me, so all will be off my mind ... Don't think I am going to take any
extraordinary pains—there are some things in the 'Tragedy' I should like
to preserve and print now, leaving the future to spring as it likes, in any
direction,—and these half-dead, half-alive works fetter it, if left behind.

On 27 February he was still working, and told her that she might
have 'to wait a little longer for my "divine Murillo" of a Tragedy',
adding that Sarianna was copying it out, 'as I give [her] the pages',
and that his head was aching. Elizabeth soon begged him to be
careful of his health, and to keep away from 'that "Soul's Tragedy"
which [had done] so much harm'. By 9 March, however, she had
the first part: 'Now I shall know what to believe when you talk of
very bad & very indifferent doings of yours', she wrote the next
day:

I read your 'Soul's Tragedy' last night & was quite possessed with it, & fell
finally into a mute wonder how you could for a moment doubt about
publishing it. It is very vivid, I think, & vital, & impressed me more than
the first act of 'Luria' did .. though I do not mean to compare such dis-
similar things... But this 'Tragedy' shows more heat from the first .. &
then, the words beat down more closely .. well! I am struck by it all as you
see. If you keep it up to this passion, if you justify this high key-note .. it is
a great work, & worthy of a place next Luria. Also do observe how excel-
lently balanced the two will be, & how the tongue of this next silver Bell
will swing from side to side. And *you* to frighten me about it—!—Yes!—
and the worst is (because it was stupid in me) the worst is that I half

believed you & took the manuscript to be something inferior . . for YOU . .
& the adviseableness of its publication, a doubtful case.

Even so, she was anxious that he should not endanger his health:

Do not think of Chiappino, leave him behind . . he has a good strong life
of his own, & can wait for you. Oh—but let me remember to say of him,
that he & the other personnages appear to me to articulate with perfect
distinctness & clearness . . you need not be afraid of having been obscure
in this first part. It is all as lucid as noon.[1]

Meanwhile he had been hard at work. On 18 March he wrote:

all the morning I have been going for once and for ever thro' the Tragedy,
and it is *done*—(done *for*). Perhaps I may bring it tomorrow—if my sister
can copy all—I cut out a huge kind of sermon from the middle and
reserve it for a better time—still it is very long; so long![2]

He was afraid that both plays were failures: she vehemently dis-
agreed, to his surprise and delight. On 29 March she wrote at
length:

It is a new work with your mark on it. That is . . it would make some six or
sixteen works for other people, if 'cut up into little stars'—rolled out . .
diluted with rain-water. But it is your work as it is . . . full of power & sig-
nificance—& I am not at all sure . . . that if I knew you now first & only by
these two productions, . . Luria and the Tragedy, . . I should not involun-
tarily attribute more power and a higher faculty to the writer of the last . . .
Such thoughts, you have, in this second part of the Tragedy!—a 'Soul's
Tragedy' indeed! No one *thinks* like you—other poets talk like the merest
women in comparison.

She went on:

Certainly I think you were right (though you know I doubted & cried out)
I think now you were right in omitting the theological argument you told
me of, from this second part. It would clog the action . . & already I am
half inclined to fancy it a little clogged in one or two places—but if this is
true even, it would be easy to lighten it. Your Ogniben (here is my only
criticism in the way of objection) seems to me almost too wise for a crafty

[1] Kintner, i. 493, 501, 522, 525–6.
[2] Kintner, i. 546. Cf. EBB's conclusion that Browning had been right, after all, 'in omit-
ting the theological argument': Kintner, ii. 570.

worldling—tell me if he is not!—Such thoughts, for the rest, you are prodigal of! That about the child, . . . do you remember how you brought it to me in your first visit, nearly a year ago.[1]

He was surprised and encouraged:

It seems as if, having got out of the present trouble, I shall never fall into its fellow—I will strike, for the future, on the glowing, malleable metal; afterward, *filing* is quite another process from hammering, and a more difficult one: note, that 'filing' is the wrong word,—and the rest of it, the wrong simile,—and all of it, in its stupid wrongness very characteristic of what I try to illustrate—oh, the better, better days are before me *there* as in all else![2]

That same day Elizabeth returned the proof of *Luria* and 'the two parts of the Soul's Tragedy'. She would have liked to reread the second part of the latter, but was unwilling to retain it, although he had given her 'leave'. 'I think of the printers—& you will let me have the proof, in this case also.'[3] 'I shall be anxious to hear your own thoughts of the "Soul's Tragedy" when you have it in print,' she wrote the following day.[4] Surely he would then like it better: 'It *strikes* me. It is original, as they say. There is something in it awakening .. striking:—and when it has awakened, it wont let you go to sleep again immediately.' The following day he told her that he had 'put in a few phrases in the second part . . . where Ogniben speaks', and hoped that they

give a little more insight as to his character—which I meant for that of a man of wide speculation and narrow practice,—universal understanding of men & sympathy with them, yet professionally restricted claims for himself, for his own life. *There*, was the theology to have come in! He should have explained, 'the belief in a future state, with me modifies every feeling derivable from this present life—I consider *that* as dependent on foregoing *this*—consequently, I may see that your principles are perfectly right and proper to be embraced so far as concerns this world, tho' I believe there is an eventual gain, to be obtained elsewhere, in either opposing or disregarding them,—in not availing myself of the advantages

---

[1] Kintner, ii. 569–70. We agree with Kintner that the passage 'about the child' is probably that at II. 314 ff.

[2] Kintner, ii. 572.

[3] Kintner, ii. 573.

[4] Kintner, ii. 577.

they procure'. Do you see?—as a man may not choose to drink wine, for his health's sake, or from a scruple of conscience, &c.—and yet may be a good judge of what wine should be, how it *ought* to taste—Something like this was *meant*—and when it is forgotten almost, and only the written thing with a shadow of the meaning stays,—you wonder that the written thing gets to look better in time?[1]

Four days later Elizabeth returned proofs of *A Soul's Tragedy*, because Browning might choose 'perhaps to bring the sheet corrected into town' for Moxon, on his next visit to her.

Tomorrow I shall force you to tell me how you like the Tragedy NOW! For my part, it delights me—& must raise your reputation as a poet & thinker . . *must*. Chiappino is highly dramatic in that first part, & speaks so finely sometimes that it is a wrench to one's sympathies to find him overthrown.[2]

On 7 April he complained that he had been sent one proof only,

so I have been correcting everything as fast as possible, that, returning it at once, a *revise* might arrive, fit to send, for *this* that comes is just as bad as if I had let it alone in the first instance. All your corrections are golden . . . As for that point we spoke of yesterday—it seems 'past praying for'—if I make the speech an 'aside', I *commit* Ogniben to that opinion:—did you notice, at the beginning of the second part, that on this Ogniben's very entry, (as described by a bystander) he is made to say, for first speech, 'I have known so many leaders of revolts'—*'laughing gently to himself'*? This, which was wrongly printed in Italics, as if a comment of the Bystander's own, was a characteristic circumstance, as I meant it—All these opinions should be delivered with a 'gentle laughter to himself'—but—as is said elsewhere,—we profess & we perform![3]

Elizabeth was delighted with the dedication of the pamphlet to Landor, as already recorded, and added: 'As to Ogniben, you understand best of course—*I* understood the "laughing gently to himself," though I omitted to notice the Italics—I perfectly understood that it was the bystander's observation.' When she received her copy, on 13 April, she wrongly supposed that the position of the note about the title of the series, on the reverse of the title-page of *A Soul's Tragedy*, meant that it was excluded: a mistake immediately corrected by Browning. On the 16th she wrote again in praise of

---

[1] Kintner, ii. 579.   [2] Kintner, ii. 589.   [3] Kintner, ii. 597–8.

both works: 'The Soul's Tragedy is wonderful—it suggests the idea of more various power than was necessary to the completion of Luria .. though in itself not a comparable work. But you never wrote more vivid dramatic dialogue than that first part—it is exquisite art, it appears to me.' A few days later she mentioned that she had made hardly any comments on individual passages (in marked contrast to her detailed criticism of *Luria*). On the 27th she wrote:

That *Tragedy* has wonderful things in it—thoughts, suggestions, . . and more & more I feel, that you never did better dialogue than in the first part—Every pulse of it is alive & individual—dramatic dialogue of the best. Nobody in the world could write such dialogue—now, you know, you must be patient & 'meke as maid,' being in the course of the fortynine days of enduring praises.[1]

In fact there was very little praise to endure. Unlike several later critics, most of the reviewers showed little or no interest in the piece. The exception was the anonymous writer of the review in *Douglas Jerrold's Shilling Magazine* in which *Luria* too was highly praised:

The "Soul's Tragedy" is one of the most intensely dramatic works ever penned. The deepest emotions and the nicest traits of character are developed by the mere external conduct and expression. The villain of the piece is a thorough human villain, and the unfolding his villany is a masterly exposition of the degradations and weakness of human nature. The truly good and the noble are equally powerfully portrayed, and Mr. Browning has fulfilled the mission of the poet and the dramatist by giving new and valuable illustrations of our human nature.[2]

The work was not intended for the theatre. 'The theatre and Mr. Browning's dramas are never likely to come in contact,' the reviewer commented; 'not at all events until, as in the early days of our true drama, the most refined minds, and therefore the comparatively few, again visit the playhouse as a place to study nature and philosophy.'[2]

The Text

Neither the original manuscript nor Sarianna's fair copy appears to have survived. In his own copy of the *Bells and Pomegranates* (as

---

[1] Kintner, ii. 599; 628 (cf. 643); 659.   [2] June 1846, p. 574.

issued in volume form)[1] Browning corrected 'love' to 'lose' at II. 212. After 1846 *A Soul's Tragedy* was reprinted in all his collected editions, with a few revisions in each. An interesting change in *1849* is from Stiatta's 'new tragedy' to 'new poem' (II. 446), perhaps a reflection of Browning's own preoccupations at this time. The exclamation 'My God!' (I. 275) was removed in *1868*. The spelling 'Goliahs' for 'Goliaths' (II. 360), was finally eliminated in *1875*. All seven of the substantive alterations made by Browning in the Gordon N. Ray copy of vol. v of *1870* (now in the Pierpont Morgan Library) are made correctly in *1888*; since none is made in *1875*, it seems that Browning did most of his work on *A Soul's Tragedy* for the final edition after 1875.

*   *   *   *

On 13 July, just three months after the publication of the last of the *Bells*, Browning wrote to Domett to thank him for the 'cautions and warnings' which he had sent him from New Zealand:

As to the obscurity and imperfect expression, the last number . . . which you get with this, must stand for the best I could do, *four or five months* ago, to rid myself of these defects—and if you judge I have succeeded in any degree, you will not fancy I am likely to relax in my endeavour now. As for the necessity of such endeavour I agree with you altogether: from the beginning, I have been used to take a high ground, and say, all endeavour elsewhere is thrown away. Endeavour to *think* (the real *thought*), to *imagine*, to *create*, or whatever they call it—as well endeavour to add the cubit to your stature! *Nascitur poeta*—and that conceded to happen, the one object of labour is naturally what you recommend to me, and I to myself—nobody knows better, with what indifferent success. But here is . . . the reason why I have gone on so far although succeeding so indifferently: I felt so instinctively from the beginning that unless I tumbled out the dozen more or less of conceptions, I should bear them about forever.

He hopes that soon 'the real work [will] present itself to be done': if so he will 'begin at once and in earnest'.[2]

Joseph Arnould accurately described the two-volume *Poems* eventually published in 1849 as a revised form of 'Paracelsus & the

---

[1] The copy now belongs to Brigham Young University.
[2] *Browning and Domett*, pp. 126–8.

Bells and Pomegranates'.[1] *Pauline*, *Strafford* and *Sordello* were omitted. The contents of all eight *Bells* were included, Nos. III and VII (*Dramatic Lyrics* and *Dramatic Romances and Lyrics*) being given last, as one collection under the latter title, 'Here's to Nelson's memory!' and 'Claret and Tokay' alone being omitted. The prefatory note reads as follows:

MANY of these pieces were out of print, the rest had been withdrawn from circulation, when the corrected edition, now submitted to the reader, was prepared. The various Poems and Dramas have received the author's most careful revision.

December, 1848.

This edition of 1849 seems to have remained available until 1860, since it appears in Chapman and Hall's list of publications issued in February of that year.

---

[1] See Donald Smalley, 'Joseph Arnould and Robert Browning: New Letters . . .': PMLA (March 1965), 95.

HERE ends my first series of "Bells and Pomegranates:" and I take the opportunity of explaining, in reply to inquiries, that I only meant by that title to indicate an endeavour towards something like an alternation, or mixture, of music with discoursing, sound with sense, poetry with thought; which looks too ambitious, thus expressed, so the symbol was preferred. It is little to the purpose, that such is actually one of the most familiar of the many Rabbinical (and Patristic) acceptations of the phrase; because I confess that, letting authority alone, I supposed the bare words, in such juxta-position, would sufficiently convey the desired meaning. "Faith and good works" is another fancy, for instance, and perhaps no easier to arrive at: yet Giotto placed a pomegranate fruit in the hand of Dante, and Raffaelle crowned his Theology (in the *Camera della Segnatura*) with blossoms of the same; as if the Bellari and Vasari would be sure to come after, and explain that it was merely "*simbolo delle buone opere—il qual Pomo granato fu però usato nelle vesti del Pontefice appresso gli Ebrei*"

R.B.

For commentary on this prefatory note, which was printed opposite the first page of *A Soul's Tragedy* in *1846* (only), see Vol. III, pp. 3 ff.

A SOUL'S TRAGEDY.

ACT FIRST,
BEING WHAT WAS CALLED THE POETRY OF CHIAPPINO'S LIFE:
AND ACT SECOND, ITS PROSE.

part title *1846–65* TRAGEDY. PART FIRST, ... AND PART SECOND, *1868–75* PROSE. *London*, 1846.

PERSONS.

LUITOLFO *and* EULALIA, *betrothed lovers*.
CHIAPPINO, *their friend*.
OGNIBEN, *the Pope's Legate*.
Citizens of Faenza.

TIME, 15—. PLACE, *Faenza*.

persons (1865–89 only) 1865 OGNIBEN, *the Legate*:

    Faenza: a city some 30 miles SW of Ravenna and 30 miles SE of Bologna, which became part of the Papal States in 1509. It was governed by Rome through Ravenna.

A SOUL'S TRAGEDY.

ACT I.

SCENE.—*Inside* LUITOLFO'S *house.* CHIAPPINO, EULALIA.

Eulalia. What is it keeps Luitolfo? Night's fast falling,
And 't was scarce sunset . . . had the ave-bell
Sounded before he sought the Provost's house?
I think not: all he had to say would take
Few minutes, such a very few, to say!   5
How do you think, Chiappino? If our lord
The Provost were less friendly to your friend
Than everybody here professes him,
I should begin to tremble—should not you?
Why are you silent when so many times   10
I turn and speak to you?
   Chiappino.   That's good!
   Eulalia.   You laugh!
   Chiappino. Yes. I had fancied nothing that bears price
In the whole world was left to call my own;
And, may be, felt a little pride thereat.
Up to a single man's or woman's love,   15
Down to the right in my own flesh and blood,
There's nothing mine, I fancied,—till you spoke:
—Counting, you see, as "nothing" the permission
To study this peculiar lot of mine
In silence: well, go silence with the rest   20

section heading *1846–65* PART I.   s.d. {all editions except *1888* and *1889* omit the word 'SCENE.'} *1846–63* house at Faenza. CHIAPPINO,   11 *1846–75* laugh? 13 *1846,1849* own,   14 *1846,1849* thereat: 17 *1846–65* spoke!

  2 *ave-bell*: the bell rung when Aves (Hail Marys) are to be said, for example at dawn and about sunset (as here).

Of the world's good! What can I say, shall serve?

   Eulalia. This,—lest you, even more than needs, embitter
Our parting: say your wrongs have cast, for once,
A cloud across your spirit!

   Chiappino.   How a cloud?

   Eulalia. No man nor woman loves you, did you say?   25

   Chiappino. My God, were't not for thee!

   Eulalia.   Ay, God remains,
Even did men forsake you.

   Chiappino.   Oh, not so!
Were't not for God, I mean, what hope of truth—
Speaking truth, hearing truth, would stay with man?
I, now—the homeless friendless penniless   30
Proscribed and exiled wretch who speak to you,—
Ought to speak truth, yet could not, for my death,
(The thing that tempts me most) help speaking lies
About your friendship and Luitolfo's courage
And all our townsfolk's equanimity—   35
Through sheer incompetence to rid myself
Of the old miserable lying trick
Caught from the liars I have lived with,—God,
Did I not turn to thee! It is thy prompting
I dare to be ashamed of, and thy counsel   40
Would die along my coward lip, I know.
But I do turn to thee. This craven tongue,
These features which refuse the soul its way,
Reclaim thou! Give me truth—truth, power to speak—
And after be sole present to approve   45
The spoken truth! Or, stay, that spoken truth,
Who knows but you, too, may approve?

   Eulalia.   Ah, well—
Keep silence then, Chiappino!

   Chiappino.   You would hear,
You shall now,—why the thing we please to style

---

42 *1846,1849* thee! *1863,1865* Thee!   47 *1846–65* too, might approve?
49 *1846–65* And shall .... we're pleased to

  36 *incompetence*: inability.

My gratitude to you and all your friends   50
For service done me, is just gratitude
So much as yours was service: no whit more.
I was born here, so was Luitolfo; both
At one time, much with the same circumstance
Of rank and wealth; and both, up to this night   55
Of parting company, have side by side
Still fared, he in the sunshine—I, the shadow.
"Why?" asks the world. "Because," replies the world
To its complacent self, "these playfellows,
"Who took at church the holy-water drop   60
"Each from the other's finger, and so forth,—
"Were of two moods: Luitolfo was the proper
"Friend-making, everywhere friend-finding soul,
"Fit for the sunshine, so, it followed him.
"A happy-tempered bringer of the best   65
"Out of the worst; who bears with what's past cure,
"And puts so good a face on't—wisely passive
"Where action's fruitless, while he remedies
"In silence what the foolish rail against;
"A man to smooth such natures as parade   70
"Of opposition must exasperate;
"No general gauntlet-gatherer for the weak
"Against the strong, yet over-scrupulous
"At lucky junctures; one who won't forego
"The after-battle work of binding wounds,   75
"Because, forsooth he'd have to bring himself
"To side with wound-inflictors for their leave!"

52 *1846–75* service—and no more.   57 *1846,1849* shadow: 58 *1846–65*
world: "Because,"   59 *1863* playfellows.   61 *1846–63* One from
64 *1846,1849* him;   77 *1846,1849* with their inflictors

    63 *Friend-making . . . friend-finding*: both perhaps Browning's coinages, though OED has
one example (1580) of 'friendmaker'.

    67 *wisely passive*: cf. Wordsworth, 'Expostulation and Reply', 24.

    72 *gauntlet-gatherer*: no other example in OED. One who accepts the challenge.

    74 *won't forego*: earlier Browning had 'dont': EBB commented: 'Strictly speaking, is not
"does'nt" the right abbreviation for only the *third* person? I dont—he does'nt—"who *wont*
go" you might say with accuracy perhaps.' Cf. 'The Flight of the Duchess', 817.

—Why do you gaze, nor help me to repeat
What comes so glibly from the common mouth,
About Luitolfo and his so-styled friend?   80
    Eulalia. Because that friend's sense is obscured ...
    Chiappino.   I thought
You would be readier with the other half
Of the world's story, my half! Yet, 't is true,
For all the world does say it. Say your worst!
True, I thank God, I ever said "you sin,"   85
When a man did sin: if I could not say it,
I glared it at him; if I could not glare it,
I prayed against him; then my part seemed over.
God's may begin yet: so it will, I trust.
    Eulalia. If the world outraged you, did we?
    Chiappino.   What's "me"   90
That you use well or ill? It's man, in me,
All your successes are an outrage to,
You all, whom sunshine follows, as you say!
Here's our Faenza birthplace; they send here
A provost from Ravenna: how he rules,   95
You can at times be eloquent about.
"Then, end his rule!"—"Ah yes, one stroke does that!
"But patience under wrong works slow and sure.
"Must violence still bring peace forth? He beside,
"Returns so blandly one's obeisance! ah—   100
"Some latent virtue may be lingering yet,
"Some human sympathy which, once excite,

---

*83 {reading of *1846–75*} *1888,1889* true.   84 *1846–65* it!   88 *1846–65* over;
89 *1846–65* trust!   97 *1846* rule"! ah *1849* ah   98 *1846,1849* sure:
100 *1846,1849* obeisance—

   82–3 *the other half / Of the world's story*: cf. the titles of Books II and III of *The Ring and the Book*: 'Half-Rome' and 'The Other Half-Rome'.

   90 *What's "me"*: EBB commented: '"Who's 'me'—" It sounds awkward—What's I"—yet I doubt, altogether. What a fine part of the dialogue all this is—Would "What's 'me'" sound less awkward—"What's 'me'"—"It's man in me". Yes, I think it would be "what" .. for the relation of the "It" afterwards.'

   95 *Ravenna*: a city in NE Italy, some 45 miles E of Bologna. It is an archiepiscopal see, and has Faenza in its province.

"And all the lump were leavened quietly:
"So, no more talk of striking, for this time!"
But I, as one of those he rules, won't bear   105
These pretty takings-up and layings-down
Our cause, just as you think occasion suits.
Enough of earnest, is there? You'll play, will you?
Diversify your tactics, give submission,
Obsequiousness and flattery a turn,   110
While we die in our misery patient deaths?
We all are outraged then, and I the first:
I, for mankind, resent each shrug and smirk,
Each beck and bend, each . . . all you do and are,
I hate!

    Eulalia. We share a common censure, then.   115
'T is well you have not poor Luitolfo's part
Nor mine to point out in the wide offence.

    Chiappino. Oh, shall I let you so escape me, lady?
Come, on your own ground, lady,—from yourself,
(Leaving the people's wrong, which most is mine)   120
What have I got to be so grateful for?
These three last fines, no doubt, one on the other
Paid by Luitolfo?

    Eulalia.   Shame, Chiappino!

    Chiappino.   Shame
Fall presently on who deserves it most!
—Which is to see. He paid my fines—my friend,   125
Your prosperous smooth lover presently,
Then, scarce your wooer,—soon, your husband: well—
I loved you.

104 *1846,1849* time!   107 *1846–65* suits!   112 *1846–65* first!
115 *1846,1849* then!   *116 (reading of *1846–75*) *1888, 1889* T is   117 *1846,*
1849 Or mine   120 *1846* Leaving . . . . mine,   125 *1846* see:
126 *1846,1849* smooth husband presently,   127 *1846,1849* wooer,—now your
lover: well—   128 *1846,1849* you!

114 *beck and bend*: Jamieson tells us that 'A great deal of *becking* and *beenging*' was a
satirical phrase 'still used among the vulgar, to denote much ceremony at meeting': *An
Etymological Dictionary of the Scottish Language*, by John Jamieson, 2 vols., 1808, s.v. 'Beck'.

Eulalia. Hold!

Chiappino.   You knew it, years ago.
When my voice faltered and my eye grew dim
Because you gave me your silk mask to hold—   130
My voice that greatens when there's need to curse
The people's Provost to their heart's content,
—My eye, the Provost, who bears all men's eyes,
Banishes now because he cannot bear,—
You knew . . . but you do your parts—my part, I: 135
So be it! You flourish, I decay: all's well.

    Eulalia. I hear this for the first time.

    Chiappino.   The fault's there?
Then my days spoke not, and my nights of fire
Were voiceless? Then the very heart may burst,
Yet all prove nought, because no mincing speech   140
Tells leisurely that thus it is and thus?
Eulalia, truce with toying for this once!
A banished fool, who troubles you to-night
For the last time—why, what's to fear from me?
You knew I loved you!

    Eulalia.   Not so, on my faith!   145
You were my now-affianced lover's friend—
Came in, went out with him, could speak as he.
All praise your ready parts and pregnant wit;
See how your words come from you in a crowd!
Luitolfo's first to place you o'er himself   150
In all that challenges respect and love:
Yet you were silent then, who blame me now.
I say all this by fascination, sure:

              \

---

128 *1846,1849* ago;   129 *1846–63* my eyes grew   133 *1846–63* —My eyes,
the   134 *1846,1849* bear!   135 *1846,1849* I!   136 *1846,1849* decay!
1863,1865 decay.   *1846–65* well!   137 *1846* time! *Ch.* Oh, the fault was there?
1849 time!   142 *1863,1865* Eulalia!   *1846,1849* once—   144 *1846,1849*
time—Oh, what's   147 *1846,1849* he;   152 *1846,1849* now!

    148 *pregnant wit*: a phrase common in the sixteenth and seventeenth centuries, as OED
notes.

    153 *by fascination*: i.e. I am bewitched.

I, all but wed to one I love, yet listen!
It must be, you are wronged, and that the wrongs   155
Luitolfo pities . . .
    Chiappino.   —You too pity? Do!
But hear first what my wrongs are; so began
This talk and so shall end this talk. I say,
Was't not enough that I must strive (I saw)
To grow so far familiar with your charms   160
As next contrive some way to win them—which
To do, an age seemed far too brief—for, see!
We all aspire to heaven; and there lies heaven
Above us: go there! Dare we go? no, surely!
How dare we go without a reverent pause,   165
A growing less unfit for heaven? Just so,
I dared not speak: the greater fool, it seems!
Was't not enough to struggle with such folly,
But I must have, beside, the very man
Whose slight free loose and incapacious soul   170
Gave his tongue scope to say whate'er he would
—Must have him load me with his benefits
—For fortune's fiercest stroke?
    Eulalia.   Justice to him
That's now entreating, at his risk perhaps,
Justice for you! Did he once call those acts   175
Of simple friendship—bounties, benefits?
    Chiappino. No: the straight course had been to call them thus.
Then, I had flung them back, and kept myself

154 *1846–75* I am all   *1846,1849* listen—   159 *1846* I saw,   161 *1846,*
1849 As to contrive   162 *1846–75* too little—for,   163 *1846–75* there is
Heaven   166 *1846–75* Heaven?—Even so,   173 *1846,1849* stroke!
177 *1846–63* them so— *1865* them so; *1868–75* them so.

    159–62 *Was't not enough*: EBB quotes with 'I said,' at the end of 159 and 'all you' at the
end of 160, followed by: 'As find & take some way to get you—which / To do, an age
seemed far too little', commenting: 'There is something obscure, as it strikes me, in the
expression of this—"As *to* find" seems necessary to the construction. But "*all you*" (besides)
appears to lead the thought from Eulalia—& you mean Eulalia, . . I think. The reader will
doubt here, & have first & second thoughts.'
    162 *an age seemed far too brief*: cf. Rochester, 'The Mistress. A Song', 1–2.
    170 *incapacious*: 'Narrow; of small content': Johnson.

Unhampered, free as he to win the prize
We both sought. But "the gold was dross," he said: 180
"He loved me, and I loved him not: why spurn
"A trifle out of superfluity?
"He had forgotten he had done as much."
So had not I! Henceforth, try as I could
To take him at his word, there stood by you   185
My benefactor; who might speak and laugh
And urge his nothings, even banter me
Before you—but my tongue was tied. A dream!
Let's wake: your husband . . . how you shake at that!
Good—my revenge!
   Eulalia.   Why should I shake? What forced   190
Or forces me to be Luitolfo's bride?
   Chiappino. There's my revenge, that nothing forces you.
No gratitude, no liking of the eye
Nor longing of the heart, but the poor bond
Of habit—here so many times he came,   195
So much he spoke,—all these compose the tie
That pulls you from me. Well, he paid my fines,
Nor missed a cloak from wardrobe, dish from table;
He spoke a good word to the Provost here,
Held me up when my fortunes fell away   200
—It had not looked so well to let me drop—
Men take pains to preserve a tree-stump, even,
Whose boughs they played beneath—much more a friend.
But one grows tired of seeing, after the first,
Pains spent upon impracticable stuff   205
Like me. I could not change: you know the rest.

---

180 *1846–63* sought— *1865* sought: *1846–65* said, 181 *1846–63* not—to
spurn 182 *1846–63* superfluity: 183 *1846* much"! *1849* much!"
192 *1846,1849,1865* you! 197 *1846,1849* me! 203 *1846,1849* friend!
206 *1846–65* me:

 198 *Nor missed a cloak*: EBB quotes with 'nor a dish from table' and the query: 'Why such
a dragging line just here? An oversight probably—The second *"nor a"* might drop out to
advantage.'

 205 *impracticable*: 'Untractable; unmanageable; stubborn': Johnson.

I've spoke my mind too fully out, by chance,
This morning to our Provost; so, ere night
I leave the city on pain of death. And now
On my account there's gallant intercession   210
Goes forward—that's so graceful!—and anon
He'll noisily come back: "the intercession
"Was made and fails; all's over for us both;
"'T is vain contending; I would better go."
And I do go—and straight to you he turns   215
Light of a load; and ease of that permits
His visage to repair the natural bland
Œconomy, sore broken late to suit
My discontent. Thus, all are pleased—you, with him,
He with himself, and all of you with me   220
—"Who," say the citizens, "had done far better
"In letting people sleep upon their woes,
"If not possessed with talent to relieve them
"When once awake;—but then I had," they'll say,
"Doubtless some unknown compensating pride   225
"In what I did; and as I seem content
"With ruining myself, why, so should they be."
And so they are, and so be with his prize
The devil, when he gets them speedily!
Why does not your Luitolfo come? I long   230
To don this cloak and take the Lugo path.
It seems you never loved me, then?
    Eulalia.   Chiappino!
    Chiappino. Never?
    Eulalia.   Never.

---

207 *1846–65* out, for once,   209 *1846,1849* death— *1863,1865* death:
212 *1846,1849* the   214 *1846,1849* I had better go: 215 *1846–65* and so to
216 *1846,1849* load,   217 *1846–65* repair its natural   219 *1846,1849* dis-
content: so all   221 *1846–63* —Who, ... had   224 *1846–65* once they
woke;—but   *1846–63* had,   225 *1846–63* Doubtless   227 *1846,1849* be,
1863 be: *1865* be:"

216 *Light*: lightened.
218 *Œconomy*: management, here expression.
231 *Lugo*: about 10 miles N of Faenza.

Chiappino. That's sad. Say what I might,
There was no help from being sure this while
You loved me. Love like mine must have return, 235
I thought: no river starts but to some sea.
And had you loved me, I could soon devise
Some specious reason why you stifled love,
Some fancied self-denial on your part,
Which made you choose Luitolfo; so, excepting 240
From the wide condemnation of all here,
One woman. Well, the other dream may break!
If I knew any heart, as mine loved you,
Loved me, though in the vilest breast 't were lodged,
I should, I think, be forced to love again: 245
Else there's no right nor reason in the world.
    Eulalia. "If you knew," say you,—but I did not know.
That's where you're blind, Chiappino!—a disease
Which if I may remove, I'll not repent
The listening to. You cannot, will not, see 250
How, place you but in every circumstance
Of us, you are just now indignant at,
You'd be as we.
    Chiappino. I should be? . . . that; again!
I, to my friend, my country and my love,
Be as Luitolfo and these Faentines? 255
    Eulalia. As we.
    Chiappino. Now, I'll say something to remember.
I trust in nature for the stable laws
Of beauty and utility.—Spring shall plant,
And Autumn garner to the end of time:
I trust in God—the right shall be the right 260

---

233 *1846,1849* sad— *1863,1865* sad: 234 *1846–63* no helping being
235 *1846–63* me— *1865* me; 236 *1846,1849* sea! 242 *1846,1849* woman!
246 *1846,1849* world! 247 *1846,1849* know— *1863,1865* know: 250 *1846,*
1849 to: 253 *1846* that *1849–70* that, 256 *1846–65* remember!

236 *no river starts*: proverbial. Cf. *Edward III* (perhaps partly by Shakespeare), v. i. 92: 'All
riuers haue recourse vnto the Sea'.
255 *Faentines*: people of Faenza.

And other than the wrong, while he endures:
I trust in my own soul, that can perceive
The outward and the inward, nature's good
And God's: so, seeing these men and myself,
Having a right to speak, thus do I speak.   265
I'll not curse—God bears with them, well may I—
But I—protest against their claiming me.
I simply say, if that's allowable,
I would not (broadly) do as they have done.
—God curse this townful of born slaves, bred slaves,   270
Branded into the blood and bone, slaves! Curse
Whoever loves, above his liberty,
House, land or life! and . . .   [*A knocking without.*
                    —bless my hero-friend,
Luitolfo!
     Eulalia. How he knocks!
     Chiappino.   The peril, lady!
"Chiappino, I have run a risk—a risk!   275
"For when I prayed the Provost (he's my friend)
"To grant you a week's respite of the sentence
"That confiscates your goods, exiles yourself,
"He shrugged his shoulder—I say, shrugged it! Yes,
"And fright of that drove all else from my head.   280
"Here's a good purse of *scudi:* off with you,
"Lest of that shrug come what God only knows!
"The *scudi*—friend, they're trash—no thanks, I beg!
"Take the north gate,—for San Vitale's suburb,
"Whose double taxes you appealed against,   285
"In discomposure at your ill-success
"Is apt to stone you: there, there—only go!

---

265 *1846,1849* I speak: 267 *1846,1849* me!   269 *1846–65* not . . broadly . . .
272 *1846–65* Whoever loved, above   275 *1846–65* risk! My God!   276 *1846–*
65 "How when   277 *1846–65* of his sentence   278 *1846–65* goods, and
exiles you,   281 *1846–63* you!   282 *1846,1849* come—what
283 *1846,1849* beg—

     270 *townful*: antedates the first example in OED.
     281 *scudi*: coins of some value, usually of silver, but sometimes of gold.
     284 *San Vitale's suburb*: this is so common a place-name that identification is impossible.

"Beside, Eulalia here looks sleepily.
"Shake . . . oh, you hurt me, so you squeeze my wrist!"
—Is it not thus you'll speak, adventurous friend?   290
          [*As he opens the door*, LUITOLFO *rushes in, his garments disordered.*

    Eulalia. Luitolfo! Blood?
    Luitolfo.   There's more—and more of it!
Eulalia—take the garment! No—you, friend!
You take it and the blood from me—you dare!
    Eulalia. Oh, who has hurt you? where's the wound?
    Chiappino.   "Who," say you?
The man with many a touch of virtue yet!   295
The Provost's friend has proved too frank of speech,
And this comes of it. Miserable hound!
This comes of temporizing, as I said!
Here's fruit of your smooth speeches and soft looks!
Now see my way! As God lives, I go straight   300
To the palace and do justice, once for all!
    Luitolfo. What says he?
    Chiappino.   I'll do justice on him.
    Luitolfo.   Him?
    Chiappino. The Provost.
    Luitolfo.   I've just killed him.
    Eulalia.   Oh, my God!
    Luitolfo. My friend, they're on my trace; they'll have me—now!
They're round him, busy with him: soon they'll find   305
He's past their help, and then they'll be on me!
Chiappino, save Eulalia! I forget . . .
Were you not bound for . . .
    Chiappino.   Lugo?
    Luitolfo.   Ah—yes—yes!
That was the point I prayed of him to change.

292 *1846–65* garment ..   299 *1846–65* and fair looks!   302 *1846,1849* on him!   303 *1846,1849* him!   307 *1846–65* Eulalia ..   *1865* I forgot .. 308 *1846–65* bound ..   *1846–65* Lugo!   *1846–65* yes—yes—   309 *1865* change,

304 *trace*: track.

Well, go—be happy! Is Eulalia safe?   310
They're on me!
    Chiappino.   'T is through me they reach you, then!
Friend, seem the man you are! Lock arms—that's right!
Now tell me what you've done; explain how you
That still professed forbearance, still preached peace,
Could bring yourself . . .
    Luitolfo.   What was peace for, Chiappino?   315
I tried peace: did that promise, when peace failed,
Strife should not follow? All my peaceful days
Were just the prelude to a day like this.
I cried "You call me 'friend': save my true friend!
"Save him, or lose me!"
    Chiappino.   But you never said   320
You meant to tell the Provost thus and thus.
    Luitolfo. Why should I say it? What else did I mean?
    Chiappino. Well? He persisted?
    Luitolfo.   —"Would so order it
"You should not trouble him too soon again."
I saw a meaning in his eye and lip;   325
I poured my heart's store of indignant words
Out on him: then—I know not! He retorted,
And I . . . some staff lay there to hand—I think
He bade his servants thrust me out—I struck . . .
Ah, they come! Fly you, save yourselves, you two!   330
The dead back-weight of the beheading axe!
The glowing trip-hook, thumbscrews and the gadge!

---

310 *1846–65* happy . .   312 *1846–63* right.   316 *1846,1849* that say that
when   321 *1846–65* and thus!   323 *1846,1849* . . Would   324 *1846,*
1849 again—   327 *1846,1849* not.—

   331 *back-weight*: not in OED.

   332 *trip-hook . . . gadge*: OED considers the former 'perhaps an error': it obviously stands
for some instrument of torture. On 5 April 1846 EBB wrote: 'By the way (talking of St.
Catherine's wheels & the like torments) you wrote "gag" . . . did you not? . . where the proof
says "gadge"—I did not alter it.' Browning replied: 'gadge is a real name (in Johnson, too)
for a torturing iron—it is part of the horror of such things that they should be mysteriously
named,—indefinitely . . .'. She replied: 'you are perfectly right about "gadge" & in the view
you take of the effect of such words. You misunderstood me if you fancied that I objected
. . . it was simply my ignorance . . . Of course, the horror of those specialities is heightened

Eulalia. They do come! Torches in the Place! Farewell,
Chiappino! You can work no good to us—
Much to yourself; believe not, all the world　　　　　335
Must needs be cursed henceforth!
　　Chiappino.　　　　　　　　　And you?
　　Eulalia.　　　　　　　　　　　　　　I stay.
　　Chiappino. Ha, ha! Now, listen! I am master here!
This was my coarse disguise; this paper shows
My path of flight and place of refuge—see—
Lugo, Argenta, past San Nicolo,　　　　　340
Ferrara, then to Venice and all's safe!
Put on the cloak! His people have to fetch
A compass round about. There's time enough
Ere they can reach us, so you straightway make
For Lugo . . . nay, he hears not! On with it—　　　　345
The cloak, Luitolfo, do you hear me? See—
He obeys he knows not how. Then, if I must—
Answer me! Do you know the Lugo gate?
　　Eulalia. The north-west gate, over the bridge?
　　Luitolfo.　　　　　　　　　　　　　I know.　　　349
　　Chiappino. Well, there—you are not frightened? all my route
Is traced in that: at Venice you escape
Their power. Eulalia, I am master here!
　　　　　[*Shouts from without. He pushes out* LUITOLFO, *who complies*
　　　　　　　　　　　　　　　　　　　mechanically.
In time! Nay, help me with him—so! He's gone.
　　Eulalia. What have you done? On you, perchance, all know
The Provost's hater, will men's vengeance fall　　　　　355
As our accomplice.
　　Chiappino.　　　　Mere accomplice? See!
　　　　　　　　　　　[*Putting on* LUITOLFO's *vest.*

349 *1846–65* bridge! .... know!　　　351 *1846–65* you'll escape　　　352 *1846,*
1849 power!　　　356 *1846,1849* our accomplice . .

by the very want of distinct understanding they meet with in us:—it is the rack in the
shadow of the vault': Kintner, ii. 590–1, 593–4, 620. Oddly enough, the word is not in
Johnson.

341 *then to Venice*: Chiappino's route is dictated by his need to keep to places which are
politically safe for him.

Now, lady, am I true to my profession,
Or one of these?
    Eulalia.   You take Luitolfo's place?
    Chiappino. Die for him.
    Eulalia.   Well done!   [*Shouts increase.*
    Chiappino.   How the people tarry!
I can't be silent; I must speak: or sing—   360
How natural to sing now!
    Eulalia.   Hush and pray!
We are to die; but even I perceive
'T is not a very hard thing so to die.
My cousin of the pale-blue tearful eyes,
Poor Cesca, suffers more from one day's life   365
With the stern husband; Tisbe's heart goes forth
Each evening after that wild son of hers,
To track his thoughtless footstep through the streets:
How easy for them both to die like this!
I am not sure that I could live as they.   370
    Chiappino. Here they come, crowds! They pass the gate? Yes!—
    No!—
One torch is in the courtyard. Here flock all.
    Eulalia. At least Luitolfo has escaped. What cries!
    Chiappino. If they would drag one to the market-place,
One might speak there!
    Eulalia.   List, list!
    Chiappino.   They mount the steps.   375

          Enter the Populace.

    Chiappino. I killed the Provost!
    The Populace [*speaking together*]. 'T was Chiappino, friends!
Our saviour! The best man at last as first!
He who first made us feel what chains we wore,

359 *1846,1849* him!   368 *1865* the street: 372 *1846,1849* all!
373 *1846,1849* escaped!   375 *1846,1849* steps!   377 *1846–65* saviour.—
378 *1846–65* us see what

357 *my profession*: what I said I would do.
363 *'T is not a very hard thing*: cf. Byron, *Manfred*, III. 411: "tis not so difficult to die'.
365 *Cesca*: a familiar form of the name Francesca.

He also strikes the blow that shatters them,
He at last saves us—our best citizen!   380
—Oh, have you only courage to speak now?
My eldest son was christened a year since
"Cino" to keep Chiappino's name in mind—
Cino, for shortness merely, you observe!
The city's in our hands. The guards are fled.   385
Do you, the cause of all, come down—come up—
Come out to counsel us, our chief, our king,
Whate'er rewards you! Choose your own reward!
The peril over, its reward begins!
Come and harangue us in the market-place!   390
   Eulalia. Chiappino?
   Chiappino.   Yes—I understand your eyes!
You think I should have promptlier disowned
This deed with its strange unforeseen success,
In favour of Luitolfo. But the peril,
So far from ended, hardly seems begun.   395
To-morrow, rather, when a calm succeeds,
We easily shall make him full amends:
And meantime—if we save them as they pray,
And justify the deed by its effects?
   Eulalia. You would, for worlds, you had denied at once.   400
   Chiappino. I know my own intention, be assured!
All's well. Precede us, fellow-citizens!

---

385 *1846,1849* fled— *1863* fled;   386 *1846–65* down—come down—
387 *1846–65* Come forth to   391 *1846–65* Chiappino!   395 *1846,1849*
begun!   400 *1846,1849* once!   401 *1865 Eu.* I know   402 *1846–65*
well!

382 *My eldest son*: one particular citizen is speaking here.

ACT II.

SCENE.—*The Market-place.* LUITOLFO *in disguise mingling with the* Populace *assembled opposite the* Provost's *Palace.*

1st Bystander [*to* LUITOLFO]. You, a friend of Luitolfo's? Then, your friend is vanished,—in all probability killed on the night that his patron the tyrannical Provost was loyally suppressed here, exactly a month ago, by our illustrious fellow-citizen, thrice-noble saviour, and new Provost that is like to be, this very morning,— 5 Chiappino!

Luitolfo. He the new Provost?

2nd Bystander. Up those steps will he go, and beneath yonder pillar stand, while Ogniben, the Pope's Legate from Ravenna, reads the new dignitary's title to the people, according to established 10 custom: for which reason, there is the assemblage you inquire about.

Luitolfo. Chiappino—the late Provost's successor? Impossible! But tell me of that presently. What I would know first of all is, wherefore Luitolfo must so necessarily have been killed on that 15 memorable night?

3rd Bystander. You were Luitolfo's friend? So was I. Never, if you will credit me, did there exist so poor-spirited a milksop. He, with all the opportunities in the world, furnished by daily converse with our oppressor, would not stir a finger to help us: and, when 20 Chiappino rose in solitary majesty and ... how does one go on saying? ... dealt the godlike blow,—this Luitolfo, not unreasonably fearing the indignation of an aroused and liberated people, fled precipitately. He may have got trodden to death in the press at the

part title *1846–65* PART II.   s.d. {all editions except *1888* and *1889* omit the word 'SCENE.'}   1 *1849* Luitolfo's!   7 *1846–63* He   10–11 *1846,1849* established usage.—For *1863,1865* established usage: for   13 *1846–65* the old Provost's   18 *1846–65* milk-sop!   20 *1846,1849* us: so when 24 *1846,1849* precipitately:

9 *Legate*: 'An ecclesiastic deputed to represent the Pope and armed with his authority': OED.

25 south-east gate, when the Provost's guards fled through it to
Ravenna, with their wounded master,—if he did not rather hang
himself under some hedge.

Luitolfo. Or why not simply have lain perdue in some quiet
corner,—such as San Cassiano, where his estate was,—receiving
30 daily intelligence from some sure friend, meanwhile, as to the turn
matters were taking here—how, for instance, the Provost was not
dead, after all, only wounded—or, as to-day's news would seem to
prove, how Chiappino was not Brutus the Elder, after all, only the
new Provost—and thus Luitolfo be enabled to watch a favourable
35 opportunity for returning? Might it not have been so?

3rd Bystander. Why, he may have taken that care of himself,
certainly; for he came of a cautious stock. I'll tell you how his uncle,
just such another gingerly treader on tiptoes with finger on lip,—
how he met his death in the great plague-year: *dico vobis!* Hearing
40 that the seventeenth house in a certain street was infected, he
calculates to pass it in safety by taking plentiful breath, say, when he
shall arrive at the eleventh house; then scouring by, holding that
breath, till he be got so far on the other side as number twenty-
three, and thus elude the danger.—And so did he begin; but, as he
45 arrived at thirteen, we will say,—thinking to improve on his
precaution by putting up a little prayer to St. Nepomucene of
Prague, this exhausted so much of his lungs' reserve, that at sixteen
it was clean spent,—consequently at the fatal seventeen he inhaled
with a vigour and persistence enough to suck you any latent venom
50 out of the heart of a stone—Ha, ha!

Luitolfo [*aside*]. (If I had not lent that man the money he wanted
last spring, I should fear this bitterness was attributable to me.)
Luitolfo is dead then, one may conclude?

3rd Bystander. Why, he had a house here, and a woman to whom

---

28 *1846 perdue*   35 *1846–65* returning—   38 *1865* on tiptoe with
51 *1865* If   52–3 *1865* me. †[*Aloud.*]† Luitolfo   53 *1846,1849* conclude!

28 *perdue*: hidden.

33 *Brutus the Elder*: Lucius Junius Brutus, the legendary founder of the Roman Republic,
said to have led the rebellion against Tarquin the Proud. See *Sordello*, iv. 981 ff. (with n.) and
vi. 455. He is called 'the Elder' to distinguish him from Julius Caesar's assassin.

39 *dico vobis!*: I say to you!   42 *scouring*: rushing.

46 *St. Nepomucene*: the patron-saint of Bohemia.

he was affianced; and as they both pass naturally to the new Provost, 55
his friend and heir ...

Luitolfo. Ah, I suspected you of imposing on me with your
pleasantry! I know Chiappino better.

1*st Bystander.* (Our friend has the bile! After all, I do not dislike
finding somebody vary a little this general gape of admiration at 60
Chiappino's glorious qualities.) Pray, how much may you know of
what has taken place in Faenza since that memorable night?

Luitolfo. It is most to the purpose, that I know Chiappino to have
been by profession a hater of that very office of Provost, you now
charge him with proposing to accept. 65

1*st Bystander.* Sir, I'll tell you. That night was indeed memorable.
Up we rose, a mass of us, men, women, children; out fled the
guards with the body of the tyrant; we were to defy the world: but,
next grey morning, "What will Rome say?" began everybody. You
know we are governed by Ravenna, which is governed by Rome. 70
And quietly into the town, by the Ravenna road, comes on mule-
back a portly personage, Ogniben by name, with the quality of
Pontifical Legate; trots briskly through the streets humming a "*Cur
fremuere gentes*," and makes directly for the Provost's Palace—there
it faces you. "One Messer Chiappino is your leader? I have known 75
three-and-twenty leaders of revolts!" (laughing gently to him-
self)—"Give me the help of your arm from my mule to yonder steps
under the pillar—So! And now, my revolters and good friends,
what do you want? The guards burst into Ravenna last night bearing
your wounded Provost; and, having had a little talk with him, I take 80
on myself to come and try appease the disorderliness, before Rome,
hearing of it, resort to another method: 't is I come, and not another,
from a certain love I confess to, of composing differences. So, do

58 *1846,1849* pleasantry— .... better!   66 *1846,1849* memorable— *1863,1865*
memorable;   69 *1846,1849* say,"   *1846–65* everybody—(you   70 *1846–*
65 Rome).   *72 {reading of *1846-75*,DC,*1889*} *1888* Ogniben by with name, the
quality of   82 *1846* it, resorts to

59 *has the bile*: is angry, peevish.
73–4 "*Cur fremuere gentes*": the beginning of Ps. 2 in the Vulgate version: 'Why do the
heathen rage ...?'
75 *Messer*: Master.
76–7 (*laughing gently to himself*): see Browning's comment on this passage, quoted on
p. 276 above.

you understand, you are about to experience this unheard-of
85 tyranny from me, that there shall be no heading nor hanging, no
confiscation nor exile: I insist on your simply pleasing yourselves.
And now, pray, what does please you? To live without any govern-
ment at all? Or having decided for one, to see its minister murdered
by the first of your body that chooses to find himself wronged, or
90 disposed for reverting to first principles and a justice anterior to all
institutions,—and so will you carry matters, that the rest of the
world must at length unite and put down such a den of wild beasts?
As for vengeance on what has just taken place,—once for all, the
wounded man assures me he cannot conjecture who struck him;
95 and this so earnestly, that one may be sure he knows perfectly well
what intimate acquaintance could find admission to speak with him
late last evening. I come not for vengeance therefore, but from pure
curiosity to hear what you will do next." And thus he ran on, on,
easily and volubly, till he seemed to arrive quite naturally at the
100 praise of law, order, and paternal government by somebody from
rather a distance. All our citizens were in the snare, and about to be
friends with so congenial an adviser; but that Chiappino suddenly
stood forth, spoke out indignantly, and set things right again.

   Luitolfo. Do you see? I recognize him there!

105   *3rd Bystander*. Ay but, mark you, at the end of Chiappino's
longest period in praise of a pure republic,—"And by whom do I
desire such a government should be administered, perhaps, but by
one like yourself?"—returns the Legate: thereupon speaking for a
quarter of an hour together, on the natural and only legitimate
110 government by the best and wisest. And it should seem there was
soon discovered to be no such vast discrepancy at bottom between
this and Chiappino's theory, place but each in its proper light. "Oh,
are you there?" quoth Chiappino: "Ay, in that, I agree," returns
Chiappino: and so on.

86 *1846–65* yourselves,—   96–7 *1846,1849* him so late that evening—
98–9 *1846* thus ran he on easily *1849–65* ran on, easily   101 *1846,1849* distance:
103 *1846,1849* again . . .   110 *1846,1849* Wisest—   113–14 *1846–65* Chi-
appino:—"In . . . . Chiappino,

   85 *heading*: beheading, as in *Measure for Measure*, II. i. 225 ('heading and hanging').
   106 *period*: sentence.
   113 *are you there?*: is *that* what you mean?

Luitolfo. But did Chiappino cede at once to this?   115

1st *Bystander.* Why, not altogether at once. For instance, he said that the difference between him and all his fellows was, that they seemed all wishing to be kings in one or another way,—"whereas what right," asked he, "has any man to wish to be superior to another?"—whereat, "Ah, sir," answers the Legate, "this is the death   120 of me, so often as I expect something is really going to be revealed to us by you clearer-seers, deeper-thinkers—this—that your right-hand (to speak by a figure) should be found taking up the weapon it displayed so ostentatiously, not to destroy any dragon in our path, as was prophesied, but simply to cut off its own fellow left-hand: 125 yourself set about attacking yourself. For see now! Here are you who, I make sure, glory exceedingly in knowing the noble nature of the soul, its divine impulses, and so forth; and with such a know-ledge you stand, as it were, armed to encounter the natural doubts and fears as to that same inherent nobility, which are apt to waylay   130 us, the weaker ones, in the road of life. And when we look eagerly to see them fall before you, lo, round you wheel, only the left-hand gets the blow; one proof of the soul's nobility destroys simply another proof, quite as good, of the same, for you are found delivering an opinion like this! Why, what is this perpetual yearning   135 to exceed, to subdue, to be better than, and a king over, one's fellows,—all that you so disclaim,—but the very tendency yourself are most proud of, and under another form, would oppose to it,—only in a lower stage of manifestation? You don't want to be vulgarly superior to your fellows after their poor fashion—to have   140 me hold solemnly up your gown's tail, or hand you an express of the last importance from the Pope, with all these bystanders noticing how unconcerned you look the while: but neither does our gaping friend, the burgess yonder, want the other kind of kingship, that consists in understanding better than his fellows this and similar   145 points of human nature, nor to roll under his tongue this sweeter

116 *1846,1849* once—   118–19 *1846,1849* —whereas .... right,   119–20 *1846,1849* has .... another?   126 *1846–65* yourself—   130 *1846–75* nobility, that are   131 *1846,1849* Life,—   134 *1846–65* same,—you 146 *1846,1849* under the tongue

141 *an express*: an urgent message.

morsel still,—the feeling that, through immense philosophy, he does *not* feel, he rather thinks, above you and me!" And so chatting, they glided off arm-in-arm.

150   *Luitolfo*. And the result is . . .

1st Bystander. Why that, a month having gone by, the indomitable Chiappino, marrying as he will Luitolfo's love—at all events succeeding to Luitolfo's wealth—becomes the first inhabitant of Faenza, and a proper aspirant to the Provostship; which we assemble
155   here to see conferred on him this morning. The Legate's Guard to clear the way! He will follow presently.

Luitolfo [*withdrawing a little*]. I understand the drift of Eulalia's communications less than ever. Yet she surely said, in so many words, that Chiappino was in urgent danger: wherefore, disregard-
160   ing her injunction to continue in my retreat and await the result of—what she called, some experiment yet in process—I hastened here without her leave or knowledge: how could I else? But if this they say be true—if it were for such a purpose, she and Chiappino kept me away . . . Oh, no, no! I must confront him and her before I
165   believe this of them. And at the word, see!

Enter CHIAPPINO *and* EULALIA.

Eulalia. We part here, then? The change in your principles would seem to be complete.

Chiappino. Now, why refuse to see that in my present course I
170   change no principles, only re-adapt them and more adroitly? I had despaired of, what you may call the material instrumentality of life; of ever being able to rightly operate on mankind through such a deranged machinery as the existing modes of government: but now, if I suddenly discover how to inform these perverted institutions
175   with fresh purpose, bring the functionary limbs once more into immediate communication with, and subjection to, the soul I am about to bestow on them—do you see? Why should one desire to invent, as long as it remains possible to renew and transform? When

153 *1846–65* Luitolfo's goods,—becomes   156 *1846,1849* presently!
158 *1846,1849* ever—   160 *1846,1849* her injunctions to   *1846,1849* and wait
the   162 *1846–65* knowledge—what could *1868–75* knowledge: what could
162–3 *1846,1849* else?—Yet if what they *1863,1865* if what they   165 *1846,1849*
them—   168 *1846,1849* complete!   178 *1846,1849* invent, so long

all further hope of the old organization shall be extinct, then, I grant
you, it may be time to try and create another.   180

Eulalia. And there being discoverable some hope yet in the
hitherto much-abused old system of absolute government by a
Provost here, you mean to take your time about endeavouring to
realize those visions of a perfect State, we once heard of?

Chiappino. Say, I would fain realize my conception of a palace, for 185
instance, and that there is, abstractedly, but a single way of erecting
one perfectly. Here, in the market-place is my allotted building-
ground; here I stand without a stone to lay, or a labourer to help me,—
stand, too, during a short day of life, close on which the night comes.
On the other hand, circumstances suddenly offer me (turn and see it!) 190
the old Provost's house to experiment upon—ruinous, if you please,
wrongly constructed at the beginning, and ready to tumble now. But
materials abound, a crowd of workmen offer their services; here,
exists yet a Hall of Audience of originally noble proportions, there a
Guest-chamber of symmetrical design enough: and I may restore,   195
enlarge, abolish or unite these to heart's content. Ought I not make
the best of such an opportunity, rather than continue to gaze discon-
solately with folded arms on the flat pavement here, while the sun
goes slowly down, never to rise again? Since you cannot understand
this nor me, it is better we should part as you desire.   200

Eulalia. So, the love breaks away too!

Chiappino. No, rather my soul's capacity for love widens—needs
more than one object to content it,—and, being better instructed,
will not persist in seeing all the component parts of love in what is
only a single part,—nor in finding that so many and so various loves 205
are all united in the love of a woman,—manifold uses in one instru-
ment, as the savage has his sword, staff, sceptre and idol, all in one
club-stick. Love is a very compound thing. The intellectual part of
my love I shall give to men, the mighty dead or the illustrious living;

180 *1846,1849* it will be   187 *1846,1849* perfectly;   190 *1846–65* me . . . . . .
it . . *1868–75* it)   192 *1846,1849* now—   196 *1846,1849* content—
1846–63 not rather make   197 *1846–63* opportunity, than   199–
200 *1846,1849* again? But you . . . . me: 205–6 *1846–65* finding the so . . . . loves,
united   206 *1846,1849* woman,—finding all uses   207 *1846–75* sword,
sceptre   208–9 *1846–63* thing. I shall give the intellectual part of my love to Men,
209 *1846–65* or illustrious

210 and determine to call a mere sensual instinct by as few fine names as possible. What do I lose?

Eulalia. Nay, I only think, what do I lose? and, one more word—which shall complete my instruction—does friendship go too? What of Luitolfo, the author of your present prosperity?

215 *Chiappino*. How the author?

Eulalia. That blow now called yours . . .

Chiappino. Struck without principle or purpose, as by a blind natural operation: yet to which all my thought and life directly and advisedly tended. I would have struck it, and could not: he would

220 have done his utmost to avoid striking it, yet did so. I dispute his right to that deed of mine—a final action with him, from the first effect of which he fled away,—a mere first step with me, on which I base a whole mighty superstructure of good to follow. Could he get good from it?

225 *Eulalia*. So we profess, so we perform!

Enter OGNIBEN. EULALIA *stands apart*.

Ogniben. I have seen three-and-twenty leaders of revolts. By your leave, sir! Perform? What does the lady say of performing?

Chiappino. Only the trite saying, that we must not trust profes-

230 sion, only performance.

Ogniben. She'll not say that, sir, when she knows you longer; you'll instruct her better. Ever judge of men by their professions! For though the bright moment of promising is but a moment and cannot be prolonged, yet, if sincere in its moment's extravagant

235 goodness, why, trust it and know the man by it, I say—not by his performance; which is half the world's work, interfere as the world needs must, with its accidents and circumstances: the profession was purely the man's own. I judge people by what they might be,—not are, nor will be.

240 *Chiappino*. But have there not been found, too, performing natures, not merely promising?

Ogniben. Plenty. Little Bindo of our town, for instance, promised

his friend, great ugly Masaccio, once, "I will repay you!"—for a
favour done him. So, when his father came to die, and Bindo
succeeded to the inheritance, he sends straightway for Masaccio and   245
shares all with him—gives him half the land, half the money, half
the kegs of wine in the cellar. "Good," say you: and it is good. But
had little Bindo found himself possessor of all this wealth some five
years before—on the happy night when Masaccio procured him
that interview in the garden with his pretty cousin Lisa—instead of   250
being the beggar he then was,—I am bound to believe that in the
warm moment of promise he would have given away all the wine-
kegs and all the money and all the land, and only reserved to himself
some hut on a hill-top hard by, whence he might spend his life in
looking and seeing his friend enjoy himself: he meant fully that   255
much, but the world interfered.—To our business! Did I under-
stand you just now within-doors? You are not going to marry your
old friend's love, after all?

Chiappino. I must have a woman that can sympathize with, and
appreciate me, I told you.   260

Ogniben. Oh, I remember! you, the greater nature, needs must
have a lesser one (—avowedly lesser—contest with you on that score
would never do)—such a nature must comprehend you, as the
phrase is, accompany and testify of your greatness from point to
point onward. Why, that were being not merely as great as yourself,   265
but greater considerably! Meantime, might not the more bounded
nature as reasonably count on your appreciation of it, rather?—on
your keeping close by it, so far as you both go together, and then
going on by yourself as far as you please? Thus God serves us.

Chiappino. And yet a woman that could understand the whole of   270
me, to whom I could reveal alike the strength and the weakness—

Ogniben. Ah, my friend, wish for nothing so foolish! Worship

---

243 *1846* you"!   244 *1846–65* him: 247 *1846,1849* good:
256 *1846,1849* interfered!—   *1846,1849* business—   263 *1846–65* do!)—
265 *1846,1849* onward: 269 *1846,1849* please? So God   *1846–63* us!

249 *Masaccio*: 'accio' is a pejorative suffix. The reference is not to the early fifteenth-
century painter, but to an imaginary youth who earns the suffix by being ugly, as the
painter did by being awkward or slovenly. Cf. Mrs Foster's translation of Vasari's *Lives*,
i. 403 n.

your love, give her the best of you to see; be to her like the western
lands (they bring us such strange news of) to the Spanish Court;
275 send her only your lumps of gold, fans of feathers, your spirit-like
birds, and fruits and gems! So shall you, what is unseen of you, be
supposed altogether a paradise by her,—as these western lands by
Spain: though I warrant there is filth, red baboons, ugly reptiles and
squalor enough, which they bring Spain as few samples of as pos-
280 sible. Do you want your mistress to respect your body generally?
Offer her your mouth to kiss: don't strip off your boot and put your
foot to her lips! You understand my humour by this time? I help
men to carry out their own principles: if they please to say two and
two make five, I assent, so they will but go on and say, four and four
285 make ten.

Chiappino. But these are my private affairs; what I desire you to
occupy yourself about, is my public appearance presently: for when
the people hear that I am appointed Provost, though you and I may
thoroughly discern—and easily, too—the right principle at bottom
290 of such a movement, and how my republicanism remains thoroughly
unaltered, only takes a form of expression hitherto commonly
judged (and heretofore by myself) incompatible with its exist-
ence,—when thus I reconcile myself to an old form of government
instead of proposing a new one ...

295 *Ogniben.* Why, you must deal with people broadly. Begin at a
distance from this matter and say,—New truths, old truths! sirs,
there is nothing new possible to be revealed to us in the moral
world; we know all we shall ever know: and it is for simply remind-
ing us, by their various respective expedients, how we do know this
300 and the other matter, that men get called prophets, poets and the
like. A philosopher's life is spent in discovering that, of the half-
dozen truths he knew when a child, such an one is a lie, as the world
states it in set terms; and then, after a weary lapse of years, and

276 *1846–65* gems—   283 *1846,1849* own principle: if   284 *1846,1849*
assent, if they   285 *1846–63* ten!   292 *1846–63* judged .. .... myself ..
296–7 *1846,1849* truths! why there   298 *1846–65* know,   299 *1849–65 do*
301 *1846* like:

273–4 *the western lands*: a reference to the discoveries of the great explorers of the fif-
teenth and sixteenth centuries. Like Columbus himself (born in Genoa, but supported in
the end by Spain), they brought back such 'rarities' as gold, exotic birds, and jewels.

plenty of hard-thinking, it becomes a truth again after all, as he
happens to newly consider it and view it in a different relation with 305
the others: and so he restates it, to the confusion of somebody else in
good time. As for adding to the original stock of truths,—impos-
sible! Thus, you see the expression of them is the grand business:—
you have got a truth in your head about the right way of governing
people, and you took a mode of expressing it which now you 310
confess to be imperfect. But what then? There is truth in falsehood,
falsehood in truth. No man ever told one great truth, that I know,
without the help of a good dozen of lies at least, generally
unconscious ones. And as when a child comes in breathlessly and
relates a strange story, you try to conjecture from the very falsities in 315
it, what the reality was,—do not conclude that he saw nothing in
the sky, because he assuredly did not see a flying horse there as he
says,—so, through the contradictory expression, do you see, men
should look painfully for, and trust to arrive eventually at, what you
call the true principle at bottom. Ah, what an answer is there! to 320
what will it not prove applicable?—"Contradictions? Of course
there were," say you!

 Chiappino. Still, the world at large may call it inconsistency, and
what shall I urge in reply?

 Ogniben. Why, look you, when they tax you with tergiversation 325
or duplicity, you may answer—you begin to perceive that, when
all's done and said, both great parties in the State, the advocators of
change in the present system of things, and the opponents of it,
patriot and anti-patriot, are found working together for the
common good; and that in the midst of their efforts for and against 330
its progress, the world somehow or other still advances: to which
result they contribute in equal proportions, those who spend their
life in pushing it onward, as those who give theirs to the business of

307–8 *1846,1849* impossible!—So you 311 *1846–65* imperfect— 314 *1846–*
65 ones: 321 *1846–65* applicable!—"Contradictions?"— 322 *1846–65*
were, *1865* you? 324 *1846,1849* I say in *1865* reply! 330 *1846–65*
good, 332 *1846–65* who spent their 333 *1846–65* who gave theirs

 314 *when a child*: 'Such thoughts ... you are prodigal of!', EBB wrote on 29 March 1846.
'That about the child, ... do you remember how you brought it to me in your first visit,
nearly a year ago[?]': Kintner, ii. 570.

 327 *advocators*: no other example, in this sense, in OED.

pulling it back. Now, if you found the world stand still between the
335 opposite forces, and were glad, I should conceive you: but it steadily
advances, you rejoice to see! By the side of such a rejoicer, the man
who only winks as he keeps cunning and quiet, and says, "Let
yonder hot-headed fellow fight out my battle! I, for one, shall win
in the end by the blows he gives, and which I ought to be giving"—
340 even he seems graceful in his avowal, when one considers that he
might say, "I shall win quite as much by the blows our antagonist
gives him, blows from which he saves me—I thank the antagonist
equally!" Moreover, you may enlarge on the loss of the edge of
party-animosity with age and experience . . .
345   *Chiappino*. And naturally time must wear off such asperities: the
bitterest adversaries get to discover certain points of similarity
between each other, common sympathies—do they not?
    Ogniben. Ay, had the young David but sat first to dine on his
cheeses with the Philistine, he had soon discovered an abundance of
350 such common sympathies. He of Gath, it is recorded, was born of a
father and mother, had brothers and sisters like another man,—
they, no more than the sons of Jesse, were used to eat each other.
But, for the sake of one broad antipathy that had existed from the
beginning, David slung the stone, cut off the giant's head, made a
355 spoil of it, and after ate his cheeses alone, with the better appetite,
for all I can learn. My friend, as you, with a quickened eye-sight, go
on discovering much good on the worse side, remember that the
same process should proportionably magnify and demonstrate to
you the much more good on the better side! And when I profess no
360 sympathy for the Goliaths of our time, and you object that a large
nature should sympathize with every form of intelligence, and see
the good in it, however limited—I answer, "So I do; but preserve the
proportions of my sympathy, however finelier or widelier I may
extend its action." I desire to be able, with a quickened eye-sight, to

334 *1846,1849* back—   338 *1846–65* battle;   342 *1846–65* him, and from
343 *1846,1849* you must enlarge   352 *1846,1849* other;   359 *1846,1849*
side—   *1863,1865* side.   360 *1846–70* the Goliahs of   362 *1846–65* so
364 *1846–65* action.

    348 *the young David*: we read in 1 Sam. 17 how the champion of the Philistines, Goliath
of Gath, was opposed and killed by David, the youngest of the eight sons of Jesse.

descry beauty in corruption where others see foulness only: but I 365
hope I shall also continue to see a redoubled beauty in the higher
forms of matter, where already everybody sees no foulness at all. I
must retain, too, my old power of selection, and choice of appropri-
ation, to apply to such new gifts; else they only dazzle instead of
enlightening me. God has his archangels and consorts with them: 370
though he made too, and intimately sees what is good in, the worm.
Observe, I speak only as you profess to think and, so, ought to speak:
I do justice to your own principles, that is all.

Chiappino. But you very well know that the two parties do, on
occasion, assume each other's characteristics. What more disgust- 375
ing, for instance, than to see how promptly the newly emancipated
slave will adopt, in his own favour, the very measures of precaution,
which pressed soreliest on himself as institutions of the tyranny he
has just escaped from? Do the classes, hitherto without opinion, get
leave to express it? there follows a confederacy immediately, from 380
which—exercise your individual right and dissent, and woe be to
you!

Ogniben. And a journey over the sea to you! That is the generous
way. Cry—"Emancipated slaves, the first excess, and off I go!" The
first time a poor devil, who has been bastinadoed steadily his whole 385
life long, finds himself let alone and able to legislate, so, begins pet-
tishly, while he rubs his soles, "Woe be to whoever brings anything
in the shape of a stick this way!"—you, rather than give up the very
innocent pleasure of carrying one to switch flies with,—you go
away, to everybody's sorrow. Yet you were quite reconciled to stay- 390
ing at home while the governors used to pass, every now and then,
some such edict as "Let no man indulge in owning a stick which is
not thick enough to chastise our slaves, if need require!" Well, there
are pre-ordained hierarchies among us, and a profane vulgar
subjected to a different law altogether; yet I am rather sorry you 395

367 *1846* forms, where   373 *1849* all!   375 *1846,1849* characteristics:
379 *1846,1849* from.—   380 *1846–65* there is a   384 *1846,1849* way. Say—
emancipated *1863,1865* emancipated   *1846–65* go!   388 *1846,1849* way,"—
390 *1846,1849* sorrow!   393 *1846–65* require."

385 *bastinadoed*: beaten on the soles of the feet, by way of punishment or torture.
394 *a profane vulgar*: an echo of Horace's *Odes*, III. i. 1: 'Odi profanum vulgus et arceo': I
hate and avoid the unhallowed mob.

should see it so clearly: for, do you know what is to—all but save you at the Day of Judgment, all you men of genius? It is this: that, while you generally began by pulling down God, and went on to the end of your life, in one effort at setting up your own genius in his
400 place,—still, the last, bitterest concession wrung with the utmost unwillingness from the experience of the very loftiest of you, was invariably—would one think it?—that the rest of mankind, down to the lowest of the mass, stood not, nor ever could stand, just on a level and equality with yourselves. That will be a point in the favour
405 of all such, I hope and believe.

Chiappino. Why, men of genius are usually charged, I think, with doing just the reverse; and at once acknowledging the natural inequality of mankind, by themselves participating in the universal craving after, and deference to, the civil distinctions which repre-
410 sent it. You wonder they pay such undue respect to titles and badges of superior rank.

Ogniben. Not I (always on your own ground and showing, be it noted!) Who doubts that, with a weapon to brandish, a man is the more formidable? Titles and badges are exercised as such a weapon,
415 to which you and I look up wistfully. We could pin lions with it moreover, while in its present owner's hands it hardly prods rats. Nay, better than a mere weapon of easy mastery and obvious use, it is a mysterious divining rod that may serve us in undreamed-of ways. Beauty, strength, intellect—men often have none of these,
420 and yet conceive pretty accurately what kind of advantages they would bestow on the possessor. We know at least what it is we make up our mind to forego, and so can apply the fittest substitute

---

403 *1846* mass, was not, nor ever could be, just   405 *1846–65* believe!
407 *1846* reverse,   411 *1846,1849* rank!   412 *1846–65* I!   418 *1846,*
1849 serve you in   421–2 *1846,1849* possessor.—You know at least what it is you
make up your mind

406 *Why, men of genius*: in a letter Browning comments on this speech, and reveals a revision: 'Chiappino remarks that men of genius usually do the *reverse* . . of beginning by dethroning &c and so arriving with utmost reluctancy at the acknowledgement of a natural & unalterable *inequality* of Mankind—instead of *that*, they begin *at once*, he says, by recognizing it in their adulation &c &c—I have supplied the words "*at once*," and taken out "*virtually*," which was unnecessary; so that the parallel possibly reads clearlier': Kintner, ii. 594.
417 *of easy mastery*: easy to master.

in our power. Wanting beauty, we cultivate good humour; missing
wit, we get riches: but the mystic unimaginable operation of that
gold collar and string of Latin names which suddenly turned poor   425
stupid little peevish Cecco of our town into natural lord of the best
of us—a Duke, he is now—there indeed is a virtue to be reverenced!

Chiappino. Ay, by the vulgar: not by Messere Stiatta the poet,
who pays more assiduous court to him than anybody.

Ogniben. What else should Stiatta pay court to? He has talent, not   430
honour and riches: men naturally covet what they have not.

Chiappino. No, or Cecco would covet talent, which he has not,
whereas he covets more riches, of which he has plenty, already.

Ogniben. Because a purse added to a purse makes the holder twice
as rich: but just such another talent as Stiatta's, added to what he   435
now possesses, what would that profit him? Give the talent a purse
indeed, to do something with! But lo, how we keep the good people
waiting! I only desired to do justice to the noble sentiments which
animate you, and which you are too modest to duly enforce. Come,
to our main business: shall we ascend the steps? I am going to   440
propose you for Provost to the people; they know your antecedents,
and will accept you with a joyful unanimity: whereon I confirm
their choice. Rouse up! Are you nerving yourself to an effort?
Beware the disaster of Messere Stiatta we were talking of! who,
determining to keep an equal mind and constant face on whatever   445
might be the fortune of his last new poem with our townsmen,
heard too plainly "hiss, hiss, hiss," increase every moment. Till at last
the man fell senseless: not perceiving that the portentous sounds
had all the while been issuing from between his own nobly clenched
teeth, and nostrils narrowed by resolve.   450

Chiappino. Do you begin to throw off the mask?—to jest with
me, having got me effectually into your trap?

Ogniben. Where is the trap, my friend? You hear what I engage

---

423 *1846,1849* in your power; wanting Beauty, you cultivate good Humour, *1863,1865*
power;   424 *1846,1849* Wit, you get   426 *1846* our own town
427 *1846–65* now!   438 *1846–65* waiting.   443 *1846,1849* up! you are nerv-
ing   444 *1846,1849* of— *1863,1865* of;   446 *1846* new tragedy with
447 *1846,1849* moment, *1863,1865* moment: 450 *1846,1849* resolve!

  426 *Cecco*: a familiar form of Francesco.
  428 *Messere Stiatta*: Master Stiatta, an imaginary poet.

to do, for my part: you, for yours, have only to fulfil your promise
455 made just now within doors, of professing unlimited obedience to
Rome's authority in my person. And I shall authorize no more than
the simple re-establishment of the Provostship and the conferment
of its privileges upon yourself: the only novel stipulation being a
birth of the peculiar circumstances of the time.
460 *Chiappino.* And that stipulation?
Ogniben. Just the obvious one—that in the event of the discovery
of the actual assailant of the late Provost . . .
Chiappino. Ha!
Ogniben. Why, he shall suffer the proper penalty, of course; what
465 did you expect?
Chiappino. Who heard of this?
Ogniben. Rather, who needed to hear of this?
Chiappino. Can it be, the popular rumour never reached you . . .
Ogniben. Many more such rumours reach me, friend, than I
470 choose to receive; those which wait longest have best chance. Has
the present one sufficiently waited? Now is its time for entry with
effect. See the good people crowding about yonder palace-steps—
which we may not have to ascend, after all. My good friends! (nay,
two or three of you will answer every purpose)—who was it fell
475 upon and proved nearly the death of your late Provost? His
successor desires to hear, that his day of inauguration may be graced
by the act of prompt bare justice we all anticipate. Who dealt the
blow that night, does anybody know?
Luitolfo [*coming forward*]. I!
480 *All.* Luitolfo!
Luitolfo. I avow the deed, justify and approve it, and stand forth
now, to relieve my friend of an unearned responsibility. Having
taken thought, I am grown stronger: I shall shrink from nothing
that awaits me. Nay, Chiappino—we are friends still: I dare say
485 there is some proof of your superior nature in this starting aside,
strange as it seemed at first. So, they tell me, my horse is of the right
stock, because a shadow in the path frightens him into a frenzy,

456 *1846,1849* person—   461 *1846,1849* Ogni. Oh, the   470 *1846,1849*
chance—   472 *1846* people crowded about   473 *1846–75* all!   *1846–65*
friends—   477 *1846,1849* anticipate?   486 *1846,1849* it seems at

makes him dash my brains out. I understand only the dull mule's way of standing stockishly, plodding soberly, suffering on occasion a blow or two with due patience.   490

Eulalia. I was determined to justify my choice, Chiappino,—to let Luitolfo's nature vindicate itself. Henceforth we are undivided, whatever be our fortune.

Ogniben. Now, in these last ten minutes of silence, what have I been doing, deem you? Putting the finishing stroke to a homily of   495 mine, I have long taken thought to perfect, on the text, "Let whoso thinketh he standeth, take heed lest he fall." To your house, Luitolfo! Still silent, my patriotic friend? Well, that is a good sign however. And you will go aside for a time? That is better still. I understand: it would be easy for you to die of remorse here on the   500 spot and shock us all, but you mean to live and grow worthy of coming back to us one day. There, I will tell everybody; and you only do right to believe you must get better as you get older. All men do so: they are worst in childhood, improve in manhood, and get ready in old age for another world. Youth, with its beauty and   505 grace, would seem bestowed on us for some such reason as to make us partly endurable till we have time for really becoming so of ourselves, without their aid; when they leave us. The sweetest child we all smile on for his pleasant want of the whole world to break up, or suck in his mouth, seeing no other good in it—would be rudely   510 handled by that world's inhabitants, if he retained those angelic infantine desires when he had grown six feet high, black and bearded. But, little by little, he sees fit to forego claim after claim on the world, puts up with a less and less share of its good as his proper portion; and when the octogenarian asks barely a sup of gruel and a   515 fire of dry sticks, and thanks you as for his full allowance and right

498 *1846* Luitolfo.—   *1868–75* Still,   499 *1846,1849* however!
501 *1846,1849* you will live   503 *1846,1849* you will get .... older!
505 *1846* world: 506 *1846* would really seem   508 *1846,1849* aid,
510 *1846* it—he would   512 *1846* he got six *1849–65* he has grown
513 *1846–65* bearded: 516 *1846* and will thank you

    489 *stockishly*: no other example in OED, which also cites 'stockishness' in *Strafford*,
III. iii. 27.

    496–7 *Let whoso thinketh*: 1 Cor. 10:12: 'Wherefore let him that thinketh he standeth
take heed lest he fall.'

in the common good of life,—hoping nobody may murder him,—
he who began by asking and expecting the whole of us to bow down
in worship to him,—why, I say he is advanced, far onward, very far,
520 nearly out of sight like our friend Chiappino yonder. And now—
(ay, good-bye to you! He turns round the north-west gate: going to
Lugo again? Good-bye!)—and now give thanks to God, the keys of
the Provost's palace to me, and yourselves to profitable meditation
at home! I have known *Four*-and-twenty leaders of revolts.

520 *1846,1849* yonder!   522 *1846* bye)!—   524 *1846–65* home.   *1846,*
1849 revolts!—

INTRODUCTION TO *CHRISTMAS-EVE AND EASTER-DAY*

EXCEPT 'The Guardian Angel',[1] later published in *Men and Women*, Browning is not known to have written any new poems between September 1846, when he and his wife left England for Italy, and late in 1849. He worked hard, intermittently, on the revision of the best of his work for the two-volume *Poems . . . A New Edition*, which eventually appeared in 1849.[2] But then, in November of that year, he began the first of the two poems which became *Christmas-Eve and Easter-Day*.

Two events which had occurred in March had a profound effect on Browning, leading him to reflect on the problems of life and death: the birth of his son on the 9th, and the death of his mother on the 18th. His sister Sarianna, knowing the depth of his feelings for their mother, sought to prepare him for bad news by sending him two letters telling him that she was ill when in fact she was already dead. Without these letters, Elizabeth wrote to her sister Arabel in April, she did not dare to think how the news 'might have affected him in body & soul'.[3] She continued: 'I never saw a *man* so overcome & wrung to the soul—The bursts of convulsive weeping, the recapitulation of all her goodness & tenderness in words that made the heart ache, & then the recovery of composure with such a ghastly violence, that you wished the agitation back again—these things, I shall not try to describe.' Early in June she told Arabel that Browning still 'breaks suddenly into tears', adding: 'I observe that his soul is much with God.'[4] On 2 July he wrote to Sarianna to tell her of the baptism of their child, mentioning that Elizabeth had made the arrangements, and continuing: 'I have been thinking over nothing else, these last three months, than Mama and all about her, and catching at any little fancy of finding something which it would

---

[1] This religious and highly personal poem was written in Ancona in 1848.
[2] See Vol. III, pp. 6 ff., and pp. 278–9, above.
[3] PK 49:22.
[4] PK 49:32.

have pleased her I should do.'[1] In October, when they were back in Florence after a four months' holiday near Bagni di Lucca, his emotional state had improved, and the following month he began a new poem.[2]

In January 1850 Elizabeth told Arabel that they had been 'very busy with his new book, which comes out at easter':

I hope you will like at least some things in it . . . Dont knit your brows, I beg of you, till you get to the end, & see the scope of the whole. The opening will introduce you to a dissenting chapel of the poorest & lowest description, . . of the Methodist Whitfieldite order: an extreme case is taken to make the ultimate decision stronger. I expect an outcry from nearly all classes of readers, for my part. I dare say, the merely literary reader will call the writer a methodist and the religious one will accuse him of some levity in the treatment of his subject: I am prepared for those drawbacks. At the same time, the fact will remain, of the recognition of Christ's faith in its simplicity—and men who can understand how the individuality of a writer is a proof of his earnestness, will not find fault with the mode. Both poems (there are two in the book) are dramatic in a sense—they express certain aspects of Christian experience. Mr Forster, to whom they have been sent, on their way to Chapman & Hall, will open his eyes wide at them, I prophesy—and I feel rather uneasy about what is likely to be the next word from him. There are very noble & grand things in the poems, let him say what he pleases![3]

Browning himself referred to the poems in a letter to H. F. Chorley dated 11 March:

I sent off two days ago the second half of a poem I have been writing since November—the first part preceding it by a week: I wanted to begin again with as much effect as might be attainable—and the fancy occurred of writing a Christmas Story *in verse*—but it grew in the doing and I could not send it off in time—I then thought of Easter as *next* season—and finding that my poem would suffer by any change for the purpose of

---

[1] *Letters*, p. 23.

[2] DeVane (p. 197) suggests that Clough may have met the Brownings when he was in Florence in 1849: 'He had written that year in Italy his *Epi-Straussium* and his *Easter-Day, Naples, 1849*, and his talk may have been the final touch which put Browning's poem in motion.' We do not know of any meeting, however. EBB told Miss Mitford, on 1 December, that Browning and she had 'had the sight of Clough & Burbidge', but the reference is not to the men but to their joint volume of poems, *Ambarvalia*, and neither of these poems is included in it. Cf. Raymond and Sullivan, iii. 286 and n. 11.   [3] PK 50:12.

adapting it to the latter festival, I wrote another as supplement or complement, and the two make what I suppose you will soon see now. I make no doubt I shall give many well-meaning people offence—such have a knack of being sure that everybody else is ill-meaning—but I care rather less than usual about *that*, perhaps from being rather more than usual certain of my own purpose and feeling. In any case, I have no incli-nation to do anything more in this way, let it please or not please. I hope to be able for some time to come to write regularly now, and so "fulfil my destiny," as they say, for good or bad—& this is the beginning. Forster, to whom I applied in the first instance for an opinion of the thing's feasible-ness, answered very promptly & kindly, and will manage the business.[1]

Forster read the proofs, and the book was published on 1 April, the day after Easter. By a series of oversights, the Brownings did not receive a copy for many weeks. On 22 September Elizabeth told Mrs Ogilvy that they were still without a copy: 'It was trusted to some-body, who took it into his head to send it by sea & travel by land himself'.[2] Soon after that, it seems, a single copy arrived, but in November she told Miss Mitford that they did not have a copy to give away.[3]

Before they had seen the published book the Brownings eagerly awaited news of its reception from London. Elizabeth was anxious. 'Whether you will like Robert's new book I don't know,' she had written to Mrs Jameson on 2 April, 'but I am sure you will admit the originality and power in it. I wish we had the option of giving it to you, but Chapman & Hall never seem to think of our giving copies away, nor leave them at our disposal. There is nothing *Italian* in the book; poets are apt to be most present with the distant.'[4] On 6 April the *Athenæum* acknowledged that the book was 'the work of a poet', but added: 'if this fact should gain but a limited recognition, the writer will have only himself to blame', adding that 'while dealing with the highest themes of imagination and indicating his com-petency to treat them, [Browning] has recklessly impaired the dignity of his purpose by the vehicle chosen for its development.

---

[1] PK 50:11.
[2] *Elizabeth Barrett Browning's Letters to Mrs. David Ogilvy*, ed. Peter N. Heydon and Philip Kelley (1974), p. 30.
[3] Raymond and Sullivan, iii. 315.
[4] *Letters of EBB*, i. 441–2.

The form of doggrel—carried to excess by strange and offensive oddities of versification—is not that in which the mysteries of faith, doubt, and eternity can be consistently treated.'[1] Writing to Arabel at the beginning of May, Elizabeth attributed the 'virulence' of this review to 'Unitarian influence, which, we hear, is predominant in it of late':

We hear that the book is 'much talked of' in London, and 'accused of irreligion'. There's the effect of writing a religious book! . . . At the same time I can understand how much . . . is open to misunderstanding with the ordinary run of readers. Then, the last part, which on some accounts, I, too, prefer, I think much too *ascetic*—I told Robert so at the time . . but he answered that it was one view of the subject . . . Robert *sees things passionately*:—that's his characteristic: to feel passionately is more common. Certainly the poem does not represent his own permanent state of mind, which was what I meant when I told you it was dramatic.[2]

Other reviews had already proved more favourable than that in the *Athenæum*. On 6 April 'a burning panegyric of six columns' had appeared in the *Examiner*, as Elizabeth wrote to Miss Mitford.[3] The writer considered that 'As an emanation of thought in verse' this was 'every way a most remarkable production', rejoicing that Browning had been 'steadily reclaiming his genius, of late years, from the "vague and formless infinite" into which at one time it seemed to be falling', referring to the 'not scant or insufficient audience now accustomed to expect from Mr Browning a combination of the analytic and imaginative powers such as poets have rarely manifested', and prophesying that he would 'yet win and wear his laurel, and be admitted for what he truly is, one of the most original poets of his time'. Three weeks later the *Leader* had also been enthusiastic, commenting that 'In the bold and artful mingling of the ludicrous with the intensely serious' Browning recalled Carlyle, and observing that 'Since Butler no English poet has exhibited the same daring propensity and facility in rhyming.' Near the end of April, in the 'May' number of *The Germ*, W. M. Rossetti did not name particular poems but defended Browning strongly

[1] P. 370.   [2] PK 50:27.
[3] Raymond and Sullivan, iii. 298; *Examiner*, pp. 213, 211; *Leader*, p. 111; *The Germ*, pp. 187 ff.; *English Review*, xiv. 92.

against ill-judged criticism of his style. In September a writer in the *English Review* was to be more specific: 'On the whole, . . . this contribution of Browning's to our poetical literature is a great work, and is gladly hailed by us as such. Essentially different as it is in all respects from *In Memoriam*, they are both destined to an earthly immortality.' For the most perceptive review of all he had to wait until the issue of the *Revue des deux mondes* for 15 August 1851. Joseph Milsand devoted the second of his articles on 'La poésie anglaise depuis Byron' to Browning's work, and included a long account of these two poems.

At the end of April 1850 Elizabeth was able to report that 'Two hundred copies went off in the first fortnight',[1] but sales soon declined. On 23 September 1851 Browning told Edward Chapman (of Chapman and Hall, the publishers) that he was 'vexed at the ill luck of *Christmas-Eve* etc.'[2] He asked: 'Was the price [6/—] too high? Could anything be done by judicious advertizing at the seasons the book treats of? Could one put in some illustrations, even now? I might get you a few good ones.' On 16 January 1852 he wrote again: 'I noticed the other day that you prefix to an advertisement of *Christmas Eve*, an opinion from a journal—if that is the best course (of which I have doubts)—why not take your extract from some real authority in the matter', suggesting that 'admirable critic' Joseph Milsand.[3] On 12 April 1853 Browning told Forster that 'poor *Christmas Eve* . . . hasn't paid printing yet'. Chapman had copies of the original printing in stock for many years.[4] The book was pirated in America, but in England it became so hard to sell that bibliographers are still trying to enumerate the various bindings in which it may be found.

Elizabeth had less reason than most readers to be perplexed by the poems. 'And talking of Italy & the cardinals', she had written to Browning in July 1845, '. . . did you ever hear that I was one of

---

[1] Raymond and Sullivan, iii. 298.
[2] *New Letters*, p. 52.
[3] Ibid., pp. 53–4, 61. See too p. 58.
[4] Ibid., p. 392, shows that copies were still unsold on 29 January 1864. See John Carter, *Binding Variants in English Publishing 1820–1900* (1932), which lists three bindings: his working copy of the book, in Eton College Library, adds two more.

"those schismatiques / of Amsterdam" whom your Dr. Donne w^d
have put into the dykes?—unless he meant the Baptists, instead of
the Independents, the holders of the Independent church principle':

No—not '*schismatical*,' I hope—hating as I do from the roots of my heart
all that rending of the garment of Christ ... & caring very little for most
dogmas & doxies in themselves ... & believing that there is only one
church in heaven & earth, with one divine High Priest to it,—let exclusive
religionists build what walls they please & bring out what chrisms—But I
used to go with my father always, when I was able, to the nearest dissent-
ing chapel of the Congregationalists—from liking the simplicity of that
praying and speaking without books—& a little too from disliking the
theory of state churches. There is a narrowness among the dissenters
which is wonderful,—an arid, grey Puritanism in the clefts of their souls:
but it seems to me clear that they know what the 'liberty of Christ' *means*,
far better than those who do call themselves 'churchmen'; & so stand
altogether, as a body, on higher ground.[1]

Browning was delighted:

Can it be you ... *you* are a schismatic and frequenter of Independent
Dissenting Chapels? And you confess this to *me*—whose father and
mother went this morning to the very Independent Chapel where they
took me, all those years back, to be baptized—and where they heard, this
morning, a sermon preached by the very minister who officiated on that
other occasion!

Even more relevant is Elizabeth's letter of 15 August 1846, in which
she told him that she was 'unwilling, for [her] own part, to put on
any of the liveries of the sects':

The truth, as God sees it, must be so different from these opinions about
truth—these systems which fit different classes of men like their coats, &
wear brown at the elbows always!—I believe in what is divine & floats at
highest, in all these different theologies—& because the really Divine
draws together souls, & tends so to a unity, I could pray anywhere & with
all sorts of worshippers, from the Sistine Chapel to Mr. Fox's, those kneel-
ing & those standing. Wherever you go, in all religious societies, there is a
little to revolt, & a good deal to bear with—but it is not otherwise in the

---

[1] Kintner, i. 140–1, followed by i. 143, ii. 962–3 and 969. DeVane pointed out that
EBB's letter of 15 August 1846 'anticipated the matter of her [future] husband's poem':
Handbook, p. 198. In fact it clearly influenced it.

world without,—&, *within*, you are especially reminded that God has to be more patient than yourself after all. Still you go quickest there, where your sympathies are least ruffled & disturbed—& I like, beyond comparison best, the simplicity of the dissenters . . the unwritten prayer, . . the sacraments administered quietly & without charlatanism! & the principle of a church, as they hold it, *I* hold it too, quite apart from state-necessities . . pure from the Law. Well—there is enough to dissent from among the dissenters—the Formula is rampant among them as among others—you hear things like the buzzing of flies in proof of a corruption—& see every now & then something divine set up like a post for men of irritable minds & passions to rub themselves against, calling it a holy deed—you feel moreover bigotry & ignorance pressing on you on all sides, till you gasp for breath like one strangled—But better this, even, than what is elsewhere—*this* being elsewhere too in different degrees, besides the evil of the place. Public & social prayer is right & desirable—& I would prefer, as a matter of custom, to pray in one of those chapels, where the minister is simple-minded & not controversial—certainly w^d prefer it. Not exactly in the Socinian chapels, nor yet in Mr. Fox's—not by preference. The Unitarians seem to me to throw over what is most beautiful in the Christian Doctrine; but the Formulists, on the other side, stir up a dust, in which it appears excusable not to see. When the veil of the body falls, how we shall look into each other's faces, astonished, . . after one glance at God's!

She added that their wedding ceremony would be just as Browning wished,

& you will see by this profession of faith that I am not likely much to care either way. There are some solemn & beautiful things in the Ch. of England Marriage-service, as I once heard it read, the only time I was present at such a ceremony—but I heard it then in the abbreviated customary form . . & not as the Puseyites (who always bring up the old lamps against a new) choose to read it.

Browning replied that he understood her 'very, very meaning', and responded to it with his whole soul:

those are my own feelings, my convictions beside—instinct confirmed by reason. . . ∴ If in a meeting house, with the blank white walls, and a simple doctrinal exposition,—all the senses should turn (from where they lie neglected) to all that sunshine in the Sistine with its music and painting, which would lift them at once to Heaven,—why should you not go forth?—to return just as quickly, when they are nourished into a luxuriance that extinguishes, what is called, Reason's pale wavering light.

It is not to be supposed that the Independent Chapel at Walworth, which had become the family church of the Brownings through the influence of his mother (his father having been brought up in the Church of England), had anything in common with the Zion Chapel of *Christmas-Eve*. Mrs Browning, described by Carlyle as 'the true type of a Scottish gentlewoman',[1] joined the Congregational Church when she came to England, considering it the nearest equivalent to the Church of Scotland. George Clayton, the minister of York Street Congregational Church (as it came to be known), had no more in common with the ignorant preacher of the poem than had his congregation with the motley crowd described in Zion Chapel. John Maynard has pointed out that Camberwell was at this time a district where religion and religious issues were subjects of keen interest and debate: there were more than twenty different churches and sects in the area,[2] and Clayton was one of the most intelligent and eloquent of the ministers. He more often termed himself an evangelical preacher than a Congregationalist, seeing 'his main role [as] that of an evangelist in the larger movement which was awakening a new religious and moral sensibility in English life'.

For the baptism of their son Browning took pains to find a service which had as much as possible in common with Clayton's (and would therefore have given pleasure to his mother). He told his sister that the child had been baptized 'at the French Evangelical Protestant Church, being the chapel at the Prussian Legation at Florence', adding: 'Ba and I particularly congratulate ourselves on having managed the matter as we did: the service was very simple and evangelical—just the same as at Mr. Clayton's, except that there is a form of prayer and service. I saw the minister, a very simple, good and sincere man apparently.'[3] In a letter to Arabel, Elizabeth mentioned that M. Drouin had told Browning that he must forgive

[1] *Life*, p. 18.
[2] 'Robert Browning's Evangelical Heritage': BIS 3 (1975), 2, 6.
[3] *Letters*, p. 23, followed by PK 49:40.

him for asking, 'as we were English, what were our reasons for preferring the French Lutheran to the English church[?]' Browning had 'entered with detail into our reasons:—after which, he observed that we were perfectly justified & right in his opinion, & that he sh.ᵈ have great pleasure in baptizing our child. He seemed to understand the state of religious parties in England, & talked about them with melancholy.'

The fact that *Christmas-Eve* was written as 'a Christmas Story' helps to explain its structure and intention. Like *A Christmas Carol* and *The Chimes* it and its sequel incorporate an element of the supernatural. The narrative begins and ends among the poorest of the people, and we notice that the narrator moves from contempt for Zion Chapel and its slum-dwelling worshippers to a seasonably charitable frame of mind. It describes, as Mrs Orr observes of each of the poems, 'a spiritual experience appropriate to the day, and lived through in a vision of Christ'. In this 'probable or obvious hallucination', the speaker, of whom we learn no more than that he has come up from Manchester by train and has never been in Italy, has a vision of Christ and finds himself transported to Rome, where he sees the inside of St Peter's, and thence to an unnamed university city in Germany where he listens to a dryasdust address delivered by a Higher Critic, a 'hawk-nosed high-cheek-boned Professor'. Tempted to adopt 'a mild indifferentism', he yet manages to catch again at Christ's garment, which transports him back to the Chapel.[1] There he joins in the simple worship.

The speaker in *Easter-Day* refers to 'The common, where the chapel was, / Our friend spoke of, the other day', but that is almost as much as we learn about him. Although the poem is formally a dialogue, the other friend whom he addresses (as they sit up one Easter night) is little more than a rhetorical convenience. Theological debate is more overt than in *Christmas-Eve*.[2] After describing a dream or hallucination in the course of which he believed that he

---

[1] *Christmas-Eve*, 1229. Matt. 9:20–1 (with 14:36) is the source for the healing power of Christ's garment, which is associated with faith. It is central to the poem.

[2] Cf. too EBB's remark that *Easter-Day* is 'much too *ascetic*', quoted above, p. 320. It is more ascetic than Browning's own habitual temper.

was addressed by Christ, the speaker ends by acknowledging the supremacy of Love over Knowledge.

Like 'Waring', a single poem in two parts and with two speakers, this pair of poems reminds us of Browning's early friends, 'the Colloquials'. Mrs. Orr observes that the humorous tone and levity of *Christmas-Eve* 'is alone enough to prove that the author is not depicting himself', and the same is true of *Easter-Day*. If there were some more convincing suggestion of a social setting it would be easier for the reader to accept the rhyme 'a sight' and 'Aphrodite' in the former poem, or the flatness of ll. 227 ff. in the latter. It is helpful to recall Wordsworth's defensive remark that 'The Thorn' 'is not supposed to be spoken in the author's own person' but in that of a narrator whose character 'sufficiently shew[s] itself in the course of the story'.[1] Whatever conclusion we may reach about that poem, it is clear that the element of dramatization in *Christmas-Eve and Easter-Day* is inadequate.

Mrs Orr observes that *Christmas-Eve*, like its successor, contains 'much which is in harmony with Mr. Browning's known views; and it is difficult at first sight to regard them . . . as proceeding from an imaginary person who is only feeling his way to the truth. This, however, they prove . . . to be.' They are the expression of a troubled mind searching for some approximation to certainty.[2] It is no chance that they are the first work Browning produced after the birth of his son and the death of his mother.

The Text

One manuscript version of *Christmas-Eve and Easter-Day*, the printer's copy, has survived and is now in the Forster Collection of the Victoria and Albert Museum. It is in Browning's hand, with the

---

[1] 'Advertisement' to *Lyrical Ballads* (1798), last para.

[2] As early as 25 April 1850 Arnould told Browning that he completely agreed with all he had written 'about German Professorships & Straussism' (Donald Smalley: 'Joseph Arnould and Robert Browning', PMLA 80, 1965, 100). It has often been conjectured that Browning read George Eliot's translation (1846) of the 4th edition of Strauss's *Das Leben Jesu, kritisch bearbeitet*. In '"See the Christ stand!": Browning's Religion' (Drew, pp. 72–95), Kingsbury Badger lists some striking parallels. In any event Browning is certain to have known of Strauss's main arguments, which were widely canvassed in conversation and in the Reviews: see, for example, the *Westminster Review* for April 1847.

exception of ll. 731–813, 966–1017, and 1253–359 of *Christmas-Eve*, which are in the hand of EBB. *Christmas-Eve* (38 pages in the manuscript) is a fair copy with some neat additions and substitutions; *Easter-Day* (33 pages) is more boldly and untidily written and has more alterations. There is a small hole on p. 26 of *Christmas-Eve* (at l. 965) where a word has been scratched out, and a lacuna on p. 25 of *Easter-Day* (between ll. 767 and 768) where about seven lines have been removed. A slip of paper with ll. 1062–87 has been pasted on to p. 30 of *Christmas-Eve*: underneath, the page is blank. The manuscript is in ink, with an occasional addition in pencil in Browning's hand. The right-hand margin of *Christmas-Eve* has been numbered in pencil every hundred lines; all except 100 and 1200 are a few lines out.

Some of the more interesting of Browning's slips and second thoughts which are still legible are as follows. At l. 105 of *Christmas-Eve* the last three letters of 'perform' are inserted diagonally before 'the Grand-Inquisitor'. The initial 'p' is unchanged but the other three letters of the original word are illegible: Browning's first thought may have been 'play', rejected because of the awkward chime with 'way' earlier in the line. At l. 58 of *Easter-Day* what looks like 'way' (and would therefore alliterate both with 'well' and with the 'wink' of the previous line) has been changed to 'path'. Similarly, 'end' (l. 283), which is too near 'Hand', has been changed to 'close'. A repeated 'that' (l. 475) becomes 'all'. Even Browning seems to have found it hard to keep the speakers separate in *Easter-Day*: at l. 493 'You' is cancelled and replaced with 'I' in the manuscript only to be restored in *1863*. Two significant word changes are 'complement' for 'supplement' (l. 587) and 'variegate' for 'decorate' (l. 751).

The first edition was accurately set up from the manuscript, with only one error, where the printer mis-read 'ends' (badly written) as 'suds' (*Christmas-Eve*, 65); Browning corrected this and the spelling 'Buonarotti's' in a copy now in the William Andrews Clark Memorial Library at UCLA. Most of the manuscript's old-fashioned spellings—'flavors', 'siezed', 'prophecied', 'frankincence'—were regularized, though 'color' occasionally slipped through, and 'honor', 'stedfast', 'extacy' and 'extatic', 'mistakeable', 'unevadeable', and 'befals' persisted (the last in all printed editions until *1888*).

Ampersands were generally eliminated, and hyphens inserted in compounds. Most capitalizations were retained. At the head of each section, Browning's arabic numerals were replaced by roman numerals. The printer followed Browning's punctuation faithfully, only tidying up apostrophes (flocks' > flock's, camps > camp's), rationalizing single and double inverted commas, and moving punctuation inside quotation marks ("shares"! > 'shares!'). In a proof copy of the first edition, now in the Berg Collection of the New York Public Library, Browning tried out two variants which were never adopted and which appear nowhere else: in Section VII of *Christmas-Eve* he altered 'to be ever here.' to 'ever to be here.' (l. 412) and 'the show above me' to 'the scene above me' (l. 420). In Section VIII he altered 'is it' to 'is't' in the text (l. 474), but failed to indicate the alteration correctly in the margin.

In the collected edition of 1863 there are four printer's errors in the text of *Christmas-Eve and Easter-Day*: 'semed' (*Christmas-Eve*, 78), 'T'wixt' (*Christmas-Eve*, 532), 'overheard' for 'overhead' (*Easter-Day*, 523) and 'clap' deleted instead of 'and' (*Christmas-Eve*, 718). All these were put right in the 1865 edition. Further regularization of spelling took place in *1863* and there were a number of minor changes in style: the suffix '-ize' generally replaced '-ise', and elisions were printed with a space to indicate word-boundaries ('T was). Two grammatical slips (*Christmas-Eve*, 685 and 1150) were put right. Capital letters—used extensively in the manuscript and first edition not only for He, His, Thou, and Thy, but for such words as Love, Nature, Art, Dread, Hell, Voice, Book, Quick, Dead—became less frequent, though many remained to be removed in *1868*. There were also changes in substantives which indicate a shift in Browning's attitude to his subject-matter. A more immediate sense of time and place ('those fountains' > 'these fountains') reinforced an admission of a more direct personal involvement ('I, as one who' > 'I, a man who'; 'we allege' > 'I allege'; 'your very blood' > 'my very blood'; 'veritable listeners' > 'a live actual listener'). Pace and tone were relaxed by the removal of several exclamation-marks and the replacement of colons and semi-colons by full stops. Livy was transformed into Sallust (*Christmas-Eve*, 664) and *lepidopteræ* into *coleoptera* (*Easter-Day*, 154). In *1863* Browning removed one line (*Christmas-Eve*, 769a) which may have been an uncancelled alternative. He also tried out a new opening for *Christmas-Eve*. 'Out of the little chapel I flung' makes, with l. 186, a satisfying chiasmus which frames the first section of the poem, but Browning may have felt that an interval of 186 lines put too much strain on the reader's memory and powers of anticipation, or that it was a pity to lose the dramatic effect of 'I burst'. Whatever the reason, the original reading was restored in *1868*.

Three short excerpts from *Christmas-Eve and Easter-Day* were chosen by Browning for *A Selection* of his works published by Moxon in 1865: 'Epitaph in the Catacombs' (*Easter-Day*, 275–88), 'The Common Lot' (*Christmas-Eve*, 1211–27) and 'Michelagnolo' (*Easter-Day*, 796–807). A corrected proof of *A Selection*, now in the Robert H. Taylor Collection at Princeton, shows that 'Epitaph in the Catacombs' was cut from a copy of the first edition, altered by Browning in accordance with the changes in *1863*, and inserted at page 209, after 'Rabbi Ben Ezra'. 'Michelagnolo', its two final question-marks replaced by more assertive exclamation-marks, took its place at the end of *A Selection* between 'Prospice' and 'One Word More'.

The edition of 1865 introduced a dozen substantive alterations and one printer's error ('aright' for 'a right', *Christmas-Eve*, 878). Some of these alterations begin a process, accelerated in *1868*, of removing unstressed monosyllables from the line and thereby tightening up the metre ('for the senses' > 'for sense's'; 'may the truth' > 'may truth'; 'of its posturings' > 'of posturings'). Although A. C. Dooley concludes that the changes in *1868* are generally fewer and simpler than those in *1865*, the *1868* text of *Christmas-Eve and Easter-Day* has, if anything, more variants than that of *1865*. As well as taking out unstressed words, Browning consistently removed italics, words in upper-case, and exclamation marks. In an attempt to make it easier to identify the speakers in the dialogue, he inserted quotation-marks (often removed again in *1888*) at lines 640–730, 732–68, 1062–131, 1138, and 1140–157 of *Christmas-Eve*; at lines 443–7 and 597–600 a change from indirect to direct speech is accompanied by a change in tense from past to present. There seems to be only one new printer's error in *1868*: 'years' for 'ears' (*Christmas-Eve*, 606); it was put right in *1870*, when the edition was reset.

Otherwise, Browning made only a few minor alterations in *1870*. In a copy of vol. v of *1870*, however, now in the Gordon N. Ray Collection of the Pierpont Morgan Library, he made two substantive changes in *Christmas-Eve* (151 and 247) that were not made in *1875* but were to be incorporated in *1888*. He also tried out a new and unique variant of *Christmas-Eve*, 149, one of the most frequently-altered lines in the poem:

No sooner had our friend an inkling

(*MS,1850*)

No sooner got our friend an inkling

(*1863–8*)

Our friend no sooner had got an inkling

(RB's MS alteration in the Ray copy of

1870)

No sooner our friend had got an inkling

(*1888,1889*)

In the collected edition of 1888, Browning made some interesting changes, particularly in *Easter-Day*: substituting, for instance, the discreeter 'a woman yet . . . . Shall look on me' for 'Shall live with me' (941–3); 'living men and women' for 'loving men and women' (937); 'faith might flap her wings' for 'clap her wings' (183). Several other changes were listed by W. Robertson Nicoll and Thomas J. Wise (see p. 345 n. below). The major change in *Christmas-Eve* in *1888* was the introduction of line-indentation to indicate the rhyme-scheme. All seven of the changes inserted by Browning in the Dykes Campbell and Brown University copies of *1888* (most importantly l. 17 of *Christmas-Eve*) have been adopted here.

CHRISTMAS-EVE & EASTER-DAY.

CHRISTMAS-EVE.

I.

Out of the little chapel I burst
   Into the fresh night-air again.
Five minutes full, I waited first
   In the doorway, to escape the rain
That drove in gusts down the common's centre   5
   At the edge of which the chapel stands,
Before I plucked up heart to enter.
   Heaven knows how many sorts of hands
Reached past me, groping for the latch
   Of the inner door that hung on catch   10
More obstinate the more they fumbled,
   Till, giving way at last with a scold
Of the crazy hinge, in squeezed or tumbled
   One sheep more to the rest in fold,
And left me irresolute, standing sentry   15
In the sheepfold's lath-and-plaster entry,
   Six feet long by three feet wide,
   Partitioned off from the vast inside—

title *1850* DAY. A POEM.   *MS* Christmas Eve & Easter Day. *1863,1865* DAY. FLOR-
ENCE, 1850. *subtitle (reading of *1850–75*) *MS* Christmas Eve. *1888,1889* CHRISTMAS
EVE.   1 *1863,1865* I flung,   3 *MS,1850* I had waited a good five minutes
first *1863,1865* Five minutes I waited, held my tongue   7 *MS,1850* enter:
16 *MS* sheepfolds'   *17 (reading of DC,BrU,*1889*) *MS–1888* Four feet long by two
feet wide,

   1 *the little chapel*: imaginary: cf. 385 n. below.
   13 *crazy*: 'Broken; decrepit': Johnson.
   16 *sheepfold's*: the word was often used for a church, or place of worship. Ruskin's *Notes
on the Construction of Sheepfolds* appeared in 1851. Cf. John 10.
   17 *Six feet long*: no doubt revised because an entry 'four feet long by two feet wide' is
implausible. It is hard to avoid believing, with Pettigrew, that there is a hit at Wordsworth's
'I've measured it from side to side; / 'Tis three feet long, and two feet wide', in early texts of
'The Thorn', ll. 32–3.

I blocked up half of it at least.
No remedy; the rain kept driving.   20
    They eyed me much as some wild beast,
That congregation, still arriving,
Some of them by the main road, white
A long way past me into the night,
Skirting the common, then diverging;   25
Not a few suddenly emerging
From the common's self thro' the paling-gaps,
—They house in the gravel-pits perhaps,
Where the road stops short with its safeguard border
Of lamps, as tired of such disorder;—   30
But the most turned in yet more abruptly
    From a certain squalid knot of alleys,
Where the town's bad blood once slept corruptly,
    Which now the little chapel rallies
And leads into day again,—its priestliness   35
Lending itself to hide their beastliness
So cleverly (thanks in part to the mason),
And putting so cheery a whitewashed face on
Those neophytes too much in lack of it,
    That, where you cross the common as I did,   40
    And meet the party thus presided,
"Mount Zion" with Love-lane at the back of it,
They front you as little disconcerted
As, bound for the hills, her fate averted,
And her wicked people made to mind him,   45
Lot might have marched with Gomorrah behind him.

---

20 *MS,1850* driving: 23 *MS,1850* mainroad,   40 *MS* That, when you

33 *bad blood*: scum, 'the lowest of the low'. Cf. 'blue blood'.
39 *neophytes*: converts.
41 *presided*: cf. *Sordello*, vi. 736 n.
42 *"Mount Zion"*: cf. 261, below.
46 *Lot*: 'when God destroyed the cities of the plain [Sodom and Gomorrah] ... God remembered Abraham, and sent Lot out of the midst of the overthrow, when he overthrew the cities in the which Lot dwelt': Gen. 19:29.

II.

Well, from the road, the lanes or the common,
In came the flock: the fat weary woman,
Panting and bewildered, down-clapping
    Her umbrella with a mighty report,   50
Grounded it by me, wry and flapping,
    A wreck of whalebones; then, with a snort,
Like a startled horse, at the interloper
(Who humbly knew himself improper,
But could not shrink up small enough)   55
—Round to the door, and in,—the gruff
Hinge's invariable scold
Making my very blood run cold.
Prompt in the wake of her, up-pattered
On broken clogs, the many-tattered   60
Little old-faced peaking sister-turned-mother
Of the sickly babe she tried to smother
Somehow up, with its spotted face,
From the cold, on her breast, the one warm place;
She too must stop, wring the poor ends dry   65
Of a draggled shawl, and add thereby
Her tribute to the door-mat, sopping
Already from my own clothes' dropping,
Which yet she seemed to grudge I should stand on:
    Then, stooping down to take off her pattens,   70
She bore them defiantly, in each hand one,
Planted together before her breast
And its babe, as good as a lance in rest.

54–5 *MS,1850* Who . . . . enough,   58 *MS,1850* Making your very   65 *1850*
poor suds dry

51 *wry*: twisted, out of shape.
61 *old-faced*: as in *King John*, II. i. 259.
    peaking: Johnson defines 'To Peak' as 'To look sickly'.
62–3 *to smother* / . . . *up*: to cover for warmth.
70 *pattens*: a kind of overshoe 'worn to raise the ordinary shoes out of the mud or wet': OED.
73 *a lance in rest*: since lances were heavy, a knight would ride into battle with his lance supported by a rest attached to his armour.

Close on her heels, the dingy satins
Of a female something, past me flitted,   75
    With lips as much too white, as a streak
    Lay far too red on each hollow cheek;
And it seemed the very door-hinge pitied
All that was left of a woman once,
Holding at least its tongue for the nonce.   80
Then a tall man, like the Penitent Thief,
With his jaw bound up in a handkerchief,
And eyelids screwed together tight,
Led himself in by some inner light.
And, except from him, from each that entered,   85
    I got the same interrogation—
    "What, you the alien, you have ventured
    "To take with us, the elect, your station?
"A carer for none of it, a Gallio!"—
    Thus, plain as print, I read the glance   90
At a common prey, in each countenance
    As of huntsman giving his hounds the tallyho.
And, when the door's cry drowned their wonder,
    The draught, it always sent in shutting,
Made the flame of the single tallow candle   95
In the cracked square lantern I stood under,
    Shoot its blue lip at me, rebutting
As it were, the luckless cause of scandal:
I verily fancied the zealous light
(In the chapel's secret, too!) for spite   100

---

78 *1863* it semed the   86 *MS,1850* I had the   88 *MS* with us elect your sta-
tion— *1850* with us, elect,   89 *MS–1863* a Gallio?"—   92 *MS,1850* tallyho:
93 *1868* wonder   96 *MS,1850* square lanthorn I   99 *MS,1850* verily thought
the
___

81 *the Penitent Thief*: one of the two thieves hanged at the same time as Christ: Luke
23:40ff.

84 *some inner light*: a reference to the use of 'light' by Quakers and other religious sects:
OED 'Light', *sb.* 7b.

88 *the elect*: those chosen by God for salvation: a favourite phrase with the dissenters. Cf.
Titus 1:1.

89 *a Gallio*: a man who is culpably indifferent. Acts 18:12–17.

Would shudder itself clean off the wick,
With the airs of a Saint John's Candlestick.
There was no standing it much longer.
"Good folks," thought I, as resolve grew stronger,
"This way you perform the Grand-Inquisitor   105
"When the weather sends you a chance visitor?
"You are the men, and wisdom shall die with you,
"And none of the old Seven Churches vie with you!
"But still, despite the pretty perfection
    "To which you carry your trick of exclusiveness,   110
"And, taking God's word under wise protection,
    "Correct its tendency to diffusiveness,
"And bid one reach it over hot ploughshares,—
    "Still, as I say, though you've found salvation,
"If I should choose to cry, as now, 'Shares!'—   115
    "See if the best of you bars me my ration!
"I prefer, if you please, for my expounder
"Of the laws of the feast, the feast's own Founder;
"Mine's the same right with your poorest and sickliest
    "Supposing I don the marriage vestiment: 120

---

102 *MS,1850* St. John's   104 *MS* folks", said I, *1850* folks," said I,   113 *MS,*
1850 "Bidding one   115 *MS* "Shares"!—   117 *MS,1850* Because I prefer for
118 *MS* feasts'

   102 *a Saint John's Candlestick*: a candlestick bearing seven candles, with reference to Rev.
1:12 ff., where the speaker sees seven golden candlesticks and is told that they signify 'the
seven churches'. Cf. 108, below.
   105 *The Grand-Inquisitor*: *Inquisitores ad conquirendos et eruendos hereticos*, 'inquisitors for
searching out and rooting out heretics', were first appointed in 382 ... But the name is
chiefly associated with the Spanish Inquisition as reconstituted in the end of the 15th c.':
OED. Cf. 'How It Strikes a Contemporary', 38–9.
   107 *"You are the men*: cf. Job 12:2 (Porter and Clarke).
   108 *Seven Churches*: John was commanded to write the epistles contained in the second
and third chapters of Revelation to the angels (ministers) of seven places there named.
   113 *over hot ploughshares*: the ploughshare is the blade of a plough, which cuts into the
earth. Walking barefoot over ploughshares was a form of trial by ordeal. Cf. 'The Flight of
the Duchess', 751.
   115 *'Shares!'*: an exclamation (often by a child) demanding to be allowed to share some-
thing found by another person. Cf. *The Ring and the Book*, xi. 841.
   118 *the feast's own Founder*: Christ, with reference to the Last Supper. Cf. Matt. 22:11–13.
   120 *the marriage vestiment*: cf. Matt. 22:11 ff. ('wedding garment'). 'Vestiment', from L.
'vestimentum', is an old form of 'vestment'.

"So, shut your mouth and open your Testament,
"And carve me my portion at your quickliest!"
Accordingly, as a shoemaker's lad
   With wizened face in want of soap,
   And wet apron wound round his waist like a rope,   125
(After stopping outside, for his cough was bad,
To get the fit over, poor gentle creature,
And so avoid disturbing the preacher)
—Passed in, I sent my elbow spikewise
At the shutting door, and entered likewise,   130
Received the hinge's accustomed greeting,
   And crossed the threshold's magic pentacle,
   And found myself in full conventicle,
—To wit, in Zion Chapel Meeting,
On the Christmas-Eve of 'Forty-nine,   135
   Which, calling its flock to their special clover,
   Found all assembled and one sheep over,
Whose lot, as the weather pleased, was mine.

III.

I very soon had enough of it.
   The hot smell and the human noises,   140
And my neighbour's coat, the greasy cuff of it,
   Were a pebble-stone that a child's hand poises,
Compared with the pig-of-lead-like pressure
   Of the preaching man's immense stupidity,
As he poured his doctrine forth, full measure,   145
   To meet his audience's avidity.

126–8 MS,1850 After .... preacher,   132 MS,1850 Crossed the   137 MS,
1850 Found them assembled   144 MS–1875 preaching-man's

132 pentacle: a five-pointed star-shaped figure used as a magical symbol.
133 conventicle: 'An assembly for worship. Generally used in an ill sense, including heresy or schism': Johnson.
135 On the Christmas-Eve: Berdoe pointed out that Christmas-Eve fell on a Monday in 1849. As Porter and Clarke observe, 'This is a sufficient indication of the purely imaginary nature of the experience', since most dissenters at this time did not celebrate Christmas Eve.
142 poises: lifts, balances, holds.
143 pig-of-lead-like: Browning's compound. A pig of metal is a mass moulded into a shape for storage and handling.

You needed not the wit of the Sibyl
   To guess the cause of it all, in a twinkling:
   No sooner our friend had got an inkling
Of treasure hid in the Holy Bible,   150
(Whene'er 't was the thought first struck him,
How death, at unawares, might duck him
Deeper than the grave, and quench
The gin-shop's light in hell's grim drench)
Than he handled it so, in fine irreverence,   155
   As to hug the book of books to pieces:
And, a patchwork of chapters and texts in severance,
   Not improved by the private dog's-ears and creases,
Having clothed his own soul with, he'd fain see equipt yours,—
So tossed you again your Holy Scriptures.   160
And you picked them up, in a sense, no doubt:
   Nay, had but a single face of my neighbours
   Appeared to suspect that the preacher's labours
Were help which the world could be saved without,
'T is odds but I might have borne in quiet   165
A qualm or two at my spiritual diet,
Or (who can tell?) perchance even mustered
   Somewhat to urge in behalf of the sermon:
But the flock sat on, divinely flustered,
   Sniffing, methought, its dew of Hermon   170
With such content in every snuffle,
As the devil inside us loves to ruffle.

---

149 *MS,1850* No sooner had our friend an inkling *1863–75* No sooner got our friend an inkling   151 *MS,1850* (Whenever it was *1863–75* (Whene'er 't was that the 155 *1870* Then he   156 *MS,1850* Book   158 *MS* by [the] private 165 *MS,1850* 'Tis odds but I had borne   166 *MS,1850* diet;   167 *MS,1850* Or, who can tell? had even mustered

   147 *the Sibyl*: in classical mythology the Sibyls knew the future.

   152 *at unawares*: as in *Sordello*, ii. 545.

   157 *in severance*: without relation to each other.

   169 *flustered*: Johnson states that the verb means 'To make hot and rosy with drinking; to make half drunk', citing *Othello*, II. iii. 54.

   170 *dew of Hermon*: 'Behold, how good and how pleasant it is for brethren to dwell together in unity!... As the dew of Hermon': Ps. 133:1, 3.

My old fat woman purred with pleasure,
   And thumb round thumb went twirling faster,
While she, to his periods keeping measure,   175
   Maternally devoured the pastor.
The man with the handkerchief untied it,
Showed us a horrible wen inside it,
Gave his eyelids yet another screwing,
And rocked himself as the woman was doing.   180
The shoemaker's lad, discreetly choking,
Kept down his cough. 'T was too provoking!
My gorge rose at the nonsense and stuff of it;
   So, saying like Eve when she plucked the apple,
   "I wanted a taste, and now there's enough of it,"   185
I flung out of the little chapel.

IV.

There was a lull in the rain, a lull
   In the wind too; the moon was risen,
And would have shone out pure and full,
   But for the ramparted cloud-prison,   190
Block on block built up in the West,
For what purpose the wind knows best,
Who changes his mind continually.
And the empty other half of the sky
Seemed in its silence as if it knew   195
What, any moment, might look through
A chance gap in that fortress massy:—
   Through its fissures you got hints
   Of the flying moon, by the shifting tints,
Now, a dull lion-colour, now, brassy   200
Burning to yellow, and whitest yellow,
Like furnace-smoke just ere flames bellow,

183 *MS–1863* it,   184 *MS,1850* And saying,   202 *MS–1875* ere the flames
  176 *devoured*: perhaps suggested by *Othello*, i. iii. 150.
  185 *enough of it*: unscriptural, but see *Paradise Lost*, ix. 791.
  190 *ramparted*: as in Coleridge's 'Ode to the Departing Year', 128.
     cloud-prison: cf. Shelley, *Prometheus Unbound*, iv. 376.

All a-simmer with intense strain
To let her through,—then blank again,
At the hope of her appearance failing.   205
Just by the chapel, a break in the railing
Shows a narrow path directly across;
'T is ever dry walking there, on the moss—
Besides, you go gently all the way uphill.
    I stooped under and soon felt better;   210
My head grew lighter, my limbs more supple,
    As I walked on, glad to have slipt the fetter.
My mind was full of the scene I had left,
    That placid flock, that pastor vociferant,
    —How this outside was pure and different!   215
The sermon, now—what a mingled weft
Of good and ill! Were either less,
    Its fellow had coloured the whole distinctly;
But alas for the excellent earnestness,
    And the truths, quite true if stated succinctly,   220
But as surely false, in their quaint presentment,
However to pastor and flock's contentment!
Say rather, such truths looked false to your eyes,
    With his provings and parallels twisted and twined,
Till how could you know them, grown double their size   225
    In the natural fog of the good man's mind,
Like yonder spots of our roadside lamps,
Haloed about with the common's damps?
Truth remains true, the fault's in the prover;
    The zeal was good, and the aspiration;   230
And yet, and yet, yet, fifty times over,

---

209 *MS,1850* uphill: 211 *MS–1863* grew light, my   212 *MS,1850* fetter;
222 *MS* flocks'   *223 {reading of *MS–1875*,DC,BrU,*1889*} *1888* eyes.
226 *MS,1850* mind?   228 *MS,1850* damps.

  203 *a-simmer*: first recorded by OED in *Blackwood's Magazine*, June 1849, p. 767.
  212 *slipt the fetter*: cf. *The Return of the Druses*, v. 63.
  214 *vociferant*: shouting, bawling.
  217 *good and ill*: cf. *All's Well that Ends Well*, iv. iii. 67 (Pettigrew and Collins).
  221 *presentment*: presentation.

Pharaoh received no demonstration,
By his Baker's dream of Baskets Three,
Of the doctrine of the Trinity,—
Although, as our preacher thus embellished it,   235
Apparently his hearers relished it
With so unfeigned a gust—who knows if
They did not prefer our friend to Joseph?
But so it is everywhere, one way with all of them!
    These people have really felt, no doubt,   240
A something, the motion they style the Call of them;
    And this is their method of bringing about,
By a mechanism of words and tones,
(So many texts in so many groans)
A sort of reviving and reproducing,   245
    More or less perfectly, (who can tell?)
The mood itself, which strengthens by using;
    And how that happens, I understand well.
A tune was born in my head last week,
Out of the thump-thump and shriek-shriek   250
    Of the train, as I came by it, up from Manchester;
And when, next week, I take it back again,
My head will sing to the engine's clack again,
    While it only makes my neighbour's haunches stir,
—Finding no dormant musical sprout   255
In him, as in me, to be jolted out.
'T is the taught already that profits by teaching;
He gets no more from the railway's preaching
    Than, from this preacher who does the rail's office, I:

---

245 *MS–1863* reviving or reproducing,   247 *MS–1875* Of the mood itself, that
strengthens   248 *MS–1875* how it happens,   257 *MS,1850* that profit by
259 *MS,1850* I, *1863* I;

232 *Pharaoh*: Gen. 40:16 ff. describes the dream of Pharaoh's baker, correctly interpreted
by Joseph as an omen that the man would be executed in three days. The preacher here
attempts to interpret this in terms of the New Testament.

241 *Call*: divine summons.

251 *the train*: the 1840s was the decade of the 'railway mania' during which the principal
cities of England were first linked by railway-lines.

253 *clack*: insistently repeated sound.

259 *does the rail's office*: by making a 'clack'.

Whom therefore the flock cast a jealous eye on. 260
Still, why paint over their door "Mount Zion,"
    To which all flesh shall come, saith the prophecy?

v.

But wherefore be harsh on a single case?
    After how many modes, this Christmas-Eve,
Does the self-same weary thing take place? 265
    The same endeavour to make you believe,
And with much the same effect, no more:
    Each method abundantly convincing,
As I say, to those convinced before,
    But scarce to be swallowed without wincing 270
By the not-as-yet-convinced. For me,
I have my own church equally:
And in this church my faith sprang first!
    (I said, as I reached the rising ground,
And the wind began again, with a burst 275
    Of rain in my face, and a glad rebound
From the heart beneath, as if, God speeding me,
I entered his church-door, nature leading me)
—In youth I looked to these very skies,
    And probing their immensities, 280
I found God there, his visible power;
    Yet felt in my heart, amid all its sense
    Of the power, an equal evidence
That his love, there too, was the nobler dower.
For the loving worm within its clod, 285

260 *MS,1850* flock casts a   265 *MS–1875* selfsame   267 *MS,1850* And
much with the   272 *MS,1850* equally.   273 *MS–1865 this*   283 *MS–
1863* Of that power,

262 *the prophecy*: 'Praise waiteth for thee, O God, in Sion: and unto thee shall the vow be
performed. / O thou that hearest prayer, unto thee shall all flesh come': Ps. 65:1–2.

284 *dower*: 'Endowment; gift': Johnson.

285 *the loving worm*: Pettigrew and Collins cite Shelley, *Epipsychidion*, 128–9: 'The spirit
of the worm beneath the sod / In love and worship, blends itself with God', noting that the
lines are quoted in the Essay on Shelley: see p. 441 below.

Were diviner than a loveless god
Amid his worlds, I will dare to say.
    You know what I mean: God's all, man's nought:
    But also, God, whose pleasure brought
Man into being, stands away   290
    As it were a handbreadth off, to give
Room for the newly-made to live,
And look at him from a place apart,
And use his gifts of brain and heart,
Given, indeed, but to keep for ever.   295
Who speaks of man, then, must not sever
Man's very elements from man,
Saying, "But all is God's"—whose plan
Was to create man and then leave him
Able, his own word saith, to grieve him,   300
But able to glorify him too,
As a mere machine could never do,
That prayed or praised, all unaware
Of its fitness for aught but praise and prayer,
Made perfect as a thing of course.   305
Man, therefore, stands on his own stock
Of love and power as a pin-point rock:
And, looking to God who ordained divorce
Of the rock from his boundless continent,
Sees, in his power made evident,   310
Only excess by a million-fold
O'er the power God gave man in the mould.
For, note: man's hand, first formed to carry
A few pounds' weight, when taught to marry

---

291 *MS,1850* were, an handbreadth   307 *MS–1875* rock,   313 *MS,1850*
For, see: Man's

    300 *his own word saith*: Gen. 3:22 ff. Cf. *Paradise Lost*, iii. 98 ff.
    305 *as a thing of course*: as a matter of course.
    307 *pin-point*: this is the first example of the compound as an adjective in OED.
    312 *in the mould*: on earth, in this life.

Its strength with an engine's, lifts a mountain, 315
   —Advancing in power by one degree;
   And why count steps through eternity?
But love is the ever-springing fountain:
Man may enlarge or narrow his bed
For the water's play, but the water-head— 320
How can he multiply or reduce it?
   As easy create it, as cause it to cease;
He may profit by it, or abuse it,
   But 't is not a thing to bear increase
As power does: be love less or more 325
   In the heart of man, he keeps it shut
   Or opes it wide, as he pleases, but
Love's sum remains what it was before.
So, gazing up, in my youth, at love
As seen through power, ever above 330
All modes which make it manifest,
My soul brought all to a single test—
That he, the Eternal First and Last,
Who, in his power, had so surpassed
All man conceives of what is might,— 335
Whose wisdom, too, showed infinite,
—Would prove as infinitely good;
Would never, (my soul understood,)
With power to work all love desires,
Bestow e'en less than man requires; 340
That he who endlessly was teaching,
Above my spirit's utmost reaching,
What love can do in the leaf or stone,
(So that to master this alone,
This done in the stone or leaf for me, 345

323 *MS,1850* abuse it;   325 *MS,1850* power will: be   327 *MS,1850* wide as
338 *MS,1850* my . . . . understood,

  315 *lifts a mountain*: probably a reminiscence of the saying of Archimedes: 'Give me a place to stand and I will move the earth'. The 'engine' would be a lever.
  318 *the ever-springing fountain*: cf. Jer. 2:13.
  333 *First and Last*: Rev. 1:11.

I must go on learning endlessly)
Would never need that I, in turn,
   Should point him out defect unheeded,
And show that God had yet to learn
   What the meanest human creature needed,   350
—Not life, to wit, for a few short years,
Tracking his way through doubts and fears,
While the stupid earth on which I stay
   Suffers no change, but passive adds
   Its myriad years to myriads,   355
Though I, he gave it to, decay,
Seeing death come and choose about me,
And my dearest ones depart without me.
No: love which, on earth, amid all the shows of it,
   Has ever been seen the sole good of life in it,   360
The love, ever growing there, spite of the strife in it,
   Shall arise, made perfect, from death's repose of it.
And I shall behold thee, face to face,
O God, and in thy light retrace
How in all I loved here, still wast thou!   365
Whom pressing to, then, as I fain would now,
I shall find as able to satiate
   The love, thy gift, as my spirit's wonder
Thou art able to quicken and sublimate,
   With this sky of thine, that I now walk under,   370
And glory in thee for, as I gaze
Thus, thus! Oh, let men keep their ways
Of seeking thee in a narrow shrine—
Be this my way! And this is mine!

VI.

For lo, what think you? suddenly   375
The rain and the wind ceased, and the sky

348   MS–1863 out a defect   350 MS needed⟨.⟩ [,—] 1850–68 needed,—
359 MS–1865 No!   362 MS–1865 it!   368 MS spirits'   371 MS,
1850 And glory in Thee as thus I gaze,   374 MS–1865 is
  363 *face to face*: cf. 1 Cor. 13:12, Gen. 32:30, etc.

Received at once the full fruition
Of the moon's consummate apparition.
The black cloud-barricade was riven,
Ruined beneath her feet, and driven 380
Deep in the West; while, bare and breathless,
    North and South and East lay ready
For a glorious thing that, dauntless, deathless,
    Sprang across them and stood steady.
'T was a moon-rainbow, vast and perfect, 385
From heaven to heaven extending, perfect
As the mother-moon's self, full in face.
It rose, distinctly at the base
    With its seven proper colours chorded,
Which still, in the rising, were compressed, 390
Until at last they coalesced,
    And supreme the spectral creature lorded
In a triumph of whitest white,—
Above which intervened the night.
But above night too, like only the next, 395
    The second of a wondrous sequence,
    Reaching in rare and rarer frequence,
Till the heaven of heavens were circumflexed,
Another rainbow rose, a mightier,
Fainter, flushier and flightier,— 400

378 *MS* moons'   391 *1850* coälesced, *MS,1863–68* coälesced,   395 *MS,*
1850 like the next,   398 *MS,1850* heavens be circumflext, *1863,1865* were circum-
flext,

385 *moon-rainbow*: Browning told W. G. Kingsland that 'all the incidents' of the poem
were 'imaginary—save the lunar rainbow: I saw that': *Literary Anecdotes of the Nineteenth
Century*, ed. W. Robertson Nicoll and Thomas J. Wise (2 vols., 1895–6), i. 456.

389 *its seven proper colours*: there are seven spectral colours: red, orange, yellow, green,
blue, indigo, and violet.

    chorded: this appears to be the only example of the word in relation to colours.

392 *lorded*: without 'it' this is a rare and obsolete use.

393 *whitest white*: because, as Newton showed, the spectral colours together produce
white.

398 *the heaven of heavens*: a biblical phrase: see e.g., 2 Chron. 6:18.

    circumflexed: arched over.

400 *flushier*: probably a nonce-word.

    flightier: presumably 'more fleeting', another nonce-word.

Rapture dying along its verge.
Oh, whose foot shall I see emerge,
Whose, from the straining topmost dark,
On to the keystone of that arc?

VII.

This sight was shown me, there and then,—   405
Me, one out of a world of men,
Singled forth, as the chance might hap
To another if, in a thunderclap
Where I heard noise and you saw flame,
Some one man knew God called his name.   410
For me, I think I said, "Appear!
"Good were it to be ever here.
"If thou wilt, let me build to thee
"Service-tabernacles three,
"Where, forever in thy presence,   415
"In ecstatic acquiescence,
"Far alike from thriftless learning
"And ignorance's undiscerning,
"I may worship and remain!"
      Thus at the show above me, gazing   420
With upturned eyes, I felt my brain
      Glutted with the glory, blazing
Throughout its whole mass, over and under,
Until at length it burst asunder
And out of it bodily there streamed   425
The too-much glory, as it seemed,
Passing from out me to the ground,
Then palely serpentining round
Into the dark with mazy error.

401 MS–1865 verge!   403 MS–1865 WHOSE,   415 1850 for ever
*423 {reading of MS–1875,DC,BrU} 1888,1889 under   *425 {reading of MS–1865}
1868–89 streamed,

    414 Service-tabernacles three: cf. Matt. 17:4, Mark 9:5, Luke 9:33.
    418 ignorance's undiscerning: cf. Steele, Spectator, no. 157: 'The Ignorance and Undiscern-
ing of the Generality of Schoolmasters'.
    429 with mazy error: echoing Paradise Lost, iv. 239: 'error', wandering course.

VIII.

All at once I looked up with terror.   430
He was there.
He himself with his human air,
On the narrow pathway, just before.
I saw the back of him, no more—
He had left the chapel, then, as I.   435
I forgot all about the sky.
No face: only the sight
Of a sweepy garment, vast and white,
With a hem that I could recognize.
I felt terror, no surprise;   440
My mind filled with the cataract,
At one bound, of the mighty fact.
"I remember, he did say,
    "Doubtless that, to this world's end,
"Where two or three should meet and pray,   445
    "He would be in the midst, their friend;
"Certainly he was there with them!"
    And my pulses leaped for joy
    Of the golden thought without alloy,
That I saw his very vesture's hem.   450
Then rushed the blood back, cold and clear,
With a fresh enhancing shiver of fear;
And I hastened, cried out while I pressed
To the salvation of the vest,
"But not so, Lord! It cannot be   445
"That thou, indeed, art leaving me—
"Me, that have despised thy friends!

---

*432 {reading of *MS–1868*} *1870* human hair, *1875–89* air.   433 *MS,1850* before:
*442 {reading of *MS–1863*} *1865–89* bound   443 *MS–1865* I remembered, He
447 *MS–1863* them. *1865* them,   452 *MS–1865* fear,   456 *MS* "Th⟨ou⟩[at]
[Thou,] indeed,   457 *MS–1865* friends.

434 *the back of him, no more*: cf. Exod. 33:23.
438 *white*: cf. Matt. 17:2; Mark 9:3; Luke 9:29.
439 *a hem*: see Introduction, p. 325 n. 1 above.
445 *Where two or three*: Matt. 18:20.

"Did my heart make no amends?
"Thou art the love of God—above
"His power, didst hear me place his love,   460
"And that was leaving the world for thee.
"Therefore thou must not turn from me
"As I had chosen the other part!
"Folly and pride o'ercame my heart.
"Our best is bad, nor bears thy test;   465
"Still, it should be our very best.
"I thought it best that thou, the spirit,
    "Be worshipped in spirit and in truth,
"And in beauty, as even we require it—
    "Not in the forms burlesque, uncouth,   470
"I left but now, as scarcely fitted
"For thee: I knew not what I pitied.
"But, all I felt there, right or wrong,
    "What is it to thee, who curest sinning?
"Am I not weak as thou art strong?   475
    "I have looked to thee from the beginning,
"Straight up to thee through all the world
"Which, like an idle scroll, lay furled
"To nothingness on either side:
"And since the time thou wast descried,   480
"Spite of the weak heart, so have I
"Lived ever, and so fain would die,
"Living and dying, thee before!
"But if thou leavest me——"

IX.

Less or more,
I suppose that I spoke thus.   485

461 MS,1850 Thee! 1868–75 thee: 463 MS–1865 "As if I . . . . part. 1868–75 part.
472 MS,1850 pitied:

463 the other part: 'For he that is not against us is on our part': Mark 9:40.
468 Be worshipped: John 4:23: 'the true worshippers shall worship the Father in spirit and
in truth'.
478 like an idle scroll: cf. Isa. 34:4 and Rev. 6:14.

When,—have mercy, Lord, on us!
The whole face turned upon me full.
   And I spread myself beneath it,
   As when the bleacher spreads, to seethe it
In the cleansing sun, his wool,—   490
Steeps in the flood of noontide whiteness
   Some defiled, discoloured web—
So lay I, saturate with brightness.
   And when the flood appeared to ebb,
Lo, I was walking, light and swift,   495
   With my senses settling fast and steadying,
But my body caught up in the whirl and drift
   Of the vesture's amplitude, still eddying
On, just before me, still to be followed,
   As it carried me after with its motion: 500
What shall I say?—as a path were hollowed
   And a man went weltering through the ocean,
Sucked along in the flying wake
Of the luminous water-snake.
Darkness and cold were cloven, as through   505
I passed, upborne yet walking too.
And I turned to myself at intervals,—
"So he said, so it befalls.
"God who registers the cup
   "Of mere cold water, for his sake   510
"To a disciple rendered up,
   "Disdains not his own thirst to slake
"At the poorest love was ever offered:
"And because my heart I proffered,

500 *MS* motion,   508 *MS,1850* said, and so it befals. *1863–75* it befals.
514 *MS–1865* because it was my

493 *saturate with brightness*: cf. Henry More, annotation to Joseph Glanvill, *Lux Orientalis* (1682): 'All will be turned into a more full and saturate Brightness and Glory.' On Browning and More, see our notes on *Sordello*, i. 748 and v. 43, in Vol. II.

495 *I was walking*: cf. 771.

504 *the luminous water-snake*: cf. Coleridge, 'The Ancient Mariner', 272–6. Cf. *Paracelsus*, i. 444 n., and below, 771 ff.

509 *the cup*: Matt. 10:42.

"With true love trembling at the brim,   515
"He suffers me to follow him
"For ever, my own way,—dispensed
"From seeking to be influenced
"By all the less immediate ways
     "That earth, in worships manifold,   520
"Adopts to reach, by prayer and praise,
     "The garment's hem, which, lo, I hold!"

                         x.

And so we crossed the world and stopped.
     For where am I, in city or plain,
     Since I am 'ware of the world again?   525
And what is this that rises propped
With pillars of prodigious girth?
Is it really on the earth,
This miraculous Dome of God?
Has the angel's measuring-rod   530
Which numbered cubits, gem from gem,
'Twixt the gates of the New Jerusalem,
Meted it out,—and what he meted,
Have the sons of men completed?
—Binding, ever as he bade,   535
Columns in the colonnade
With arms wide open to embrace
The entry of the human race
To the breast of . . . what is it, yon building,

---

517 MS "Forever,   527 MS girth⟨—⟩[?]   532 1863 T'wixt   536 MS–
1865 in this colonnade

    520 *worships*: modes of worship.
    529 *Dome of God*: St Peter's in Rome, the greatest church in the world. It was designed by
Michelangelo, more or less following the plan of Bramante: a huge church, centred round
a dome, without a long nave. In the early seventeenth century a long nave was added.
    530 *the angel's measuring-rod*: Rev. 21:15 ff.
    532 *the New Jerusalem*: 'And I John saw the holy city, new Jerusalem, coming down from
God out of heaven, prepared as a bride adorned for her husband': Rev. 21:2.
    533 *Meted*: measured.
    536 *the colonnade*: in the mid-seventeenth century Giovanni Bernini constructed colon-
nades surrounding the piazza in front of St Peter's.

Ablaze in front, all paint and gilding,   540
With marble for brick, and stones of price
For garniture of the edifice?
Now I see; it is no dream;
It stands there and it does not seem:
For ever, in pictures, thus it looks,   545
And thus I have read of it in books
Often in England, leagues away,
And wondered how these fountains play,
Growing up eternally
Each to a musical water-tree,   550
Whose blossoms drop, a glittering boon,
Before my eyes, in the light of the moon,
To the granite lavers underneath.
Liar and dreamer in your teeth!
I, the sinner that speak to you,   555
Was in Rome this night, and stood, and knew
Both this and more. For see, for see,
The dark is rent, mine eye is free
To pierce the crust of the outer wall,
And I view inside, and all there, all,   560
As the swarming hollow of a hive,
The whole Basilica alive!
Men in the chancel, body and nave,
Men on the pillars' architrave,
Men on the statues, men on the tombs   565
With popes and kings in their porphyry wombs,

---

548 *MS,1850* how those fountains   557 *MS,1850* more!

548 *these fountains*: the fountains on either side of the obelisk in St Peter's Square.

550 *water-tree*: perhaps Browning's coinage.

553 *lavers*: basins.

554 *Liar and dreamer in your teeth!*: i.e. I reject your charge that I am a liar and a dreamer!

562 *Basilica*: 'a large oblong building or hall, with double colonnades and a semicircular apse at the end': OED. Here, St Peter's.

563 *chancel, body and nave*: the chancel is the eastern part of a church, in which the altar is placed, and the nave the main part of it, exclusive of the aisles or wings. The 'body' of a church is the nave, so the speaker seems imprecise.

564 *architrave*: the lowest part of the entablature which is placed above a column.

All famishing in expectation
Of the main-altar's consummation.
For see, for see, the rapturous moment
Approaches, and earth's best endowment   570
Blends with heaven's; the taper-fires
Pant up, the winding brazen spires
Heave loftier yet the baldachin;
The incense-gaspings, long kept in,
Suspire in clouds; the organ blatant   575
Holds his breath and grovels latent,
As if God's hushing finger grazed him,
(Like Behemoth when he praised him)
At the silver bell's shrill tinkling,
Quick cold drops of terror sprinkling   580
On the sudden pavement strewed
With faces of the multitude.
Earth breaks up, time drops away,
In flows heaven, with its new day
Of endless life, when He who trod,   585
Very man and very God,
This earth in weakness, shame and pain,
Dying the death whose signs remain
Up yonder on the accursed tree,—
Shall come again, no more to be   590
Of captivity the thrall,

567 *famishing*: the only example of the figurative use of the word in OED is from *Colombe's Birthday*, I. 58: 'You famish for promotion'.

573 *baldachin*: 'A piece of architecture, in form of a canopy, supported with columns, and serving as a covering to an altar': Johnson. The great bronze canopy in St Peter's was designed by Bernini. Like the spiral columns which support it, it is made of bronze.

574 *incense-gaspings*: no doubt a nonce-word.

575 *Suspire*: breathe out.   *blatant*: loud, clamorous.

576 *latent*: concealed, or hiding itself.

577 *God's hushing finger*: 'The finger of God *signifies his power, his operation*': Cruden, *Concordance*.

578 *Behemoth*: see Job 40:15 ff. Any large animal, often taken to be the elephant. Cf. *Paradise Lost*, vii. 471.

579 *the silver bell's shrill tinkling*: at the elevation of the Host (sacrament) in the Roman Catholic Church, a bell is rung and the worshippers fall on their knees.

583 *Earth breaks up*: Rev. 21. 1.

But the one God, All in all,
King of kings, Lord of lords,
As His servant John received the words,
"I died, and live for evermore!"   595

XI.

Yet I was left outside the door.
"Why sit I here on the threshold-stone
"Left till He return, alone
"Save for the garment's extreme fold
"Abandoned still to bless my hold?"   600
My reason, to my doubt, replied,
As if a book were opened wide,
And at a certain page I traced
Every record undefaced,
Added by successive years,—   605
The harvestings of truth's stray ears
Singly gleaned, and in one sheaf
Bound together for belief.
Yes, I said—that he will go
And sit with these in turn, I know.   610
Their faith's heart beats, though her head swims
Too giddily to guide her limbs,
Disabled by their palsy-stroke
From propping mine. Though Rome's gross yoke
Drops off, no more to be endured,   615
Her teaching is not so obscured
By errors and perversities,
That no truth shines athwart the lies:

---

593 *MS,1850* kings, and Lord   597 *MS–1865* Why sate I there on   598 *MS,*
1850 He returns, alone   599 *MS* Garments'   600 *MS–1865* hold?—
606 *1868* stray years   614 *MS–1875* propping me. Though   618 *MS* ⟨But
that a⟩ [That no] truth shines ⟨through⟩ [athwart] the

593 *King of kings, Lord of lords*: Rev. 19:16.
595 *"I died*: in Rev. 1:18–19 the Lord speaks to St John the Divine: 'I am he that liveth,
and was dead; and, behold, I am alive for evermore.'
597 *the threshold-stone*: cf. Scott, *The Lay of the Last Minstrel*, i. i. 7.
618 *athwart*: through, a meaning considered by Johnson and OED 'not proper'.

And he, whose eye detects a spark
Even where, to man's, the whole seems dark,   620
May well see flame where each beholder
Acknowledges the embers smoulder.
But I, a mere man, fear to quit
The clue God gave me as most fit
To guide my footsteps through life's maze,   625
Because himself discerns all ways
Open to reach him: I, a man
Able to mark where faith began
To swerve aside, till from its summit
Judgment drops her damning plummet,   630
Pronouncing such a fatal space
Departed from the founder's base:
He will not bid me enter too,
But rather sit, as now I do,
Awaiting his return outside.   635
—'T was thus my reason straight replied
And joyously I turned, and pressed
The garment's skirt upon my breast,
Until, afresh its light suffusing me,
My heart cried—What has been abusing me   640
That I should wait here lonely and coldly,
Instead of rising, entering boldly,
Baring truth's face, and letting drift
Her veils of lies as they choose to shift?
Do these men praise him? I will raise   645
My voice up to their point of praise!
I see the error; but above
The scope of error, see the love.—
Oh, love of those first Christian days!
—Fanned so soon into a blaze,   650

628 *MS,1850* He gave to   638 *MS* Garments'   640 *1868–75* cried "What
643 *MS* truths'

630 *plummet*: 'A weight of lead hung at a string, by which depths are sounded, and per-
pendicularity is discerned': Johnson. Browning is obviously thinking of the Leaning Tower
of Pisa.
641 *lonely*: used (improperly) as an adverb.

From the spark preserved by the trampled sect,
That the antique sovereign Intellect
Which then sat ruling in the world,
Like a change in dreams, was hurled
From the throne he reigned upon: 655
You looked up and he was gone.
Gone, his glory of the pen!
—Love, with Greece and Rome in ken,
Bade her scribes abhor the trick
Of poetry and rhetoric,   660
And exult with hearts set free,
In blessed imbecility
Scrawled, perchance, on some torn sheet,
Leaving Sallust incomplete.
Gone, his pride of sculptor, painter!   665
—Love, while able to acquaint her
With the thousand statues yet
Fresh from chisel, pictures wet
From brush, she saw on every side,
Chose rather with an infant's pride   670
To frame those portents which impart
Such unction to true Christian Art.
Gone, music too! The air was stirred
By happy wings: Terpander's bird

656 *MS–1865* gone!   *663 {reading of *MS–1863*} *1865–89* sheet   664 *MS,
1850* Leaving Livy incomplete.   *667 {reading of *MS–1865*} *1868–89* While the
670 *MS* infants'

652 *the antique sovereign Intellect*: as in the poem 'Cleon', in *Men and Women*.

658 *in ken*: within its field of vision or consideration.

662 *imbecility*: 'feebleness of mind or body': Johnson.

664 *Sallust*: while minor works by Gaius Sallustius Crispus (86–*c*. 34 BC) remain, his *His-
toriae* survive only in fragments. He has an unusual and striking style. The revision from
'Livy' was probably to avoid pointless alliteration.

665 *his*: Intellect's.

672 *unction*: 'Any thing that excites piety and devotion': Johnson.

674 *Terpander's bird*: Terpander was 'a lyric poet and musician of Antissa in Lesbos, 675
BC. It is said that he appeased a tumult at Sparta by the melody and sweetness of his notes':
Lemprière. The bird is probably the nightingale, to which any Greek poet could be com-
pared, unless indeed Terpander is a mistake for Ibycus, the poet whose murder was
avenged by cranes.

(That, when the cold came, fled away)   675
Would tarry not the wintry day,—
As more-enduring sculpture must,
Till filthy saints rebuked the gust
With which they chanced to get a sight
Of some dear naked Aphrodite   680
They glanced a thought above the toes of,
By breaking zealously her nose off.
Love, surely, from that music's lingering,
Might have filched her organ-fingering,
Nor chosen rather to set prayings   685
To hog-grunts, praises to horse-neighings.
Love was the startling thing, the new:
Love was the all-sufficient too;
And seeing that, you see the rest:
As a babe can find its mother's breast   690
As well in darkness as in light,
Love shut our eyes, and all seemed right.
True, the world's eyes are open now:
—Less need for me to disallow
Some few that keep Love's zone unbuckled,   695
Peevish as ever to be suckled,
Lulled by the same old baby-prattle
With intermixture of the rattle,
When she would have them creep, stand steady
Upon their feet, or walk already,   700
Not to speak of trying to climb.
I will be wise another time,
And not desire a wall between us,
      When next I see a church-roof cover

676 *MS* wint⟨er⟩[ry] day,—   678 *MS–1865* Till a filthy saint rebuked
679 *MS–1865* which he chanced   681 *MS–1865* He glanced   683 *MS*
lingering.   685 *MS,1850* Nor chose rather   689 *MS,1850* rest.
693 *MS* worlds'   699 *MS* When ⟨when⟩ she

   678 *gust*: sensual enjoyment.
   680 *Aphrodite*: Browning himself would not have pronounced the name of the Greek
Venus without its final syllable.
   684 *organ-fingering*: not in OED.

So many species of one genus,   705
    All with foreheads bearing *lover*
Written above the earnest eyes of them;
    All with breasts that beat for beauty,
Whether sublimed, to the surprise of them,
    In noble daring, steadfast duty,   710
The heroic in passion, or in action,—
Or, lowered for sense's satisfaction,
To the mere outside of human creatures,
Mere perfect form and faultless features.
What? with all Rome here, whence to levy   715
    Such contributions to their appetite,
With women and men in a gorgeous bevy,
    They take, as it were, a padlock, clap it tight
On their southern eyes, restrained from feeding
On the glories of their ancient reading,   720
On the beauties of their modern singing,
On the wonders of the builder's bringing,
On the majesties of Art around them,—
    And, all these loves, late struggling incessant,
When faith has at last united and bound them,   725
    They offer up to God for a present?
Why, I will, on the whole, be rather proud of it,—
    And, only taking the act in reference
To the other recipients who might have allowed of it,
    I will rejoice that God had the preference.   730

                        XII.

So I summed up my new resolves:
    Too much love there can never be.

706 *MS* with ⟨?their⟩ foreheads   708 *MS* with ⟨?hearts⟩ [breasts] that
712 *MS–1863* for the senses' *1865* senses'   715 *MS,1850* What!
718 *MS,1850* padlock, and clap *1863* padlock, and it tight   726 *MS,1850* present!
*729 ⟨reading of *MS–1865*⟩ *1868–75* allowed it, *1888,1889* allowed it   730 *MS,1850*
preference! *1868–75* preference."   732 *1868–75* "Too

    709 *sublimed*: sublimated.

And where the intellect devolves
   Its function on love exclusively,
I, a man who possesses both,   735
Will accept the provision, nothing loth,
—Will feast my love, then depart elsewhere,
That my intellect may find its share.
And ponder, O soul, the while thou departest,
And see thou applaud the great heart of the artist,   740
Who, examining the capabilities
   Of the block of marble he has to fashion
   Into a type of thought or passion,—
Not always, using obvious facilities,
Shapes it, as any artist can,   745
Into a perfect symmetrical man,
Complete from head to foot of the life-size,
Such as old Adam stood in his wife's eyes,—
But, now and then, bravely aspires to consummate
A Colossus by no means so easy to come at,   750
And uses the whole of his block for the bust,
   Leaving the mind of the public to finish it,
Since cut it ruefully short he must:
On the face alone he expends his devotion,
   He rather would mar than resolve to diminish it,   755
—Saying, "Applaud me for this grand notion
"Of what a face may be! As for completing it
   "In breast and body and limbs, do that, you!"
All hail! I fancy how, happily meeting it,
   A trunk and legs would perfect the statue,   760
Could man carve so as to answer volition.
   And how much nobler than petty cavils,
   Were a hope to find, in my spirit-travels,
Some artist of another ambition,

735 *MS,1850* I, as one who   752 *MS–1863* the minds of   754 *MS,1850*
devotion;   758 *MS–1865 that*,   763 *MS,1850* | A hope

750 *A Colossus*: a statue of great size, particularly 'a celebrated brazen image at Rhodes, which passed for one of the seven wonders of the world... It was 70 cubits, or 105 feet high': Lemprière. It was destroyed by an earthquake about 224 BC.

Who having a block to carve, no bigger,   765
　　Has spent his power on the opposite quest,
　　And believed to begin at the feet was best—
For so may I see, ere I die, the whole figure!

XIII.

No sooner said than out in the night!
My heart beat lighter and more light: 770
And still, as before, I was walking swift,
　　With my senses settling fast and steadying,
But my body caught up in the whirl and drift
　　Of the vesture's amplitude, still eddying
On just before me, still to be followed,   775
　　As it carried me after with its motion,
—What shall I say?—as a path were hollowed,
　　And a man went weltering through the ocean,
Sucked along in the flying wake
Of the luminous water-snake.   780

XIV.

Alone! I am left alone once more—
　　(Save for the garment's extreme fold
　　Abandoned still to bless my hold)
Alone, beside the entrance-door
Of a sort of temple,—perhaps a college,   785
—Like nothing I ever saw before
At home in England, to my knowledge.
The tall old quaint irregular town!
　　It may be ... though which, I can't affirm ... any
　　Of the famous middle-age towns of Germany;   790
And this flight of stairs where I sit down,

768 *1868–75* figure!"   769a *MS,1850* And still as we swept through storm and
night,   771 *MS,1850* And lo, as   *789 {editors' emendation; all versions have
two dots after 'be' and 'affirm'} *MS–1865 which*,

　771 *And still, as before*: cf. 495, above. This line prepares us for the fact that 772–80
repeat, word for word, 496–504. The repetition strengthens our impression that the
speaker is earnest in his desire to describe what actually befell him. The same is true of the
repetition of 599–600 in 782–3.

Is it Halle, Weimar, Cassel, Frankfort
Or Göttingen, I have to thank for't?
It may be Göttingen,—most likely.
Through the open door I catch obliquely   795
Glimpses of a lecture-hall;
    And not a bad assembly neither,
Ranged decent and symmetrical
    On benches, waiting what's to see there;
Which, holding still by the vesture's hem,   800
I also resolve to see with them,
Cautious this time how I suffer to slip
The chance of joining in fellowship
With any that call themselves his friends;
    As these folk do, I have a notion.   805
    But hist—a buzzing and emotion!
All settle themselves, the while ascends
By the creaking rail to the lecture-desk,
    Step by step, deliberate
    Because of his cranium's over-freight,   810
Three parts sublime to one grotesque,
If I have proved an accurate guesser,
The hawk-nosed high-cheek-boned Professor.
I felt at once as if there ran
A shoot of love from my heart to the man—   815
    That sallow virgin-minded studious
    Martyr to mild enthusiasm,

---

792 *MS–1865* Cassel or Frankfort,   793 *MS–1865* Or Göttingen, that I
804 *MS–1865* friends,   805 *MS–1875* these folks do,

794 *Göttingen*: Pettigrew rightly observes that Strauss had no connection with the University of Göttingen.

795 *obliquely*: the pronunciation of this word has changed. In 1842 Tennyson rhymed 'oblique' with 'strike' and 'Ixion-like', in 'The Two Voices', 193–5.

813 *Professor*: Maynard suggests that this description may have been influenced by the appearance of Professor von Mühlenfels, some of whose lectures Browning attended at the London University: pp. 277–8.

815 *A shoot of love*: cf. Carlyle, *French Revolution*, vol. i, book vii, para. 3: 'Many things . . . grow by shoots and fits'.

816 *virgin-minded*: this antedates the first example in OED.

817 *enthusiasm*: in the old sense, 'A vain belief of private revelation' (Johnson), though here used of a rationalizing Higher Critic.

As he uttered a kind of cough-preludious
    That woke my sympathetic spasm,
(Beside some spitting that made me sorry)   820
And stood, surveying his auditory
With a wan pure look, well nigh celestial,—
    Those blue eyes had survived so much!
    While, under the foot they could not smutch,
Lay all the fleshly and the bestial.   825
Over he bowed, and arranged his notes,
Till the auditory's clearing of throats
Was done with, died into a silence;
    And, when each glance was upward sent,
    Each bearded mouth composed intent,   830
And a pin might be heard drop half a mile hence,—
He pushed back higher his spectacles,
Let the eyes stream out like lamps from cells,
And giving his head of hair—a hake
    Of undressed tow, for colour and quantity—   835
One rapid and impatient shake,
    (As our own Young England adjusts a jaunty tie
When about to impart, on mature digestion,
Some thrilling view of the surplice-question)
—The Professor's grave voice, sweet though hoarse,   840
Broke into his Christmas-Eve discourse.

---

828 *MS* with {illeg.}[,] died into [a] silence;   *835 {reading of *MS–1875*,DC,BrU,
1889} *1888* quantity   *837 {reading of DC,*1889*} *MS–1888* young England
841 *MS–1865* his Christmas-Eve's discourse.

  818 *cough-preludious*: no doubt a nonce-word. Cleveland and others have 'preludious'.

  824 *smutch*: stain.

  834 *hake*: apparently for 'hank'.

  837 *Young England*: in 1843 Disraeli and others, whom it was fashionable to call 'Young England', found themselves at odds with Sir Robert Peel. A good account of their party may be found in Disraeli's *Coningsby* and *Sybil*. Like Disraeli himself, some of his followers were dandies, and some had strong sympathies with the new High Church party.

  839 *the surplice-question*: a surplice is a loose white outer garment worn by clerics and others during a church service. The wearing of surplices became a 'question' by the 1840s. In 1850 mobs who regarded surplices, like candles and the processional cross, as signs of undue Roman Catholic influence, besieged churches in Knightsbridge and Pimlico.

XV.

And he began it by observing
   How reason dictated that men
Should rectify the natural swerving,
   By a reversion, now and then,   845
To the well-heads of knowledge, few
And far away, whence rolling grew
The life-stream wide whereat we drink,
Commingled, as we needs must think,
With waters alien to the source;   850
To do which, aimed this eve's discourse;
Since, where could be a fitter time
For tracing backwards to its prime
This Christianity, this lake,
This reservoir, whereat we slake,   855
From one or other bank, our thirst?
So, he proposed inquiring first
Into the various sources whence
   This Myth of Christ is derivable;
Demanding from the evidence,   860
   (Since plainly no such life was liveable)
How these phenomena should class?
Whether 't were best opine Christ was,
Or never was at all, or whether
He was and was not, both together—   865
It matters little for the name,
So the idea be left the same.
Only, for practical purpose' sake,
'T was obviously as well to take
The popular story,—understanding   870
   How the ineptitude of the time,

---

851 *MS,1850* discourse. *1863* discourse: 867 *MS,1850* same:

   859 *This Myth of Christ*: the story of Christ, with its mythical elements. It is unlikely that even this follower of the Higher Criticism would have maintained that Christ himself did not exist. It was (and is) another matter to argue that a great deal in the accounts of Christ which we possess is mythological in nature. Strauss regarded the miracles as myths.

And the penman's prejudice, expanding
   Fact into fable fit for the clime,
Had, by slow and sure degrees, translated it
   Into this myth, this Individuum,—   875
Which, when reason had strained and abated it
   Of foreign matter, left, for residuum,
A Man!—a right true man, however,
Whose work was worthy a man's endeavour:
Work, that gave warrant almost sufficient   880
   To his disciples, for rather believing
He was just omnipotent and omniscient,
   As it gives to us, for as frankly receiving
His word, their tradition,—which, though it meant
Something entirely different   885
From all that those who only heard it,
In their simplicity thought and averred it,
Had yet a meaning quite as respectable:
For, among other doctrines delectable,
Was he not surely the first to insist on   890
   The natural sovereignty of our race?—
   Here the lecturer came to a pausing-place.
And while his cough, like a drouthy piston,
Tried to dislodge the husk that grew to him,
I seized the occasion of bidding adieu to him,   895
The vesture still within my hand.

XVI.

I could interpret its command.
This time he would not bid me enter

---

877 *MS–1865* matter, gave, for   878 *1865* aright   879 *MS,1850* endeavour!
887 *MS* simplicity [thought and] averred

   875 *Individuum*: something indivisible.
   876 *abated*: 'abate of' is rare and obsolete: in *King Lear*, II. iv. 157 it means 'deprive', but
here 'purify'.
   891 *our race*: i.e. the human race.
   893 *drouthy*: thirsty, dry (Scots).
   894 *husk*: huskiness.

The exhausted air-bell of the Critic.
Truth's atmosphere may grow mephitic   900
When Papist struggles with Dissenter,
Impregnating its pristine clarity,
—One, by his daily fare's vulgarity,
    Its gust of broken meat and garlic;
—One, by his soul's too-much presuming   905
To turn the frankincense's fuming
    And vapours of the candle starlike
Into the cloud her wings she buoys on.
    Each, that thus sets the pure air seething,
      May poison it for healthy breathing—   910
But the Critic leaves no air to poison;
Pumps out with ruthless ingenuity
Atom by atom, and leaves you—vacuity.
Thus much of Christ does he reject?
And what retain? His intellect?   915
What is it I must reverence duly?
Poor intellect for worship, truly,
Which tells me simply what was told
    (If mere morality, bereft
    Of the God in Christ, be all that's left)   920
Elsewhere by voices manifold;
With this advantage, that the stater
    Made nowise the important stumble
    Of adding, he, the sage and humble,
Was also one with the Creator.   925
You urge Christ's followers' simplicity:
    But how does shifting blame, evade it?

---

908 *MS,1850* on: 909 *MS,1850* And each that sets   910 *MS,1850* Poisoning
it   912 *MS–1865* out by a ruthless

    899 *The exhausted air-bell*: a bell-jar from which air is removed, during a scientific
experiment. The compound, not in OED, will not be Browning's coinage. Cf. Edward
Young, *Love of Fame*, v. 177–8: 'Like cats in air-pumps, to subsist we strive / On joys too thin
to keep the soul alive'. Cf. 912, below.
    900 *mephitic*: foul, stinking.
    902 *pristine*: original.

Have wisdom's words no more felicity?
    The stumbling-block, his speech—who laid it?
How comes it that for one found able   930
To sift the truth of it from fable,
Millions believe it to the letter?
Christ's goodness, then—does that fare better?
Strange goodness, which upon the score
    Of being goodness, the mere due   935
Of man to fellow-man, much more
    To God,—should take another view
Of its possessor's privilege,
And bid him rule his race! You pledge
Your fealty to such rule? What, all—   940
From heavenly John and Attic Paul,
And that brave weather-battered Peter,
Whose stout faith only stood completer
For buffets, sinning to be pardoned,
As, more his hands hauled nets, they hardened,— 945
All, down to you, the man of men,
Professing here at Göttingen,
Compose Christ's flock! They, you and I,
Are sheep of a good man! And why?
The goodness,—how did he acquire it?   950
Was it self-gained, did God inspire it?
Choose which; then tell me, on what ground
Should its possessor dare propound
His claim to rise o'er us an inch?
    Were goodness all some man's invention,   955
    Who arbitrarily made mention

---

931 *MS* {illeg.} [To] sift the truth [of it] from fable,   945 *MS–1865* As the more
948 *MS,1850* flock! So, you

    928 *felicity*: happiness of expression, and hence force.
    929 *who laid it?*: cf. Thomas Burton, *Diary* [1656–9] (1828), iii. 398: 'Dutch and Dane are not wanting to lay stumbling-blocks'.
    941 *heavenly John and Attic Paul*: John the Divine, author of Revelation, and St Paul, who preached in Athens.
    942 *weather-battered Peter*: St Peter was a fisherman: see e.g. Matt. 4:18.
    944 *sinning to be pardoned*: by denying Jesus: Matt. 26:69ff.

What we should follow, and whence flinch,—
What qualities might take the style
     Of right and wrong,—and had such guessing
     Met with as general acquiescing   960
As graced the alphabet erewhile,
When A got leave an Ox to be,
No Camel (quoth the Jews) like G,—
For thus inventing thing and title
Worship were that man's fit requital.   965
But if the common conscience must
Be ultimately judge, adjust
Its apt name to each quality
Already known,—I would decree
Worship for such mere demonstration   970
     And simple work of nomenclature,
Only the day I praised, not nature,
     But Harvey, for the circulation.
I would praise such a Christ, with pride
And joy, that he, as none beside,   975
Had taught us how to keep the mind
God gave him, as God gave his kind,
Freer than they from fleshly taint:
I would call such a Christ our Saint,
As I declare our Poet, him   980
Whose insight makes all others dim:
A thousand poets pried at life,
And only one amid the strife
Rose to be Shakespeare: each shall take
His crown, I'd say, for the world's sake—   985

---

957 *MS–1865* and where flinch,—   965 *MS* Worship were {hole in manuscript}
that man's [fit] requital.   978 *MS,1850* taint!   984 *MS,1850* Shakespeare!

   958 *style*: name, title.
   962 *When A got leave*: the Hebrew letters aleph (not A, as sometimes supposed, but the
glottal stop) and gimel (G) were thought to have originated in stylized representations of ox
and camel.
   973 *Harvey*: William Harvey (1578–1657), who proved conclusively how the blood
circulates in the human body, in his *De Motu Cordis*.
   984 *each*: each poet.

Though some objected—"Had we seen
"The heart and head of each, what screen
"Was broken there to give them light,
"While in ourselves it shuts the sight,
"We should no more admire, perchance, 990
"That these found truth out at a glance,
"Than marvel how the bat discerns
"Some pitch-dark cavern's fifty turns,
"Led by a finer tact, a gift
"He boasts, which other birds must shift 995
"Without, and grope as best they can."
No, freely I would praise the man,—
Nor one whit more, if he contended
That gift of his, from God descended.
Ah friend, what gift of man's does not? 1000
No nearer something, by a jot,
Rise an infinity of nothings
    Than one: take Euclid for your teacher:
Distinguish kinds: do crownings, clothings,
    Make that creator which was creature? 1005
Multiply gifts upon man's head,
And what, when all's done, shall be said
But—the more gifted he, I ween!
    That one's made Christ, this other, Pilate,
And this might be all that has been,— 1010
    So what is there to frown or smile at?
What is left for us, save, in growth
Of soul, to rise up, far past both,

1006 *MS–1865* upon his head,   1008 *MS,1850* But .. the   1009 *MS,1850*
Christ, another, Pilate,

987 *what screen*: i.e. how comparatively slight a screen.

990 *admire*: be astonished.

993 *a gift*: i.e. the 'sonar' system of bats.

994 *other birds*: cf. *Sordello*, ii. 228–9, where too the bat is described as a bird.

1003 *take Euclid for your teacher*: study geometry (and perhaps more generally mathematics).

1009 *Pilate*: Pontius Pilate, the governor of Judaea from AD 26 to 36, under whom Christ was crucified. See Matt. 27:2 ff.

From the gift looking to the giver,
And from the cistern to the river,   1015
And from the finite to infinity,
And from man's dust to God's divinity?

XVII.

Take all in a word: the truth in God's breast
Lies trace for trace upon ours impressed:
Though he is so bright and we so dim,   1020
We are made in his image to witness him:
And were no eye in us to tell,
    Instructed by no inner sense,
The light of heaven from the dark of hell,
    That light would want its evidence,—   1025
Though justice, good and truth were still
Divine, if, by some demon's will,
Hatred and wrong had been proclaimed
Law through the worlds, and right misnamed.
No mere exposition of morality   1030
Made or in part or in totality,
Should win you to give it worship, therefore:
And, if no better proof you will care for,
—Whom do you count the worst man upon earth?
    Be sure, he knows, in his conscience, more   1035
Of what right is, than arrives at birth
    In the best man's acts that we bow before:
This last knows better—true, but my fact is,
'T is one thing to know, and another to practise.
And thence I conclude that the real God-function   1040
Is to furnish a motive and injunction
For practising what we know already.
And such an injunction and such a motive

1024 MS from [the] dark   1038 MS,1850 knows better—true; 1863,1865 knows
1039 MS,1850 practise;

  1015 cistern: reservoir.
  1035 he knows, in his conscience: cf. Sordello, iii. 786 ff.
  1040 God-function: not in OED.

As the God in Christ, do you waive, and "heady,
"High-minded," hang your tablet-votive   1045
Outside the fane on a finger-post?
Morality to the uttermost,
Supreme in Christ as we all confess,
Why need we prove would avail no jot
To make him God, if God he were not?   1050
What is the point where himself lays stress?
Does the precept run "Believe in good,
"In justice, truth, now understood
"For the first time?"—or, "Believe in me,
"Who lived and died, yet essentially   1055
"Am Lord of Life?" Whoever can take
The same to his heart and for mere love's sake
Conceive of the love,—that man obtains
A new truth; no conviction gains
Of an old one only, made intense   1060
By a fresh appeal to his faded sense.

                          XVIII.

Can it be that he stays inside?
    Is the vesture left me to commune with?
    Could my soul find aught to sing in tune with
Even at this lecture, if she tried?   1065
Oh, let me at lowest sympathize
With the lurking drop of blood that lies
In the desiccated brain's white roots
Without throb for Christ's attributes,
As the lecturer makes his special boast!   1070
If love's dead there, it has left a ghost.

1049 *MS–1865* we   *1054 {reading of *MS*} *1850–89* time?"   *MS–1865* ME,
*1056 {reading of *MS*} *1850–89* Life?"   1062 *1868–75* "Can   1069 *MS–*
1865 Without a throb

    1044–5 *"heady, / "High-minded"*: as people will say.
    1045 *tablet-votive*: no doubt a nonce-word. A votive tablet is an inscription recording
devotion, or a particular vow.
    1046 *fane*: temple (here church).
    1054 *Believe in me*: John 14:1.

Admire we, how from heart to brain
　　(Though to say so strike the doctors dumb)
One instinct rises and falls again,
　　Restoring the equilibrium.   1075
And how when the Critic had done his best,
And the pearl of price, at reason's test,
Lay dust and ashes levigable
On the Professor's lecture-table,—
When we looked for the inference and monition   1080
That our faith, reduced to such condition,
Be swept forthwith to its natural dust-hole,—
　　He bids us, when we least expect it,
Take back our faith,—if it be not just whole,
　　Yet a pearl indeed, as his tests affect it,   1085
Which fact pays damage done rewardingly,
So, prize we our dust and ashes accordingly!
"Go home and venerate the myth
"I thus have experimented with—
"This man, continue to adore him   1090
"Rather than all who went before him,
"And all who ever followed after!"—
　　Surely for this I may praise you, my brother!
Will you take the praise in tears or laughter?
　　That's one point gained: can I compass another? 1095
Unlearned love was safe from spurning—
Can't we respect your loveless learning?
Let us at least give learning honour!
What laurels had we showered upon her,
Girding her loins up to perturb   1100
Our theory of the Middle Verb;

1081 MS That [our] faith,   MS–1865 such a condition,   1084 MS Take [back]
our   1086 MS pays [the] damage 1850–65 pays the damage   *1092 (reading
of MS–1875) 1888,1889 'And . . . . after!'—

　　1077 the pearl of price: Matt. 13:45–6.
　　1078 dust and ashes: Gen. 18:27. Cf. 'A Toccata of Galuppi's', 35, 43.
　　　　levigable: that can be reduced to powder, a rare word. From Med. L. levigabilis.
　　1101 the Middle Verb: there are three 'voices' of the Greek verb, active, middle, and pas-
sive. In the middle voice the subject acts upon himself, or in some manner which concerns
himself.

Or Turk-like brandishing a scimitar
O'er anapæsts in comic-trimeter;
Or curing the halt and maimed 'Iketides,'
While we lounged on at our indebted ease: 1105
Instead of which, a tricksy demon
Sets her at Titus or Philemon!
When ignorance wags his ears of leather
And hates God's word, 't is altogether;
Nor leaves he his congenial thistles   1110
To go and browse on Paul's Epistles.
—And you, the audience, who might ravage
The world wide, enviably savage,
Nor heed the cry of the retriever,
More than Herr Heine (before his fever),—   1115
I do not tell a lie so arrant
    As say my passion's wings are furled up,
And, without plainest heavenly warrant,
    I were ready and glad to give the world up—
But still, when you rub brow meticulous,   1120
    And ponder the profit of turning holy

1104 *MS–1865* Iketides,   1118 *MS–1865* without the plainest   1119 *MS–*
1865 give this world   1120 *MS–1865* rub the brow

1103 *anapæsts in comic-trimeter*: in Greek comedy any of the first five of the six pairs of elements in an iambic trimeter may take the form of an anapaest. This markedly distinguishes the rhythm of comedy from that of tragedy.

1104 *'Iketides'*: 'The "Iketides" (Suppliants) . . . is a Tragedy by Æschylus, the earliest extant: and of which the text is especially incomplete: hence, halting, and "maimed"': *Handbook*, 183 n.–4 n., perhaps from Browning's own account. (We now know that the *Hiketides*, or *Supplices*, is not the earliest extant play.)

1106 *tricksy*: mischievous: cf. *The Tempest*, v. i. 226.

1107 *Titus or Philemon*: two epistles from Paul in the New Testament, often the subject of debate among theologians. Although the Professor is characterized by 'loveless learning', learning is yet to be respected.

1108 *ears of leather*: signifying stupidity.

1110 *thistles*: eaten by donkeys.

1114 *retriever*: in a religious sense. Cf. John Wesley, in *Hymns*, 1738: 'Now my poor soul Thou wouldst retrieve' ('Father, I stretch my hands').

1115 *Herr Heine*: in 1848 Heinrich Heine, the German poet, was found to be suffering from a spinal tuberculosis of syphilitic origin. He spent his last eight years paralysed and bed-ridden, but faced his fate with courage and wrote some of his finest poetry. He had become a Catholic.

If not for God's, for your own sake solely,
—God forbid I should find you ridiculous!
Deduce from this lecture all that eases you,
Nay, call yourselves, if the calling pleases you,   1125
"Christians,"—abhor the deist's pravity,—
Go on, you shall no more move my gravity
Than, when I see boys ride a-cockhorse,
I find it in my heart to embarrass them
By hinting that their stick's a mock horse,   1130
And they really carry what they say carries them.

XIX.

So sat I talking with my mind.
    I did not long to leave the door
    And find a new church, as before,
But rather was quiet and inclined   1135
To prolong and enjoy the gentle resting
From further tracking and trying and testing.
"This tolerance is a genial mood!"
(Said I, and a little pause ensued).
"One trims the bark 'twixt shoal and shelf,   1140
    "And sees, each side, the good effects of it,
"A value for religion's self,
    "A carelessness about the sects of it.
"Let me enjoy my own conviction,
    "Not watch my neighbour's faith with fretfulness,   1145
"Still spying there some dereliction
    "Of truth, perversity, forgetfulness!
"Better a mild indifferentism,
    "Teaching that both our faiths (though duller
"His shine through a dull spirit's prism)   1150

1131 *1868–75* them."   1138 *MS–1865* This .... mood!   1139 *MS* ensued)
1140 *MS–1865* One   1149 *MS,1850* To teach that all our *1863,1865* Teaching that
all our   1150 *MS,1850* His shines through

1126 *pravity*: 'Corruption; badness; malignity': Johnson.

1148 *indifferentism*: 'The principle that differences of religious belief are of no import-
ance': OED, which first finds the term in 1827–8.

"Originally had one colour!
"Better pursue a pilgrimage
    "Through ancient and through modern times
    "To many peoples, various climes,
"Where I may see saint, savage, sage   1155
"Fuse their respective creeds in one
"Before the general Father's throne!"

XX.

—'T was the horrible storm began afresh!
The black night caught me in his mesh,
Whirled me up, and flung me prone.   1160
I was left on the college-step alone.
I looked, and far there, ever fleeting
Far, far away, the receding gesture,
And looming of the lessening vesture!—
Swept forward from my stupid hand,   1165
While I watched my foolish heart expand
In the lazy glow of benevolence,
    O'er the various modes of man's belief.
I sprang up with fear's vehemence.
    Needs must there be one way, our chief   1170
Best way of worship: let me strive
To find it, and when found, contrive
My fellows also take their share!
This constitutes my earthly care:
God's is above it and distinct.   1175
For I, a man, with men am linked
And not a brute with brutes; no gain
That I experience, must remain
Unshared: but should my best endeavour
To share it, fail—subsisteth ever   1180
God's care above, and I exult
That God, by God's own ways occult,

1151 MS color— 1850–65 colour—   1152 MS–1865 Sending me on a
1157 MS–1865 throne!   1158 MS,1850 .. 'Twas   1164 MS,1850 vesture,
1170 1868–75 "Needs   1173 MS,1850 share.   1175 MS,1850 distinct!

May—doth, I will believe—bring back
All wanderers to a single track.
Meantime, I can but testify   1185
God's care for me—no more, can I—
It is but for myself I know;
 The world rolls witnessing around me
 Only to leave me as it found me;
Men cry there, but my ear is slow: 1190
Their races flourish or decay
—What boots it, while yon lucid way
Loaded with stars divides the vault?
But soon my soul repairs its fault
When, sharpening sense's hebetude,   1195
She turns on my own life! So viewed,
No mere mote's-breadth but teems immense
With witnessings of providence:
And woe to me if when I look
Upon that record, the sole book   1200
Unsealed to me, I take no heed
Of any warning that I read!
Have I been sure, this Christmas-Eve,
God's own hand did the rainbow weave,
Whereby the truth from heaven slid   1205
Into my soul?—I cannot bid
The world admit he stooped to heal
My soul, as if in a thunder-peal
Where one heard noise, and one saw flame,
I only knew he named my name: 1210
But what is the world to me, for sorrow
Or joy in its censure, when to-morrow

1184 *MS,1850* track! 1187 *MS,1850 know.* 1863,1865 *know;* 1190 *MS,*
1850 slow. 1194 *MS,1850* How soon 1195 *MS,1850* senses'
1210 *MS,1850* name. 1211 *MS,1850* And what 1212 *MS,1850* its censures,
when

 1192 *What boots it*: cf. 'Lycidas', 64. *lucid*: shining, resplendent.
 1195 *hebetude*: dullness, lethargy.
 1205–6 *the truth from heaven slid / Into my soul*: cf. Coleridge, 'The Ancient Mariner', 295–6.

It drops the remark, with just-turned head
Then, on again, 'That man is dead'?
Yes, but for me—my name called,—drawn   1215
As a conscript's lot from the lap's black yawn,
He has dipt into on a battle-dawn:
Bid out of life by a nod, a glance,—
Stumbling, mute-mazed, at nature's chance,—
With a rapid finger circled round,   1220
Fixed to the first poor inch of ground
To fight from, where his foot was found;
Whose ear but a minute since lay free
To the wide camp's buzz and gossipry—
Summoned, a solitary man   1225
To end his life where his life began,
From the safe glad rear, to the dreadful van!
Soul of mine, hadst thou caught and held
By the hem of the vesture!—

XXI.

And I caught
At the flying robe, and unrepelled   1230
    Was lapped again in its folds full-fraught
With warmth and wonder and delight,
God's mercy being infinite.
For scarce had the words escaped my tongue,
When, at a passionate bound, I sprung,   1235
Out of the wandering world of rain,
Into the little chapel again.

1214 *MS,1850* —That man is dead? *1863,1865* —that man is dead? *1868–75* dead?'
1215 *MS,1850* Yes,—but   1224 *MS* camps   1229 *MS,1850* Vesture ...
1868–75 vesture!—"   1234 *MS,1850* And scarce

   1216 *the lap's black yawn*: cf. Prov. 16:33: 'The lot is cast into the lap; but the whole dis-
posing thereof is of the LORD.' Cf. *The Ring and the Book*, ii. 393 and vii. 563.
   1217 *battle-dawn*: not in OED.
   1219 *mute-mazed*: struck dumb. Apparently Browning's coinage.
   1224 *gossipry*: gossiping.
   1233 *God's mercy*: cf. Num. 14:18, etc.

XXII.

How else was I found there, bolt upright
   On my bench, as if I had never left it?
—Never flung out on the common at night,   1240
   Nor met the storm and wedge-like cleft it,
Seen the raree-show of Peter's successor,
Or the laboratory of the Professor!
For the Vision, that was true, I wist,
True as that heaven and earth exist.   1245
There sat my friend, the yellow and tall,
   With his neck and its wen in the selfsame place;
Yet my nearest neighbour's cheek showed gall.
   She had slid away a contemptuous space:
And the old fat woman, late so placable,   1250
Eyed me with symptoms, hardly mistakable,
Of her milk of kindness turning rancid.
In short, a spectator might have fancied
That I had nodded, betrayed by slumber,
Yet kept my seat, a warning ghastly,   1255
Through the heads of the sermon, nine in number,
And woke up now at the tenth and lastly.
But again, could such disgrace have happened?
   Each friend at my elbow had surely nudged it;
And, as for the sermon, where did my nap end?   1260
   Unless I heard it, could I have judged it?
Could I report as I do at the close,
First, the preacher speaks through his nose:
Second, his gesture is too emphatic:

1238 *1868–75* upright.   1244 *MS–1865 that*   1245 *MS* [True] As that ⟨?the⟩
heaven   1248 *MS–1875* gall,   1252 *MS,1850* rancid: 1254 *MS,*
1850 by a slumber,   1257 *MS,1850* To wake up   1258 *MS–1865* such a
disgrace

1241 *wedge-like*: as in *Sordello*, vi. 52.
1242 *raree-show*: peepshow, spectacle.
1250 *placable*: forgiving, capable of being placated, as in *Paradise Lost*, xi. 151.
1252 *milk of kindness*: cf. *Macbeth*, i. v. 14.

Thirdly, to waive what's pedagogic,   1265
    The subject-matter itself lacks logic:
Fourthly, the English is ungrammatic.
Great news! the preacher is found no Pascal,
Whom, if I pleased, I might to the task call
Of making square to a finite eye   1270
The circle of infinity,
And find so all-but-just-succeeding!
Great news! the sermon proves no reading
Where bee-like in the flowers I bury me,
Like Taylor's the immortal Jeremy!   1275
And now that I know the very worst of him,
What was it I thought to obtain at first of him?
Ha! Is God mocked, as he asks?
Shall I take on me to change his tasks,
And dare, despatched to a river-head   1280
    For a simple draught of the element,
Neglect the thing for which he sent,
    And return with another thing instead?—
Saying, "Because the water found
"Welling up from underground,   1285
"Is mingled with the taints of earth,
"While thou, I know, dost laugh at dearth,
"And couldst, at wink or word, convulse
"The world with the leap of a river-pulse,—
"Therefore I turned from the oozings muddy,   1290
    "And bring thee a chalice I found, instead:

1274 *MS–1875* I may bury me,   1288 *MS–1865* couldest, at a word,
1289 *MS–1863* of its river-pulse,—

1265 *pedagogic*: academic.

1268 *Pascal*: Blaise Pascal (1623–62), the French philosopher and physicist, now best remembered for his *Pensées*, showed a precocious taste for mathematics, rediscovering many of the propositions of Euclid, and writing a treatise on conic sections at the age of sixteen. It is impossible to draw a square exactly equal in area to a given circle.

1274 *bee-like*: cf. Byron, *Don Juan*, xi. 63.

1275 *the immortal Jeremy!*: Jeremy Taylor, author of *The Rule and Exercises of Holy Living* (1650). Browning owned a copy of an edition published in 1813: Kelley and Coley, A 2259.

1278 *Is God mocked*: 'Be not deceived; God is not mocked': Gal. 6:7.

1289 *river-pulse*: the welling-up of a river. A nonce-word: cf. 'Epilogue' to *Dramatis Personæ*, 39: 'Like a fountain's sickening pulse'.

"See the brave veins in the breccia ruddy!
　"One would suppose that the marble bled.
"What matters the water? A hope I have nursed:
"The waterless cup will quench my thirst."   1295
—Better have knelt at the poorest stream
　That trickles in pain from the straitest rift!
For the less or the more is all God's gift,
Who blocks up or breaks wide the granite-seam.
And here, is there water or not, to drink?   1300
　I then, in ignorance and weakness,
Taking God's help, have attained to think
　My heart does best to receive in meekness
That mode of worship, as most to his mind,
Where earthly aids being cast behind,   1305
His All in All appears serene
With the thinnest human veil between,
　Letting the mystic lamps, the seven,
　　The many motions of his spirit,
Pass, as they list, to earth from heaven.   1310
　　For the preacher's merit or demerit,
It were to be wished the flaws were fewer
　In the earthen vessel, holding treasure
Which lies as safe in a golden ewer;
　But the main thing is, does it hold good measure?   1315
Heaven soon sets right all other matters!—
　Ask, else, these ruins of humanity,
This flesh worn out to rags and tatters,
　This soul at struggle with insanity,

1294 *MS–1868* nursed,　　　1295 *MS–1863* "That the　　　1297 *MS,1865–75* the
straightest rift!　　　1304 *MS,1850* This mode　　　1314 *MS* ewer,

　1292 *breccia*: rough plaster containing gravel; a composition of rough stones. Browning
(or the speaker) may have supposed the word to mean a kind of marble.
　1297 *straitest*: narrowest.
　1308 *the mystic lamps*: Rev. 1:12 ff.
　1309 *motions of his spirit*: inward promptings or impulses: 'a working of God in the soul'
('obs.', OED): a phrase common among dissenters at the time.
　1313 *earthen vessel*: a phrase from the Authorized Version, e.g. Lev. 6:28, 2 Cor. 4:7.

Who thence take comfort—can I doubt?—   1320
Which an empire gained, were a loss without.
May it be mine! And let us hope
That no worse blessing befall the Pope,
Turned sick at last of to-day's buffoonery,
    Of posturings and petticoatings,   1325
    Beside his Bourbon bully's gloatings
In the bloody orgies of drunk poltroonery!
Nor may the Professor forego its peace
    At Göttingen presently, when, in the dusk
Of his life, if his cough, as I fear, should increase,   1330
    Prophesied of by that horrible husk—
When thicker and thicker the darkness fills
The world through his misty spectacles,
And he gropes for something more substantial
    Than a fable, myth or personification,—   1335
May Christ do for him what no mere man shall,
    And stand confessed as the God of salvation!
Meantime, in the still recurring fear
    Lest myself, at unawares, be found,
    While attacking the choice of my neighbours round,   1340
With none of my own made—I choose here!
The giving out of the hymn reclaims me;
I have done: and if any blames me,

1320 MS–1865 comfort, can I doubt, 1868–75 comfort, can I doubt?   1324 MS–
1863 of the day's buffoonery,   1325 MS,1850 Of his posturings and his petticoat-
ings, 1863 Of its posturings and its petticoatings,   1326 MS,1850 Beside the
Bourbon   1332 MS,1850 And when,   1341 MS–1863 Without my
1343 MS–1863 done!—And

  1321 were a loss: cf. Matt. 16:26.
  1325 petticoatings: not in OED, which has several examples of 'petticoated'.
  1326 his Bourbon bully's gloatings: 'this is probably Ferdinand II. of Naples and Sicily, who
was [nicknamed] King Bomba. He was fiercely opposed to the Italian liberals and to Pope
Pius IX. for his concessions to them': Porter and Clarke. He dissolved the national parlia-
ment in March 1849: his bombarding of the chief cities of Sicily won him his nickname. By
the time of this poem, however, Pius IX had thrown in his lot with the reaction.
  1327 poltroonery: base cowardice.
  1331 husk: see above, 894 n.
  1340 round: round about me.
  1342 The giving out of the hymn: a possibly fictitious example of a long-winded 'giving
out' or announcement of the number of the final hymn.

Thinking that merely to touch in brevity
   The topics I dwell on, were unlawful,—   1345
Or worse, that I trench, with undue levity,
   On the bounds of the holy and the awful,—
I praise the heart, and pity the head of him,
And refer myself to THEE, instead of him,
Who head and heart alike discernest,   1350
   Looking below light speech we utter,
   When frothy spume and frequent sputter
Prove that the soul's depths boil in earnest!
May truth shine out, stand ever before us!
I put up pencil and join chorus   1355
To Hepzibah Tune, without further apology,
   The last five verses of the third section
   Of the seventeenth hymn of Whitfield's Collection,
To conclude with the doxology.

1352 MS–1865 When the frothy   1354 MS–1863 May the truth   1358 MS–
1863 hymn in Whitfield's

   1356 Hepzibah Tune: we are indebted to the Revd Dr Ivor H. Jones of Wesley House, Cambridge, for a copy of this tune (p. 381), written by J. Husband (for several years Clerk of Surrey Chapel, London). The copy reproduced here is from the Rippon Tune Collection (1791), given in three-part harmony and assuming a continuo accompaniment. Among the hymns set to this tune are 'Jerusalem, thou happy place' and 'All hail the great Immanuel's name'.

   1357–8 The last five verses. . . . Whitfield's Collection: Browning may not have had a specific hymn in mind. Of the many editions of George Whit(e)field's Hymns for Social Worship Collected from Various Authors, and more particularly design'd for the use of the Tabernacle Congregation in London (1753), none seems to fit both with the details of 'giving out' and with 'Hepzibah Tune'. Linda H. Peterson suggests that Browning had in mind hymn 17 in part two of Whitefield's seventh edition: 'Come we that Love the Lord': 'Biblical Typology and the Self-Portrait of the Poet in Robert Browning', in George P. Landow, ed., Approaches to Victorian Autobiography (Athens, Ohio, 1979), p. 242.

   1359 doxology: a verse or other form of words glorifying God: specifically 'Glory be to the Father, and to the Son, and to the Holy Ghost; As it was in the beginning, is now, and evermore shall be, world without end, Amen.'

EASTER-DAY.

I.

How very hard it is to be
A Christian! Hard for you and me,
—Not the mere task of making real
That duty up to its ideal,
Effecting thus, complete and whole,   5
A purpose of the human soul—
For that is always hard to do;
But hard, I mean, for me and you
To realize it, more or less,
With even the moderate success   10
Which commonly repays our strife
To carry out the aims of life.
"This aim is greater," you will say,
"And so more arduous every way."
—But the importance of their fruits   15
Still proves to man, in all pursuits,
Proportional encouragement.
"Then, what if it be God's intent
"That labour to this one result
"Should seem unduly difficult?"   20
Ah, that's a question in the dark—
And the sole thing that I remark
Upon the difficulty, this;
We do not see it where it is,
At the beginning of the race: 25
As we proceed, it shifts its place,
And where we looked for crowns to fall,
We find the tug's to come,—that's all.

subtitle MS Easter Day.   13 MS,1850 you may say,   15 MS,1850 of the
fruits   20 MS,1850 "Shall seem   24 MS–1865 is,   27 MS,1850 for
palms to

27 *crowns*: signalizing victory. Cf. l. 65. Cf. 1 Cor. 9:25, 2 Tim. 4:8.
28 *the tug*: the greatest effort.

II.

At first you say, "The whole, or chief
"Of difficulties, is belief.   30
"Could I believe once thoroughly,
"The rest were simple. What? Am I
"An idiot, do you think,—a beast?
"Prove to me, only that the least
"Command of God is God's indeed,   35
"And what injunction shall I need
"To pay obedience? Death so nigh,
"When time must end, eternity
"Begin,—and cannot I compute,
"Weigh loss and gain together, suit   40
"My actions to the balance drawn,
"And give my body to be sawn
"Asunder, hacked in pieces, tied
"To horses, stoned, burned, crucified,
"Like any martyr of the list?   45
"How gladly!—if I make acquist,
"Through the brief minute's fierce annoy,
"Of God's eternity of joy."

III.

—And certainly you name the point
Whereon all turns: for could you joint   50
This flexile finite life once tight
Into the fixed and infinite,
You, safe inside, would spurn what's out,
With carelessness enough, no doubt—

33 *MS,1850* think?   39 *MS,1850* compute?   40 *MS,1850* together?
46 *MS,1850* gladly,   *MS–1865* I made acquist,   47 *MS,1850* minutes'
48 *MS* joy!"

   46 *acquist*: 'Acquirement; attainment; gain. Not in use': Johnson. Cf. *Samson Agonistes*,
1755. Browning also uses the word in *Sordello* and elsewhere.
   47 *annoy*: injury, suffering.
   51 *flexile*: flexible, capable of varied adaptation.

Would spurn mere life: but when time brings   55
To their next stage your reasonings,
Your eyes, late wide, begin to wink
Nor see the path so well, I think.

IV.

You say, "Faith may be, one agrees,
"A touchstone for God's purposes,   60
"Even as ourselves conceive of them.
"Could he acquit us or condemn
"For holding what no hand can loose,
"Rejecting when we can't but choose?
"As well award the victor's wreath   65
"To whosoever should take breath
"Duly each minute while he lived—
"Grant heaven, because a man contrived
"To see its sunlight every day
"He walked forth on the public way.   70
"You must mix some uncertainty
"With faith, if you would have faith be.
"Why, what but faith, do we abhor
"And idolize each other for—
"Faith in our evil or our good,   75
"Which is or is not understood
"Aright by those we love or those
"We hate, thence called our friends or foes?
"Your mistress saw your spirit's grace,
"When, turning from the ugly face,   80
"I found belief in it too hard;
"And she and I have our reward.
"—Yet here a doubt peeps: well for us
"Weak beings, to go using thus

55 *MS* but ⟨where⟩ [when] time *1850* but where time   58 *MS* the ⟨way⟩ [path] so
69 *MS,1850* see the sunlight   72 *MS–1865* be.   79 *MS* spirits'
82 *MS,1850* And both of us have

65–6 "*As well award . . . take breath*: Browning's observation in a letter to EBB: 'Provid-
ence . . . might have . . . revealed the articles of belief as certainly as that condition . . . by
which we breathe so many times in a minute': Kintner, i. 213.

"A touchstone for our little ends,   85
"Trying with faith the foes and friends;
"—But God, bethink you! I would fain
"Conceive of the Creator's reign
"As based upon exacter laws
"Than creatures build by with applause.   90
"In all God's acts—(as Plato cries
"He doth)—he should geometrize.
"Whence, I desiderate . . ."

                         V.

                              I see!
You would grow as a natural tree,
Stand as a rock, soar up like fire.   95
The world's so perfect and entire,
Quite above faith, so right and fit!
Go there, walk up and down in it!
No. The creation travails, groans—
Contrive your music from its moans,   100
Without or let or hindrance, friend!
That's an old story, and its end
As old—you come back (be sincere)
With every question you put here
(Here where there once was, and is still,   105
We think, a living oracle,

---

86 *MS,1850* "And try with   90 *1870,1875* build up with   92 *MS–1865*
should   94 *MS,1850* grow smoothly as a tree,   95 *MS,1850* Soar heaven-
ward, straightly (*MS* straightly) up like fire—   96 *MS,1850* God bless you—there's
your world entire   97 *MS,1850* Needing no faith, if you think fit;   99 *MS,
1850* | The whole creation

   91 *as Plato cries*: see Plutarch's *Moralia* (Loeb ed.), vol. ix, ed. Edwin L. Minar and others
(1961), p. 119. Question 2 in 'Table-Talk' is headed: 'What Plato meant by saying that God
is always doing geometry.' One of the speakers immediately comments that while this
statement is not made explicitly in any of Plato's writings, it is well enough attested and 'in
harmony with his character'.
   98 *walk up and down in it!*: cf. Zech. 10:12: 'And I will strengthen them in the LORD; and
they shall walk up and down in his name, saith the Lord.'
   99 *The creation travails*: cf. Rom. 8:22: 'For we know that the whole creation groaneth and
travaileth in pain together until now.'

Whose answers you stand carping at)
This time flung back unanswered flat,—
Beside, perhaps, as many more
As those that drove you out before,   110
Now added, where was little need.
Questions impossible, indeed,
To us who sat still, all and each
Persuaded that our earth had speech,
Of God's, writ down, no matter if   115
In cursive type or hieroglyph,—
Which one fact freed us from the yoke
Of guessing why He never spoke.
You come back in no better plight
Than when you left us,—am I right?   120

VI.

So, the old process, I conclude,
Goes on, the reasoning's pursued
Further. You own, "'T is well averred,
"A scientific faith's absurd,
"—Frustrates the very end 't was meant   125
"To serve. So, I would rest content
"With a mere probability,
"But, probable; the chance must lie
"Clear on one side,—lie all in rough,
"So long as there be just enough   130
"To pin my faith to, though it hap
"Only at points: from gap to gap

---

107 *MS,1850* you stood carping   109 *MS–1863* Besides, perhaps,   111 *MS–*
1865 need!   117 *MS,1850* fact frees us   123 *MS,1850* "Tis   126 *MS,*
1850 serve: so   130 *MS,1850* there is just

108 *flat*: without qualification.

116 *In cursive type or hieroglyph*: as the Ohio editor has pointed out, the speaker is no
doubt alluding to the Rosetta Stone, which has been in the British Museum since 1802. It
bears three inscriptions of the same decree in two languages, one of which is Greek. This
proved the clue to the hieroglyphic script of the ancient Egyptians, deciphered by J. F.
Champollion in 1822 and subsequently. The third inscription, in demotic, is also in the
Egyptian language: its script is cursive.

129 *in rough*: in rough form. Cf. *Sordello*, ii. 467.

"One hangs up a huge curtain so,
"Grandly, nor seeks to have it go
"Foldless and flat along the wall.					135
"What care I if some interval
"Of life less plainly may depend
"On God? I'd hang there to the end;
"And thus I should not find it hard
"To be a Christian and debarred				140
"From trailing on the earth, till furled
"Away by death.—Renounce the world!
"Were that a mighty hardship? Plan
"A pleasant life, and straight some man
"Beside you, with, if he thought fit,				145
"Abundant means to compass it,
"Shall turn deliberate aside
"To try and live as, if you tried
"You clearly might, yet most despise.
"One friend of mine wears out his eyes,			150
"Slighting the stupid joys of sense,
"In patient hope that, ten years hence,
"'Somewhat completer,' he may say,
"'My list of *coleoptera!*'
"While just the other who most laughs			155
"At him, above all epitaphs
"Aspires to have his tomb describe
"Himself as sole among the tribe
"Of snuffbox-fanciers, who possessed
"A Grignon with the Regent's crest.				160

---

135 *MS,1850* wall: 136 *MS,1850* I that some   137 *MS,1850* plainly might
depend   142 *MS,1850* death! .... world? *1870* world   153–4 *MS,1850*
"Somewhat completer he may see | His list of *lepidopteræ*:

154 *coleoptera*: 'A large and important order of insects, distinguished by having the
anterior pair of wings converted into . . . hard sheaths which cover the other pair when not
in use': OED. Commonly beetles. Here pronounced, as by scientists of the time, to rhyme
with 'say'.

160 *A Grignon*: 'a snuff-box made by the French metal-worker Pierre Grignon (1723–
1784) bearing the crest of the Duke of Orleans, regent for Louis XV': Porter and Clarke.

"So that, subduing, as you want,
"Whatever stands predominant
"Among my earthly appetites
"For tastes and smells and sounds and sights,
"I shall be doing that alone,   165
"To gain a palm-branch and a throne,
"Which fifty people undertake
"To do, and gladly, for the sake
"Of giving a Semitic guess,
"Or playing pawns at blindfold chess."   170

VII.

Good: and the next thing is,—look round
For evidence enough! 'T is found,
No doubt: as is your sort of mind,
So is your sort of search: you'll find
What you desire, and that's to be   175
A Christian. What says history?
How comforting a point it were
To find some mummy-scrap declare
There lived a Moses! Better still,
Prove Jonah's whale translatable   180
Into some quicksand of the seas,
Isle, cavern, rock, or what you please,
That faith might flap her wings and crow
From such an eminence! Or, no—
The human heart's best; you prefer   185
Making that prove the minister

*166 {reading of *MS–1875*} *1888,1889* throne.   171 *MS–1865* Good!
172 *MS–1865* enough.   176 *MS,1850* Christian: 183 *MS–1875* might clap
her
___

166 *a palm-branch*: in sign of victory.

169 *a Semitic guess*: a hypothesis about some difficult point in Hebrew, or some other Semitic language.

173–4 *as is* . . . / *So is*: a Latin construction.

178 *some mummy-scrap*: some inscribed scrap of papyrus used in the swathing of an Egyptian mummy.

180 *Jonah's whale*: Jonah 1:17: 'Now the LORD had prepared a great fish to swallow up Jonah. And Jonah was in the belly of the fish three days and three nights.' This 'fish' is usually supposed to have been a whale. The story has been variously interpreted.

To truth; you probe its wants and needs,
And hopes and fears, then try what creeds
Meet these most aptly,—resolute
That faith plucks such substantial fruit 190
Wherever these two correspond,
She little needs to look beyond,
And puzzle out who Orpheus was,
Or Dionysius Zagrias.
You'll find sufficient, as I say, 195
To satisfy you either way;
You wanted to believe; your pains
Are crowned—you do: and what remains?
"Renounce the world!"—Ah, were it done
By merely cutting one by one 200
Your limbs off, with your wise head last,
How easy were it!—how soon past,
If once in the believing mood!
"Such is man's usual gratitude,
"Such thanks to God do we return, 205
"For not exacting that we spurn
"A single gift of life, forego
"One real gain,—only taste them so
"With gravity and temperance,
"That those mild virtues may enhance 210

189 MS most aplty,—resolute   193 MS,1850 To puzzle out what Orpheus was,
196 MS,1850 way.   199 MS,1850 Renounce the world!—   204 MS,1850
Such___   210 MS That (?these) [those] mild

193 *Orpheus*: his myth is one of the most obscure and symbolic in Greek mythology. It exerted some influence on early Christian belief, and on Christian iconography. He is the type of the singer, musician, and poet. The story of his descent into the Underworld to fetch Eurydice is told in Virgil's fourth *Georgic*.
194 *Dionysius Zagrias*: a clear account of the little that can be conjectured about Zagrias or Zagreus, an obscure god in Orphism identified with Dionysus, may be found in *The Dictionary of Classical Mythology*, by Pierre Grimal, trans. A. R. Maxwell-Hyslop (1986).
200 *By merely cutting*: 'all passive obedience and implicit submission of will and intellect is by far too easy . . . to be the course prescribed by God to Man in this life of probation—for they *evade* probation altogether, tho' foolish people think otherwise: chop off your legs, you will never go astray,—stifle your reason altogether and you will find it is difficult to reason ill': Browning to EBB (Kintner, i. 213).

"Such pleasures, rather than abstract—
"Last spice of which, will be the fact
"Of love discerned in every gift;
"While, when the scene of life shall shift,
"And the gay heart be taught to ache,   215
"As sorrows and privations take
"The place of joy,—the thing that seems
"Mere misery, under human schemes,
"Becomes, regarded by the light
"Of love, as very near, or quite   220
"As good a gift as joy before.
"So plain is it that, all the more
"A dispensation's merciful,
"More pettishly we try and cull
"Briers, thistles, from our private plot,   225
"To mar God's ground where thorns are not!"

VIII.

Do you say this, or I?—Oh, you!
Then, what, my friend?—(thus I pursue
Our parley)—you indeed opine
That the Eternal and Divine   230
Did, eighteen centuries ago,
In very truth . . . Enough! you know
The all-stupendous tale,—that Birth,
That Life, that Death! And all, the earth
Shuddered at,—all, the heavens grew black   235
Rather than see; all, nature's rack
And throe at dissolution's brink
Attested,—all took place, you think,

---

223 MS–1875 God's dispensation's   225 MS ⟨Thorns⟩ [Briars], 1850–68 Briars,
thistles,   226 MS,1850 not!   228 MS,1850 friend,—(so 1 1863,1865 friend,
238 MS Attested,—it ⟨all⟩ took

   223 dispensation: divine judgement or decision. Cf. Samson Agonistes, 60–1.
   236–7 all, nature's rack / And throe: all that which was attested by the sufferings and throes
of nature at the point of dissolution. Cf. Luke 23:44–5. For 'rack' (a mass of cloud driven
before the wind in the upper air), cf. Hamlet, II. ii. 478.

Only to give our joys a zest,
And prove our sorrows for the best?   240
We differ, then! Were I, still pale
And heartstruck at the dreadful tale,
Waiting to hear God's voice declare
What horror followed for my share,
As implicated in the deed,   245
Apart from other sins,—concede
That if He blacked out in a blot
My brief life's pleasantness, 't were not
So very disproportionate!
Or there might be another fate—   250
I certainly could understand
(If fancies were the thing in hand)
How God might save, at that day's price,
The impure in their impurities,
Give licence formal and complete   255
To choose the fair and pick the sweet.
But there be certain words, broad, plain,
Uttered again and yet again,
Hard to mistake or overgloss—
Announcing this world's gain for loss,   260
And bidding us reject the same:
The whole world lieth (they proclaim)
In wickedness,—come out of it!
Turn a deaf ear, if you think fit,
But I who thrill through every nerve   265
At thought of what deaf ears deserve—
How do you counsel in the case?

IX.

"I'd take, by all means, in your place,
"The safe side, since it so appears:

242 *1870* tale   245 *MS* in ⟨that⟩ [the] deed,   255 *MS,1850* Leave formal
licence and *1863–75* Give formal licence and   259 *MS,1850* mistake, to overgloss—

242 *heartstruck*: as in *King Lear*, III. i. 17.
259 *overgloss*: gloss over.
263 *come out of it*: cf. 2 Cor. 6:17.

"Deny myself, a few brief years,   270
"The natural pleasure, leave the fruit
"Or cut the plant up by the root.
"Remember what a martyr said
"On the rude tablet overhead!
"'I was born sickly, poor and mean,   275
"'A slave: no misery could screen
"'The holders of the pearl of price
"'From Cæsar's envy; therefore twice
"'I fought with beasts, and three times saw
"'My children suffer by his law;   280
"'At last my own release was earned:
"'I was some time in being burned,
"'But at the close a Hand came through
"'The fire above my head, and drew
"'My soul to Christ, whom now I see.   285
"'Sergius, a brother, writes for me
"'This testimony on the wall—
"'For me, I have forgot it all.'
"You say right; this were not so hard!
"And since one nowise is debarred   290
"From this, why not escape some sins
"By such a method?"

X.

Then begins
To the old point revulsion new—
(For 't is just this I bring you to)

---

274 *MS,1850* overhead—   283 *MS* the ⟨end⟩ [close] a

273 *a martyr*: a corrected proof of ll. 275–88 in the Robert H. Taylor collection at
Princeton, for *A Selection*, 1865, bears the title, in Browning's hand, 'Epitaph in the Cata-
combs'. It is possible, if hardly likely, that Browning was remembering some transcription
of an actual inscription.

277 *the pearl of price*: Matt. 13:46.

279 *I fought with beasts*: like St Paul: see 1 Cor. 15:32.

286 *Sergius*: there seems no reason to believe that he is to be identified with any histori-
cal person.

293 *revulsion*: turning back.

If after all we should mistake,   295
And so renounce life for the sake
Of death and nothing else? You hear
Each friend we jeered at, send the jeer
Back to ourselves with good effect—
"There were my beetles to collect!   300
"My box—a trifle, I confess,
"But here I hold it, ne'ertheless!"
Poor idiots, (let us pluck up heart
And answer) we, the better part
Have chosen, though 't were only hope,—   305
Nor envy moles like you that grope
Amid your veritable muck,
More than the grasshoppers would truck,
For yours, their passionate life away,
That spends itself in leaps all day   310
To reach the sun, you want the eyes
To see, as they the wings to rise
And match the noble hearts of them!
Thus the contemner we contemn,—
And, when doubt strikes us, thus we ward   315
Its stroke off, caught upon our guard,
—Not struck enough to overturn
Our faith, but shake it—make us learn
What I began with, and, I wis,
End, having proved,—how hard it is   320
To be a Christian!

XI.
            "Proved, or not,
"Howe'er you wis, small thanks, I wot,

298 MS–1875 Our friends we   300 MS–1865 were   314 MS,1850 So, the
315 MS,1850 us, so, we

300 my beetles: cf. above, 154 ff.
308 truck: give in exchange.
316 upon our guard: an idiom from fencing.
322 you wis . . . I wot: the second speaker is mocking the language of the first.

"You get of mine, for taking pains
"To make it hard to me. Who gains
"By that, I wonder? Here I live   325
"In trusting ease; and here you drive
"At causing me to lose what most
"Yourself would mourn for had you lost!"

XII.

But, do you see, my friend, that thus
You leave Saint Paul for Æschylus?   330
—Who made his Titan's arch-device
The giving men *blind hopes* to spice
The meal of life with, else devoured
In bitter haste, while lo, death loured
Before them at the platter's edge!   335
If faith should be, as I allege,
Quite other than a condiment
To heighten flavours with, or meant
(Like that brave curry of his Grace)
To take at need the victuals' place?   340
If, having dined, you would digest
Besides, and turning to your rest
Should find instead . . .

XIII.

                    Now, you shall see
And judge if a mere foppery
Pricks on my speaking! I resolve   345
To utter—yes, it shall devolve

---

326 *MS,1850* and do you   328 *MS,1850* for when 'twas lost?"   330 *MS–*
1875 St. Paul   334 *MS–1865* lo!   336 *MS–1850* as we allege,

326–7 *drive / At*: work hard at.

330 *You leave Saint Paul for Æschylus*: for St Paul's promise of immortality see I Cor.
15:12 ff. Juvenal describes Prometheus as a Titan (*Satires*, xiv. 35). In the *Prometheus Bound*
of Æschylus, 252, Prometheus tells the chorus that he saved mortals from looking forward
to their doom by sending them τυφλὰς . . . ἐλπίδας (blind hopes).

345 *Pricks on*: spurs on. Cf. *Two Gentlemen of Verona*, III. i. 8.

On you to hear as solemn, strange
And dread a thing as in the range
Of facts,—or fancies, if God will—
E'er happened to our kind! I still   350
Stand in the cloud and, while it wraps
My face, ought not to speak perhaps;
Seeing that if I carry through
My purpose, if my words in you
Find a live actual listener,   355
My story, reason must aver
False after all—the happy chance!
While, if each human countenance
I meet in London day by day,
Be what I fear,—my warnings fray   360
No one, and no one they convert,
And no one helps me to assert
How hard it is to really be
A Christian, and in vacancy
I pour this story!

XIV.

                I commence   365
By trying to inform you, whence
It comes that every Easter-night
As now, I sit up, watch, till light,
Upon those chimney-stacks and roofs,
Give, through my window-pane, grey proofs   370
That Easter-day is breaking slow.
On such a night three years ago,
It chanced that I had cause to cross
The common, where the chapel was,

---

353 *MS* that ⟨if⟩ [as] I *1850* that as I   355 *MS,1850* Find veritable listeners,
356 *MS,1850* reason's self avers   357 *MS,1850* Must needs be false—the
359 *MS,1850* London streets all day,   365 *MS* ⟨Hearing⟩ {rest of deletion illegible} I
pour   367 *MS* Easter night   369 *MS,1850* Shall break, those

360 *fray*: 'fright; terrify': Johnson.
364 *in vacancy*: idly, or without anyone to listen.
372 *three years ago*: i.e. in 1846, the year Browning left England.

Our friend spoke of, the other day—   375
You've not forgotten, I dare say.
I fell to musing of the time
So close, the blessed matin-prime
All hearts leap up at, in some guise—
One could not well do otherwise.   380
Insensibly my thoughts were bent
Toward the main point; I overwent
Much the same ground of reasoning
As you and I just now. One thing
Remained, however—one that tasked   385
My soul to answer; and I asked,
Fairly and frankly, what might be
That History, that Faith, to me
—Me there—not me in some domain
Built up and peopled by my brain,   390
Weighing its merits as one weighs
Mere theories for blame or praise,
—The kingcraft of the Lucumons,
Or Fourier's scheme, its pros and cons,—
But my faith there, or none at all.   395
"How were my case, now, did I fall
"Dead here, this minute—should I lie
"Faithful or faithless?" Note that I

384 *MS,1850* now: 395 *MS,1850* But as *my* faith, or *1863,1865* But *my* faith *there*,
or ___   396 *MS,1850* now, should I   397 *MS,1850* minute—do I

378 *matin-prime*: as in 'Sibrandus Schafnaburgensis' ('Garden-Fancies II'), 7. Not in
OED.

382 *overwent*: went over.

393 *the Lucumons*: rulers of the Etruscans who were at once priests and princes. In *The
Pentameron*, iii (1837), Landor makes Boccaccio contrast 'such power as the kings of Rome
and the lucumons of Etruria are contented with' with 'Asiatic practices'. Macaulay refers to
the Lucumons in 'Horatius', xxiii, and Tennyson in *The Princess*, ii. 113.

394 *Fourier's scheme*: Charles Fourier (1772–1837) evolved a scheme for a Utopian com-
munity in which groups of one hundred families were to live in complete physical and
moral harmony, in a co-operative system including free love for the women. The chief
work of Fourierist literature was Victor Considérant's *Destinée sociale* (1834). The over-
sophisticated speaker in *Prince Hohenstiel-Schwangau* refers to 'Fourier, Comte, and all that
ends in smoke!' (439).

Inclined thus ever!—little prone
For instance, when I lay alone   400
In childhood, to go calm to sleep
And leave a closet where might keep
His watch perdue some murderer
Waiting till twelve o'clock to stir,
As good authentic legends tell: 405
"He might: but how improbable!
"How little likely to deserve
"The pains and trial to the nerve
"Of thrusting head into the dark!"—
Urged my old nurse, and bade me mark   410
Beside, that, should the dreadful scout
Really lie hid there, and leap out
At first turn of the rusty key,
Mine were small gain that she could see,
Killed not in bed but on the floor,   415
And losing one night's sleep the more.
I tell you, I would always burst
The door ope, know my fate at first.
This time, indeed, the closet penned
No such assassin: but a friend   420
Rather, peeped out to guard me, fit
For counsel, Common Sense, to wit,
Who said a good deal that might pass,—
Heartening, impartial too, it was,
Judge else: "For, soberly now,—who   425
"Should be a Christian if not you?"
(Hear how he smoothed me down.) "One takes
"A whole life, sees what course it makes
"Mainly, and not by fits and starts—

---

400 *MS,1850* I slept alone   405 *MS,1850* tell   406 *MS,*1850 He might
{underlining of 'might' cancelled in *MS*} —'But how   409 *MS* dark,—' *1850*
dark,'—   410 *MS* ⟨So⟩ urged my [old] nurse,   411 *MS,1850* Besides, that,
412 *MS* there, ⟨&⟩ [to] leap *1850* there, to leap   414 *MS,1850* It were
415 *MS,1850* In being killed upon the floor   427 *MS* down) *1850* down).

403 *perdue*: hidden. Cf. *A Soul's Tragedy*, II. 28.
429 *Mainly*: in general, as a whole.

"In spite of stoppage which imparts   430
"Fresh value to the general speed.
"A life, with none, would fly indeed:
"Your progressing is slower—right!
"We deal with progress and not flight.
"Through baffling senses passionate,   435
"Fancies as restless,—with a freight
"Of knowledge cumbersome enough
"To sink your ship when waves grow rough,
"Though meant for ballast in the hold,—
"I find, 'mid dangers manifold,   440
"The good bark answers to the helm
"Where faith sits, easier to o'erwhelm
"Than some stout peasant's heavenly guide,
"Whose hard head could not, if it tried,
"Conceive a doubt, nor understand   445
"How senses hornier than his hand
"Should 'tice the Christian off his guard.
"More happy! But shall we award
"Less honour to the hull which, dogged
"By storms, a mere wreck, waterlogged,   450
"Masts by the board, her bulwarks gone
"And stanchions going, yet bears on,—
"Than to mere life-boats, built to save,
"And triumph o'er the breaking wave?
"Make perfect your good ship as these,   455
"And what were her performances!"
I added—"Would the ship reach home!
"I wish indeed 'God's kingdom come—'

431 *MS,1850* speed: 434 *MS,1850* with progressing, not   439 *MS,1850*
'Not serve as ballast   440 *MS* mid   445 *MS* doubt, ⟨n⟩or understand *1850*
doubt, or understand   447 *1868–75* tice   451 *MS,1850* board, and bulwarks
457 *MS,1850* ship reached home!

441 *The good bark*: there may be a reminiscence here of Matthew Green's poem *The Spleen*, 814 ff.

446 *hornier*: horns are associated with devils, and with lechery and other sins.

447 *'tice*: obsolete except in dialect.

451 *by the board*: down by the side, overboard.

458 *'God's kingdom come'*: an echo of the Lord's prayer.

"The day when I shall see appear
"His bidding, as my duty, clear   460
"From doubt! And it shall dawn, that day,
"Some future season; Easter may
"Prove, not impossibly, the time—
"Yes, that were striking—fates would chime
"So aptly! Easter-morn, to bring   465
"The Judgment!—deeper in the spring
"Than now, however, when there's snow
"Capping the hills; for earth must show
"All signs of meaning to pursue
"Her tasks as she was wont to do   470
"—The skylark, taken by surprise
"As we ourselves, shall recognize
"Sudden the end. For suddenly
"It comes; the dreadfulness must be
"In that; all warrants the belief—   475
"'At night it cometh like a thief.'
"I fancy why the trumpet blows;
"—Plainly, to wake one. From repose
"We shall start up, at last awake
"From life, that insane dream we take   480
"For waking now, because it seems.
"And as, when now we wake from dreams,
"We laugh, while we recall them, 'Fool,
"'To let the chance slip, linger cool
"'When such adventure offered! Just   485
"'A bridge to cross, a dwarf to thrust
"'Aside, a wicked mage to stab—
"'And, lo ye, I had kissed Queen Mab!'

471 *MS,1850* '—The lark, as taken   473 *MS,1850* end: 475 *MS* warrants
⟨that⟩ [the] belief,—   483 *MS,1850* 'We say, while

476 *At night it cometh*: 'But the day of the Lord will come as a thief in the night; in the
which the heavens shall pass away with a great noise'. 2 Pet. 3:10.
481 *it seems*: unusual without a predicate: cf. OED, 'seem', $v.^2$, 5.
487 *mage*: magician, as in *Sordello*, vi. 98.
488 *Queen Mab*: the Queen of the Fairies.

"So shall we marvel why we grudged
"Our labour here, and idly judged   490
"Of heaven, we might have gained, but lose!
"Lose? Talk of loss, and I refuse
"To plead at all! You speak no worse
"Nor better than my ancient nurse
"When she would tell me in my youth   495
"I well deserved that shapes uncouth
"Frighted and teased me in my sleep:
"Why could I not in memory keep
"Her precept for the evil's cure?
"'Pinch your own arm, boy, and be sure   500
"'You'll wake forthwith!'"

xv.

                              And as I said
This nonsense, throwing back my head
With light complacent laugh, I found
Suddenly all the midnight round
One fire. The dome of heaven had stood   505
As made up of a multitude
Of handbreadth cloudlets, one vast rack
Of ripples infinite and black,
From sky to sky. Sudden there went,   510
Like horror and astonishment,
A fierce vindictive scribble of red
Quick flame across, as if one said

---

490 *MS* 'Our labours here; *1850* 'Our labours here,   493 *MS* all! ⟨You⟩ [I] speak
1850 all! I speak   497 *MS,1850* 'Should fright and tease me   498 *MS,1850*
'Why did I

505 *One fire*: this storm (the same as that described at 1015 ff.) is said to have occurred
'three years ago', i.e. in 1846, which may associate it with the terrific thunderstorm of
1 August in that year, shortly before the Brownings were married and left England. Huge
hailstones did great damage, the roof of the picture-gallery at Buckingham Palace being
totally destroyed.

507 *handbreadth*: not recorded in OED as an adjective.
    cloudlets: as in *Paracelsus*, iv. 511.
    rack: cf. above, 236–7.

(The angry scribe of Judgment) "There—
"Burn it!" And straight I was aware
That the whole ribwork round, minute   515
Cloud touching cloud beyond compute,
Was tinted, each with its own spot
Of burning at the core, till clot
Jammed against clot, and spilt its fire
Over all heaven, which 'gan suspire   520
As fanned to measure equable,—
Just so great conflagrations kill
Night overhead, and rise and sink,
Reflected. Now the fire would shrink
And wither off the blasted face   525
Of heaven, and I distinct might trace
The sharp black ridgy outlines left
Unburned like network—then, each cleft
The fire had been sucked back into,
Regorged, and out it surging flew   530
Furiously, and night writhed inflamed,
Till, tolerating to be tamed
No longer, certain rays world-wide
Shot downwardly. On every side
Caught past escape, the earth was lit;   535
As if a dragon's nostril split
And all his famished ire o'erflowed;
Then, as he winced at his lord's goad,

---

522 *MS–1863* As when great   523 *1863* Night overheard, and   526 *MS,*
1850 distinct could trace   534 *MS,1850* downwardly,   535 *MS,1850* escape;
*538 [reading of *MS–1865*,DC,BrU,*1889*] *1868–88* Then as

513 *The angry scribe of Judgment*: cf. Rev. 20:12, 21:27.
514 *"Burn it!"*: reminiscent of paintings by John Martin, e.g. 'The Fall of Nineveh'.
518 *clot*: cf. 'Artemis Prologizes', 95.
520 *suspire*: sigh, breathe deeply.
521 *equable*: equal (a sense not recorded in OED).
536 *a dragon's nostril*: Browning may be remembering some painting or engraving in the same iconographical tradition as Uccello's 'St George and the Dragon'. Mrs Angelina M. Bacon kindly informs us that that painting did not reach the National Gallery until 1959. Its early provenance is obscure.

Back he inhaled: whereat I found
The clouds into vast pillars bound,   540
Based on the corners of the earth,
Propping the skies at top: a dearth
Of fire i' the violet intervals,
Leaving exposed the utmost walls
Of time, about to tumble in   545
And end the world.

XVI.

I felt begin
The Judgment-Day: to retrocede
Was too late now. "In very deed,"
(I uttered to myself) "that Day!"
The intuition burned away   550
All darkness from my spirit too:
There, stood I, found and fixed, I knew,
Choosing the world. The choice was made;
And naked and disguiseless stayed,
And unevadable, the fact.   555
My brain held all the same compact
Its senses, nor my heart declined
Its office; rather, both combined
To help me in this juncture. I
Lost not a second,—agony   560
Gave boldness: since my life had end
And my choice with it—best defend,
Applaud both! I resolved to say,
"So was I framed by thee, such way
"I put to use thy senses here!   565
"It was so beautiful, so near,

548 *MS,1850* deed,   553 *MS–1865 Choosing the world.*   556 *MS–1875* held
ne'ertheless compact   561 *MS,1850* boldness: there my   563 *MS,1850*
Applaud them! I   564 *MS,1850* by Thee, this way

541 *the corners of the earth*: cf. Rev. 7:1: 'And after these things I saw four angels standing
on the four corners of the earth', and Donne's sonnet, 'At the round earth's imagin'd
corners'.
554 *disguiseless*: perhaps Browning's coinage.

"Thy world,—what could I then but choose
"My part there? Nor did I refuse
"To look above the transient boon
"Of time; but it was hard so soon   570
"As in a short life, to give up
"Such beauty: I could put the cup
"Undrained of half its fulness, by;
"But, to renounce it utterly,
"—That was too hard! Nor did the cry   575
"Which bade renounce it, touch my brain
"Authentically deep and plain
"Enough to make my lips let go.
"But Thou, who knowest all, dost know
"Whether I was not, life's brief while,   580
"Endeavouring to reconcile
"Those lips (too tardily, alas!)
"To letting the dear remnant pass,
"One day,—some drops of earthly good
"Untasted! Is it for this mood,   585
"That Thou, whose earth delights so well,
"Hast made its complement a hell?"

XVII.

A final belch of fire like blood,
Overbroke all heaven in one flood
Of doom. Then fire was sky, and sky   590
Fire, and both, one brief ecstasy,
Then ashes. But I heard no noise
(Whatever was) because a voice
Beside me spoke thus, "Life is done,
"Time ends, Eternity's begun,   595
"And thou art judged for evermore."

567 *MS,1850* I do but   570 *MS,1850* 'In time—   572 *MS,1850* I had put
578 *1865* go,   582 *MS–1850* —too tardily alas!   587 *MS* its ⟨supplement⟩
[complement] a   589 *MS* ⟨?Overhurried⟩ [Overbroke] all, next, in *1850* all, next, in
591 *MS,1850* Was fire, and both, one extacy,   594 *MS,1850* thus, 'All is
596 *MS* evermore'! *1850* evermore!"

XVIII.

I looked up; all seemed as before;
Of that cloud-Tophet overhead
No trace was left: I saw instead
The common round me, and the sky　　　　600
Above, stretched drear and emptily
Of life. 'T was the last watch of night,
Except what brings the morning quite;
When the armed angel, conscience-clear,
His task nigh done, leans o'er his spear　　　　605
And gazes on the earth he guards,
Safe one night more through all its wards,
Till God relieve him at his post.
"A dream—a waking dream at most!"
(I spoke out quick, that I might shake　　　　610
The horrid nightmare off, and wake.)
"The world gone, yet the world is here?
"Are not all things as they appear?
"Is Judgment past for me alone?
"—And where had place the great white throne?　　　　615
"The rising of the quick and dead?
"Where stood they, small and great? Who read
"The sentence from the opened book?"
So, by degrees, the blood forsook
My heart, and let it beat afresh;　　　　620
I knew I should break through the mesh
Of horror, and breathe presently:
When, lo, again, the voice by me!

597 *MS,1850* all was as　　　602 *MS,1850* life:　　　603 *MS,1850* quite,
612 *MS,1850* 'The world's gone,

598 *cloud-Tophet*: at Tophet the children of Judah sacrificed infants to strange gods: Jer.
7:31; 19:4–6. Later, refuse was burnt there, and it became a symbol for Hell: Isa. 30:33.

604 *When the armed angel*: cf. *Paradise Lost*, iv. 561–3, 576.

609 *a waking dream*: cf. Keats, 'Ode to a Nightingale', 79. Cf. below, 1010.

615 *the great white throne*: Rev. 20:11.

616 *the quick and dead*: cf. 2 Tim. 4:1, 1 Pet. 4:5. Cf. the English version of the Creed:
'From thence he shall come to judge the quick and the dead.'

618 *the opened book*: 'the book of life': Rev. 20:12.

XIX.

I saw ... Oh brother, 'mid far sands
The palm-tree-cinctured city stands,   625
Bright-white beneath, as heaven, bright-blue,
Leans o'er it, while the years pursue
Their course, unable to abate
Its paradisal laugh at fate!
One morn,—the Arab staggers blind   630
O'er a new tract of death, calcined
To ashes, silence, nothingness,—
And strives, with dizzy wits, to guess
Whence fell the blow. What if, 'twixt skies
And prostrate earth, he should surprise   635
The imaged vapour, head to foot,
Surveying, motionless and mute,
Its work, ere, in a whirlwind rapt
It vanish up again?—So hapt
My chance. HE stood there. Like the smoke   640
Pillared o'er Sodom, when day broke,—
I saw Him. One magnific pall
Mantled in massive fold and fall
His head, and coiled in snaky swathes
About His feet: night's black, that bathes   645
All else, broke, grizzled with despair,
Against the soul of blackness there.

---

627 *MS,1850* Above it,   629 *MS,1850* fate: 633 *MS,1850* Striving, with
634 *MS,1850* blow: *644 {reading of *1889*} *MS–1888* His dread, and

625 *The palm-tree-cinctured city*: as Pettigrew points out, Browning answered a question
about this. 'As you surmise, the "Palm-cinctured City" is merely typical,—"such a thing
might be, and doubtless has been"—enough for an illustration, that's all.' The letter is
printed by Thomas J. Collins, 'Letters from Robert Browning to the Revd. J. D. Williams,
1874–1889': BIS 4 (1976), 46. Cf. 'The Glove', 95, and *The Two Poets of Croisic*, 244.
630 *blind*: i.e. sand-blind, as in *Paracelsus*, iii. 204.
631 *calcined*: burnt.
641 *Sodom*: 'And he looked toward Sodom and Gomorrah, and toward all the land of the
plain, and beheld, and, lo, the smoke of the country went up as the smoke of a furnace':
Gen. 19:28. Cf. Exod. 13:21 ('a pillar of fire').
643 *fall*: cf. OED, 'Fall', *sb.*, 23.c., for the word in relation to dress.

A gesture told the mood within—
That wrapped right hand which based the chin,
That intense meditation fixed   650
On His procedure,—pity mixed
With the fulfilment of decree.
Motionless, thus, He spoke to me,
Who fell before His feet, a mass,
No man now.

XX.

        "All is come to pass.   655
"Such shows are over for each soul
"They had respect to. In the roll
"Of Judgment which convinced mankind
"Of sin, stood many, bold and blind,
"Terror must burn the truth into: 660
"Their fate for them!—thou hadst to do
"With absolute omnipotence,
"Able its judgments to dispense
"To the whole race, as every one
"Were its sole object. Judgment done,   665
"God is, thou art,—the rest is hurled
"To nothingness for thee. This world,
"This finite life, thou hast preferred,
"In disbelief of God's plain word,
"To heaven and to infinity.   670
"Here the probation was for thee,
"To show thy soul the earthly mixed
"With heavenly, it must choose betwixt.
"The earthly joys lay palpable,—
"A taint, in each, distinct as well;   675
"The heavenly flitted, faint and rare,
"Above them, but as truly were
"Taintless, so, in their nature, best.
"Thy choice was earth: thou didst attest

648 *MS* ⟨One⟩ [a] gesture   665 *MS,1850* object: that is done: 669 *MS–1875*
God's own word,

"'T was fitter spirit should subserve   680
"The flesh, than flesh refine to nerve
"Beneath the spirit's play. Advance
"No claim to their inheritance
"Who chose the spirit's fugitive
"Brief gleams, and yearned, 'This were to live   685
"'Indeed, if rays, completely pure
"'From flesh that dulls them, could endure,—
"'Not shoot in meteor-light athwart
"'Our earth, to show how cold and swart
"'It lies beneath their fire, but stand   690
"'As stars do, destined to expand,
"'Prove veritable worlds, our home!'
"Thou saidst,—'Let spirit star the dome
"'Of sky, that flesh may miss no peak,
"'No nook of earth,—I shall not seek   695
"'Its service further!' Thou art shut
"Out of the heaven of spirit; glut
"Thy sense upon the world: 't is thine
"For ever—take it!"

XXI.

"How? Is mine,
"The world?" (I cried, while my soul broke   700
Out in a transport.) "Hast Thou spoke
"Plainly in that? Earth's exquisite
"Treasures of wonder and delight,
"For me?"

XXII.

The austere voice returned,—
"So soon made happy? Hadst thou learned   705

685 *MS,1850* and thought, 'This   686 *MS* if ⟨gleams⟩ [rays], completely
687 *MS,1850* them, should endure,—   691 *MS,1850* stars should, destined
701 *MS,1850* transport) *1863,1865* transport,)

697–8 *glut / Thy sense*: cf. Keats, 'Ode on Melancholy', 15.

"What God accounteth happiness,
"Thou wouldst not find it hard to guess
"What hell may be his punishment
"For those who doubt if God invent
"Better than they. Let such men rest   710
"Content with what they judged the best.
"Let the unjust usurp at will:
"The filthy shall be filthy still:
"Miser, there waits the gold for thee!
"Hater, indulge thine enmity!   715
"And thou, whose heaven self-ordained
"Was, to enjoy earth unrestrained,
"Do it! Take all the ancient show!
"The woods shall wave, the rivers flow,
"And men apparently pursue   720
"Their works, as they were wont to do,
"While living in probation yet.
"I promise not thou shalt forget
"The past, now gone to its account;
"But leave thee with the old amount   725
"Of faculties, nor less nor more,
"Unvisited, as heretofore,
"By God's free spirit, that makes an end.
"So, once more, take thy world! Expend
"Eternity upon its shows,   730
"Flung thee as freely as one rose
"Out of a summer's opulence,
"Over the Eden-barrier whence
"Thou art excluded. Knock in vain!"

XXIII.

I sat up. All was still again.   735
I breathed free: to my heart, back fled
The warmth. "But, all the world!"—I said.

---

722 *MS,1850* yet: 724 *MS* past, ⟨is⟩ [now] gone   *MS,1850* account,
729 *MS,1850* world;   737 *MS–1865* (I said)

713 *The filthy*: cf. Rev. 22:11: 'he which is filthy, let him be filthy still'.

I stooped and picked a leaf of fern,
And recollected I might learn
From books, how many myriad sorts   740
Of fern exist, to trust reports,
Each as distinct and beautiful
As this, the very first I cull.
Think, from the first leaf to the last!
Conceive, then, earth's resources! Vast   745
Exhaustless beauty, endless change
Of wonder! And this foot shall range
Alps, Andes,—and this eye devour
The bee-bird and the aloe-flower?

XXIV.

Then the voice, "Welcome so to rate   750
"The arras-folds that variegate
"The earth, God's antechamber, well!
"The wise, who waited there, could tell
"By these, what royalties in store
"Lay one step past the entrance-door.   755
"For whom, was reckoned, not too much,
"This life's munificence? For such
"As thou,—a race, whereof scarce one
"Was able, in a million,
"To feel that any marvel lay   760
"In objects round his feet all day;
"Scarce one, in many millions more,
"Willing, if able, to explore
"The secreter, minuter charm!
"—Brave souls, a fern-leaf could disarm   765

741 *MS,1850* | Exist, if one may trust reports,   750 *MS,1850* And the
751 *MS* that ⟨decorate⟩ [variegate]   758 *MS,1850* whereof not one   762 *MS,
1850* "Nor one,

740 *myriad sorts / Of fern*: many thousands have been identified.

749 *The bee-bird*: 'the humming-bird, *colubri*, of the tropics, formerly supposed to feed
only on honey, the buzzing of whose . . . wings is like the hum of the bee, and the night-
blooming aloe that dies at cock-crow, . . . wonders of bird and plant-life': Porter and
Clarke.

754 *royalties*: splendours (archaic).

"Of power to cope with God's intent,—
"Or scared if the south firmament
"With north-fire did its wings refledge!
"All partial beauty was a pledge
"Of beauty in its plenitude: 770
"But since the pledge sufficed thy mood,
"Retain it! plenitude be theirs
"Who looked above!"

XXV.

     Though sharp despairs
Shot through me, I held up, bore on.
"What matter though my trust were gone   775
"From natural things? Henceforth my part
"Be less with nature than with art!
"For art supplants, gives mainly worth
"To nature; 't is man stamps the earth—
"And I will seek his impress, seek   780
"The statuary of the Greek,
"Italy's painting—there my choice
"Shall fix!"

XXVI.

    "Obtain it!" said the voice,
"—The one form with its single act,
"Which sculptors laboured to abstract,   785
"The one face, painters tried to draw,
"With its one look, from throngs they saw.
"And that perfection in their soul,
"These only hinted at? The whole,
"They were but parts of? What each laid   790
"His claim to glory on?—afraid

772 *MS,1850* it—   775 *MS,1850* "What is it though my trust is gone
783 *MS,1850* it" 787 *MS,1850* saw! 790 *MS* "(These) [They] were
791 *MS* "His (his) claim

768 *north-fire*: cf. below, 1016.
 768 *refledge*: as in Southey, 'The Pilgrim to Compostella . . . A Christmas Tale', ii. 86.

"His fellow-men should give him rank
"By mere tentatives which he shrank
"Smitten at heart from, all the more,
"That gazers pressed in to adore!   795
"'Shall I be judged by only these?'
"If such his soul's capacities,
"Even while he trod the earth,—think, now,
"What pomp in Buonarroti's brow,
"With its new palace-brain where dwells   800
"Superb the soul, unvexed by cells
"That crumbled with the transient clay!
"What visions will his right hand's sway
"Still turn to forms, as still they burst
"Upon him? How will he quench thirst,   805
"Titanically infantine,
"Laid at the breast of the Divine?
"Does it confound thee,—this first page
"Emblazoning man's heritage?—
"Can this alone absorb thy sight,   810
"As pages were not infinite,—
"Like the omnipotence which tasks
"Itself to furnish all that asks
"The soul it means to satiate?
"What was the world, the starry state   815
"Of the broad skies,—what, all displays
"Of power and beauty intermixed,
"Which now thy soul is chained betwixt,—
"What else than needful furniture
"For life's first stage? God's work, be sure,   820

---

793 *MS–1875* "By the poor tentatives he shrank   799 *MS,1850* in Buonarotti's
brow,   804 *MS–1875* to form, as   811 *MS,1850* "As if they were

793 *tentatives*: attempts, experiments. Browning rewrote the line to place the stress on
the second syllable, as probably in *The Ring and the Book*, ix. 1539 and x. 1820, and
'Cenciaja', 182. Yet Johnson stresses the first syllable, and OED gives no alternative.

799 *Buonarroti's brow*: a reference to Michelangelo Buonarroti (1475–1564), the great
Florentine artist.

809 *Emblazoning*: celebrating.

820 *life's first stage*: cf. *Pauline*, 885; *Paracelsus*, v. 712; and *Sordello*, vi. 65.

"No more spreads wasted, than falls scant!
"He filled, did not exceed, man's want
"Of beauty in this life. But through
"Life pierce,—and what has earth to do,
"Its utmost beauty's appanage,   825
"With the requirement of next stage?
"Did God pronounce earth 'very good'?
"Needs must it be, while understood
"For man's preparatory state;
"Nought here to heighten nor abate;   830
"Transfer the same completeness here,
"To serve a new state's use,—and drear
"Deficiency gapes every side!
"The good, tried once, were bad, retried.
"See the enwrapping rocky niche,   835
"Sufficient for the sleep in which
"The lizard breathes for ages safe:
"Split the mould—and as light would chafe
"The creature's new world-widened sense,
"Dazzled to death at evidence   840
"Of all the sounds and sights that broke
"Innumerous at the chisel's stroke,—
"So, in God's eye, the earth's first stuff
"Was, neither more nor less, enough
"To house man's soul, man's need fulfil.   845
"Man reckoned it immeasurable?
"So thinks the lizard of his vault!
"Could God be taken in default,

---

821 *MS–1865* scant: 823 *MS,1850* life. And pass   824 *MS,1850* "Life's
line,—and   826 *MS,1850* the requirements of   830 *MS–1875* "Nothing to
831 *MS,1850* "But transfer the completeness   838 *MS–1875* as this would
840 *MS,1850* "One minute after you dispense *1863–75* "One minute after day dispense
841 *MS–1875* "The thousand sounds   842 *MS–1875* "In on him at   843 *MS,*
1850 God's eyes, the   846 *MS,1850* "You reckoned it immeasurable:

825 *appanage*: 'Lands set apart by princes for the maintenance of their younger children':
Johnson. Hence perquisite.
827 *'very good'*: Gen. 1:31.
838 *chafe*: distress.
842 *Innumerous*: as in *Paradise Lost*, vii. 455.

"Short of contrivances, by you,—
"Or reached, ere ready to pursue   850
"His progress through eternity?
"That chambered rock, the lizard's world,
"Your easy mallet's blow has hurled
"To nothingness for ever; so,
"Has God abolished at a blow   855
"This world, wherein his saints were pent,—
"Who, though found grateful and content,
"With the provision there, as thou,
"Yet knew he would not disallow
"Their spirit's hunger, felt as well,—   860
"Unsated,—not unsatable,
"As paradise gives proof. Deride
"Their choice now, thou who sit'st outside!"

XXVII.

I cried in anguish, "Mind, the mind,
"So miserably cast behind,   865
"To gain what had been wisely lost!
"Oh, let me strive to make the most
"Of the poor stinted soul, I nipped
"Of budding wings, else now equipped
"For voyage from summer isle to isle!   870
"And though she needs must reconcile
"Ambition to the life on ground,
"Still, I can profit by late found
"But precious knowledge. Mind is best—
"I will seize mind, forego the rest,   875
"And try how far my tethered strength
"May crawl in this poor breadth and length.

---

860   *MS,1850* spirits'   869 *MS,1850* else well equipt *1863,1865* else now equipt
874 *1865* knowledge. Mine is

861   *unsatable*: insatiable: not in OED.
868   *stinted*: for 'stunted', as in *Pauline*, 956, and elsewhere in Browning.
868–9 *nipped* / *Of*: deprived of.

"Let me, since I can fly no more,
"At least spin dervish-like about
"(Till giddy rapture almost doubt   880
"I fly) through circling sciences,
"Philosophies and histories!
"Should the whirl slacken there, then verse,
"Fining to music, shall asperse
"Fresh and fresh fire-dew, till I strain   885
"Intoxicate, half-break my chain!
"Not joyless, though more favoured feet
"Stand calm, where I want wings to beat
"The floor. At least earth's bond is broke!"

XXVIII.

Then, (sickening even while I spoke)   890
"Let me alone! No answer, pray,
"To this! I know what Thou wilt say!
"All still is earth's,—to know, as much
"As feels its truths, which if we touch
"With sense, or apprehend in soul,   895
"What matter? I have reached the goal—
"'Whereto does knowledge serve!' will burn
"My eyes, too sure, at every turn!
"I cannot look back now, nor stake
"Bliss on the race, for running's sake.   900
"The goal's a ruin like the rest!"—
"And so much worse thy latter quest,"
(Added the voice) "that even on earth—
"Whenever, in man's soul, had birth
"Those intuitions, grasps of guess,   905

*889 {reading of *1868–75*} MS–1865 broke!' *1888,1889* broke!   MS floor(!)[?]
1850 floor?   893 MS earths',—   897 MS serve?'   *901 {editors'
emendation} MS–1865 rest!— *1868–89* rest!—   902 MS–1865 quest,
904 MS mans'

884 *Fining*: refining, rarefying.
       asperse: sprinkle, scatter. Cf. Southey, *Roderick, The Last of the Goths*, xxv. 487.
885 *fire-dew*: not in OED.
905 *grasps of guess*: cf. *Troilus and Cressida*, IV. ii. 13 ('grasps of love').

"Which pull the more into the less,
"Making the finite comprehend
"Infinity,—the bard would spend
"Such praise alone, upon his craft,
"As, when wind-lyres obey the waft,   910
"Goes to the craftsman who arranged
"The seven strings, changed them and rechanged—
"Knowing it was the South that harped.
"He felt his song, in singing, warped;
"Distinguished his and God's part: whence   915
"A world of spirit as of sense
"Was plain to him, yet not too plain,
"Which he could traverse, not remain
"A guest in:—else were permanent
"Heaven on the earth its gleams were meant   920
"To sting with hunger for full light,—
"Made visible in verse, despite
"The veiling weakness,—truth by means
"Of fable, showing while it screens,—
"Since highest truth, man e'er supplied,   925
"Was ever fable on outside.
"Such gleams made bright the earth an age;
"Now the whole sun's his heritage!
"Take up thy world, it is allowed,
"Thou who hast entered in the cloud!"   930

                    XXIX.

Then I—"Behold, my spirit bleeds,
"Catches no more at broken reeds,—

906 *MS–1875* "That pull   914 *MS,1850* warped,   920 *MS* "Heaven ⟨on the⟩
[upon] earth, *1850* "Heaven upon earth, *1863–75* "heaven on earth, which its
921 *MS,1850* for the light,—   932*a MS* ⟨Able to wound it, not sustain—,⟩
932*b MS* ⟨But let me not choose all in vain!⟩

907–8 *Making the finite comprehend / Infinity*: cf. *Sordello*, vi. 499; *Christmas-Eve*, 1016; and
Parleyings ('With Bernard de Mandeville', 151–2).
910 *wind-lyres*: Æolian harps, wind harps. The word is not in OED.
    waft: breath of wind.

"But lilies flower those reeds above:
"I let the world go, and take love!
"Love survives in me, albeit those   935
"I love be henceforth masks and shows,
"Not living men and women: still
"I mind how love repaired all ill,
"Cured wrong, soothed grief, made earth amends
"With parents, brothers, children, friends!   940
"Some semblance of a woman yet
"With eyes to help me to forget,
"Shall look on me; and I will match
"Departed love with love, attach
"Old memories to new dreams, nor scorn   945
"The poorest of the grains of corn
"I save from shipwreck on this isle,
"Trusting its barrenness may smile
"With happy foodful green one day,
"More precious for the pains. I pray,—   950
"Leave to love, only!"

XXX.

At the word,
The form, I looked to have been stirred
With pity and approval, rose
O'er me, as when the headsman throws
Axe over shoulder to make end—   955
I fell prone, letting Him expend
His wrath, while thus the inflicting voice
Smote me. "Is this thy final choice?
"Love is the best? 'T is somewhat late!
"And all thou dost enumerate   960

936 *MS,1850* "I loved are henceforth   937 MS–1875 "Not loving men
943 *MS–1875* "Shall live with me;   945 *MS–1875* "Its fragments to my whole, nor
951 *MS–1875* "For love, then, only!"

938 *mind*: remember (archaic and dialectal).
949 *foodful*: as in Dryden, *Virgil's Georgics*, i. 204. Cf. *The Ring and the Book*, ix. 246.
952 *I looked to*: I expected.

"Of power and beauty in the world,
"The mightiness of love was curled
"Inextricably round about.
"Love lay within it and without,
"To clasp thee,—but in vain! Thy soul   965
"Still shrunk from Him who made the whole,
"Still set deliberate aside
"His love!—Now take love! Well betide
"Thy tardy conscience! Haste to take
"The show of love for the name's sake,   970
"Remembering every moment Who,
"Beside creating thee unto
"These ends, and these for thee, was said
"To undergo death in thy stead
"In flesh like thine: so ran the tale.   975
"What doubt in thee could countervail
"Belief in it? Upon the ground
"'That in the story had been found
"'Too much love! How could God love so?'
"He who in all his works below   980
"Adapted to the needs of man,
"Made love the basis of the plan,—
"Did love, as was demonstrated:
"While man, who was so fit instead
"To hate, as every day gave proof,—   985
"Man thought man, for his kind's behoof,
"Both could and did invent that scheme
"Of perfect love: 't would well beseem
"Cain's nature thou wast wont to praise,
"Not tally with God's usual ways!"   990

---

968 *1875* Wel betide   979 *1850* love?   *MS,1863,1865 so?' 1850 so?*
983 *MS–1865* "Did   986 *MS,1850* "You thought   987 *MS,1850* and would
invent

986 *for his kind's behoof*: for human nature's sake.

983 *demonstrated*: stressed on the second syllable, as in Johnson.

XXXI.

And I cowered deprecatingly—
"Thou Love of God! Or let me die,
"Or grant what shall seem heaven almost!
"Let me not know that all is lost,
"Though lost it be—leave me not tied   995
"To this despair, this corpse-like bride!
"Let that old life seem mine—no more—
"With limitation as before,
"With darkness, hunger, toil, distress:
"Be all the earth a wilderness!   1000
"Only let me go on, go on,
"Still hoping ever and anon
"To reach one eve the Better Land!"

XXXII.

Then did the form expand, expand—
I knew Him through the dread disguise   1005
As the whole God within His eyes
Embraced me.

XXXIII.

            When I lived again,
The day was breaking,—the grey plain
I rose from, silvered thick with dew.
Was this a vision? False or true?   1010
Since then, three varied years are spent,
And commonly my mind is bent
To think it was a dream—be sure
A mere dream and distemperature—

1000 MS wilderness;   *1003 {reading of *1868–75*} MS–*1865,1888,1889* Land!'

995–6 *tied / To this despair*: cf. Dryden, *Virgil's Æneis*, viii. 636 ff.
1010 *Was this a vision?*: cf. Keats, 'Ode to a Nightingale', 79: 'Was it a vision, or a waking dream?' Cf. 609 and n.
1014 *distemperature*: 'Perturbation of the mind': Johnson.

The last day's watching: then the night,—   1015
The shock of that strange Northern Light
Set my head swimming, bred in me
A dream. And so I live, you see,
Go through the world, try, prove, reject,
Prefer, still struggling to effect   1020
My warfare; happy that I can
Be crossed and thwarted as a man,
Not left in God's contempt apart,
With ghastly smooth life, dead at heart,
Tame in earth's paddock as her prize.   1025
Thank God, she still each method tries
To catch me, who may yet escape,
She knows,—the fiend in angel's shape!
Thank God, no paradise stands barred
To entry, and I find it hard   1030
To be a Christian, as I said!
Still every now and then my head
Raised glad, sinks mournful—all grows drear
Spite of the sunshine, while I fear
And think, "How dreadful to be grudged   1035
"No ease henceforth, as one that's judged,
"Condemned to earth for ever, shut
"From heaven!"
                            But Easter-Day breaks! But
Christ rises! Mercy every way
Is infinite,—and who can say?   1040

1037 *MS* forever,   1038 *MS,1850* Heaven' . .

  1016 *Northern Light*: two days after the Brownings left England a striking display of the Aurora Borealis was visible over the principal part of Britain. It took place a few minutes after 8 p.m. on 21 September. They are likely to have seen some, at least, of the reports published in the *Athenæum* from 26 September onwards, which may have renewed Browning's memories of the thunderstorm of 1 August (l. 505 n).

  1020–1 *to effect / My warfare*: to win my battle.

  1028 *fiend in angel's shape*: proverbial.

APPENDIX A

Browning's Essay on Shelley

In May 1851 Edward Moxon bought at auction what purported to be unpublished letters by Shelley. He decided to publish them, and asked Browning to provide an introduction. On 14 October Elizabeth told her sister that Browning was in high spirits, spending part of his time writing about Shelley.[1] Eight days later he wrote to Carlyle:

I have just done the little thing I told you of—a mere Preface to some new letters of Shelley; not admitting of much workmanship of any kind, if I had it to give. But I have put down a few thoughts that presented themselves—one or two, in respect of opinions of your own (I mean, that I was thinking of those opinions while I wrote). However it be done, it is what I was 'up to', just now, and will soon be off my mind.[2]

It is entirely understandable that DeVane wished to date the letter 'almost two months later', but further references in EBB's letters make it clear that 'done' did not mean completed. In a letter dated 31 October–2 November she told her sister that he had 'done his Shelley, except something of the writing out part',[3] and that the arrival of his father and sister had stopped his work meanwhile. On 1 December she reported that he had finished, and was sending the essay off; and four days later she wrote that it 'is off his hands today'. By the 17th he had heard of Moxon's receipt of the manuscript, and hoped that the publisher would be 'no loser by [his] very handsome behavior'.[4] He continued: 'You gain my best thanks, at all events, for it—whatever they may be worth. I will spare no pains with the proofs, or anything else I can do in connection with the matter.'

It is not surprising that Moxon should have turned to Browning, although he was no longer his publisher. He knew of Browning's deep

[1] PK 51:64.
[2] *Letters*, p. 36. Browning was always to remain proud of the essay, described by Carlyle as 'a solid, well-wrought, massive, manful bit of discourse' which he hoped might prove 'the first of very many' pieces in prose. Carlyle liked 'the grave expressiveness of style (a *little* too elaborate here and there), and the dignified tone', concluding that the essay 'and another little word by Emerson' were the only new things he had read 'with real pleasure for a great while past': *Letters*, p. 367.
[3] PK 51:72, 51:76, 51:77.
[4] *New Letters*, pp. 52–3.

interest in Shelley, and must have reflected that he was making a shrewd choice as well as doing a kindness to a poet whose work still appealed to him. *Letters of Percy Bysshe Shelley. With an introductory essay, by Robert Browning* duly appeared in February 1852.[1]

On 23 February Moxon received a letter from Sir Francis Palgrave which told him that his son, on a visit to the Tennysons, had seen a copy of the book and had noticed that one of the 'letters' was based on an article which his father had contributed to the *Quarterly Review* in 1840.[2] A detailed account of the matter may be found in the issue of the *Athenæum* for 6 March 1852 (pp. 278–9) and 20 March (pp. 325–6). The forger is now known to have been an impostor who called himself 'Major George Gordon Byron'. Moxon withdrew the book from sale, and it is extremely scarce.

A few years after the publication of the essay Browning's view of Shelley as a man was profoundly altered when Thomas J. Hookham showed him Harriet's letters to himself revealing the cruelty with which Shelley had treated her.[3] Browning's disillusionment was confirmed when he read the first part of Peacock's memoirs of Shelley in *Fraser's Magazine* for July 1858. He continued to think highly of him as a poet, though at times (as a late letter to Furnivall reveals) he found that the shattering of his early image of the man tended to influence even that: 'I painfully contrast my notions of Shelley the man and Shelley—well, even the poet,—with what they were sixty years ago, when I only had his works, for a certainty, and took his character on trust.'[4] He was not prepared to become President of the Shelley Society.

In 1881, with Browning's permission, Furnivall had reprinted the essay as the first publication of the Browning Society, with a title of the editor's devising: *On the Poet Objective and Subjective: On the Latter's Aim: On Shelley as Man and Poet*. In the 'Foretalk' Furnivall remarks that he values the work because it gives us Browning's own utterances, 'and not those of any one of the "so many imaginary persons" behind whom he insists on so often hiding himself, and whose necks I, for one, should continually like to wring . . . in order to get face to face with the poet himself'. 'Straight speaking', he observes in this remarkable passage, 'straight hitting, suit me best.' He went so far as to supply each page with a running headline, as

---

[1] It was reviewed in the *Athenæum* for 21 February, p. 214: 'There is not much in these new Letters of Shelley:—there is too much in the prefatory pages by Mr. Browning. . . .'

[2] Vol. 66, pp. 313–54: 'The Fine Arts in Florence'.

[3] See William O. Raymond, *The Infinite Moment* (2nd ed., Toronto 1965), pp. 236 ff.

[4] *Trumpeter*, pp. 126–7. Cf. *Dearest Isa*, p. 328.

Browning himself had done when he reprinted *Sordello* in 1863. In 1886 Browning politely refused Ernest Rhys permission to reprint the essay,[1] but when W. Tyas Harden reprinted it two years later, as one of the publications of the Shelley Society, Browning presented copies to Theodore Watts and to two other friends.[2] Since that time the essay has frequently been reprinted.

[1] See Ernest Rhys, *Letters from Limbo* (1936), p. 19.
[2] Kelley and Coley, C 306–8.

ESSAY ON SHELLEY

AN opportunity having presented itself for the acquisition of a series of
unedited letters by Shelley, all more or less directly supplementary to and
illustrative of the collection already published by Mr. Moxon, that gentle-
man has decided on securing them. They will prove an acceptable addi-
tion to a body of correspondence, the value of which towards a right
understanding of its author's purpose and work, may be said to exceed
that of any similar contribution exhibiting the worldly relations of a poet
whose genius has operated by a different law.

   Doubtless we accept gladly the biography of an objective poet, as the
phrase now goes; one whose endeavour has been to reproduce things
external (whether the phenomena of the scenic universe, or the mani-
fested action of the human heart and brain) with an immediate reference,
in every case, to the common eye and apprehension of his fellow men,
assumed capable of receiving and profiting by this reproduction. It has
been obtained through the poet's double faculty of seeing external objects
more clearly, widely, and deeply, than is possible to the average mind, at
the same time that he is so acquainted and in sympathy with its narrower
comprehension as to be careful to supply it with no other materials than it
can combine into an intelligible whole. The auditory of such a poet will

5

10

15

---

3 *the collection*: *Essays, Letters from Abroad, Translations and Fragments*, ed. Mary Shelley,
had appeared in two volumes in 1840 (hereafter *Essays*).

4 *has decided*: this sounds as if Browning began the essay before the purchase had been
made, or before he had confirmation of it.

9 *an objective poet*: 'You have in your vision two worlds', EBB had written to Browning in
her second letter to him, '—or to use the language of the schools of the day, you are both
subjective & objective in the habits of your mind. You can deal both with abstract thought
& with human passion in the most passionate sense': Kintner, i. 9. An excellent account of
the German origins of the terms and of their early history in England may be found in
M. H. Abrams, *The Mirror and the Lamp* (OUP, New York, 1953), pp. 235 ff. In 1817
Coleridge wrote that he had 'ventured to re-introduce' the words '*objective* and *subjective*, of
such constant recurrence in the schools of yore' (*Biographia Literaria*, ed. J. Shawcross, 2
vols., 1907, i. 109, 174 ff.). The terms became more and more popular, without becoming
at all clear. 'Enough of what is now generally called the subjective style of writing', Fitz-
Gerald wrote to Frederick Tennyson in 1840. 'This word has made considerable progress in
England during the year you have been away, so that people begin to fancy they understand
what it means': *The Letters of Edward FitzGerald*, ed. A. McK. and A. B. Terhune (4 vols.,
Princeton, NJ, 1980), i. 250. In 1846 he 'damn[ed] the word!': ibid., p. 528.

15 *the poet's double faculty*: see *Sordello*, iii. 862 ff.

include, not only the intelligences which, save for such assistance, would
have missed the deeper meaning and enjoyment of the original objects,
but also the spirits of a like endowment with his own, who, by means of
his abstract, can forthwith pass to the reality it was made from, and either
corroborate their impressions of things known already, or supply them- 5
selves with new from whatever shows in the inexhaustible variety of exist-
ence may have hitherto escaped their knowledge. Such a poet is properly
the ποιητής, the fashioner; and the thing fashioned, his poetry, will of
necessity be substantive, projected from himself and distinct. We are
ignorant what the inventor of "Othello" conceived of that fact as he 10
beheld it in completeness, how he accounted for it, under what known
law he registered its nature, or to what unknown law he traced its coincid-
ence. We learn only what he intended we should learn by that particular
exercise of his power,—the fact itself,—which, with its infinite signi-
ficances, each of us receives for the first time as a creation, and is hereafter 15
left to deal with, as, in proportion to his own intelligence, he best may.
We are ignorant, and would fain be otherwise.

Doubtless, with respect to such a poet, we covet his biography. We
desire to look back upon the process of gathering together in a lifetime,
the materials of the work we behold entire; of elaborating, perhaps under 20
difficulty and with hindrance, all that is familiar to our admiration in the
apparent facility of success. And the inner impulse of this effort and
operation, what induced it? Did a soul's delight in its own extended sphere
of vision set it, for the gratification of an insuppressible power, on labour,
as other men are set on rest? Or did a sense of duty or of love lead it to 25
communicate its own sensations to mankind? Did an irresistible sympathy
with men compel it to bring down and suit its own provision of know-
ledge and beauty to their narrow scope? Did the personality of such an one
stand like an open watch-tower in the midst of the territory it is erected to
gaze on, and were the storms and calms, the stars and meteors, its watch- 30
man was wont to report of, the habitual variegation of his every-day life,
as they glanced across its open roof or lay reflected on its four-square
parapet? Or did some sunken and darkened chamber of imagery witness,
in the artificial illumination of every storied compartment we are per-
mitted to contemplate, how rare and precious were the outlooks through 35

1 *assistance*: misprinted 'assist-/tance'.

8 ποιητής: a maker, and thence a poet. Cf. Scots *makar*. We have supplied the accent,
omitted by the printer.

33 *darkened chamber of imagery*: a reminiscence of Plato's allegory of the cave: *Republic*,
vii. 514A–521B. Browning knew Plato well (Maynard, p. 234), to whom Shelley's thought
owed a great deal.

here and there an embrasure upon a world beyond, and how blankly
would have pressed on the artificer the boundary of his daily life, except
for the amorous diligence with which he had rendered permanent by art
whatever came to diversify the gloom? Still, fraught with instruction and
5 interest as such details undoubtedly are, we can, if needs be, dispense with
them. The man passes, the work remains. The work speaks for itself, as we
say: and the biography of the worker is no more necessary to an under-
standing or enjoyment of it, than is a model or anatomy of some tropical
tree, to the right tasting of the fruit we are familiar with on the market-
10 stall,—or a geologist's map and stratification, to the prompt recognition
of the hill-top, our land-mark of every day.

We turn with stronger needs to the genius of an opposite tendency—
the subjective poet of modern classification. He, gifted like the objective
poet with the fuller perception of nature and man, is impelled to embody
15 the thing he perceives, not so much with reference to the many below as
to the one above him, the supreme Intelligence which apprehends all
things in their absolute truth,—an ultimate view ever aspired to, if but
partially attained, by the poet's own soul. Not what man sees, but what
God sees—the *Ideas* of Plato, seeds of creation lying burningly on the
20 Divine Hand—it is toward these that he struggles. Not with the combina-
tion of humanity in action, but with the primal elements of humanity he
has to do; and he digs where he stands,—preferring to seek them in his
own soul as the nearest reflex of that absolute Mind, according to the
intuitions of which he desires to perceive and speak. Such a poet does not
25 deal habitually with the picturesque groupings and tempestuous tossings
of the forest-trees, but with their roots and fibres naked to the chalk and
stone. He does not paint pictures and hang them on the walls, but rather
carries them on the retina of his own eyes: we must look deep into his
human eyes, to see those pictures on them. He is rather a seer, accordingly,
30 than a fashioner, and what he produces will be less a work than an efflu-
ence. That effluence cannot be easily considered in abstraction from his
personality,—being indeed the very radiance and aroma of his per-
sonality, projected from it but not separated. Therefore, in our approach
to the poetry, we necessarily approach the personality of the poet; in
35 apprehending it we apprehend him, and certainly we cannot love it

6 *The man passes*: cf. *Adonais*, 460: 'The One remains, the many change and pass.'
8 *anatomy*: dissection.
19 *the* Ideas *of Plato*: in the philosophy of Plato an 'idea' is the eternal archetype of any
class of things, of which an individual instance is merely an imperfect copy.
31 *effluence*: effulgence. Cf. *Paradise Lost*, iii. 6, and *Adonais*, 406–7.

without loving him. Both for love's and for understanding's sake we desire to know him, and as readers of his poetry must be readers of his biography also.

I shall observe, in passing, that it seems not so much from any essential distinction in the faculty of the two poets or in the nature of the objects 5 contemplated by either, as in the more immediate adaptability of these objects to the distinct purpose of each, that the objective poet, in his appeal to the aggregate human mind, chooses to deal with the doings of men, (the result of which dealing, in its pure form, when even description, as suggesting a describer, is dispensed with, is what we call dramatic 10 poetry), while the subjective poet, whose study has been himself, appealing through himself to the absolute Divine mind, prefers to dwell upon those external scenic appearances which strike out most abundantly and uninterruptedly his inner light and power, selects that silence of the earth and sea in which he can best hear the beating of his individual heart, and 15 leaves the noisy, complex, yet imperfect exhibitions of nature in the manifold experience of man around him, which serve only to distract and suppress the working of his brain. These opposite tendencies of genius will be more readily descried in their artistic effect than in their moral spring and cause. Pushed to an extreme and manifested as a deformity, 20 they will be seen plainest of all in the fault of either artist, when subsidiarily to the human interest of his work his occasional illustrations from scenic nature are introduced as in the earlier works of the originative painters—men and women filling the foreground with consummate mastery, while mountain, grove and rivulet show like an anticipatory 25 revenge on that succeeding race of landscape-painters whose "figures" disturb the perfection of their earth and sky. It would be idle to inquire, of these two kinds of poetic faculty in operation, which is the higher or even rarer endowment. If the subjective might seem to be the ultimate requirement of every age, the objective, in the strictest state, must still retain its 30 original value. For it is with this world, as starting point and basis alike, that we shall always have to concern ourselves: the world is not to be learned and thrown aside, but reverted to and relearned. The spiritual comprehension may be infinitely subtilised, but the raw material it operates upon, must remain. There may be no end of the poets who 35

23 *originative*: Browning is referring to the Italian masters of the Renaissance.

25 *mountain, grove and rivulet*: cf. Wordsworth, 'Ode: Intimations of Immortality', 1.

26 *landscape-painters*: landscape-painting developed later (in the western world) than painting in which landscape serves as a background to figures.

32–3 *the world is not to be . . . thrown aside*: cf. 'Fra Lippo Lippi', 313–15.

communicate to us what they see in an object with reference to their own individuality; what it was before they saw it, in reference to the aggregate human mind, will be as desirable to know as ever. Nor is there any reason why these two modes of poetic faculty may not issue hereafter from the
5   same poet in successive perfect works, examples of which, according to what are now considered the exigences of art, we have hitherto possessed in distinct individuals only. A mere running-in of the one faculty upon the other, is, of course, the ordinary circumstance. Far more rarely it happens that either is found so decidedly prominent and superior, as to be
10 pronounced comparatively pure: while of the perfect shield, with the gold and the silver side set up for all comers to challenge, there has yet been no instance. Either faculty in its eminent state is doubtless conceded by Providence as a best gift to men, according to their especial want. There is a time when the general eye has, so to speak, absorbed its fill of the
15 phenomena around it, whether spiritual or material, and desires rather to learn the exacter significance of what it possesses, than to receive any augmentation of what is possessed. Then is the opportunity for the poet of loftier vision, to lift his fellows, with their half-apprehensions, up to his own sphere, by intensifying the import of details and rounding the
20 universal meaning. The influence of such an achievement will not soon die out. A tribe of successors (Homerides) working more or less in the same spirit, dwell on his discoveries and reinforce his doctrine; till, at unawares, the world is found to be subsisting wholly on the shadow of a reality, on sentiments diluted from passions, on the tradition of a fact, the
25 convention of a moral, the straw of last year's harvest. Then is the imperative call for the appearance of another sort of poet, who shall at once replace this intellectual rumination of food swallowed long ago, by a supply of the fresh and living swathe; getting at new substance by breaking up the assumed wholes into parts of independent and unclassed
30 value, careless of the unknown laws for recombining them (it will be the business of yet another poet to suggest those hereafter), prodigal of objects for men's outer and not inner sight, shaping for their uses a new and different creation from the last, which it displaces by the right of life over death,—to endure until, in the inevitable process, its very sufficiency to
35 itself shall require, at length, an exposition of its affinity to something higher,—when the positive yet conflicting facts shall again precipitate

21 *Homerides*: (L. *Homeridae*) a guild of poets in Chios 'who claimed descent from Homer and a hereditary property in the Homeric poems, which they recited publicly' (OED).

23–4 *the shadow of a reality*: cf. above, p. 426, l. 19 n.

themselves under a harmonising law, and one more degree will be
apparent for a poet to climb in that mighty ladder, of which, however
cloud-involved and undefined may glimmer the topmost step, the world
dares no.longer doubt that its gradations ascend.

   Such being the two kinds of artists, it is naturally, as I have shown, with 5
the biography of the subjective poet that we have the deeper concern.
Apart from his recorded life altogether, we might fail to determine with
satisfactory precision to what class his productions belong, and what
amount of praise is assignable to the producer. Certainly, in the face of
any conspicuous achievement of genius, philosophy, no less than sym- 10
pathetic instinct, warrants our belief in a great moral purpose having
mainly inspired even where it does not visibly look out of the same. Great-
ness in a work suggests an adequate instrumentality; and none of the
lower incitements, however they may avail to initiate or even effect many
considerable displays of power, simulating the nobler inspiration to which 15
they are mistakenly referred, have been found able, under the ordinary
conditions of humanity, to task themselves to the end of so exacting a
performance as a poet's complete work. As soon will the galvanism that
provokes to violent action the muscles of a corpse, induce it to cross the
chamber steadily: sooner. The love of displaying power for the display's 20
sake, the love of riches, of distinction, of notoriety,—the desire of a
triumph over rivals, and the vanity in the applause of friends,—each and
all of such whetted appetites grow intenser by exercise and increasingly
sagacious as to the best and readiest means of self-appeasement,—while
for any of their ends, whether the money or the pointed finger of the 25
crowd, or the flattery and hate to heart's content, there are cheaper prices
to pay, they will all find soon enough, than the bestowment of a life upon a
labour, hard, slow, and not sure. Also, assuming the proper moral aim to
have produced a work, there are many and various states of an aim: it may
be more intense than clear-sighted, or too easily satisfied with a lower 30
field of activity than a steadier aspiration would reach. All the bad poetry
in the world (accounted poetry, that is, by its affinities) will be found to
result from some one of the infinite degrees of discrepancy between the

2 *that mighty ladder*: as J. B. Bury pointed out, the idea of Progress penetrated the general
consciousness 'in the period 1820 to 1850' (*The Idea of Progress*, 1920, p. 324). Cf. Georg
Roppen, *Evolution and Poetic Belief* (Oslo, 1956). In Browning's poetry the image of ascent is
ubiquitous, from the French footnote to *Pauline*, 811, through 'A Grammarian's Funeral',
and on to his later poetry.

   18 *galvanism*: the application of electric currents to the tissues, living or dead (called
after Luigi Galvani, 1737–98). Cf. *The Ring and the Book*, i. 740.

   20–1 *power for the display's sake*: like Eglamor in *Sordello*, at ii. 195 ff., e.g., or iii. 616 ff.

attributes of the poet's soul, occasioning a want of correspondency between his work and the verities of nature,—issuing in poetry, false under whatever form, which shows a thing not as it is to mankind generally, nor as it is to the particular describer, but as it is supposed to be for some unreal neutral mood, midway between both and of value to neither, and living its brief minute simply through the indolence of whoever accepts it or his incapacity to denounce a cheat. Although of such depths of failure there can be no question here we must in every case betake ourselves to the review of a poet's life ere we determine some of the nicer questions concerning his poetry,—more especially if the performance we seek to estimate aright, has been obstructed and cut short of completion by circumstances,—a disastrous youth or a premature death. We may learn from the biography whether his spirit invariably saw and spoke from the last height to which it had attained. An absolute vision is not for this world, but we are permitted a continual approximation to it, every degree of which in the individual, provided it exceed the attainment of the masses, must procure him a clear advantage. Did the poet ever attain to a higher platform than where he rested and exhibited a result? Did he know more than he spoke of?

I concede however, in respect to the subject of our study as well as some few other illustrious examples, that the unmistakeable quality of the verse would be evidence enough, under usual circumstances, not only of the kind and degree of the intellectual but of the moral constitution of Shelley: the whole personality of the poet shining forward from the poems, without much need of going further to seek it. The "Remains"— produced within a period of ten years, and at a season of life when other men of at all comparable genius have hardly done more than prepare the eye for future sight and the tongue for speech—present us with the complete enginery of a poet, as signal in the excellence of its several adaptitudes as transcendent in the combination of effects,—examples, in fact, of the whole poet's function of beholding with an understanding keenness the universe, nature and man, in their actual state of perfection in imperfection,—of the whole poet's virtue of being untempted by the manifold partial developments of beauty and good on every side, into leaving them

---

9 *nicer*: more difficult.

25 *The "Remains"*: his writings in general: not the title of a specific book.

29 *enginery*: equipment.

   adaptitudes: aptitudes for a particular purpose. The only other example known to OED occurs in EBB's *The Greek Christian Poets and the English Poets*, first published in the *Athenæum* in 1842. The word recurs on p. 439 below.

the ultimates he found them,—induced by the facility of the gratification
of his own sense of those qualities, or by the pleasure of acquiescence in
the short-comings of his predecessors in art, and the pain of disturbing
their conventionalisms,—the whole poet's virtue, I repeat, of looking
higher than any manifestation yet made of both beauty and good, in order 5
to suggest from the utmost actual realisation of the one a corresponding
capability in the other, and out of the calm, purity and energy of nature,
to reconstitute and store up for the forthcoming stage of man's being, a
gift in repayment of that former gift, in which man's own thought and
passion had been lavished by the poet on the else-incompleted mag- 10
nificence of the sunrise, the else-uninterpreted mystery of the lake,—so
drawing out, lifting up, and assimilating this ideal of a future man, thus
descried as possible, to the present reality of the poet's soul already arrived
at the higher state of development, and still aspirant to elevate and extend
itself in conformity with its still-improving perceptions of, no longer the 15
eventual Human, but the actual Divine. In conjunction with which noble
and rare powers, came the subordinate power of delivering these attained
results to the world in an embodiment of verse more closely answering to
and indicative of the process of the informing spirit, (failing as it occa-
sionally does, in art, only to succeed in highest art),—with a diction more 20
adequate to the task in its natural and acquired richness, its material
colour and spiritual transparency,—the whole being moved by and
suffused with a music at once of the soul and the sense, expressive both of
an external might of sincere passion and an internal fitness and con-
sonancy,—than can be attributed to any other writer whose record is 25
among us. Such was the spheric poetical faculty of Shelley, as its own self-
sufficing central light, radiating equally through immaturity and accom-
plishment, through many fragments and occasional completion, reveals it
to a competent judgment.

But the acceptance of this truth by the public, has been retarded by 30
certain objections which cast us back on the evidence of biography, even
with Shelley's poetry in our hands. Except for the particular character of
these objections, indeed, the non-appreciation of his contemporaries
would simply class, now that it is over, with a series of experiences which
have necessarily happened and needlessly been wondered at, ever since the 35
world began, and concerning which any present anger may well be
moderated, no less in justice to our forerunners than in policy to our-
selves. For the misapprehensiveness of his age is exactly what a poet is sent

---

38 *misapprehensiveness*: aptness to misapprehend. Cf. *The Ring and the Book*, ix. 1526.

to remedy; and the interval between his operation and the generally perceptible effect of it, is no greater, less indeed, than in many other departments of the great human effort. The "E pur si muove" of the astronomer was as bitter a word as any uttered before or since by a poet over his rejected living work, in that depth of conviction which is so like despair.

But in this respect was the experience of Shelley peculiarly unfortunate—that the disbelief in him as a man, even preceded the disbelief in him as a writer; the misconstruction of his moral nature preparing the way for the misappreciation of his intellectual labours. There existed from the beginning,—simultaneous with, indeed anterior to his earliest, noticeable works, and not brought forward to counteract any impression they had succeeded in making,—certain charges against his private character and life, which, if substantiated to their whole breadth, would materially disturb, I do not attempt to deny, our reception and enjoyment of his works, however wonderful the artistic qualities of these. For we are not sufficiently supplied with instances of genius of his order, to be able to pronounce certainly how many of its constituent parts have been tasked and strained to the production of a given lie, and how high and pure a mood of the creative mind may be dramatically simulated as the poet's habitual and exclusive one. The doubts, therefore, arising from such a question, required to be set at rest, as they were effectually, by those early authentic notices of Shelley's career and the corroborative accompaniment of his letters, in which not only the main tenor and principal result of his life, but the purity and beauty of many of the processes which had conduced to them, were made apparent enough for the general reader's purpose,—whoever lightly condemned Shelley first, on the evidence of reviews and gossip, as lightly acquitting him now, on that of memoirs and correspondence. Still, it is advisable to lose no opportunity of strengthening and completing the chain of biographical testimony; much more, of

3 *'E pur si muove'*: ('and yet it does move'): the words traditionally supposed to have been pronounced by Galileo (1564–1642) after his submission to the Inquisition, and profession that he still held to the Ptolemaic theory by which the sun moves round the earth. The story is apocryphal.

10–11 *from the beginning*: Shelley was sent down from Oxford in 1811, for distributing copies of his little pamphlet, *The Necessity of Atheism* (written with T. J. Hogg) to the bishops and heads of colleges. Soon scandalous rumours of his private life were in circulation. The earliest of his 'noticeable works' may be said to be *Alastor* (1816).

22–3 *early authentic notices*: such as those by Thomas Jefferson Hogg in the *New Monthly Magazine* for 1832–3 (repr. by R. A. Streatfeild as *Shelley at Oxford*, 1904), and those in the notes to Mary Shelley's edition of *The Poetical Works* (4 vols., 1839). Many of his letters were published by Mary Shelley in 1840, in *Essays*.

course, for the sake of the poet's original lovers, whose volunteered sacrifice of particular principle in favour of absorbing sympathy we might desire to dispense with, than for the sake of his foolish haters, who have long since diverted upon other objects their obtuseness or malignancy. A full life of Shelley should be written at once, while the materials for it 5 continue in reach; not to minister to the curiosity of the public, but to obliterate the last stain of that false life which was forced on the public's attention before it had any curiosity on the matter,—a biography, composed in harmony with the present general disposition to have faith in him, yet not shrinking from a candid statement of all ambiguous passages, 10 through a reasonable confidence that the most doubtful of them will be found consistent with a belief in the eventual perfection of his character, according to the poor limits of our humanity. Nor will men persist in confounding, any more than God confounds, with genuine infidelity and an atheism of the heart, those passionate, impatient struggles of a boy 15 towards distant truth and love, made in the dark, and ended by one sweep of the natural seas before the full moral sunrise could shine out on him. Crude convictions of boyhood, conveyed in imperfect and inapt forms of speech,—for such things all boys have been pardoned. There are growing-pains, accompanied by temporary distortion, of the soul also. And it 20 would be hard indeed upon this young Titan of genius, murmuring in divine music his human ignorances, through his very thirst for knowledge, and his rebellion, in mere aspiration to law, if the melody itself substantiated the error, and the tragic cutting short of life perpetuated into sins, such faults as, under happier circumstances, would have been 25 left behind by the consent of the most arrogant moralist, forgotten on the lowest steps of youth.

The responsibility of presenting to the public a biography of Shelley, does not, however[,] lie with me: I have only to make it a little easier by arranging these few supplementary letters, with a recognition of the value 30 of the whole collection. This value I take to consist in a most truthful conformity of the Correspondence, in its limited degree, with the moral and intellectual character of the writer as displayed in the highest manifestations of this genius. Letters and poems are obviously an act of the same mind, produced by the same law, only differing in the applica- 35 tion to the individual or collective understanding. Letters and poems may

7 *that false life*: a general reference.

15 *atheism*: in 1816 Shelley wrote the word ἄθεος in a hotel register in Chamonix, and in another at Montavert.

19–20 *There are growing-pains*: cf. Keats, in the preface to *Endymion*.

be used indifferently as the basement of our opinion upon the writer's character; the finished expression of a sentiment in the poems, giving light and significance to the rudiments of the same in the letters, and these, again, in their incipiency and unripeness, authenticating the exalted mood and reattaching it to the personality of the writer. The musician speaks on the note he sings with; there is no change in the scale, as he diminishes the volume into familiar intercourse. There is nothing of that jarring between the man and the author, which has been found so amusing or so melancholy; no dropping of the tragic mask, as the crowd melts away; no mean discovery of the real motives of a life's achievement, often, in other lives, laid bare as pitifully as when, at the close of a holiday, we catch sight of the internal lead-pipes and wood-valves, to which, and not to the ostensible conch and dominant Triton of the fountain, we have owed our admired waterwork. No breaking out, in household privacy, of hatred anger and scorn, incongruous with the higher mood and suppressed artistically in the book: no brutal return to self-delighting, when the audience of philanthropic schemes is out of hearing: no indecent stripping off the grander feeling and rule of life as too costly and cumbrous for every-day wear. Whatever Shelley was, he was with an admirable sincerity. It was not always truth that he thought and spoke; but in the purity of truth he spoke and thought always. Everywhere is apparent his belief in the existence of Good, to which Evil is an accident; his faithful holding by what he assumed to be the former, going everywhere in company with the tenderest pity for those acting or suffering on the opposite hypothesis. For he was tender, though tenderness is not always the characteristic of very sincere natures; he was eminently both tender and sincere. And not only do the same affection and yearning after the well-being of his kind, appear in the letters as in the poems, but they express themselves by the same theories and plans, however crude and unsound. There is no reservation of a subtler, less costly, more serviceable remedy for his own ill, than he had proposed for the general one; nor does he ever contemplate an object on his own account, from a less elevation than he uses in exhibiting it to the world. How shall we help believing Shelley to have been, in his ultimate attainment, the splendid spirit of his own best poetry, when we find even his carnal speech to agree faithfully, at faintest as at strongest, with the tone and rhythm of his most oracular utterances?

For the rest, these new letters are not offered as presenting any new

1 *basement*: groundwork, basis.
36 *carnal*: ordinary, human.

feature of the poet's character. Regarded in themselves, and as the substantive productions of a man, their importance would be slight. But they possess interest beyond their limits, in confirming the evidence just dwelt on, of the poetical mood of Shelley being only the intensification of his habitual mood; the same tongue only speaking, for want of the special 5 excitement to sing. The very first letter, as one instance for all, strikes the key-note of the predominating sentiment of Shelley throughout his whole life—his sympathy with the oppressed. And when we see him at so early an age, casting out, under the influence of such a sympathy, letters and pamphlets on every side, we accept it as the simple exemplification of 10 the sincerity, with which, at the close of his life, he spoke of himself, as—

> "One whose heart a stranger's tear might wear
> As water-drops the sandy fountain stone;
> Who loved and pitied all things, and could moan
> For woes which others hear not, and could see   15
> The absent with the glass of phantasy,
> And near the poor and trampled sit and weep,
> Following the captive to his dungeon deep—
> One who was as a nerve o'er which do creep
> The else-unfelt oppressions of this earth."   20

Such sympathy with his kind was evidently developed in him to an extraordinary and even morbid degree, at a period when the general intellectual powers it was impatient to put in motion, were immature or deficient.

I conjecture, from a review of the various publications of Shelley's 25 youth, that one of the causes of his failure at the outset, was the peculiar *practicalness* of his mind, which was not without a determinate effect on his progress in theorising. An ordinary youth, who turns his attention to similar subjects, discovers falsities, incongruities, and various points for amendment, and, in the natural advance of the purely critical spirit 30

6 *The very first letter*: two importance sentences of this letter, here dated 22 February 1811 and addressed to the editor of the *Statesman* (John Hunt), are taken from Shelley's letter to the editor of the *Examiner* (Leigh Hunt), dated 2 March 1811. The genuine letter had been published in the *Westminster Review* for April 1841, pp. 308–9. The text may be found in *The Letters of Shelley*, ed. Frederick L. Jones (2 vols., 1964), i. 54–5.

11 *at the close of his life*: in fact this poem, 'Julian and Maddalo', was written in 1818, though not published until 1824, among the *Posthumous Poems*.

12 *One whose heart*: Shelley, 'Julian and Maddalo', 442–50 (slightly adapted). Maddalo (Byron) is describing himself to Julian (Shelley).

27 *practicalness*: Browning is thinking of the early political pamphlets, and perhaps the notes to *Queen Mab*.

unchecked by considerations of remedy, keeps up before his young eyes
so many instances of the same error and wrong, that he finds himself
unawares arrived at the startling conclusion, that all must be changed—or
nothing: in the face of which plainly impossible achievement, he is apt
(looking perhaps a little more serious by the time he touches at the deci-
sive issue), to feel, either carelessly or considerately, that his own attempt-
ing a single piece of service would be worse than useless even, and to refer
the whole task to another age and person—safe in proportion to his
incapacity. Wanting words to speak, he has never made a fool of himself
by speaking. But, in Shelley's case, the early fervour and power to *see*, was
accompanied by as precocious a fertility to *contrive:* he endeavoured to
realise as he went on idealising; every wrong had simultaneously its
remedy, and, out of the strength of his hatred for the former, he took the
strength of his confidence in the latter—till suddenly he stood pledged to
the defence of a set of miserable little expedients, just as if they repre-
sented great principles, and to an attack upon various great principles,
really so, without leaving himself time to examine whether, because they
were antagonistical to the remedy he had suggested, they must therefore
be identical or even essentially connected with the wrong he sought to
cure,—playing with blind passion into the hands of his enemies, and
dashing at whatever red cloak was held forth to him, as the cause of the
fireball he had last been stung with—mistaking Churchdom for Chris-
tianity, and for marriage, "the sale of love" and the law of sexual
oppression.

Gradually, however, he was leaving behind him this low practical
dexterity, unable to keep up with his widening intellectual perception;
and, in exact proportion as he did so, his true power strengthened and
proved itself. Gradually he was raised above the contemplation of spots
and the attempt at effacing them, to the great Abstract Light, and,
through the discrepancy of the creation, to the sufficiency of the First
Cause. Gradually he was learning that the best way of removing abuses is
to stand fast by truth. Truth is one, as they are manifold; and innumerable
negative effects are produced by the upholding of one positive principle. I

6 *considerately*: after careful consideration.

21–2 *red cloak . . . fireball*: an allusion to bull-fighting. If the bull is cowardly, 'banderillas
de fuego' (fire-darts), furnished with fulminating crackers which explode with terrific
noise, are brought into play.

22 *Churchdom*: only one other example of the word is given in OED².

23 *the sale of love*: cf. *Queen Mab*, v. 189 ('Even love is sold'), and Shelley's note on the
passage.

29 *the great Abstract Light*: cf. *Adonais*, 460–4.

shall say what I think,—had Shelley lived he would have finally ranged himself with the Christians; his very instinct for helping the weaker side (if numbers make strength), his very "hate of hate," which at first mistranslated itself into delirious Queen Mab notes and the like, would have got clearer-sighted by exercise. The preliminary step to following Christ, is the leaving the dead to bury their dead—not clamouring on His doctrine for an especial solution of difficulties which are referable to the general problem of the universe. Already he had attained to a profession of "a worship to the Spirit of good within, which requires (before it sends that inspiration forth, which impresses its likeness upon all it creates) devoted and disinterested homage, *as Coleridge says,"*—and Paul likewise. And we find in one of his last exquisite fragments, avowedly a record of one of his own mornings and its experience, as it dawned on him at his soul and body's best in his boat on the Serchio—that as surely as

> "The stars burnt out in the pale blue air,
> And the thin white moon lay withering there—
> Day had kindled the dewy woods,
> And the rocks above, and the stream below,
> And the vapours in their multitudes,
> And the Apennine's shroud of summer snow—
> Day had awakened all things that be;"

just so surely, he tells us (stepping forward from this delicious dance-music, choragus-like, into the grander measure befitting the final enunciation),

> "All rose to do the task He set to each,
> Who shaped us to his ends and not our own;
> The million rose to learn, and One to teach
> What none yet ever knew or can be known."

No more difference than this, from David's pregnant conclusion so long ago!

3 *his very "hate of hate"*: as the Ohio editor points out, the phrase 'hate of hate' occurs in 'The Poet' (l. 3), included in Tennyson's *Poems, Chiefly Lyrical* (1830).

6 *leaving the dead*: Luke 9:60.

9 *a worship to the Spirit of good within*: Professor Timothy Webb points out that this is a rearranged quotation from a letter from Shelley to Maria Gisborne, dated 'October 13th or 14th, 1819' (*Letters*, ed. Jones, ii. 125: *Essays*, ii. 234). Browning has capitalized 'Spirit'.

11 *as Coleridge says*: untraced.

and Paul likewise: Rom. 8:9, and elsewhere in his Epistles.

15 *The stars burnt out*: 'The Boat on the Serchio', 7–8, 11–14, and 17. Written in 1821, the poem was first published in *Posthumous Poems*, 1824. The other four lines are 30–3.

23 *choragus-like*: the choragus was the leader of the Chorus in an ancient Greek play.

28 *David's pregnant conclusion*: throughout the Psalms: see e.g. the first and the last.

Meantime, as I call Shelley a moral man, because he was true, simple-hearted, and brave, and because what he acted corresponded to what he knew, so I call him a man of religious mind, because every audacious negative cast up by him against the Divine, was interpenetrated with a
5   mood of reverence and adoration,—and because I find him everywhere taking for granted some of the capital dogmas of Chritianity, while most vehemently denying their historical basement. There is such a thing as an efficacious knowledge of and belief in the politics of Junius, or the poetry of Rowley, though a man should at the same time dispute the title of
10   Chatterton to the one, and consider the author of the other, as Byron wittily did, "really, truly, nobody at all."* There is even such a thing, we come to learn wonderingly in these very letters, as a profound sensibility

*Or, to take our illustrations from the writings of Shelley himself, there is such a thing as admirably appreciating a work by Andrea Verocchio,—and fancifully characterising the Pisan Torre Guelfa by the Ponte a Mare, black against the sunsets,—and consummately painting the islet of San Clemente with its penitentiary for rebellious priests, to the west between Venice and the Lido—while you believe the first to be a fragment of an antique sarcophagus,—the second, Ugolino's Tower of Famine (the vestiges of which should be sought for in the Piazza de' Cavalieri)—and the third (as I convinced myself last summer at Venice), San Servolo with its madhouse—which, far from being "windowless," is as full of windows as a barrack.

4 *interpenetrated*: the first transitive use of the verb in OED is from Shelley's 'Lines Written among the Euganean Hills', 313.

7 *basement*: cf. note to p. 434, l. 1, above.

8 *Junius*: the authorship of *The Letters of Junius* is a celebrated mystery. They were first collected in two volumes in 1772, and are believed to be the work of Sir Philip Francis (1740–1818).

8–9 *the poetry of Rowley*: Thomas Chatterton (1752–70) claimed to have found poems by a fifteenth-century Bristol monk, Thomas Rowley, in a chest in a church in Bristol. He committed suicide. In 1777 and 1778 T. Tyrwhitt proved, what had been suspected, that they were forgeries. Like Shelley, Browning was fascinated by Chatterton, making him the main subject of his review of a book on Tasso, published in the *Foreign Quarterly Review* for July 1842 and reprinted in 1948 as *Browning's Essay on Chatterton* (ed. Donald Smalley, Cambridge, Mass.).

11 *nobody at all*: in *The Vision of Judgment*, st. lxxx, Byron reveals his 'hypothesis' that Junius 'Was *really*, *truly*, nobody at all'.

note *a work by Andrea Verocchio*: see the description of 'A Bas-Relief: probably the sides of a sarcophagus', in 'Remarks on some of the Statues in the Gallery of Florence': *Essays, Letters from Abroad*, ii. 271 ff. The relief is now in the Museo Nazionale in Florence.

the Pisan Torre Guelfa by the Ponte a Mare: in *The Poetical Works* (4 vols., 1839), iv. 46 the brief poem, 'The Tower of Famine', has a note, by Shelley himself or his wife: 'At Pisa there still exists the prison of Ugolino, which goes by the name of "La Torre della Fame" . . . It is situated near the Ponte al Mare on the Arno.'

San Servolo: San Servolo is an island set aside in 1725 for 'maniacs of noble family'. Browning is referring to 'Julian and Maddalo', 96 ff., where the building is said to be 'windowless'.

and adaptitude for art, while the science of the percipient is so little advanced as to admit of his stronger admiration for Guido (and Carlo Dolce!) than for Michael Angelo. A Divine Being has Himself said, that "a word against the Son of man shall be forgiven to a man," while "a word against the Spirit of God" (implying a general deliberate preference of perceived evil to perceived good) "shall not be forgiven to a man." Also, in religion, one earnest and unextorted assertion of belief should outweigh, as a matter of testimony, many assertions of unbelief. The fact that there is a gold-region is established by the finding of one lump, though you miss the vein never so often.

He died before his youth ended. In taking the measure of him as a man, he must be considered on the whole and at his ultimate spiritual stature, and not be judged of at the immaturity and by the mistakes of ten years before: that, indeed, would be to judge of the author of "Julian and Maddalo" by "Zastrozzi." Let the whole truth be told of his worst mistake. I believe, for my own part, that if anything could now shame or grieve Shelley, it would be an attempt to vindicate him at the expense of another.

In forming a judgment, I would, however, press on the reader the simple justice of considering tenderly his constitution of body as well as mind, and how unfavourable it was to the steady symmetries of conventional life; the body, in the torture of incurable disease, refusing to

1 *adaptitude*: as above, p. 430.
   science: knowledge.
2–3 *Guido (and Carlo Dolce!)*: Shelley's *Essays* contain numerous laudatory references to Guido Reni (1575–1642), whom he more than once yokes with Raphael. Carlo Dolci (1616–86) was a minor Florentine painter. The passage may have been suggested by an observation by Keats: 'A year ago I could not understand . . . Raphael's Cartoons; now I begin to read them a little. And how did I learn to do so? By seeing something done in quite an opposite spirit; I mean a picture of Guido's, in which all the Saints, instead of that heroic simplicity and unaffected grandeur, which they inherit from Raphael, had, each of them, . . . all the canting, solemn, melo-dramatic mawkishness of Mackenzie's Father Nicholas': *Life, Letters, and Literary Remains of John Keats*, ed. Richard Monckton Milnes (2 vols., 1848), i. 255. Moxon sent Browning a presentation copy: Kelley and Coley, A 1603.
   While Shelley 'agree[d] with the whole world' in thinking Raphael 'the finest painter', he reacted 'with astonishment and indignation [to] the common notion' that Michelangelo equalled or even surpassed him: *Essays*, ii. 224 (*Letters*, ed. F. L. Jones, ii. 112).
3 *A Divine Being*: see Luke 12:10.
15 *"Zastrozzi"*: this romance, by 'P.B.S.', was Shelley's first publication, in 1810.
17 *another*: his first wife, Harriet Westbrook, whom he left for Mary Godwin. Harriet killed herself, and early defenders of Shelley, including Leigh Hunt, were sometimes unfair to Harriet. Browning is probably thinking particularly of Thomas Medwin's *The Shelley Papers* (1833) and *Life of Shelley* (2 vols., 1847).
21 *incurable disease*: Shelley was a hypochondriac, and was sometimes thought to be consumptive. He seems to have suffered from a chronic kidney and bladder disease.

give repose to the bewildered soul, tossing in its hot fever of the fancy,— and the laudanum-bottle making but a perilous and pitiful truce between these two. He was constantly subject to "that state of mind" (I quote his own note to "Hellas") "in which ideas may be supposed to assume the force of sensation, through the confusion of thought with the objects of thought, and excess of passion animating the creations of the imagination": in other words, he was liable to remarkable delusions and hallucinations. The nocturnal attack in Wales, for instance, was assuredly a delusion; and I venture to express my own conviction, derived from a little attention to the circumstances of either story, that the idea of the enamoured lady following him to Naples, and of the "man in the cloak" who struck him at the Pisan post-office, were equally illusory,—the mere projection, in fact, from himself, of the image of his own love and hate.

"To thirst and find no fill—to wail and wander
With short unsteady steps—to pause and ponder—
To feel the blood run through the veins and tingle
When busy thought and blind sensation mingle,—
To nurse the image of *unfelt caresses*
Till dim imagination just possesses
The half-created shadow"—

of unfelt caresses,—and of unfelt blows as well: to such conditions was his genius subject. It was not at Rome only (where he heard a mystic voice exclaiming, "Cenci, Cenci," in reference to the tragic theme which occupied him at the time),—it was not at Rome only that he mistook the cry of "old rags." The habit of somnambulism is said to have extended to the very last days of his life.

2 *the laudanum-bottle*: occasionally, and reluctantly, Shelley took laudanum to help him in nervous attacks.

3 *that state of mind*: from Shelley's note to *Hellas*, 814–15.

8 *The nocturnal attack*: during the night of 26/7 February 1813 the house at Tremadoc in Wales where Shelley was staying was disturbed by the firing of several shots. He believed there had been an attempt to assassinate him. Hogg, Peacock, and others believed he was suffering from hallucination. See H. M. Dowling, 'The Attack at Tanyrallt', *Keats–Shelley Memorial Bulletin* (1961).

10–11 *the enamoured lady*: see Medwin's *Life*, i. 324 ff.

11 *the "man in the cloak"*: ibid. ii. 9 ff.

14 *To thirst*: fragment first printed by Mary Shelley in *The Poetical Works* (1839), iii. 69. Browning's italics.

23 *"Cenci, Cenci,"*: Medwin states that Shelley told him that while he was writing *The Cenci* 'he heard in the street the oft-repeated cry, "Cenci, Cenci," which he at first thought the echo of his own soul, but soon learnt was one of the cries of Rome—Cenci meaning old rags': *Life*, i. 344. In *Pacchiarotto and Other Poems* (1876) Browning published a poem entitled 'Cenciaja', a trifle (bundle of rags), relating to Shelley's work.

Let me conclude with a thought of Shelley as a poet. In the hierarchy of creative minds, it is the presence of the highest faculty that gives first rank, in virtue of its kind, not degree; no pretension of a lower nature, whatever the completeness of development or variety of effect, impeding the precedency of the rarer endowment though only in the germ. The contrary is sometimes maintained; it is attempted to make the lower gifts (which are potentially included in the higher faculty) of independent value, and equal to some exercise of the special function. For instance, should not a poet possess common sense? Then the possession of abundant common sense implies a step towards becoming a poet. Yes; such a step as the lapidary's, when, strong in the fact of carbon entering largely into the composition of the diamond, he heaps up a sack of charcoal in order to compete with the Koh-i-noor. I pass at once, therefore, from Shelley's minor excellencies to his noblest and predominating characteristic.

This I call his simultaneous perception of Power and Love in the absolute, and of Beauty and Good in the concrete, while he throws, from his poet's station between both, swifter, subtler, and more numerous films for the connexion of each with each, than have been thrown by any modern artificer of whom I have knowledge; proving how, as he says,

> "The spirit of the worm within the sod,
> In love and worship blends itself with God."

I would rather consider Shelley's poetry as a sublime fragmentary essay towards a presentment of the correspondency of the universe to Deity, of the natural to the spiritual, and of the actual to the ideal, than I would isolate and separately appraise the worth of many detachable portions which might be acknowledged as utterly perfect in a lower moral point of view, under the mere conditions of art. It would be easy to take my stand on successful instances of objectivity in Shelley: there is the unrivalled "Cenci;" there is the "Julian and Maddalo" too; there is the magnificent "Ode to Naples:" why not regard, it may be said, the less organised matter as the radiant elemental foam and solution, out of which would have been evolved, eventually, creations as perfect even as those? But I prefer to look for the highest attainment, not simply the high,—and, seeing it, I hold by

13 *the Koh-i-noor*: a very large oval diamond from India, which had become part of the British Crown Jewels in 1849.

17 *while he throws*: cf. the opening of Shelley's 'Letter to Maria Gisborne', *Sordello*, i. 665 ff., and the letter cited in our note ad loc.

21 *The spirit of the worm*: Shelley, *Epipsychidion*, 128–9 ('within' should be 'beneath').

it. There is surely enough of the work "Shelley" to be known enduringly among men, and, I believe, to be accepted of God, as human work may; and around the imperfect proportions of such, the most elaborated productions of ordinary art must arrange themselves as inferior illustra-
5 tions.

It is because I have long held these opinions in assurance and gratitude, that I catch at the opportunity offered to me of expressing them here; knowing that the alacrity to fulfil an humble office conveys more love than the acceptance of the honour of a higher one, and that better, there-
10 fore, than the signal service it was the dream of my boyhood to render to his fame and memory, may be the saying of a few, inadequate words upon these scarcely more important supplementary letters of SHELLEY.

PARIS, *Dec. 4th*, 1851.

1 *the work "Shelley"*: cf. Browning to EBB: 'I never have begun, even, what I hope I was born to begin and end,—"R.B. a poem."': Kintner, i. 17.
10 *the dream of my boyhood*: see *Pauline*, particularly ll. 141 ff., 554 ff., and 1020 ff.

APPENDIX B

Fugitives

Schoolboy Verses

SINCE a reviewer regretted our omission of trivial fugitives from Volume I, and since it is difficult to draw the line between them and other occasional verses clearly worth preserving, we give here four fugitives relating to Browning's days at the school in Peckham run by the Revd Thomas Martin Ready and his sisters.

(1) We boys are privates in our Regiments ranks—
'Tis to our Captain that we all owe thanks!

In his *Diary* for 7 February 1873 Alfred Domett quotes these lines, which Browning recited and described as 'the two concluding lines' of a copy of verses he had written 'at 8 or 9 years of age' [*c.* 1820/1], to ingratiate himself with Mr Ready: 'great *bosh* they were', he commented. Griffin and Minchin first published them, in 1910, before the publication of the *Diary.*

(2) Within these walls and near that house of glass,
Did I, three years of hapless childhood pass—
D——d undiluted misery it was!

Browning quoted this 'epigram' to Domett on some occasion 'in the days of our early acquaintance', perhaps in the 1830s (cf. our Vol. III, p. 224). It is not clear when the epigram had been composed. Domett was uncertain of the words, particularly querying 'three', but mentioning that the last line had been spoken 'in a suddenly deepened tone'. The epigram was first published by E. A. Horsman on p. 74 of his edition of the *Diary.*

(3) 'Impromptu on hearing a sermon by the Rev. T. R— pronounced "Heavy"'

A *Heavy* Sermon!—Sure the error's great—
For not a word Tom uttered *had its weight.*

Browning gave this as a postscript to a letter to W. J. Fox in March

1833: *Correspondence*, iii. 75. Earlier composition seems likely.

(4) 'Epigram'

> "I wander from the point!" cried Tom—
> It was an idle fear—
> How could he ever wander from
> What he was never near!

Maynard (p. 382) attributes the lines to Browning, as a strong probability. They were first printed in February 1835 in the second and last issue of *The Trifler*, 'an amateur magazine edited on purely casual principles by Browning's friends'. Again, earlier composition is likely.[1]

Later Fugitives

Cockney Anthology—a specimen

[1] On Andrea del Sarto's "*Jupiter & Leda*"

Bowbell loquitur/

> Nymph, of the swelling limbs & *bosom ample**
> In your good graces I'd be Jove's succeeder—
> And tho' *twas* Jove who set me the example
> Doubt not but I'll do justice to my Leader.

> * μετὰ κούρης βαθυκόλπου κ.τ.λ
> Anacr. Od. V.

See *Collections*, Plate 10, for a reproduction of these verses. For permission to print them we are indebted to the Armstrong Browning Library.

title: 'The Cockney School of Poetry' was an abusive label applied by writers in *Blackwood's Magazine* to Leigh Hunt and others.

"*Jupiter & Leda*": see John Shearman, *Andrea del Sarto* (2 vols., 1965), vol. ii, no. 31 and plate 35b.

Bowbell loquitur: the Cockney speaks. A Cockney is a person born within the sound of Bow Bells in London.

Anacr. Od. V: like many other lyrics, this is no longer attributed to Anacreon. In traditional editions (e.g. the Foulis ed., *Anacreontis Carmina* [and Greek title], Glasgow, 1777) this is the 5th Ode. The words quoted are from l. 14.

[1] Griffin and Minchin (p. 30) tentatively ascribe to Browning, 'before he could read', the couplet: 'Good people all who wish to see / A boy take physic, look at me'. We agree with Park Honan ('The Texts of Fifteen Fugitives by Robert Browning', VP 5, 1967, 159n.) and Pettigrew and Collins (ii. 1131) that Browning's authorship is most unlikely. For our omission of other pieces which have been ascribed to him, see above, p. vi.

cui puella/

> Alas friend, to what use?
> Already you've betrayed yourself no man
>   To cope with Zeus:—
>   For *he* began
> By veiling his bright presence in a *Swan*—
>   *You*'ve made yourself—a *Goose*!

R Browning. Thursday Feby 6. 1834.

[2]   *On the deleterious effects of Tea*

"Tea, Tea, inquam, Fanny, contra tea testem suscitabo."
                              Cic. pro Roscio

> When Doctors with tirades on *Tea* affright us
> I think they miss an instance & a nice 'un:
> We've all heard talk of "weeping Heraclitus—"
> Well—Heraclitus was produced by—*Hyson*!

RB

[*THE 'MOSES' OF MICHAEL ANGELO*]

> And who is He that, sculptured in huge stone,
>   Sitteth a giant, where no works arrive
>   Of straining Art, and hath so prompt and live
> The lips, I listen to their very tone?
> Moses is He—Ay, that, makes clearly known
>   The chin's thick boast, and brow's prerogative
>   Of double ray: so did the mountain give

cui puella: to whom the nymph.

Cic. pro Roscio: Cicero, *Pro Q. Roscio Comoedo*, 37: 'Te, te inquam, Fanni, ab tuis subselliis contra te testem suscitabo': 'It is you, I say, Fannius, whom I will rouse from your benches as a witness against yourself' (translated by J. H. Freese in the Loeb ed. of Cicero, vol. vi: *Pro Publio Quinctio*, etc., London and Cambridge, Mass., 1930). Fanny Haworth, if she was the recipient of these lines, was presumably a lover of tea. Browning is punning on 'tea' and L. 'te'.

"weeping Heraclitus": according to Lemprière, Heraclitus was 'Naturally of a melancholy disposition', and so 'passed his time in a solitary and unsocial manner, and received the appellation of . . . the mourner, from his unconquerable custom of weeping at the follies, frailty, and vicissitudes of human affairs'.

Hyson: Hyson is one of the varieties of China green tea. It was also one version of the name of the father of Heraclitus.

Back to the world that visage, God was grown
Great part of! Such was he when he suspended
　Round him the sounding & vast waters; such
　　When he shut sea on sea o'er Mizraïm.
And ye, his hordes, a vile calf raised, and bended
　The knee? This Image had ye raised, not much
　　Had been your error in adoring Him.

From Zappi. RB. Given to Ba "for love's sake", Siena, Sept. 27. '50.

This sonnet, first published in the *Cornhill Magazine* for September 1914 and in *New Poems*, is here printed from the manuscript in the Thomas Fisher Rare Book Library in the University of Toronto. The words 'sculptured in' are written above an illegible deletion. The original, by Giambatista Felice Zappi, may be found in his *Rime* and in Vol. 42 of the *Parnaso Italiano* (Venice, 1789), p. 162. ('Mizraïm' is the Hebrew for 'Egypt'.)

APPENDIX C

Index of the titles and first lines of the poems in Dramatic Lyrics and Dramatic Romances and Lyrics.

The titles are in italics.

All's over, then: does truth sound bitter   IV. 59
Artemis Prologizes   III. 218
As I ride, as I ride   III. 254

Bishop orders his Tomb at Saint Praxed's Church, The   IV. 69
Boot and Saddle   III. 183
Boot, saddle, to horse, and away!   III. 183
Boy and the Angel, The   IV. 144

Cavalier Tunes   III. 180
Christ God who savest man, save most   III. 190
Claret and Tokay   IV. 151, 152
Confessional, The   IV. 89
Count Gismond   III. 190
Cristina   III. 241

Earth's Immortalities   IV. 140
Englishman in Italy, The   IV. 41

Fame   IV. 140
Flight of the Duchess, The   IV. 100
Flower's Name, The   IV. 77
Fortù, Fortù, my beloved one   IV. 41

Garden Fancies   IV. 77
Give a Rouse   III. 182
Glove, The   IV. 170
Gr-r-r—there go, my heart's abhorrence!   III. 199

Hamelin Town's in Brunswick   III. 263
'Heigho!' yawned one day King Francis   IV. 170
Here's the garden she walked across   IV. 77
Here's to Nelson's memory!   IV. 64

Home-Thoughts, from abroad   IV. 63
Home-Thoughts, from the sea   IV. 65
'How they Brought the Good News from Ghent to Aix'   IV. 19

I am a goddess of the ambrosial courts   III. 218
I could have painted pictures like that youth's   IV. 26
I know a Mount, the gracious Sun perceives   III. 237
In a Gondola   III. 205
Incident of the French Camp   III. 197
I send my heart up to thee, all my heart   III. 205
I sprang to the stirrup, and Joris, and he   IV. 19
Italian in England, The   IV. 32
It is a lie—their Priests, their Pope   IV. 89
I've a Friend, over the sea   IV. 165

Johannes Agricola in Meditation   III. 246
Just for a handful of silver he left us   IV. 56

Kentish Sir Byng stood for his King   III. 180
King Charles, and who'll do him right now?   III. 182

Laboratory, The   IV. 85
Lost Leader, The   IV. 56
Lost Mistress, The   IV. 59
Love   IV. 141

Marching Along   III. 180
Meeting at Night   IV. 149
Morning, evening, noon and night   IV. 144
My heart sank with our Claret-flask   IV. 151
My Last Duchess   III. 186

Nationality in Drinks   IV. 151
Nay but you, who do not love her   IV. 142
Nobly, nobly Cape Saint Vincent to the North-west died away   IV. 65
Now that I, tying thy glass mask tightly   IV. 85

Oh, to be in England   IV. 63

Parting at Morning   IV. 150
Pictor Ignotus   IV. 26
Pied Piper of Hamelin, The   III. 263
Plague take all your pedants, say I!   IV. 80
Porphyria's Lover   III. 250

Round the cape of a sudden came the sea   IV. 150
Rudel to the Lady of Tripoli   III. 237

Said Abner, "At last thou art come!"   IV. 156
Saul   IV. 156
See, as the prettiest graves will do in time   IV. 140
She should never have looked at me   III. 241
Sibrandus Schafnaburgensis   IV. 80
Soliloquy of the Spanish Cloister   III. 199
Song   IV. 142
So, the year's done with!   IV. 141

That's my last Duchess painted on the wall   III. 186
That second time they hunted me   IV. 32
The grey sea and the long black land   IV. 149
The rain set early in to-night   III. 250
Through the Metidja to Abd-el-Kadr   III. 254
There's heaven above, and night by night   III. 246
Time's Revenges   IV. 165

Up jumped Tokay on our table   IV. 152

Vanity, saith the preacher, vanity!   IV. 69

Waring   III. 225
What's become of Waring   III. 225

You're my friend   IV. 100
You know, we French stormed Ratisbon   III. 197

ADDITIONS AND CORRECTIONS
TO VOLUMES I–III

Volume I

(*Note*: the corrections to the first printing of Volume I listed on p. 531 of Volume II are incorporated here)

p. xix n. 2: *for* Pub. *read Papers of the*

p. xx, l. 21: *for* who may be *read* who may not be

p. 4 n. 1: *delete and read* Correspondence, iii. 265.

    n. 4: *delete last sentence and read* Cf. Correspondence, iii. 265.

p. 14, l. 11 word': *add note* He was afraid that it would be published in America: see George Monteiro, 'The Legitimizing of *Pauline*', *Browning and his Circle*, Fall 1974, pp. 56–8.

p.   31, l. 83: *add note* Cf. *Paradise Lost*, v. 896 (Pettigrew).

p.   68, l. 567 n.: *for* *itself* *read* itself

p. 110, l. 23: *the last word should be* amiable

    l. 35: *for* Those *read* those

    n. 2: *add* Correspondence, iii. 109.

    n. 3: *add* Cf. Correspondence, iii. 126.

p. 111, l. 18: *for* not turn out *read* turn out not

    n. 2: *delete and substitute* Correspondence, iii. 132. Cf. Correspondence, iii. 133, which mentions that Browning approached Murray about the poem on 4 April.

p. 119 n. 6: *delete and substitute* Correspondence, iii. 265.

p. 122, 7 ll. up: the editors have not had access to the corrected proof for the first edition, in private hands in Texas (Kelley and Coley, E 317).

p. 127, l. 28: *insert* The songs from Parts IV and V were included in the *Selection* of 1865, with a few trivial variants.

    l. 36: *insert* All but six of the revisions made by Browning in a copy of *1865* now at Baylor University were incorporated into the text of *1868*.

p. 128, l. 2: *add* The song 'Heap cassia' from Part IV was printed in the *Selections* of 1872 and 1884–8 from the text of *1868*.

    n. 2: *for* proela *read* praela. The lines are the opening of Donne's poem, 'De Libro cum mutuaretur Impresso'. There is a good translation by Edmund Blunden in 'Some Seventeenth-Century Latin Poems by English Writers': UTQ 25 (1955), 11:

> What Printing-presses yield we think good store,
> But what is writ by hand we reverence more:
> A book that with this printing-blood is dyed
> On shelves for dust and moth is set aside,
> But if 't be penned it wins a sacred grace
> And with the ancient Fathers takes its place.

p. 133: *add note on l. 15*   Cf. *Correspondence*, iii. 126.

p. 153, l. 193, textual note: *add*   *1865*   It is so, Festus?

p. 175, l. 481 n.: *for*   754   *read* III. i. 116.

p. 205 *delete n. to l. 3 and read* i.e. the city lies between me and the sunset.

p. 241, l. 368, textual note: *for* ⟨spare{?}⟩   *read* ⟨pure⟩
    l. 366, note: *add*   Cf. Gal. 6:7 (Pettigrew)

p. 245, n. to l. 425: *for* 'Elegie: Death' *read* 'An Elegy upon the Death of Mistress Boulstred'.

p. 275: *the last four textual footnotes should be numbered*   74, 75, 76, 77

p. 321 *add note to l. 603* Cf. Luther at the Diet of Worms: 'Here I stand: I can do no otherwise' (Pettigrew).

p. 339, l. 826, textual note: *add*   *Baylor 1865*   admiration ⟨will.⟩ [does.]

p. 393, l. 374, textual note: *add*   *Baylor 1865* revises to 'commands hope,'

p. 401, l. 457, textual note: *add*   *1865S* those black-bull hides,

p. 405, l. 500, textual note: *for*   *1849*   *read*   *1849,1865S*

p. 409, last line of notes: *read*   ambitiousness

p. 459, l. 424, textual note: *for*   *1849*   *read*   *1849,1865S*
    add textual note on l. 425   *1865S* Bear not

p. 489: *add note on l. 775*   *types* in the theological sense, prefigurations.

p. 495: *add note on l. 852*   Cf. *Hamlet*, IV. vii. 183.

p. 515: *add note on ll. 3–4*   *I inspected one, and am certified of the existence of other transcripts*: In a persuasive article, 'Browning's First Letter to Rossetti: a Discovery' (BIS 15, 1987, 79–90), Mark Samuels Lasner describes one such transcript, now in his personal collection, in William Allingham's Commonplace Book. There it is accompanied by a copy of a hitherto unknown letter from Browning to D. G. Rossetti, dated from 'Florence, Nov. 10, 1847'. Acknowledging that Rossetti was right in attributing *Pauline* to his authorship, Browning adds, 'beside the faults for which the author is directly answerable, the misprints are portentous—I having made my first essay at the business of correcting the proof sheets over Messers Saunders & Otley's parlour-table, to avoid breaking my incognito by giving my address & receiving the copy at home!'

p. 515 n. 1: *for*   Vol. iii   *read*   Vol. v

p. 533: *add*   Several 'Fugitives' belonging to the period of Volume I may be found in the present volume, on pp. 443–5.

Volume II

p. 4, *add to n*[2]: see too Bruce S. Busby, SBC, Fall 1977, 65–70.

p. 20, l. 4 *add the following note*:

For an account of the copy manuscript of *Strafford* dated 27 April 1837 (B.L. Additional MS 42941) submitted to the Lord Chamberlain for licensing as a stage-play, see Anneliese Meidl, 'A *Strafford* Manuscript in the Lord Chamberlain's Office Records', *Browning Institute Studies* XII (1984) pp. 163–188. To Dr. Meidl's useful analysis we add the following comments. The manuscript represents an abridgement and adaptation of the play for the stage. It is impossible to distinguish Browning's contributions to the adaptation with any certainty from those of Macready, who, with Forster's help, 'altered, omitted, and made up one new scene', advised or effected drastic cuts, and probably provided a number of bridging passages which cobble together mutilated speeches, often at the expense of the metre. Crudely emotional emphasis was added, especially in the last scene, and the balance of the play was altered to reduce the importance of Pym, played by Macready's rival, Vandenhoff. The text, especially in Acts III and IV, is frequently of 'Bad Quarto' standard, largely owing to the incompetence of the copyist, who was less literate than the transcriber of the remainder of the play, and whose copy seems to have been that of the stage-manager. It provides detailed instructions for exits and entrances, whereas Acts I, II and V lack these, giving instead interpretative comments for Strafford's speeches only. These are likely to derive from Macready, who annotated his *King John* prompt-book in a similar way.

Though the text of the Lord Chamberlain's copy is clearly corrupt, it has three readings which suggest corrections of misprints or omissions in the first and subsequent editions. See the additional notes to p. 40, l. 152, p. 57, l. 179, and p. 92, l. 51.

p. 29, l. 1, textual note: *transfer to p. 30*.

p. 40, l. 152: *emend to*   talk. The King   *and add textual note*   *152 {reading based on punctuation of *LC transcript*.} *1837–89* talk, the King

p. 57, l. 179: *after* friend! *add* WENTWORTH *takes* PYM's *hand and add textual note* *179 {s.d. based on *LC transcript*.}

p. 92, l. 51 *add before* 'But the adage' *Savile*.

A copy of the first edition of *Strafford* in the Gordon N. Ray collection at the Pierpont Morgan Library is inscribed by RB on the title-page: '—Parsloe Esq | with the Author's compts.' Some stage-directions in Acts I–III are underlined, and there are a few additional directions in an unknown hand such as 'Forward R', 'X to them', and after I. i. '*As all go up, & move* towards L.2d. W. (W.)

p. 139, l. 42 n.: *delete reference to 'Æschylus' Soliloquy'* (which is by EBB)

p. 159, 8 lines up: *delete* 'about ... 1837',[1] *and read* written on 1 July 1837,[1] *and substitute for n.* [1] *Correspondence*, iii. 256.

p. 162, l. 15: *after* 'notes.' *add* The same day he begged Landor to 'accept the accompanying little book published to-day'.

p. 173 n. 1, l. 4: *for* Whyte *read* White

p. 195, l. 4 n., line 7: *for* p. *read* i.

p. 236: *add note on l. 824* brand: sword.

p. 246, l. 3: *for* pine-trees *read* pine-tree

p. 282, l. 773 n.: *add* Cf. *Antony and Cleopatra*, III. x. 14.

p. 297, l. 76 n.: *add* Cf. below, vi. 399–400.

p. 309, l. 303 n.: *delete* Sordello *and read* the narrator

p. 338: *add note to l. 830*: *Meribah!*: see Numbers 20.13, 27.14, and Deut. 32.51.

p. 359, l. 196 n.: *add* Cf. Keats, 'I stood tip-toe', 116–17.

p. 374: *add note on l. 501* Cf. the subtitle of *The Fable of the Bees*, 'Private Vices, Public Benefits'. Bernard Mandeville was a favourite with Browning, who addressed the first of his *Parleyings* to him.

p. 375, l. 531 n.: *add* See OED, 'News', *sb.*, 3.

p. 401, l. 14 n., *second line*: *delete and read* 'Mooned' means crescent-shaped.

p. 452, l. 1 n.: *add* Cf. Byron, *Childe Harold's Pilgrimage*, IV. clxxviii–clxxxiii.

p. 493, l. 777 n.: Cf. Michael Meredith, *More than Friend* (Armstrong Browning Library and Wedgestone Press), pp. 129, 137–8.

p. 530, l. 1: *delete the three Greek words and substitute* δόξα εἰς αἰῶνα(ς).

Volume III

p. v, l. 6 up: *for*   Harold N. Lee   *read*   Harold B. Lee

p. 7, l. 22: *for*   at present',   *read*   for the present',

p. 11, third paragraph: *delete first sentence (and n. 3)*

p. 14, *add note on l. 6*: In 'A Note on the Flowers in *Pippa Passes*' (VP 14, 1976, 60–1) William R. Campbell argues that the flower images are used 'to characterize people and to point an important . . . theme of the work'.

p. 14, *add note on l. 8*: See, however, 'A New Source for the Form of *Pippa Passes*', by John Woolford and Daniel Karlin, NQ June 1989, 184–5.

p. 73, l. 164 n.: *first line should end with* in

p. 93, ll. 15 ff.: *delete from*   On 20 September Forster   *to foot of the page, and also the last four references to Macready's Diaries in n. 3.*

p. 138, *last textual note*: *for*   Exeunt singly.   *read*   *Exeunt singly.*

p. 151, l. 312 n.: *for*   pp.   *read*   p.

p. 153, l. 374: *for*   himself   *read*   himself.

p. 154, l. 376 n.: *delete* ii.

p. 173, l. 4 up: *add note*   For a contrary view, see George Bornstein, 'The Arrangement of Browning's *Dramatic Lyrics* (1842)' in Neill Fraistat (ed.), *Poems in their Place* (North Carolina, 1986).

p. 177 n.: *for*   BROWNING.   *read*   BROWNING,

p. 206, ll. 30–1 n.: *for*   your   *read*   Your

p. 224, l. 1: *for*   'Alfred Domett, or'   *read*   'Alfred Domett, Esq.'

    l. 5 n.: *for*   (London, Canada,   *read*   (London, Ontario,

    l. 5: *before*   The best   *insert*   For Domett's own comment, see his *Diary*, p. 64.

p. 247: *add note on l. 47*   Cf. Rev. 8:3–4.

p. 250: *add note on l. 12*   a point already made by George O. Marshall, Jr., in *Browning Newsletter*, Fall 1969, pp. 9–11.

p. 278, l. 22: *for*   would not   *read*   *would not*

p. 306, last line: *for*   I. vii. 29   *read*   III. iii. 216.

p. 403, textual nn.: *for*   260–6   *read*   262–6.